FIFTH EDITION

CONTACTS

Langue et culture françaises

Instructor's Resource Manual

Jean-Paul Valette

Rebecca M. Valette
BOSTON COLLEGE

HOUGHTON MIFFLIN COMPANY Boston Toronto
Dallas Geneva, Illinois Palo Alto Princeton, New Jersey

Components of the CONTACTS, Fifth Edition program:

- **For the student ...**
  Student Text
  Cahier d'activités: Workbook, Lab Manual, *Pas de problème!* Video Workbook
  Audiocassettes (Parts I & II), including Song Cassette
  Téléguide Video Workbook

- **For the instructor ...**
  Instructor's Annotated Edition
  Instructor's Resource Manual
  Test Bank
  Téléguide Instructor's Edition

- **For the institution ...**
  Audiocassettes (Parts I & II), including Song Cassette
  Computerized Study Modules
  Pas de problème! Video
  Télématin Video

Sponsoring Editor: Diane Gifford
Senior Development Editor: Katherine Gilbert
Production/Design Coordinator: Karen Rappaport
Project Editor: Amy Lawler
Manufacturing Coordinator: Sharon Pearson
Marketing Manager: George Kane

Printed in the U.S.A.

ISBN: 0-395-63796-1

123456789-CS-96 95 94 93

CONTENTS

CONTACTS

Instructor's Resource Manual

INSTRUCTOR'S GUIDE

INTRODUCTION

The Instructor's Resource Manual for the Fifth Edition of CONTACTS is intended as an aid for instructors who are preparing to teach with CONTACTS. It provides instructors with suggestions on how to plan their courses in a variety of circumstances.

The Instructor's Resource Manual offers advice on how to tailor a first-year course to a variety of scheduling situations. It gives an example of how to teach a model unit. The Manual further includes a description of how the CONTACTS program addresses each of the four skills plus culture and offers instructors advice on how to place additional emphasis on any of these areas. In addition, the Manual assists instructors in developing strategies for student evaluation. The Instructor's Resource Manual also provides information on useful sources of secondary printed material. Finally, the Instructor's Resource Manual includes 30 Transparency Masters and 10 *Chansons françaises* with correlation charts for both.

The Instructor's Resource Manual also contains a complete Tapescript for the recording program (pp. TS 1–227), transcript for the *Chansons françaises* immediately after, and an Answer Key to Lab Manual (pp. AK 1–12).

PLANNING THE COURSE

CONTACTS provides a wealth of material for both instructors and students. The text is divided into eleven units plus a brief preliminary unit. Each unit is built around a main cultural theme, such as the French-speaking world, daily life, university life, or attitudes toward the future. There are three lessons in each unit. Special sections called **Vivre en France** round out the units.

All the basic material of a lesson (structural, lexical, and cultural) is introduced in the Presentation Text. The cultural context is elaborated upon in the **Lecture Culturelle** (or **Note Culturelle**). The basic structural and lexical material of the lesson is explained in the **Structure et Vocabulaire** section. In the final section of each lesson, **Communication**, students have the opportunity to use the new structures and vocabulary in creative exchanges.

CONTACTS' organization promotes maximum flexibility for the instructor. By presenting material in relatively small sections, instructors will be able to regroup or reorganize the syllabus to meet the special needs of their students. The criterion for the organization of lessons is manageability; there is less emphasis on vocabulary acquisition when the understanding of the new grammatical patterns is more demanding, and vice versa. Since universities vary considerably in the number of classroom hours they allot to beginning language courses, CONTACTS identifies for the instructor structural, lexical, and cultural material that can be considered optional. Further, instructors interested in placing a heavier emphasis on one of the four skills or on culture may wish to present some of this optional material for passive recognition only. (For further information on how to place special emphasis on certain skills, see page IG 3.

The English explanations are included primarily for out-of-class reference so that instructors can conduct their classes entirely in French if they so desire. Direction lines for exercises appear in English through Lesson 10, when they switch to French. For the convenience of the instructor, French direction lines for the exercises in Lessons 4–10 are included in the overprinted annotations in the IAE.

The annotations in the IAE also contain supplementary information on structural points, as well as suggestions for expanding on exercises, teaching tips, etc.

Preparing a Syllabus

In preparing a syllabus for the academic year, the instructor must first determine how many classroom hours will be available for the first-year sequence. Instructors whose classes meet three times a week for two twelve-week semesters will have only 70–75 classroom hours to complete the first-year program. Those whose classes meet five times a week for two fifteen-week semesters or three ten-week quarters will have up to 150 classroom hours to devote to the first-year material. Clearly those meeting on the shorter semester schedules will have to concentrate on the basic material of the program and omit much of the optional material.

Instructors whose classes meet five times a week during twelve-week semesters or four times a week during fifteen-week semesters (or ten-week quarters) will have no difficulty devoting two to three class hours to each lesson. They will still be able to spend one full class hour on each of the **Vivre en France** end-of-unit sections and a full class hour on each of the unit tests. On the other hand, instructors whose classes meet only four times a week during twelve-week semesters or three times a week during fifteen-week semesters (or ten-week quarters) and who wish to spend at least two class hours per lesson will sometimes have to spend only one-half a class period on each **Vivre en France** section and can give only one-half hour unit tests. Alternatively, they will have to choose to teach some of the optional material for passive recognition only (or else omit it entirely from their syllabus).

Classes on a semester schedule should be able to complete the preliminary unit plus Units 1–6 during the first semester and Units 7–11 in the second semester. (However, instructors whose classes meet only three times a week may prefer a lighter syllabus which covers the preliminary unit plus Units 1–5 during the first semester and Units 6–10 during the second semester.) Classes on a quarter system can complete the preliminary unit and Units 1–3 in the first quarters, Units 4–7 in the second quarter, and Units 8–11 in the third quarter.

Teaching a Unit

There are many different ways of teaching a unit. As a general role, activities developing reading and writing skills are done at home, while activities promoting listening and speaking skills are done in the classroom and reinforced in the language laboratory. The following sample lesson plans have been prepared for Unit 3, *Problèmes d'argent*, for a class meeting four times a week for a fifteen-week semester.

	In-class activities	*Hand in...*
day 1	**Leçon 7: Le budget de Philippe** presentation text A. Les nombres de 100 à l'infini B. Le verbe **payer** C. L'expression **être à** D. La possession avec **de** [quickly present Section E]	

day 2	E. Les adjectifs possessifs Vocabulaire: *La famille et les relations personnelles* *Communication, L. 7* [quickly present Lesson 8, Section A]	Workbook, lesson 7 Lab Manual, lesson 7
day 3	**Leçon 8: Un tee-shirt qui coûte cher** presentation text A. Les verbes comme **acheter** et **préférer** [quickly present Sections B, C, D]	
day 4	B. L'adjectif interrogatif **quel** C. L'adjectif démonstratif **ce** D. Le comparatif des adjectifs *Communication, L. 8* [quickly present Lesson 9, Section A]	Workbook, L. 8 Lab Manual, L. 8
day 5	**Leçon 9: Le rêve et la réalité** presentation text A. Le verbe **faire** Voc.: *Le logement, Les prépositions de lieu* [quickly present Lesson 9, Sections B, C, D]	
day 6	B. Les adjectifs **beau, nouveau, vieux** C. Le superlatif D. Le temps *Communicating, L. 9*	Workbook, L. 9 Lab Manual, L. 9
day 7	**Vivre en France: L'argent français** [quickly review L. 7, 8, 9]	
day 8	Test: Unit 3 [quickly present L. 10, Sections A, B]	Lab Manual, Vivre en France, Unit 3

You will have noticed that the in-class lesson activities have the following distinctive features: (1) the instructor presents the new material of each lesson briefly on one day and then develops the lesson activities on the following day; and (2) every other day the workbook material for the lesson is corrected by the students in small groups at the end of the period, with the instructor circulating to check that everyone has prepared the assignment and to answer any questions that might arise. An answer key for the Workbook is provided at the back of the *Cahier d'activités*, as well as the texts of the dictation activities from the audio program. The written **Communication** activities are handed in to be corrected by the instructor. Although the presentation text opens the lesson in the student text, it need not be presented first. Some instructors may prefer to introduce the new structures in another manner and then use the presentation text as reading comprehension material or as a listening comprehension activity, in conjunction with the tape program.

FLEXIBILITY OF TEACHING STRATEGIES

CONTACTS provides practice in all four basic skills—reading, writing, listening, and speaking. Every effort is made to provide students with opportunities for self-expression using all four skills, a critical component of true functional proficiency. The sample lesson plan given below shows how the basic program addresses the four skills plus culture and how it might be modified to emphasize any one of these areas.

Reading skills

Basic program: The Presentation Text and the **Lecture Culturelle** (beginning with Unit 3) of each lesson offer students ample opportunity to practice reading skills. The Presentation Text is reinforced by comprehension questions printed in the Instructor's Annotated Edition. Comprehension questions to accompany the **Lectures Culturelles** are found on the tape program.

Additional emphasis: If your college library subscribes to French-language newspapers, magazines, or other publications, you may be able to obtain the older issues and distribute them in class from time to time so that students can learn to read advertisements, classified ads, television schedules, movie program descriptions, etc.

Writing skills

Basic program: The student Workbook component of the *Cahier d'activités* provides students with extensive writing practice. The *Communication* section of the Workbook in particular encourages extensive personalized written self-expression. The four *Révision* sections provide students with systematic review of their written skills before midterms and finals. The Lab Manual, used in conjunction with the tape program, provides written practice through short dictations and other written activities based on audio cues. Answer keys for the Workbook activities, the *Révisions,* and the dictations from the tape program are provided at the back of the *Cahier d'activités.*

Additional emphasis: The oral activities in the Student Text, especially the *questions personnelles,* can be easily adapted to written practice.

Listening skills

Basic program: Listening skills are developed through daily classroom interaction. Instructors who wish more extensive practice of listening skills should encourage their students to use the tape program. Since the tape program is available on low-cost cassettes (packaged in two parts), instructors are encouraged to make arrangements with their bookstore to allow students to buy the cassettes so that they can listen to the tape program on their own cassette players at their convenience. In addition to being exposed to audio work on all the structures and vocabulary of the lesson, students will do a dictation as well as other listening comprehension activities. They will also have the opportunity to hear both the Presentation Text and the **Lecture Culturelle** read out loud. The **Vivre en France** sections of the tape program are intended to develop listening skills applicable to authentic daily-life situations. An answer key for the Lab Manual is found in the Instructor's Resource Manual, following the tapescript.

The Fifth Edition of CONTACTS offers instructors the choice of two video programs to enhance students' listening skills. The *Pas de problème!* video was custom-shot in France. It focuses on problem-solving skills in a contemporary setting. A video workbook to accompany *Pas de problème!* is included in the *Cahier d'activités.* A transcript, timings, and a correlation chart are included on page TS 2 of this Instructor's Resource Manual.

Télématin video consists of authentic footage from the French morning program, *Télématin.* A complete transcript, suggestions for teaching with *Télématin*, and timings are all included in the Instructor's Edition of the *Téléguide* video workbook.

Additional emphasis: French-language films are shown in most large cities and are easily acquired for classroom use from a variety of sources, as are excerpts from current French television productions. Additional listening practice can be gained by using video materials from sources such as PICS (Project for International Communication Studies) at the University of Iowa.

Speaking skills

Basic program: CONTACTS' main goal is to develop communicative competency. All activities accompanying the **Structure et Vocabulaire** section are intended to be done orally in class. The paired *Communication* activities encourage students to use the structures and vocabulary of the lesson in creative exchanges. The **Vivre en France** end-of-unit sections provide students with the oral skills to function in a stated context while living or traveling in the French-speaking world. Extensive out-of-class oral practice as well as detailed instruction in pronunciation is further provided in the tape program.

Additional emphasis: In a course where the primary emphasis is placed on the spoken language, the teacher may wish to conduct the class entirely in French. Students should be referred to Appendix A, *Expressions pour la classe*. The presentation text may be used in class in conjunction with the corresponding tape recording and can be introduced at the beginning, middle, or end of the lesson.

If the instructor guides most of the oral practice in the classroom, the *questions personnelles* can be transformed into directed dialogue activities. For example, if the question reads *Avez-vous des frères?*, the instructor might say, *Bob, demandez à Nancy si elle a des frères*. Then Bob would ask Nancy, *As-tu des frères?* Similarly, the instructor could direct the exchanges of the dialogue exercises. In other oral exercises, the instructor can read the cues and call at random on students to respond.

The course emphasizing conversation will probably make heavy use of pair and small group activities. In addition to the *Communication* section at the end of each lesson, communicative activities abound throughout the text. They are indicated by the double arrow symbol. The dialogues and *questions personnelles* lend themselves as well to directed conversation by small groups of two to three students. As the various groups work through the activities orally, the instructor can move around the classroom, joining first one group and then another. The instructor may just listen in or may wish to join in the activity. As a change of pace, each group can be asked to prepare a *Communication* activity and then perform it for the class.

Culture

Basic program: A wealth of cultural material is provided to the students in the Presentation Texts and the **Lectures Culturelles**. The **Vivre en France** sections will broaden students' awareness of the French-speaking world. The full-color art program (especially the extensive photos and realia) offers students an extensive visual image of contemporary culture in France and the French-speaking world. The *Pas de problème!* video gives students a unique insight into contemporary French life.

Additional emphasis: The basic program can be supplemented with material from French-language newspapers and magazines—movie schedules, classified ads, horoscopes, etc. See page IG 7 for sources of cultural materials.

EVALUATION AND COURSE GOALS

The best way to determine and instructor's course objectives is to examine how he or she assigns course grades. For instance, an instructor may state that a course will stress conversation skills. However, if the final grade is based primarily on student performance on written tests, the students will soon realize that the course's true objectives center on writing skills.

Sample grading instructions

Each college will develop its own focus for the elementary French course. The chart that follows is an example of information concerning grades that might be given to students at the start of the semester. It represents one type of grading system that can be used for classes meeting three times a week where the intent is to cover the Preliminary Unit and Units 1–5 in the course of the first semester.

The grading system is based on the premise that regular preparation is essential for success, especially in a required course where some students may have had previous exposure to French and be inclined to minimize the need for study.

One-fifth of the student's final grade is based on classroom preparation. Approximately one-third of the grade is based on oral work, which includes classroom participation, oral tests, and general improvement in the pronunciation. In addition, a section in each unit test is directed toward listening comprehension.

Grades will be assigned as follows:

preparation and participation: 30%	
Workbook: 16 assignments at 5 pts each	80
Communication: 15 assignments at 3 pts each	45
Language lab: 16 assignments at 5 pts each	80
Class participation	95
	300 pts
tests and quizzes: 70%	
Unit tests: 5 at 50 pts each	250
Recorded pronunciation tests: 2 at 50 pts each	100
Speaking tests: 2 at 50 pts each	100
final exam	250
	700 pts
TOTAL (to be divided by 10)	**1000 pts**

Grading scale:

97–100	A+	77–79	C+		
93–96	A	73–76	C		
90–92	A-	70–72	C-		
87–89	B+	67–69	D+		
83–86	B	63–66	D		
82–82	B-	60–62	D-	below 60	F

Grading of class preparations:

complete & on time	5 pts
1–2 days late	3 pts
3–7 days late	2 pts
over 1 week late	1 pt

Participation grade:

3 absences are tolerated
each subsequent absence -10 pts

there are no make-up tests given in the course.

REALIA AND OTHER SECONDARY SOURCES

Since the emphasis in CONTACTS is on the contemporary French-speaking world, the instructor may want to enrich the course with additional contemporary materials. From prior trips to French-speaking countries, the instructor may have various realia which can supplement the material presented in the text: travel guides, TV guides, theater and movie guides, maps, political posters, illustrated handbills, etc. The university library or the departmental language center may have subscriptions to current French magazines and illustrated guidebooks, such as the *Michelin* series. The language laboratory or tape library may have recordings of folk songs or contemporary music. If the classroom has an up-to-date map of the world, this can be used frequently to point out areas of the French-speaking world as they are mentioned in the text.

Newspapers and magazines

Although beginning students will not be able to read French newspapers and magazines, especially at the outset of the course, they can increase their familiarity with the French-speaking world by thumbing through such publications, studying layouts, advertisements, and schedules of shows. If the university library does not bind French newspapers, instructors may be able to obtain old copies for classroom use.

In larger cities, French magazines and newspapers can be bought at international newsstands. Students and instructors can place subscriptions to most French publications through Dawson Fence, rue de la Prairie, V.P. 40, 91146 Villebon/Yvette, Cédex FRANCE Some of the more widely read French publications include:

Elle (fashions, current trends, advertisements)
Express (current events, advertisements)
Jours de France (cartoons, fashions, horoscopes, advertisements)
Marie Claire (fashions, current trends, advertisements)
Le Monde (daily newspaper of news and information)
Paris-Match (current events, photo articles, advertisements)
Journal français d'Amérique (bimonthly newspaper of French news, trends, and history in France and the United States)

The overseas editions of *Elle* and *Paris-Match* do not carry the same advertisements as the French versions.

Reference books

The following books, published in France, can be used for further reference.

G. Michard et G. Torrès, *Nouveau Guide France* (Paris: Hachette, 1983)
G. Quénelle et J. Tournaire, *La France dans votre poche*, 3/e (Paris: Hatier, 1979)
D. et M. Frémy, *Quid* (Paris: Laffont, 1993)

Even beginning students can gain an impression of France from the charts, maps, and pictures these books contain.

Brochures, travel guides, and other realia

Descriptive material about French-speaking countries can be obtained from national tourist offices or by writing the local chambers of commerce *(Syndicats d'Initiative)*. The following addresses and phone numbers may be helpful:

French Government Tourist Office, 610 Fifth Avenue, New York, NY 10020. Phone: 212-757-1125
Caribbean Tourism Association (for Martinique and Guadeloupe), 20 E. 46th Street, New York, NY 10017. Phone: 212-682-0435
Québec Government House, 17 West 50th Street, New York, NY 10020-2201. Phone: 800-443-7000
Canadian Office of Tourism, 1771 N Street, Washington, DC 20036. Phone: 202-682-1775

Further information may also be obtained from the embassies of the various French-speaking countries located in Washington, DC, or from their regional consulates located throughout the country. A list of consulates for a given country can be obtained by contacting the embassy in Washington.

AUDIO PROGRAM TAPESCRIPT

This Tapescript is a written transcript of the audiocassettes that accompany CONTACTS, Fifth Edition. The complete program consists of nineteen tapes. The cassettes, which can be purchased by students through the bookstore, are packaged in two sets of nine and ten cassettes. Part 1 includes the recorded material for the Preliminary Unit and Units 1–5, along with the corresponding end-of-unit sections (**Vivre en France**). Part 2 includes recorded material for Units 7–11, the corresponding **Vivre en France** sections, and ten French songs on Tape 19, Side B. These songs can be used to enliven classroom activities and provide aural comprehension practice at the same time.

The tape program for CONTACTS was carefully designed to accompany the student text. Each of the 33 lessons has approximately one half hour of tape activities. One lesson appears on each side of a cassette with each **Vivre en France** section on the same side as the last lesson of each unit. The exception is **Vivre en France 10** (after Lesson 30) which appears by itself on Tape 17, Side B. These activities provide students with intensive practice of the material, as well as the opportunity to hear a variety of native voices. The general organization of each lesson is as follows:

1. **Présentation:** A reading of the **Présentation** text from the lesson, followed by comprehension questions where appropriate.

2. **Phonétique:** Pronunciation explanations and exercises, often including a sound discrimination test.

3. **Structure et Vocabulaire:** Reading and repetition of vocabulary and verb paradigms from the text for that particular lesson, followed by a number of activities designed to reinforce the structures and vocabulary. The activities include a variety of original exercises including substitutions, transformations, and listening comprehension drills in a three-phase format: cue, pause for student response, and confirmation.

4. **Dialogue:** A series of brief conversations followed by comprehension activities in which students are often asked to respond based on illustrations.

5. **Dictée:** A brief dictation for practice of oral comprehension.

6. **Lecture culturelle:** A reading of the **Lecture culturelle** (Lessons 7–33). Instructors may wish to have students first read along as they listen, and then listen with books closed. The reading is followed by true-false comprehension questions.

The CONTACTS tape program also contains activities based on the **Vivre en France** section at the end of each unit:

1. **La bonne réponse:** Students are asked to select the appropriate response in short conversational exchanges.

2. **En France:** Students hear a conversation and use the information they hear to fill out various forms in their Lab Manual.

You will note that each audiocassette lesson is coordinated with the Lab Manual section of the *Cahier d'activités*. For most exercises, the correct responses are confirmed at the end of the tape activity, thus allowing students to check their comprehension while listening. The texts of the dictations are provided in the *Cahier d'activités*.

The following table gives the approximate timing for each lesson. Note that the Fifth Edition of CONTACTS uses 90-minute cassettes; lab directors should keep this in mind when duplicating cassettes.

Recordings: Part One

Tape	Content	Time
Tape 1A	Unité Préliminaire (A)	30 min.
Tape 1B	Unité Préliminaire (B)	29 min.
Tape 2A	Leçon 1	35 min.
Tape 2B	Leçon 2	38 min.
Tape 3A	Leçon 3 + Vivre en France 1	39 min.
Tape 3B	Leçon 4	34 min.
Tape 4A	Leçon 5	31 min.
Tape 4B	Leçon 6 + Vivre en France 2	37 min.
Tape 5A	Leçon 7	28 min.
Tape 5B	Leçon 8	30 min.
Tape 6A	Leçon 9 + Vivre en France 3	37 min.
Tape 6B	Leçon 10	30 min.
Tape 7A	Leçon 11	30 min.
Tape 7B	Leçon 12 + Vivre en France 4	41 min.
Tape 8A	Leçon 13	30 min.
Tape 8B	Leçon 14	31 min.
Tape 9A	Leçon 15 + Vivre en France 5	38 min.
Tape 9B	—	—

Recordings: Part Two

Tape	Content	Time
Tape 10A	Leçon 16	39 min.
Tape 10B	Leçon 17	34 min.
Tape 11A	Leçon 18 + Vivre en France 6	46 min.
Tape 11B	Leçon 19	29 min.
Tape 12A	Leçon 20	36 min.
Tape 12B	Leçon 21 + Vivre en France 7	40 min.
Tape 13A	Leçon 22	29 min.
Tape 13B	Leçon 23	30 min.
Tape 14A	Leçon 24 + Vivre en France 8	43 min.
Tape 14B	Leçon 25	34 min.
Tape 15A	Leçon 26	38 min.
Tape 15B	Leçon 27 + Vivre en France 9	28 min.
Tape 16A	Leçon 28	31 min.
Tape 16B	Leçon 29	33 min.
Tape 17A	Leçon 30	46 min.
Tape 17B	Vivre en France 10	8 min.
Tape 18A	Leçon 31	30 min.
Tape 18B	Leçon 32	26 min.
Tape 19A	Leçon 33	31 min.
Tape 19B	Chansons françaises	30 min.

UNITÉ PRÉLIMINAIRE: RENCONTRES

PREMIÈRE PARTIE: À L'INSTITUT DE TOURAINE

Activité 1: Introduction. As you are about to begin your study of French, we, the authors, would like to welcome you. Thousands of American students have developed proficiency in French with the first four editions of CONTACTS, and it is with their suggestions and those of their teachers that we have prepared this new edition. We hope that you will find the program challenging and informative and that your classes will afford you the joy and excitement of acquiring another means of communication.

There is a difference between *learning* a new language and *acquiring* a new language. As you study with CONTACTS, you will be "learning" how the French language works: what the French sound system is like, how sentences are put together, what words and expressions mean, how endings are used with verbs and adjectives, etc. All these aspects of the language are clearly explained with abundant examples.

But if you truly want to *acquire* French as a language of communication, you must go beyond the mere learning. You have to develop a feeling for what French sounds like, you have to understand what you hear and read, and you have to try to express your own ideas in speaking and writing.

The purpose of the tape program is to give you the opportunity of practicing listening comprehension and speaking skills. At the beginning, the most important thing is *to understand* what you hear. Take the time to play the tape over and over until you feel comfortable with each section. Listen again and again until you know what everything means. Only when what you hear begins to make sense will you be on the way to building language proficiency! *Bonne chance!*

NOTE: As you work with the tape program you will need the following things: the lab manual section of your *Cahier d'activités*, your textbook, and a pencil.

Are you ready? *Commençons.*

PRÉSENTATION

Activité 2. Lecture Open your textbook to p. 2. Follow the text.

Écoutez. Listen.

The **Institut de Touraine** is well known to thousands of American students and teachers who have studied French there. It is one of the many schools in France that offer language and civilization courses for foreign students. The **Institut** is located in Tours, the main city of Touraine, a region in central France known for its beautiful landscape and its picturesque **châteaux.** People say that the purest French is spoken in Touraine.

Today is the first day of class.

Voici Marc.
Voici Anne et voilà Monique.
Voilà Madame Lacoste.

—Qui est-ce?
—C'est Philippe.

—Bonjour, Anne.
—Bonjour, Philippe.

—Comment vous appelez-vous?
—Je m'appelle Anne Bissette.
—Bonjour, Anne.
—Bonjour, Madame.

—Au revoir, Monique.
—Au revoir, Philippe.

—Au revoir, Anne.
—Au revoir, Monique. À bientôt.

—Au revoir, Anne.
—Au revoir, Madame.

Now close your textbook and listen again. Try to understand what is being said.

(Reading is repeated, French part only.)

Activité 3. Pratique orale. Repeat the mini-dialogues after the speakers. Try to imitate their voices as closely as possible. Practice each line twice.

Ready? *Commençons.* Let's begin.

(French section of presentation text is reread. Each line is said twice, pausing for repetition.)

Vocabulaire: Bonjour!

Activité 4. Prononciation. Open your textbook to p. 3. Repeat the following expressions. Then repeat the sentences in which each expression is used.

Ready? *Commençons.* Let's begin.

Voici . . .

Voici Philippe.
Voici le taxi.
Voici Marc et Michèle.
Voici le cinéma.

Voilà . . .

Voilà Anne.
Voilà l'autobus.
Voilà Monique et Alice.
Voilà l'hôtel Novotel.

Bonjour! — Bonjour, Jacqueline!
Au revoir! — Au revoir, Sylvie!
À bientôt! — À bientôt, Thomas!

Comment vous appelez-vous? — Comment vous appelez-vous, Mademoiselle?

Je m'appelle . . . — Je m'appelle Annette.

Qui est-ce? — Qui est-ce?

C'est . . . — C'est Madame Lamy.

Activité 5. Situation: Présentations. You will hear the names of French students. Introduce each student to your friends.

Écoutez le modèle. Listen to the model.

Modèle: Philippe — Voici Philippe.

Commençons. Let's begin.

Suzanne — Voici Suzanne.
Monique — Voici Monique.
Michel — Voici Michel.
Louise — Voici Louise.
Thomas — Voici Thomas.
Anne — Voici Anne.

Now say hello to the next group of students. Listen to the model.

Modèle: Annie — Bonjour, Annie.

Ready? *Commençons!* Let's begin!

Antoine — Bonjour, Antoine.
Paul — Bonjour, Paul.
Pauline — Bonjour, Pauline.
Élisabeth — Bonjour, Élisabeth.
Pascal — Bonjour, Pascal.
Sylvie — Bonjour, Sylvie.

PHONÉTIQUE

Activité 6. Introduction à la phonétique française. Open your textbook to p. 5. Spoken French differs from English in several ways:

First, TENSENESS. English is a very relaxed language. Vowels are often glided. Some consonants may also be prolonged.
Écoutez. Listen.
Madam Michele café

French is a very tense language. Vowels are short and clipped: they do not glide. Consonants are short and distinctly pronounced.
Écoutez. Listen.
Madame Michèle café
Répétez. Repeat: Madame Michèle café

Second, RHYTHM. English rhythm is sing-songy. Some syllables are short and others are long.
Écoutez. Listen.
Good morning.
Good morning, Emily.
My name is Paul.

French rhythm is very even. Only the last syllable of a group of words is longer than others.
Écoutez. Listen.
Bonjour.
Bonjour, Émilie.
Je m'appelle Paul.
Répétez. Repeat: Bonjour. Bonjour, Émilie. Je m'appelle Paul.

Third, LINKING. In spoken English, words are usually separated. Your vocal cords may even stop vibrating an instant between words.
Écoutez. Listen.
Good-by / Eric.
Paul / arrives / at the / hotel.

In spoken French, words are not separated. In fact, within a group of words, all syllables are linked together.
Écoutez. Listen.
Au revoir Éric.
Paul arrive à l'hôtel.
Répétez. Repeat: Au revoir Éric. Paul arrive à l'hôtel.

Fourth, SYLLABLES. In spoken English, many words and syllables end on a consonant sound.
This is Paris. /s/ and /z/ are consonant sounds.

In spoken French, syllables end on a vowel sound wherever possible.
Voi-ci Pa-ris. /a/ and /i/ are vowel sounds.
Répétez. Repeat: Voici Paris.

Activité 7. Consonnes et voyelles. Now open your lab manual. For this activity you will need a pencil.

The letters "b", "t," and "v" are *consonants*.
The sounds /b/, /t/, and /v/ are *consonant sounds*.
The letters "a" and "o" are *vowels*.
The sounds /a/ and /o/ are *vowel sounds*.
In spoken French it is important to distinguish whether words end on a consonant sound or a vowel sound.

You will hear a series of French names. Listen carefully to each name. If the name ends on a vowel sound, mark row 1 in your lab manual. If the name ends on a consonant sound, mark row 2. Do not think of how the name is spelled. Simply listen to the last sound of the word.

Écoutez les modèles. Listen to the models.

Modèle A: Marie

/i/ is a vowel sound. You should have marked row 1.

Modèle B: Monique

/k/ is a consonant sound. You should have marked row 2.

Commençons. Let's begin.

1. Isabelle	consonant
2. Michel	consonant
3. Sylvie	vowel
4. Anne	consonant
5. Nicolas	vowel
6. Brigitte	consonant
7. Louise	consonant
8. Arnaud	vowel

Now listen again and check your answers.

Activité 8. Intonation (I) Open your textbook to p. 7.

As you speak, your voice rises and falls; this is called *intonation.* In French, as in English, your voice falls at the end of a declarative sentence. However, in French the voice rises after each group of words within a longer sentence, whereas in English it either falls or stays on the same pitch.

Repeat after the speaker, mimicking the same intonation patterns.

Voici.
Voici Annette.
Voici Annette Vidal.

Voilà.
Voilà Michel.
Voilà Michel et Dominique.

Voilà.
Voilà l'auto.
Voilà l'automobile.

Voilà l'automobile de Paul.
Voilà l'automobile de Pauline.
Voilà l'automobile de Pauline Duval.

Activité 9. Situation: À Paris. You are working as a tour guide in Paris. Point out the places listed on p. 7 of your textbook to the tourists in your group. Be sure that your French intonation is French!

Écoutez le modèle. Listen to the model.

Modèle: l'hôtel Napoléon	Voilà l'hôtel Napoléon.
l'Opéra	Voilà l'Opéra.
la Madeleine	Voilà la Madeleine.
la Sorbonne	Voilà la Sorbonne.
le musée d'Orsay	Voilà le musée d'Orsay.
la pyramide du Louvre	Voilà la pyramide du Louvre.
le parc de la Villette	Voilà le parc de la Villette.
la Tour Eiffel	Voilà la Tour Eiffel.
le café Bonaparte	Voilà le café Bonaparte.
la place de la Bastille	Voilà la place de la Bastille.
l'avenue Victor Hugo	Voilà l'avenue Victor Hugo.
le boulevard Saint Michel	Voilà le boulevard Saint Michel.
le boulevard Raspail	Voilà le boulevard Raspail.

DIALOGUE

Activité 10. Qui est-ce? Open your lab manual. Look at the illustrations. Imagine you are at the Institut de Touraine talking to Philippe. Other students that you know come by. Philippe asks who they are. You tell him, and then you greet each person.

Écoutez le modèle. Listen to the model.

Modèle: (Philippe): —Qui est-ce? (Vous): —C'est Michèle. Bonjour, Michèle.

Are you ready? Now you are meeting the person in the first illustration.

1. —Qui est-ce? —C'est Dominique. Bonjour, Dominique.
2. —Qui est-ce? —C'est Daniel. Bonjour, Daniel.
3. —Qui est-ce? —C'est Sylvie. Bonjour, Sylvie.
4. —Qui est-ce? —C'est Marc. Bonjour, Marc.

DICTÉE

Activité 11. Bonjour! You will hear a short dialogue. First, listen! Do not write. Try to understand what is being said.

(Text is read without pauses.)

Voici Annie et Nicole. Et voilà Pascal.
Bonjour, Annie.
Bonjour, Nicole.
Qui est-ce?
C'est Pascal.
Au revoir, Annie. À bientôt.

Now you will hear the dialogue again, with pauses after each phrase. Write down what you hear.

(Text is read again with pauses.)

Voici Annie / et Nicole. / Et voilà Pascal. /
Bonjour, Annie. /
Bonjour, Nicole. /
Qui est-ce? /
C'est Pascal. /
Au revoir, Annie. / À bientôt. /

Now listen once more and check what you wrote.

(Text is reread, without pauses.)

End of Unité Préliminaire, Part One.
(music)

DEUXIÈME PARTIE: AU CAFÉ DE L'UNIVERS

PRÉSENTATION

Activité 1. Lecture. Open your textbook to p. 8.

Écoutez. Listen.

The **Café de l'Univers** is a popular meeting place in the center of Tours. Students, tourists, shoppers, doctors, and business people stop by with friends and associates to talk and have something to drink.

—Bonjour, Monsieur.
—Bonjour, Madame. Comment allez-vous?
—Très bien, merci. Et vous?
—Pas mal, merci.

—Salut, Marc!
—Salut, Nathalie! Ça va?
—Ça va bien. Et toi?
—Ça va!

—Un chocolat, s'il vous plaît.
—Oui, Mademoiselle. Et pour Monsieur?
—Un café.

—Voici un chocolat pour Mademoiselle.
—Merci.
—Et un café pour Monsieur.
—Merci bien!
—À votre service!

Now close your textbook and listen again. Try to understand everything that is being said.

(Reading is repeated, French dialogue only.)

Activité 2. Pratique orale. Now repeat the dialogue lines after the speakers. Try to imitate their voices as closely as possible. Practice each sentence twice. Ready?

Commençons. Let's begin.

Bonjour, Monsieur.
Bonjour, Madame.
Comment allez-vous?

Bonjour, Monsieur.
Bonjour, Madame.
Comment allez-vous?

(Presentation text from Activity 1 is reread, French part only. Each sentence is read twice, pausing for repetition.)

Vocabulaire: Salutations

Activité 3. Prononciation. Open your textbook to p. 9.

Repeat the following greetings and expressions.

Bonjour, Monsieur.
Bonjour, Madame.
Bonjour, Mademoiselle.
Comment allez-vous?
Je vais très bien.
Je vais bien.
Je vais pas mal.
Je vais comme çi, comme ça.
Je vais mal.
Et vous?

Salut!
Ça va?
Ça va très bien.
Ça va bien.
Ça va pas mal.
Ça va comme çi, comme ça.
Ça va mal.
Et toi?

S'il vous plaît!
Merci!
Merci bien!
De rien.
Il n'y a pas de quoi.
À votre service!
Pardon.
Excusez-moi!
Il n'y a pas de mal.

Activité 4. Situation: Bonjour! You will hear the names of various people. Imagine that you are meeting these people in the street. Say hello to them.

Écoutez les modèles. Listen to the models.

Modèles: Paul — Bonjour, Paul.
Madame Bissette — Bonjour, Madame.

Commençons. Let's begin.

Christine — Bonjour, Christine.
Philippe — Bonjour, Philippe.
Monsieur Lenoir — Bonjour, Monsieur.
Mademoiselle Dupont — Bonjour, Mademoiselle.
Jacqueline — Bonjour, Jacqueline.
Michel — Bonjour, Michel.
Madame Duval — Bonjour, Madame.
Monsieur Maillet — Bonjour, Monsieur.
Monique — Bonjour, Monique.
Mademoiselle Michel — Bonjour, Mademoiselle.

PHONÉTIQUE

Activité 5. Les lettres muettes. Open your textbook to p. 12. Some letters in French are not pronounced, especially when they come at the end of a word. The following letters are usually silent:
—final -e
Repeat: Philippe Sylvie Annie
—final -s
Repeat: Louis Nicolas Charles
—other final consonants, except -c, -f, -l, -k, and usually -r
Repeat: Richard Robert Marc chef Paul Patrick Victor *but* Roger Olivier
—h in all positions
Repeat: Henri Thomas Nathalie

Activité 6. Situation: Au revoir. In your lab manual are listed the names of eight French students. After you hear the number corresponding to each name, say good-by to that student. Then listen for the confirmation. Be sure to respond immediately after you hear the number.

Écoutez le modèle. Listen to the model.

Modèle: Au revoir, Roger.

Commençons. Let's begin.

one	Au revoir, Nathalie.
two	Au revoir, Louise.
three	Au revoir, Robert.
four	Au revoir, Nicolas.
five	Au revoir, Bernard.
six	Au revoir, Marthe.
seven	Au revoir, Édith.
eight	Au revoir, Marc.

Activité 7. Les marques orthographiques. Open your textbook to p. 12. Accents and spelling marks are part of the spelling of a word and cannot be left out.
L'accent aigu *(acute accent)*
This accent appears only on the vowel "e."
Repeat: Cécile Frédéric café

L'accent grave *(grave accent)*
This accent may appear on "a," "e," and on the word **où.**
Repeat: Michèle voilà où

L'accent circonflexe *(circumflex)*
This accent may appear on all vowels except "y."
Repeat: mâle forêt dîner hôtel sûr

Le tréma *(dieresis)*
This accent is used on the second of two consecutive vowels and indicates that these vowels are pronounced separately.
Repeat: Noël naïf

La cédille *(cedilla)*
This spelling mark appears only under the consonant "c." It indicates that the letter is pronounced /s/.
Repeat: François français garçon

Activité 8. Orthographe. Open your lab manual. The nouns you see have not been spelled correctly. The letters that are underlined should have an accent or spelling mark. Listen to the pronunciation of each of these nouns, followed by the missing accent or spelling mark. Add this accent or spelling mark to the underlined letter.

Commençons. Let's begin.

1. hôtel, accent circonflexe
2. garçon, cédille
3. forêt, accent circonflexe
4. Léon, accent aigu
5. Joël, tréma
6. Michèle, accent grave
7. Mélanie, accent aigu
8. Danièle, accent grave
9. Françoise, cédille
10. Valérie, accent aigu

L'ALPHABET FRANÇAIS

Activité 9. Prononciation. Repeat the alphabet in French.

Commençons. Let's begin.

A - B - C - D - E - F - G - H - I - J - K - L - M - N - O - P - Q - R - S - T - U - V - W - X - Y - Z

Did you notice some differences between the French alphabet and the English? For example, the vowel "e" is pronounced / ə / and the vowel "i" is pronounced /i/. In French, the letter "g" is /ʒe/; while the letter "j" is /ʒi/. The letter "y" is *i grec* or "Greek I." Also the French think of "W" (double u) as double v: *double v.*

Now repeat the alphabet once more in groups of three letters:
ABC - DEF - GHI - JKL - MNO - PQR - STU - VWX - YZ

Activité 10. Géographie. In your lab manual you will see a map of France on which six cities are indicated. Listen to the spellings of the names of these cities. Write these names in the spaces provided. Each name will be spelled twice.

(Repeat spelling twice for each city.)

1. P - A - R - I - S
2. N - A - N - C - Y
3. B - O - R - D - E - A - U - X
4. C - H - E - R - B - O - U - R - G
5. A - V - I - G - N - O - N
6. M - O - N - T - P - E - L - L - I - E - R

Now check your work: The cities are Paris (P - A - R - I - S), Nancy (N - A - N - C - Y), Bordeaux (B - O - R - D - E - A - U - X), Cherbourg (C - H - E - R - B - O - U - R - G), Avignon (A - V - I - G - N - O - N), and Montpellier (M - O - N - T - P - E - L - L - I - E - R).

DIALOGUE

Activité 11. Ça va? In your lab manual you will see illustrations of various people. From their faces, you can tell how they are feeling today. You will hear each person being greeted. Respond to the greeting according to the picture.

Écoutez les modèles. Listen to the two models.

Modèle: A. —Bonjour, Monsieur.
Comment allez-vous? —Je vais bien, merci.

Modèle: B. —Bonjour, Michèle.
Ça va? —Non, ça va mal.

Commençons. Let's begin.

1. Bonjour, Madame.
   Comment allez-vous? Je vais très bien, merci.
2. Bonjour, Mademoiselle.
   Comment allez-vous? Je vais pas mal, merci.
3. Bonjour, Monique. Ça va? Ça va comme ci, comme ça.
4. Bonjour, Nicolas. Ça va? Ça va mal.
5. Bonjour, Roger. Ça va? Ça va bien.

DICTÉE

Activité 12. Salutations. You will hear a short dialogue. First, listen! Do not write! Try to understand what is being said.

(Text is read without pauses.)

—Bonjour, Mademoiselle.
—Bonjour, Monsieur.
—Comment allez-vous?
—Je vais très bien. Et vous?
—Je vais comme ci, comme ça.

Now you will hear the dialogue again, with pauses after each phrase. Write down what you hear.

(Text is read again with pauses.)

Now listen once more and check what you wrote.

(Text is reread without pauses.)

End of Unité Préliminaire, Part Two.
(music)

UNITÉ 1: QUI PARLE FRANÇAIS?

LEÇON 1. AU CANADA

PRÉSENTATION

Activité 1. Lecture. Open your textbook to p. 20. Follow the text as you listen to it.

(See textbook page 20.)

Activité 2. Compréhension du texte. Did you understand Paul Lavoie? You will hear a series of statements about what he said. In your lab manual, indicate whether they are true or false, by marking the appropriate row **vrai,** true, or **faux,** false.

Écoutez. Listen.

(First numbers and cues only are read. Then the cues are reread with the confirmation.)

1. Paul parle français.	(vrai)
2. Paul habite à Montréal.	(vrai)
3. Monique et Philippe habitent à Montréal.	(faux: Philippe habite à Québec.)
4. Monique parle français et anglais.	(vrai)
5. Philippe parle français et anglais aussi.	(faux: Philippe ne parle pas anglais.)

Now listen and check your answers.

PHONÉTIQUE

Activité 3. La liaison: pronom sujet + verbe. As you recall, in French, a pronoun subject and its verb are always linked together and pronounced like one long word.

Répétez. Repeat: nous dînons vous jouez je visite

When a subject pronoun ending on a silent "s" is followed by a verb beginning with a vowel sound, **liaison** occurs. This means that the "s" (representing the sound /z/) is pronounced as if it were the *first* sound of the verb. Note that liaison only occurs after plural subject pronouns.

Répétez. Repeat: nous aimons vous arrivez ils écoutent elles étudient

Vous habitez à Paris.
Nous invitons Philippe.

STRUCTURE ET VOCABULAIRE

A. *Le présent des verbes en* ***-er*** *et les pronoms sujets*

Activité 4. Prononciation. Open your textbook to p. 22. You will hear pairs of sentences containing the verbs **visiter** and **parler.** Repeat each sentence after the speaker.

Commençons. Let's begin.

Je visite Paris.
Tu visites Montréal.
Marc visite New York.
Hélène visite Boston.
Nous visitons Mexico.
Vous visitez Moscou.
Paul et Jacques visitent Québec.
Anne et Sylvie visitent Toronto.

Je parle français.
Tu parles français.
Il parle anglais.
Elle parle anglais.
Nous parlons espagnol.
Vous parlez russe.
Ils parlent français.
Elles parlent anglais.

Activité 5. Prononciation. Open your textbook to p. 25. In this activity you will practice the pronunciation of the new verbs. First repeat the infinitive. Then repeat the sentence in which the verb is used.

Commençons. Let's begin.

détester	Paul déteste Paris.
dîner	Roger dîne avec Nicole.
jouer (au tennis)	Nous jouons au tennis.
parler	Jacques parle français.
regarder	Nous regardons Suzanne.
	Tu regardes la télévision.
rentrer	Je rentre à Montréal.
téléphoner (à)	Vous téléphonez à Sylvie.
travailler	Pierre travaille.
visiter	Nous visitons Québec.

Now turn to p. 26 to practice more verbs. *Commençons.* Let's begin.

aimer	Paul aime Paris.
arriver	Nous arrivons de Bordeaux.
écouter	Vous écoutez la radio.
étudier	Ils étudient avec Sophie.
habiter	Barbara habite à Boston.
inviter	Elle invite Robert.

Activité 6. Pratique. Now you will have the opportunity to practice some of these verbs in substitution exercises. First repeat the sentence in your lab manual. Then listen to the new verb and make a new sentence using it. The voice on the tape will confirm the correct answer and then you will hear another new verb.

Commençons. Let's begin.

Marc **habite** à Paris.

travailler	Marc travaille à Paris.
dîner	Marc dîne à Paris.
étudier	Marc étudie à Paris.
arriver	Marc arrive à Paris.

Here is a new sentence.

Écoutez et répétez. Listen and repeat.

Vous **aimez** Philippe.

inviter	Vous invitez Philippe.
regarder	Vous regardez Philippe.
écouter	Vous écoutez Philippe.
détester	Vous détestez Philippe.

This time you will hear different *subjects* to use in making new sentences.

Écoutez et répétez. Listen and repeat.

Je joue au tennis.

nous	Nous jouons au tennis.
tu	Tu joues au tennis.
Paul	Paul joue au tennis.
Monique et Paul	Monique et Paul jouent au tennis.

Activité 7. Identification de structures. You will hear Paul talking about his friends. Listen carefully to each sentence and try to tell if he is speaking about one person or several people. If the verb begins with a consonant sound, it is impossible to tell. **Il téléphone(nt)** could mean *He is phoning* or *They are phoning*. But if the verb begins with a vowel sound, you can hear a difference between singular and plural. **Il étudie** means *He is studying*. In the plural, you hear the sound /z/: **ils étudient,** meaning *They are studying*. Mark the first row (**une personne**) if the speaker is definitely talking about a single person. Mark the second row (**un groupe**) if he is definitely talking about two or more people. If it is impossible to tell, mark row three (**impossible à dire).**

Commençons. Let's begin.

1. Ils habitent à Paris.
2. Elle(s) travaille(nt) à Montréal.
3. Elles arrivent de Québec.
4. Il(s) regarde(nt) la télévision.
5. Elle aime Québec.
6. Ils invitent Monique.
7. Elle(s) visite(nt) Montréal.
8. Il écoute la radio.

Now check your answers. You should have marked **une personne** for sentences 5 and 8. You should have marked **un groupe** for sentences 1, 3, and 6. You should have marked **impossible à dire** for sentences 2, 4, and 7. If you got any wrong, listen to this activity again.

B. La négation

Activité 8. Conversation: Pas moi. You will hear Michèle make a series of statements about her friends. Say that you do not do the things that her friends do.

Écoutez le modèle. Listen to the model.

Modèle: Sylvie travaille à Québec. Je ne travaille pas à Québec.

Commençons. Let's begin.

Nicole joue au tennis. — Je ne joue pas au tennis.
Henri téléphone à Suzanne. — Je ne téléphone pas à Suzanne.
Monique visite Chicago. — Je ne visite pas Chicago.
Marc étudie avec Sophie. — Je n'étudie pas avec Sophie.
Paul invite Martine. — Je n'invite pas Martine.
Marie aime Montréal. — Je n'aime pas Montréal.

Activité 9. Conversation: Contradictions. You will hear Philippe making certain statements. Contradict him by making his statements negative. Use subject pronouns.

Écoutez le modèle. Listen to the model.

Modèle: Marie parle anglais. — Ah non! Elle ne parle pas anglais.

Commençons. Let's begin.

Sophie travaille avec Marc. — Ah non! Elle ne travaille pas avec Marc.
Richard joue au tennis. — Ah non! Il ne joue pas au tennis.
Robert téléphone à Claire. — Ah non! Il ne téléphone pas à Claire.
Nous invitons Michèle. — Ah non! Nous n'invitons pas Michèle.
Nous étudions. — Ah non! Nous n'étudions pas.
Thomas et Paul écoutent la radio. — Ah non! Ils n'écoutent pas la radio.

C. *Les nombres de* 0 *à* 12

Activité 10. Compréhension. Repeat the numbers in your lab manual after the speaker.

zero, un, deux, trois, quatre, cinq, six, sept, huit, neuf, dix, onze, douze

Now, as you hear each number, cross out the corresponding digit in your lab manual.

Commençons. Let's begin.

neuf onze deux zéro dix sept trois douze un quatre six huit

You should have one number left: **cinq:** *five*.

Activité 11. Pratique. Now look in the lab manual and read each set of three numbers aloud. Then listen to the confirmation.

Écoutez le modèle. Listen to the model.

Modèle: Deux - neuf - quatre

Commençons. Let's begin.

A. trois - cinq - sept
B. huit - zéro - un
C. deux - neuf - onze
D. quatre - douze - six
E. dix - deux - douze
F. sept - huit - onze

Activité 12. Prononciation. Open your textbook to p. 29. You will first hear each number used before a word beginning with a consonant sound. Then you will hear the same number used before a word beginning with a vowel sound. Repeat each phrase after you hear it.

un moment	un instant
une minute	une heure
deux minutes	deux heures
trois minutes	trois heures
quatre minutes	quatre heures
cinq minutes	cinq heures
six minutes	six heures
sept minutes	sept heures
huit minutes	huit heures
neuf minutes	neuf heures
dix minutes	dix heures
onze minutes	onze heures
douze minutes	douze heures

Vocabulaire: L'heure

Activité 13. Prononciation. Now turn to p. 30 of your textbook. Repeat the times after the speaker.

Répétez. Repeat.

Il est une heure.	Il est midi.
Il est dix heures.	Il est minuit.

Activité 14. Conversation: L'heure. Monique is asking you what time it is. Look at the clocks in your lab manual and answer accordingly.

Écoutez le modèle. Listen to the model.

Modèle: Quelle heure est-il? — Il est trois heures.

Commençons. Let's begin.

1. Quelle heure est-il? — Il est dix heures.
2. Quelle heure est-il? — Il est cinq heures.
3. Quelle heure est-il? — Il est une heure.
4. Quelle heure est-il? — Il est huit heures.
5. Quelle heure est-il? — Il est midi.

DIALOGUE

Activité 15. Qu'est-ce que tu fais? Philippe will ask you what you do at certain hours of the day. Answer his questions according to the illustrations in your lab manual. NOTE: **Qu'est-ce que tu fais?** means *What do you do?*

Écoutez le modèle. Listen to the model.

Modèle: Qu'est-ce que tu fais à deux heures? — À deux heures, j'étudie.

Commençons. Let's begin.

1. Qu'est-ce que tu fais à onze heures? — À onze heures, j'étudie.
2. Qu'est-ce que tu fais à dix heures? — À dix heures, je regarde la télé.
3. Qu'est-ce que tu fais à six heures? — À six heures, je joue au tennis.
4. Qu'est-ce que tu fais à sept heures? — À sept heures, je dîne.
5. Qu'est-ce que tu fais à trois heures? — À trois heures, je téléphone.

DICTÉE

Activité 16. Au Canada. You are going to hear a short paragraph. First, listen! Do not write! Try to understand what is being said.

Vous habitez à Paris? J'habite à Québec avec Paul et Jacques. Nous habitons à Québec, mais nous ne travaillons pas à Québec. Je travaille à Montréal. Paul et Jacques étudient à l'Université Laval.

Now you will hear the paragraph again, broken into short phrases. Write what you hear. Note that the punctuation is already included in your lab manual, and many proper nouns are written for you.

Vous habitez à Paris? / J'habite à Québec / avec Paul et Jacques. / Nous habitons / à Québec, / mais nous ne travaillons pas / à Québec. / Je travaille / à Montréal. / Paul et Jacques / étudient / à l'Université Laval. /

Now, listen once more and check what you wrote.

(Text is reread without pauses.)

Fin de la Leçon Une.
End of Lesson One.
(music)

LEÇON 2. DAKAR

PRÉSENTATION

Activité 1. Lecture. Open your textbook to p. 32. Lamine, a student from Sénégal, introduces herself and her friend Hamadi.

(See textbook page 32.)

Activité 2. Compréhension du texte. Did you understand Lamine? You will hear a series of statements about what she said. Indicate whether they are true or false, by marking the appropriate response, **vrai,** true, or **faux,** false.

Écoutez. Listen.

1. Lamine habite à Paris.
2. Lamine habite à Dakar.
3. Lamine étudie l'architecture.
4. Lamine étudie beaucoup.
5. Lamine aime la musique.
6. Hamadi est très sportif.
7. Hamadi nage bien.
8. Lamine et Hamadi sont différents.

Now check your answers. You should have marked **vrai** for sentences 2, 3, 4, 5, and 8; and **faux** for sentences 1, 6, and 7. If you made any mistakes, listen to the **Présentation** once more, and do these questions again.

PHONÉTIQUE

Activité 3. Intonation: Questions à réponse affirmative ou négative. In French, as in English, the voice rises at the end of a yes/no question.

Compare: *Est-ce que tu travailles?* Are you working?

Repeat each question after the speaker, linking your words together and using a rising intonation.

Répétez. Repeat: Est-ce que vous voyagez?
Est-ce que tu joues au tennis?
Est-ce que Marie nage bien?

In conversational French, questions can be formed without **est-ce que** simply by using a rising intonation.

Répétez. Repeat: Vous voyagez?
Tu joues au tennis?
Marie nage bien?

Again in conversational French, if a yes answer is expected, questions can be formed by adding the tag **n'est-ce pas?** at the end of the sentence. Here the intonation falls on the main part of the sentence, and rises only on the **n'est-ce pas?**

Répétez. Repeat: Vous voyagez, n'est-ce pas?
Tu joues au tennis, n'est-ce pas?
Marie nage bien, n'est-ce pas?

STRUCTURE ET VOCABULAIRE

Vocabulaire: Activités

Activité 4. Prononciation. Open your textbook to p. 34. First repeat the **je**-forms of the verb after you hear it said by the speaker. Then listen and repeat the sample sentence.

Commençons. Let's begin.

chanter: je chante — Jean et Claire chantent.
danser: je danse — Jeanne et Richard dansent.
nager: je nage — Vous ne nagez pas.
voyager: je voyage — Paul ne voyage pas.

Now repeat each adverb and listen to the sentence in which it is used.

assez	Tu ne travailles pas assez.
aussi	J'invite Paul. J'invite Sylvie aussi.
beaucoup	Nous aimons beaucoup Dakar.
maintenant	Il travaille pour Air Afrique maintenant.
toujours	Ils parlent toujours français en classe.
souvent	Michèle ne voyage pas souvent.
bien	Tu chantes bien.
mal	Je chante mal.
assez	Vous dansez assez bien!
très	Anne ne nage pas très souvent.

Activité 5. Situation: Clarifications. You will hear what several people do. Make the statements clearer by adding the adverb suggested in your lab manual.

Écoutez le modèle. Listen to the model.

Modèle: Marie et Richard dansent. — Marie et Richard dansent bien.

Commençons. Let's begin.

1. Je chante. — Je chante mal.
2. Nous voyageons. — Nous voyageons souvent.
3. Tu travailles. — Tu travailles beaucoup.
4. Martine nage. — Martine nage maintenant.
5. Vous étudiez. — Vous étudiez toujours.
6. Claire et Louis dansent. — Claire et Louis dansent aussi.
7. Vous chantez. — Vous chantez assez bien.
8. M. et Mme Dupont voyagent. — M. et Mme Dupont voyagent très souvent.

A. *Le verbe **être***

Activité 6: Prononciation. Open your book to p. 35. **Être** is the most common verb in the French language. Repeat after the speaker, first the verb form and then the sample sentence containing that verb form.

Commençons. Let's begin.

je suis	Je suis à Québec.
tu es	Tu es à l'université.
il est/elle est	Il n'est pas avec Nathalie.
nous sommes	Nous ne sommes pas en classe.
vous êtes	Vous êtes de New York.
ils sont/elles sont	Elles ne sont pas à Paris.

Activité 7. Pratique. Now you will practice **être** in some substitution exercises. Repeat the key sentence. Then formulate new sentences using the suggested subjects.

Commençons. Let's begin.

Lamine est à Paris.

vous — Vous êtes à Paris.
tu — Tu es à Paris.
Daniel et François — Daniel et François sont à Paris.
nous — Nous sommes à Paris.

Lamine n'est pas en classe.

je — Je ne suis pas en classe.
nous — Nous ne sommes pas en classe.
Philippe — Philippe n'est pas en classe.
vous — Vous n'êtes pas en classe.

B. La construction infinitive

Activité 8. Narration: C'est vrai! You will hear what certain people do not like to do. Confirm these statements using the verb **détester.**

Écoutez le modèle. Listen to the model.

Modèle: Georges n'aime pas nager. — Georges déteste nager.

Commençons. Let's begin.

Jean n'aime pas chanter. — Jean déteste chanter.
Nous n'aimons pas travailler. — Nous détestons travailler.
Nous n'aimons pas jouer au tennis. — Nous détestons jouer au tennis.
Paul et Suzanne n'aiment pas voyager. — Paul et Suzanne détestent voyager.
Sylvie n'aime pas étudier. — Sylvie déteste étudier.
Vous n'aimez pas écouter la radio. — Vous détestez écouter la radio.
Tu n'aimes pas danser. — Tu détestes danser.

C. Questions à réponse affirmative ou négative

Activité 9. Situation: Répétition. You will hear Lamine ask several questions in an informal way, using intonation only. Repeat these questions using **est-ce que.**

Écoutez le modèle. Listen to the model.

Modèle: Vous aimez voyager? — Est-ce que vous aimez voyager?

Commençons. Let's begin.

Vous travaillez maintenant? — Est-ce que vous travaillez maintenant?
Tu danses avec Marie? — Est-ce que tu danses avec Marie?
Marc et Claire voyagent souvent? — Est-ce que Marc et Claire voyagent souvent?
Chantal déteste téléphoner? — Est-ce que Chantal déteste téléphoner?
Nous invitons Richard? — Est-ce que nous invitons Richard?
Je téléphone à Sylvie? — Est-ce que je téléphone à Sylvie?
Anne joue au tennis? — Est-ce qu'Anne joue au tennis?

Activité 10. Conversation: Souvent? Lamine is telling you what certain people do. Ask whether they do these things often. Introduce your questions with **est-ce que** and use a subject pronoun.

Écoutez le modèle. Listen to the model.

Modèle: Alain travaille. — Est-ce qu'il travaille souvent?

Commençons. Let's begin.

Philippe nage. — Est-ce qu'il nage souvent?
Marie étudie. — Est-ce qu'elle étudie souvent?
Paul voyage. — Est-ce qu'il voyage souvent?
Nathalie téléphone. — Est-ce qu'elle téléphone souvent?
Jacqueline chante. — Est-ce qu'elle chante souvent?
Pierre et Anne dansent. — Est-ce qu'ils dansent souvent?
Alice et Marguerite étudient. — Est-ce qu'elles étudient souvent?

D. *Les nombres de* 13 *à* 99

Activité 11. Compréhension: Les nombres. Repeat the following numbers after the speaker. Open your lab manual.

Commençons. Let's begin.

13 14 15 16 17 18 19 20
21 22 29 30 40 50 60
61 62 69 70 71 72 73
79 80 81 82 89 90 91 92 99

You will now hear ten numbers read. Cross out the corresponding numbers in your lab manual.

Commençons. Let's begin.

13 60 80 92 22 16 50 73 30 69

Check your answers. You should have crossed out 13, 16, 22, 30, 50, 60, 69, 73, 80, and 92.

Activité 12. Compréhension: Les adresses. Monique is giving you the addresses of her friends. Write down the house numbers in the blanks in your lab manual.

Commençons. Let's begin.

1. Paul habite 86, rue de la Pompe.
2. Véronique habite 61, rue Daru.
3. Élisabeth habite 14, avenue Daumesnil.
4. Marc habite 98, boulevard des Italiens.
5. Philippe habite 82, rue Sedaine.
6. Jean-Claude habite 76, rue de la Boétie.
7. Sylvie habite 95, rue de Sèvres.
8. Robert habite 24, avenue Foch.

Check your answers.

1. quatre-vingt-six, eighty-six
2. soixante et un, sixty-one
3. quatorze, fourteen
4. quatre-vingt-dix-huit, ninety-eight
5. quatre-vingt-deux, eighty-two
6. soixante-seize, seventy-six
7. quatre-vingt-quinze, ninety-five
8. vingt-quatre, twenty-four

Vocabulaire: Les divisions de l'heure

Activité 13. Prononciation. Open your textbook to p. 42 and repeat after the speaker.

Il est huit heures et quart.
Il est neuf heures et demie.
Il est midi moins le quart.
Il est une heure cinq.
Il est deux heures vingt.
Il est trois heures moins cinq.
Il est deux heures cinquante-cinq.
Il est quatre heures moins vingt.
Il est trois heures quarante.

Activité 14. Compréhension: La montre de Claire. Look at the times shown on the watches in your lab manual. You will hear Claire give the time. If her time corresponds to that shown on the watch, mark **oui.** If she gives a different time, mark **non.**

Écoutez le modèle. Listen to the model.

Modèle: Il est six heures.

Claire says it is six o'clock, but the watch shows five o'clock. You should have marked **non.**

Commençons. Let's begin.

1. Il est quatre heures.
2. Il est cinq heures et demie.
3. Il est dix heures moins le quart.
4. Il est minuit.
5. Il est deux heures et quart.
6. Il est une heure et demie.
7. Il est trois heures moins le quart.
8. Il est huit heures et quart.

Now check your answers. You should have marked **oui** for items 1, 3, 5, and 6; and **non** for items 2, 4, 7, and 8. If you made any mistakes, listen to these sentences again.

Activité 15. Conversation: Quelle heure est-il? Philippe is asking you the time. Answer according to the clocks you see in your lab manual.

Écoutez le modèle. Listen to the model.

Modèle: Quelle heure est-il? Il est deux heures vingt-cinq.

Commençons. Let's begin.

1. Quelle heure est-il? Il est midi moins cinq.
2. Quelle heure est-il? Il est sept heures dix.
3. Quelle heure est-il? Il est six heures moins vingt.
4. Quelle heure est-il? Il est deux heures et quart.
5. Quelle heure est-il? Il est quatre heures moins le quart.
6. Quelle heure est-il? Il est une heure vingt.
7. Quelle heure est-il? Il est neuf heures et demie.
8. Quelle heure est-il? Il est cinq heures moins dix.

DIALOGUE

Activité 16. Préférences et obligations. Lamine will ask you whether you do certain things. Answer her, using the expressions suggested in your lab manual.

Écoutez le modèle. Listen to the model.

Modèle: Tu étudies?	Oui, je dois étudier.

Commençons. Let's begin.

1. Tu voyages?	Oui, j'aime voyager.
2. Tu invites Jacqueline?	Oui, je peux inviter Jacqueline.
3. Tu téléphones à Paul?	Oui, je dois téléphoner à Paul.
4. Tu joues au tennis?	Oui, je voudrais jouer au tennis.
5. Tu dînes maintenant?	Oui, je veux dîner maintenant.
6. Tu regardes la télé?	Non, je n'aime pas regarder la télé.
7. Tu rentres?	Non, je ne veux pas rentrer.
8. Tu dînes avec nous?	Non, je ne peux pas dîner avec vous.
9. Tu travailles?	Non, je ne dois pas travailler.

DICTÉE

Activité 17. Voyages. You will hear a short paragraph. First, listen! Do not write!

J'aime voyager. Je voyage assez souvent. Maintenant je suis à Québec. Je veux aussi visiter Montréal. Est-ce que vous voyagez souvent? Est-ce que vous aimez voyager?

Now write the sentences you hear in your lab manual.

J'aime voyager. / Je voyage / assez souvent. / Maintenant / je suis à Québec. / Je veux aussi visiter Montréal. Est-ce que / vous voyagez souvent? / Est-ce que vous aimez voyager? /

Listen again and check what you wrote.
(Text is reread without pauses.)

Fin de la Leçon 2.
End of Lesson 2.
(music)

LEÇON 3. À PARIS, À L'ALLIANCE FRANÇAISE

PRÉSENTATION

Activité 1. Lecture. Open your textbook to p. 46. Follow the text as you listen to it.

(See textbook page 46.)

Activité 2. Compréhension du texte. Did you understand Janet and Claire? You will hear a series of questions about what they said. Mark your answers in your lab manual: **oui** or **non.**

Écoutez. Listen.

1. Est-ce que Janet est anglaise?
2. Est-ce que Claire est anglaise aussi?
3. Est-ce que Claire habite à Genève?
4. Est-ce que Claire étudie le français?
5. Est-ce qu'elle aime voyager?

Now check your answers. You should have marked **oui** for sentences 1, 4, and 5; and **non** for sentences 2 and 3. If you made any mistakes, listen to the **Présentation** once more and do these questions again.

PHONÉTIQUE

Activité 3. Intonation: Questions d'information. The intonation of information questions is different in French and English.

Compare: *Qu'est-ce que tu regardes?* What are you looking at?

In French information questions, the question words begin on a high pitch. Then the intonation drops, to rise slightly on the last syllable.

Répétez. Repeat: Qui joue au tennis? Comment allez-vous?

Quand est-ce que tu étudies? Où est Philippe?

STRUCTURE ET VOCABULAIRE

A. *Le pronom* ***on***

Activité 4. Prononciation. Open your textbook to p. 48. Repeat the sentences after the speakers.

Est-ce qu'on étudie beaucoup à l'université? Oui, on étudie beaucoup.
Est-ce qu'on parle allemand à Genève? Non, on ne parle pas allemand. On parle français.
Est-ce qu'on dîne maintenant? Non, on dîne à sept heures.

Activité 5. Situation: Où est-ce qu'on parle français? You will hear the names of certain cities. Say whether or not French is spoken in those cities.

Écoutez les modèles. Listen to the models.

Modèles: Paris? Oui, on parle français à Paris.
San Francisco? Non, on ne parle pas français à San Francisco.

Commençons. Let's begin.

Genève? — Oui, on parle français à Genève.
Philadelphie? — Non, on ne parle pas français à Philadelphie.
Québec? — Oui, on parle français à Québec.
Los Angeles? — Non, on ne parle pas français à Los Angeles.
Mexico? — Non, on ne parle pas français à Mexico.
Montréal? — Oui, on parle français à Montréal.

B. Questions d'information

Activité 6. Prononciation. Open your textbook to p. 50. Repeat the interrogative expressions and the sentences after the speakers.

comment? — Comment est-ce que vous voyagez? En auto ou en bus?
où? — Où est-ce que tu habites?
quand? — Quand est-ce que vous étudiez?
à quelle heure? — À quelle heure est-ce qu'il arrive?
pourquoi? — Pourquoi est-ce que tu étudies les maths?
parce que — Parce que je veux être architecte!

Now turn to p. 51.

Écoutez et répétez. Listen and repeat.

qui? — Qui est-ce que vous invitez?
à qui? — À qui est-ce que tu parles?
avec qui? — Avec qui est-ce que Jacques joue au tennis?
pour qui? — Pour qui est-ce que vous travaillez?
que? — Qu'est-ce que vous étudiez?

Activité 7. Pratique. Now we will do some substitution exercises. First repeat the key sentence. Then formulate new sentences using the suggested interrogative expression. Be sure to use French intonation.

Commençons. Let's begin.

Où est-ce que vous travaillez?
quand? — Quand est-ce que vous travaillez?
pour qui? — Pour qui est-ce que vous travaillez?
pourquoi? — Pourquoi est-ce que vous travaillez?

Quand est-ce que tu rentres?
avec qui? — Avec qui est-ce que tu rentres?
à quelle heure? — À quelle heure est-ce que tu rentres?
comment? — Comment est-ce que tu rentres?

À quelle heure est-ce qu'il téléphone?
à qui? — À qui est-ce qu'il téléphone?
pour qui? — Pour qui est-ce qu'il téléphone?
pourquoi? — Pourquoi est-ce qu'il téléphone?

Activité 8. Situation: Questions. Be nosy and ask a lot of questions. Use the suggested interrogative expressions.

Écoutez le modèle. Listen to the model.

Modèle: Pierre travaille. Pour qui? — Pour qui est-ce que Pierre travaille?

Commençons! Let's begin.

Tu voyages. Pourquoi? — Pourquoi est-ce que tu voyages?
Martine étudie. Où? — Où est-ce que Martine étudie?
Robert arrive. À quelle heure? — À quelle heure est-ce que Robert arrive?
Vous rentrez. Quand? — Quand est-ce que vous rentrez?
Luc et Claire dansent. Comment? — Comment est-ce que Luc et Claire dansent?
Sylvie téléphone. À qui? — À qui est-ce que Sylvie téléphone?
Albert chante. Avec qui? — Avec qui est-ce qu'Albert chante?

Activité 9. Conversation: Comment? Jean-Michel is telling you certain things, but you do not understand the last part of each statement. Ask a question so that the information will be repeated. In your questions, use the appropriate interrogative expression and the corresponding subject pronoun.

Écoutez le modèle. Listen to the model.

Modèle: Jacqueline habite à Paris. — Où est-ce qu'elle habite?

Commençons. Let's begin.

Robert habite à Québec. — Où est-ce qu'il habite?
Albert travaille à Zurich. — Où est-ce qu'il travaille?
Monique rentre à minuit. — À quelle heure est-ce qu'elle rentre?
Sylvie téléphone à Georges. — À qui est-ce qu'elle téléphone?
Paul invite Christine. — Qui est-ce qu'il invite?

Martine travaille pour Monsieur Duroc. — Pour qui est-ce qu'elle travaille?
Philippe étudie beaucoup parce qu'il aime étudier. — Pourquoi est-ce qu'il étudie beaucoup?

C. Les pronoms accentués

Activité 10. Situation: Avec insistance. Repeat the statements you hear, accenting the subject. Use a stress pronoun and repeat the subject pronoun as in the model.

Écoutez le modèle. Listen to the model.

Modèle: Georges arrive à midi. — Lui, il arrive à midi.

Commençons. Let's begin.

Je chante bien. — Moi, je chante bien.
Sylvie parle anglais. — Elle, elle parle anglais.
Nous ne voyageons pas. — Nous, nous ne voyageons pas.
Vous rentrez avec Michèle. — Vous, vous rentrez avec Michèle.
Tu joues au tennis. — Toi, tu joues au tennis.
Anne et Brigitte travaillent. — Elles, elles travaillent.
Philippe et Martine ne travaillent pas. — Eux, ils ne travaillent pas.

Activité 11. Conversation: Pourquoi? Paul is telling you with which friends he does certain things. Ask him why. Use a stress pronoun in each of your questions.

Écoutez le modèle. Listen to the model.

Modèle: Je joue au tennis avec Charles. — Pourquoi est-ce que tu joues avec lui?

Commençons. Let's begin.

Je joue avec Hélène. — Pourquoi est-ce que tu joues avec elle?
J'étudie avec Thomas. — Pourquoi est-ce que tu étudies avec lui?
J'étudie avec Françoise et Sylvie. — Pourquoi est-ce que tu étudies avec elles?
Je voyage avec Éric et Marc. — Pourquoi est-ce que tu voyages avec eux?
Je travaille avec Henri et Thomas. — Pourquoi est-ce que tu travailles avec eux?
Je danse avec Monique. — Pourquoi est-ce que tu danses avec elle?

D. La date

Activité 12. Prononciation. Now open your textbook to p. 54. Repeat the days of the week after the speaker.

les jours de la semaine
lundi
mardi
mercredi
jeudi
vendredi
samedi
dimanche

Now repeat the following expressions.

Quel jour est-ce?
Quel jour sommes-nous?
Aujourd'hui, nous sommes lundi.
Demain, c'est mardi.

Now repeat the months of the year.

les mois de l'année
janvier
février
mars
avril
mai
juin
juillet
août
septembre
octobre
novembre
décembre

Activité 13. Situation: Demain. You will hear what day of the week it is today. Say what day it will be tomorrow.

Écoutez le modèle. Listen to the model.

Modèle: Aujourd'hui, c'est mardi. Demain, c'est mercredi.

Commençons. Let's begin.

Aujourd'hui, c'est jeudi. Demain, c'est vendredi.
Aujourd'hui, c'est samedi. Demain, c'est dimanche.
Aujourd'hui, c'est lundi. Demain, c'est mardi.
Aujourd'hui, c'est mercredi. Demain, c'est jeudi.
Aujourd'hui, c'est dimanche. Demain, c'est lundi.
Aujourd'hui, c'est mardi. Demain, c'est mercredi.

Activité 14. Compréhension orale: Quelle est la date? You will hear various people speaking about certain events and when these events will take place. Listen carefully to the date mentioned by each person and write it down in the space provided in your lab manual. Do not worry if you do not understand every word. Concentrate on the dates.

Écoutez le modèle. Listen to the model.

Modèle: J'arrive à Zurich le douze avril. Write the date: le douze avril.

Commençons. Let's begin.

1. L'anniversaire de Georges est le 23 avril.
2. Anne-Marie arrive à Québec le 12 décembre.
3. Le 13 juin, nous rentrons de France.
4. Nous dînons au restaurant le premier juillet, n'est-ce pas?
5. Le 25 août, j'ai rendez-vous avec Marie.
6. Mon oncle rentre de Dakar le 5 janvier.
7. Cécile invite ses amis le premier février.
8. Mon anniversaire est le 18 mai.

Now check your answers.

1. le 23 avril—April 23rd
2. le 12 décembre—December 12th
3. le 13 juin—June 13th
4. le premier juillet—July first
5. le 25 août—August 25th
6. le 5 janvier—January 5th
7. le premier février—February first
8. le 18 mai—May 18th

DIALOGUE

Activité 15. Questions. Claire will ask you some questions. Answer her, basing your responses on the illustrations in your lab manual.

Écoutez le modèle. Listen to the model.

Modèle: Où est-ce que tu habites? J'habite à Paris.

Commençons. Let's begin.

1. Quand est-ce que tu arrives à Lausanne? — J'arrive à Lausanne le 3 mars.
2. Quand est-ce que tu visites Genève? — Je visite Genève le 10 juillet.
3. Quand est-ce que tu rentres à Paris? — Je rentre à Paris le premier septembre.
4. Avec qui est-ce que tu voyages? — Je voyage avec Jacqueline.
5. Où est-ce que tu dînes? — Je dîne à La Terrasse.

DICTÉE

Activité 16. Tennis. You will hear a short paragraph. First, listen! Do not write!

Avec qui est-ce que tu joues au tennis? Tu joues avec Paul et Philippe, n'est-ce pas? Pourquoi est-ce que tu joues avec eux? Pourquoi est-ce que tu ne joues pas avec moi? Moi aussi, je joue bien!

Now write the sentences in your workbook as you hear them.

Avec qui / est-ce que tu joues / au tennis? / Tu joues avec Paul et Philippe, / n'est-ce pas? / Pourquoi est-ce que / tu joues / avec eux? / Pourquoi est-ce que / tu ne joues pas / avec moi? / Moi aussi, / je joue bien! /

Listen again and check what you wrote.

(Text is reread without pauses.)

Fin de la Leçon 3.
End of Lesson 3.
(music)

VIVRE EN FRANCE 1. L'IDENTITÉ

Activité 1. La bonne réponse. You will hear a series of questions. In your lab manual you will see three possible responses for each question. Select the logical response by circling the corresponding letter.

Commençons. Let's begin.

1. Qu'est-ce que vous faites?
2. Êtes-vous célibataire?
3. Où es-tu né?
4. Qui est à l'appareil?
5. Allô, est-ce que je peux parler à Françoise?
6. Quelle est la date de ton anniversaire?
7. Est-ce que tu veux dîner avec moi lundi?
8. Allô, ici Thérèse Mercier.

Now listen to the complete exchanges and correct your work.

Écoutez. Listen.

1. Qu'est-ce que vous faites?	Je suis photographe.
2. Êtes-vous célibataire?	Non, je suis marié.
3. Où es-tu né?	À Montréal.
4. Qui est à l'appareil?	Allô! Ici André Lucas.
5. Allô, est-ce que je peux parler à Françoise?	Oui, un moment. Ne quittez pas, s'il vous plaît.
6. Quelle est la date de ton anniversaire?	Je suis né le 18 septembre.
7. Est-ce que tu veux dîner avec moi lundi?	Oui, bien sûr. À lundi.
8. Allô, ici Thérèse Mercier.	Bonjour, Thérèse, comment allez-vous?

Activité 2. En France. You will now hear a short dialogue. In this dialogue a student comes to the office of a language school in France, l'Institut de Langues Modernes, to register for summer courses. The secretary of the school asks her a few questions and fills out the registration form, **le bulletin d'inscription.** Listen carefully to the dialogue. Although you will not be able to understand every word, you should be able to understand all the information necessary to fill out the registration form in your lab manual. You will hear the dialogue twice. First listen carefully. The second time you hear the dialogue, fill in the required information in your lab manual.

Commençons. Let's begin.

Écoutez. Listen.

—Bonjour, Mademoiselle.
—Bonjour, Monsieur. Je voudrais m'inscrire aux cours de l'Institut de Langues Modernes.
—Très bien. J'ai besoin de certains renseignements pour vous inscrire. D'abord, pouvez-vous me dire comment vous vous appelez?
—Je m'appelle Denise Lavoie.
—Denise Lavoie. Vous êtes canadienne, n'est-ce pas?
—Non, je ne suis pas canadienne. Je suis américaine. Je suis née à Boston.
—Et quelle est votre adresse à Paris?
—J'habite 39, rue du Four.
—39, rue du Four. Très bien. Vous avez un numéro de téléphone?
—Oui, attendez! C'est le 43-29-20-52.
—Merci. Bon. Est-ce que vous avez une pièce d'identité?
—Oui, voici mon passeport.
—Parfait. Signez ici. . . . Vous êtes inscrite pour les cours qui commencent lundi prochain.
—Merci bien.

Écoutez à nouveau et écrivez. Listen again and write.

(Dialogue is reread.)

Fin de Vivre en France 1.
End of Vivre en France 1.
(music)

UNITÉ 2: IMAGES DE LA VIE

LEÇON 4. LA VIE EST BELLE!

PRÉSENTATION

Activité 1. Lecture. *Ouvrez votre livre à la page 62.* Open your textbook to p. 62. *Écoutez.*

(See textbook page 62.)

Activité 2. Compréhension du texte. You will hear a series of statements about the text you have just heard. Listen carefully to each statement, and mark in your lab manual whether it is **vrai,** true, or **faux,** false.

Commençons.

1. Caroline a une voiture.
2. Caroline a une mobylette.
3. Caroline a un téléviseur.
4. Caroline a une chaîne-stéréo.
5. Caroline a des disques.
6. Caroline a un copain.

Maintenant vérifiez vos réponses. Now check your answers. You should have marked **vrai** for sentences 2, 4, 5, and 6; and **faux** for sentences 1 and 3. If you got any wrong, listen to the **Présentation** once more, and do these questions again.

PHONÉTIQUE

Activité 3. Les voyelles /ɛ̃/ et /y/. The vowels /ɛ̃/ and /y/ are important to learn because they distinguish the articles **un** and **une.**

(a) *La voyelle /ɛ̃/.* The vowel /ɛ̃/ is a nasal vowel. It can be spelled **un, in,** or **ain.** As you practice it, be sure not to pronounce an "n."

Répétez: un un un
cinq quinze vingt copain invite matin
Ils invitent quinze copains.
Il est cinq heures vingt du matin.

(b) *La voyelle /y/.* The vowel /y/ does not exist in English. To pronounce /y/, round your lips as you say /i/.

Écoutez: /i/ /y/ /i/ /y/ /i/ /y/

Répétez: tu bien sûr salut calculatrice étudier utiliser
Bien sûr, tu études.
Lucie utilise une calculatrice.
Tu as une voiture.

STRUCTURE ET VOCABULAIRE

*A. Le verbe **avoir***

Activité 4. Prononciation. *Ouvrez votre livre à la page 64.* Open your textbook to p. 64. The verb **avoir** is irregular.

Repeat the forms of this verb after the speaker.

j'ai
tu as
il a
nous avons
vous avez
ils ont

Now repeat the sample sentences.

J'ai une bicyclette.
Est-ce que tu as une auto?
Philippe a une guitare.
Nous avons une Renault.
Vous avez une Fiat.
Elles ont une Toyota.

Activité 5. Pratique. Now we will do some substitution exercises. Repeat the key sentence. Then formulate new sentences using the suggested subjects.

Commençons.

J'ai une mobylette.
nous — Nous avons une mobylette.
tu — Tu as une mobylette.
Charles et Marc — Charles et Marc ont une mobylette.
vous — Vous avez une mobylette.

Est-ce que **Philippe** a une guitare?
vous — Est-ce que vous avez une guitare?
Marie et Monique — Est-ce que Marie et Monique ont une guitare?
nous — Est-ce que nous avons une guitare?

*B. Le genre des noms; l'article indéfini **un, une***

Activité 6. Identification de structures. Imagine that you are at a party for foreign students. You will hear someone mention the nationality of the guests as they come in. Can you tell from the statement whether the guest is a man or a woman? Listen carefully. If you hear the article **un,** the speaker is referring to a male. In your lab manual mark the first row **un homme.** If you hear the article **une,** the speaker is referring to a female. Mark the second row **une femme.**

Commençons.

1. Voici un Français.
2. Voilà une Portugaise.
3. C'est un Canadien.
4. Voici un Espagnol.
5. Voilà une Américaine.
6. Voici un Italien.
7. C'est un Suisse.
8. C'est une Suédoise.

Maintenant vérifiez vos réponses. Now check your answers. You should have marked **un homme** for sentences 1, 3, 4, 6, and 7, and **une femme** for sentences 2, 5, and 8. If you got any wrong, listen to this activity once more and do these questions again.

Vocabulaire: Les gens

Activité 7. Prononciation. *Ouvrez votre livre à la page 66.* Open your textbook to p. 66. Repeat the nouns after the speakers.

un ami — une amie
un camarade — une camarade
un camarade de chambre — une camarade de chambre
un copain — une copine
un étudiant — une étudiante
un garçon — une fille
un jeune homme — une jeune fille
un homme — une femme
un monsieur — une dame
un professeur — une personne

Activité 8. Pratique. Now you will practice these words in a substitution exercise. First repeat the key sentence. Then replace the nouns as suggested.

Commençons.

Je travaille avec **un garçon.**
une dame — Je travaille avec une dame.
un jeune homme — Je travaille avec un jeune homme.
une étudiante — Je travaille avec une étudiante.

Philippe téléphone à **un ami.**
une amie — Philippe téléphone à une amie.
une copine — Philippe téléphone à une copine.
un étudiant — Philippe téléphone à un étudiant.

Alice parle à **une dame.**
un professeur — Alice parle à un professeur.
un copain — Alice parle à un copain.
une femme — Alice parle à une femme.
une camarade — Alice parle à une camarade.

Activité 9. Compréhension: Qui est-ce? You will hear a series of sentences. Each of these sentences contains a noun referring to a person. These nouns belong to the vocabulary you have just practiced. Listen carefully to each sentence. In the space provided in your lab manual, write down the noun referring to a person. Do not worry if you do not understand every word. *Écoutez le modèle.*

Modèle: Voici une amie canadienne. — Did you hear the noun, **une amie?** You would have written **une amie.**

Commençons.

1. Nous avons un professeur très strict.
2. Laurent a un ami qui habite à Paris.
3. Je connais une jeune fille qui parle japonais.
4. Voici une étudiante qui étudie souvent avec moi.
5. Mlle Dumas est une femme extraordinaire.
6. Alexandre est un jeune homme très sympathique.

Maintenant vérifiez vos réponses. Now check your answers.

1. un professeur
2. un ami
3. une jeune fille
4. une étudiante
5. une femme
6. un jeune homme

Vocabulaire: Les objets

Activité 10. Prononciation. *Ouvrez votre livre à la page 67.* Open your textbook to p. 67. Repeat the nouns after the speakers.

un objet
une chose
pour la classe
un cahier
une calculatrice
un crayon
une montre
un livre
un stylo

pour le bureau
un ordinateur
une machine à écrire
un téléphone

pour le transport
un vélo
une bicyclette
un vélomoteur
une mobylette
un VTT
une moto
une auto
une voiture

l'équipement audio-visuel
un disque
un appareil-photo
un compact disque
une cassette
un CD
une chaîne-stéréo
un lecteur de cassettes
une mini-chaîne
un lecteur de compact disques
une radio
un magnétophone
une radio-cassette
un magnétoscope
une caméra
un téléviseur
une photo
un walkman

Activité 11. Pratique. Now practice these words in a substitution exercise. Repeat the key sentence. Then formulate new sentences using the suggested nouns. Be sure to use the appropriate article: **un** or **une.**

Commençons.

Nous avons une **radio.**

livre	Nous avons un livre.
bicyclette	Nous avons une bicyclette.
moto	Nous avons une moto.
disque	Nous avons un disque.

Avez-vous un **vélo?**

montre	Avez-vous une montre?
chaîne-stéréo	Avez-vous une chaîne-stéréo?
voiture	Avez-vous une voiture?
ordinateur	Avez-vous un ordinateur?
stylo	Avez-vous un stylo?
appareil-photo	Avez-vous un appareil-photo?

Monique a une **auto.**

photo	Monique a une photo.
caméra	Monique a une caméra.
magnétophone	Monique a un magnétophone.
vélomoteur	Monique a un vélomoteur.
mini-chaîne	Monique a une mini-chaîne.

*C. Le pluriel des noms; l'article indéfini **des***

Activité 12. Situation: Au grand magasin. Imagine that you are in a French department store. When you hear a number, ask the salesman if he has the objects pictured in your lab manual. Be sure to use plural nouns. *Écoutez le modèle.*

Modèle: Est-ce que vous avez des cassettes?

Commençons.

1. #	Est-ce que vous avez des montres?
2. #	Est-ce que vous avez des livres?
3. #	Est-ce que vous avez des disques?
4. #	Est-ce que vous avez des cahiers?
5. #	Est-ce que vous avez des ordinateurs?
6. #	Est-ce que vous avez des crayons?

D. L'article indéfini dans les phrases négatives

Activité 13. Conversation: Caroline. Monique is asking you whether Caroline has certain objects. Answer in the negative. *Écoutez le modèle.*

Modèle: Est-ce que Caroline a une voiture? — Non, elle n'a pas de voiture.

Commençons.

Est-ce qu'elle a une chaîne-stéréo?	Non, elle n'a pas de chaîne-stéréo.
Est-ce qu'elle a un vélo?	Non, elle n'a pas de vélo.
Est-ce qu'elle a un magnétophone?	Non, elle n'a pas de magnétophone.
Est-ce qu'elle a un appareil-photo?	Non, elle n'a pas d'appareil-photo.
Est-ce qu'elle a un magnétoscope?	Non, elle n'a pas de magnétoscope.

Activité 14. Situation: Possessions. You will hear a series of questions about what people own. Answer in the affirmative or in the negative, as indicated in your lab manual. Use subject pronouns. *Écoutez les modèles.*

Modèles:	
Est-ce que Paul a des cassettes?	Oui, il a des cassettes.
Est-ce que Sylvie et Marie ont une moto?	Non, elles n'ont pas de moto.

Commençons.

1. Est-ce que Sylvie a des disques?	Non, elle n'a pas de disques.
2. Est-ce que Marc et Alain ont une mobylette?	Non, ils n'ont pas de mobylette.
3. Est-ce que Nadine et Claire ont une machine à écrire?	Oui, elles ont une machine à écrire.
4. Est-ce que Pierre et Isabelle ont des livres?	Oui, ils ont des livres.
5. Est-ce que Robert a une radio?	Oui, il a une radio.
6. Est-ce que Sophie a une bicyclette?	Non, elle n'a pas de bicyclette.

*E. L'expression **Il y a***

Activité 15. Situation: L'appartement de Michel. Say whether or not the following objects are to be found in Michel's apartment. Use the expression **il y a** and the appropriate indefinite article: **un, une,** or **pas de.** *Écoutez les modèles.*

Modèles:	
téléviseur (oui)	Oui, il y a un téléviseur.
ordinateur (non)	Non, il n'y a pas d'ordinateur.

Commençons.

caméra (non)	Non, il n'y a pas de caméra.
chaîne-stéréo (non)	Non, il n'y a pas de chaîne-stéréo.
magnétoscope (oui)	Oui, il y a un magnétoscope.
calculatrice (oui)	Oui, il y a une calculatrice.
appareil-photo (oui)	Oui, il y a un appareil-photo.

DIALOGUE

Activité 16. Questions. Caroline will ask you several questions. Answer according to the illustrations in your lab manual. *Écoutez le modèle.*

Modèle:	
Qu'est-ce que c'est?	C'est un téléviseur.

Commençons.

1. Qu'est-ce que c'est?	C'est une calculatrice.
2. Qu'est-ce que tu as?	J'ai un stylo.
3. Qu'est-ce que tu veux?	Je veux un appareil-photo.
4. Qu'est-ce que tu écoutes?	J'écoute des disques.
5. Qu'est-ce que tu regardes?	Je regarde des photos.
6. Qu'est-ce que tu utilises?	J'utilise une machine à écrire.

DICTÉE

Activité 17. Jacqueline. You are going to hear a short paragraph. First, listen! Do not write!

Voici Jacqueline. C'est une amie. Elle a des disques, mais elle n'a pas de chaîne-stéréo. Moi, j'ai une mini-chaîne, mais elle ne marche pas. Et toi, est-ce que tu as une chaîne-stéréo?

Now write the sentences as you hear them.

Voici Jacqueline. / C'est une amie. / Elle a des disques, / mais elle n'a pas / de chaîne-stéréo. / Moi, j'ai une mini-chaîne, / mais elle ne marche pas. / Et toi, / est-ce que tu as / une chaîne-stéréo? /

Listen once more and check what you wrote.

(Text is reread without pauses.)

Fin de la Leçon 4.
End of Lesson 4.
(music)

LEÇON 5. DANS LA RUE

PRÉSENTATION

Activité 1. Lecture. *Ouvrez votre livre à la page 76.* Open your textbook to p. 76. *Écoutez.*

(See textbook page 76.)

Activité 2. Compréhension du texte. You will hear a series of sentences about the text you have just heard. Listen carefully to each sentence and indicate in your lab manual whether it is true or false by marking **vrai** or **faux.**

Commençons.

1. Il y a une jeune fille dans le café.
2. Un jeune homme passe devant le café.
3. La jeune fille est blonde.
4. La jeune fille est américaine.
5. La jeune fille est anglaise.
6. La jeune fille est canadienne.
7. La jeune fille est française.
8. Le jeune homme continue sa promenade.

Maintenant vérifiez vos réponses. Now check your answers. You should have marked **vrai** for sentences 1, 2, 3, 7, and 8; and **faux** for sentences 4, 5, and 6. If you got any wrong, listen once more to the **Présentation,** and do these questions again.

PHONÉTIQUE

Activité 3. Les voyelles / ə /, /a/, /e/. The vowels / ə /, /a/, and /e/ are important to learn because they distinguish the articles **le, la,** and **les.** The vowel / ə / is called a "mute e."

Écoutez: /ə/ /ə/ /ə/

Répétez: le je ne que de ce
au revoir demie regarder premier petit demain
Denise regarde le petit vélo.

The letter "a" in French represents the sound /a/.

Répétez: a la ami cassette caméra camarade Canada
Alice a la cassette de Madame Laval.

The vowel sound /e/ is different from its English counterpart because there is no glide in French.

Compare: les LAY des DAY

Répétez: et les des dîner premier marié réservé
Vous voulez inviter des étudiants?
Les garçons utilisent le vélo et la moto.

STRUCTURE ET VOCABULAIRE

A. *L'article défini* ***le, la, les***

Activité 4. Identification de structures. Imagine that you are at a concert and you hear a Frenchman talking about the performers. Is he referring to a man, to a woman, or to several people? Pay attention to the form of the definite article. If you hear the definite article **le,** mark the first row **un homme** in your lab manual. If you hear the article **la,** mark the second row **une femme.** If you hear the article **les,** mark the third row **des personnes.**

Commençons.

1. Qui est le guitariste?
2. Qui est la pianiste?
3. Regardez la violoncelliste!
4. Regardez les violonistes!
5. Comment s'appellent les chanteurs?
6. Comment s'appelle le trompettiste?
7. Comment s'appelle la première violoniste?
8. Écoutez les sopranos!
9. Aimez-vous le danseur principal?
10. Aimez-vous la danseuse principale?

Maintenant vérifiez vos réponses. Now check your answers. You should have marked **un homme** for sentences 1, 6, and 9; **une femme** for sentences 2, 3, 7, and 10; and **des personnes** for sentences 4, 5, and 8. If you got any wrong, listen to this activity once more, and do these questions again.

Activité 5. Narration: Une étudiante sérieuse. Monique is studying in a café. Say that she is not looking at the people or the things in the street. Use the appropriate definite article in your sentences. *Écoutez le modèle!*

Modèle: Il y a un garçon. Monique ne regarde pas le garçon.

Commençons.

Il y a une jeune fille. Monique ne regarde pas la jeune fille.
Il y a une auto. Monique ne regarde pas l'auto.
Il y a des vélos. Monique ne regarde pas les vélos.
Il y a un monsieur. Monique ne regarde pas le monsieur.
Il y a des étudiants. Monique ne regarde pas les étudiants.
Il y a une moto. Monique ne regarde pas la moto.
Il y a une étudiante. Monique ne regarde pas l'étudiante.

B. La forme des adjectifs de description

Vocabulaire: La description

Activité 6. Prononciation. *Ouvrez votre livre à la page 82.* Open your textbook to p. 82. Listen to the pronunciation of the masculine and feminine adjectives of description. Repeat each sentence as you hear it.

Il est blond. Elle est blonde.
Il est brun. Elle est brune.
Il est fort. Elle est forte.
Il est faible. Elle est faible.
Il est grand. Elle est grande.
Il est petit. Elle est petite.
Il est heureux. Elle est heureuse.
Il est triste. Elle est triste.
Il est intelligent. Elle est intelligente.
Il est idiot. Elle est idiote.
Il est intéressant. Elle est intéressante.
Il est amusant. Elle est amusante.
Il est drôle. Elle est drôle.
Il est pénible. Elle est pénible.
Il est sympathique. Elle est sympathique.
Il est désagréable. Elle est désagréable.
Il est marié. Elle est mariée.
Il est célibataire. Elle est célibataire.
Il est allemand. Elle est allemande.
Il est américain. Elle est américaine.
Il est anglais. Elle est anglaise.
Il est canadien. Elle est canadienne.
Il est espagnol. Elle est espagnole.
Il est français. Elle est française.
Il est italien. Elle est italienne.
Il est japonais. Elle est japonaise.
Il est mexicain. Elle est mexicaine.
Il est suisse. Elle est suisse.
Il est lent. Elle est lente.
Il est rapide. Elle est rapide.
Il est confortable. Elle est confortable.
Il est moderne. Elle est moderne.

Activité 7. Description: Les jumeaux. The following sets of twins resemble each other. You will hear the description of the brother. Say that the sister has the same characteristics. *Écoutez le modèle.*

Modèle: Georges est brun. Et Sylvie? Elle est brune.

Commençons.

Pierre est blond. Et Nathalie? — Elle est blonde.
Raymond est grand. Et Christine? — Elle est grande.
Bertrand est petit. Et Caroline? — Elle est petite.
Joseph est intelligent. Et Colette? — Elle est intelligente.
Gilbert est idiot. Et Alice? — Elle est idiote.

Now you will hear the description of the sister. Describe the brother. *Écoutez le modèle.*

Modèle: Sophie est française. Et Paul? — Il est français.

Commençons.

Catherine est amusante. Et Frédéric? — Il est amusant.
Suzanne est anglaise. Et Vincent? — Il est anglais.
Élisabeth est américaine. Et Marc? — Il est américain.
Jacqueline est heureuse. Et Robert? — Il est heureux.
Colette est triste. Et Henri? — Il est triste.

C. *La place des adjectifs*

Activité 8. Situation: Descriptions. You will hear a series of descriptions, each consisting of two sentences. Transform each description into a single sentence according to the model. Note that the adjectives follow the noun. *Écoutez le modèle.*

Modèle: Voici un garçon. Il est intelligent. — Voici un garçon intelligent.

Commençons.
Voici une femme. Elle est mariée. — Voici une femme mariée.
Voici un monsieur. Il est célibataire. — Voici un monsieur célibataire.
Voici un homme. Il est fort. — Voici un homme fort.
Voici une personne. Elle est heureuse. — Voici une personne heureuse.
Voici une auto. Elle est rapide. — Voici une auto rapide.
Voici des objets. Ils sont intéressants. — Voici des objets intéressants.
Voici des étudiants. Ils sont allemands. — Voici des étudiants allemands.

Now you will hear other descriptions that also consist of two sentences each. Transform them into single sentences according to the model. Here the adjectives come before the noun. *Écoutez le modèle.*

Modèle: Voilà une voiture. Elle est petite. — Voilà une petite voiture.

Commençons.

Voilà une chaîne-stéréo. Elle est grande. — Voilà une grande chaîne-stéréo.
Voilà une caméra. Elle est bonne. — Voilà une bonne caméra.
Voilà une moto. Elle est jolie. — Voilà une jolie moto.
Voilà des garçons. Ils sont jeunes. — Voilà de jeunes garçons.
Voilà des cassettes. Elles sont mauvaises. — Voilà de mauvaises cassettes.

Activité 9. Pratique. Now you can practice adjective position with some substitution exercises. Repeat the key sentence. Then formulate new sentences by adding the suggested adjectives. These new adjectives will be given in the masculine singular form. Make all necessary changes, and be sure to place the new adjective in the correct position in the sentence.

Commençons.

Thomas est un étudiant.
américain — Thomas est un étudiant américain.
marié — Thomas est un étudiant marié.
intelligent — Thomas est un étudiant intelligent.
jeune — Thomas est un jeune étudiant.
heureux — Thomas est un étudiant heureux.

Nous avons une auto.
japonais — Nous avons une auto japonaise.
petit — Nous avons une petite auto.
confortable — Nous avons une auto confortable.
rapide — Nous avons une auto rapide.
bon — Nous avons une bonne auto.

Philippe et Pierre sont des amis.
bon — Philippe et Pierre sont de bons amis.
sympathique — Philippe et Pierre sont des amis sympathiques.
amusant — Philippe et Pierre sont des amis amusants.
grand — Philippe et Pierre sont de grands amis.

D. *Il est* ou *c'est?*

Activité 10. Conversation: Opinions. You will hear a series of opinions about various people or things. Agree with each opinion according to the model. Pay attention to the position of the adjective in your sentences. *Écoutez le modèle.*

Modèle: Le professeur est sympathique. — Mais oui, c'est un professeur sympathique.

Commençons.

L'étudiant est intelligent. — Mais oui, c'est un étudiant intelligent.
Le garçon est pénible. — Mais oui, c'est un garçon pénible.
La fille est amusante. — Mais oui, c'est une fille amusante.
Le livre est intéressant. — Mais oui, c'est un livre intéressant.
Le disque est bon. — Mais oui, c'est un bon disque.
La cassette est mauvaise. — Mais oui, c'est une mauvaise cassette.
Les motos sont rapides. — Mais oui, ce sont des motos rapides.
Les ordinateurs sont modernes. — Mais oui, ce sont des ordinateurs modernes.

Activité 11. Narration: Explications. Use the information in each of the sentences you hear to make two statements. *Écoutez le modèle.*

Modèle: J'ai un petit appareil-photo. — J'ai un appareil-photo. Il est petit.

Commençons.

J'ai une grande voiture. J'ai une voiture. Elle est grande.
J'ai une moto anglaise. J'ai une moto. Elle est anglaise.
J'ai un walkman japonais. J'ai un walkman. Il est japonais.
J'ai des photos amusantes. J'ai des photos. Elles sont amusantes.
J'ai des cassettes espagnoles. J'ai des cassettes. Elles sont espagnoles.
J'ai des amis français. J'ai des amis. Ils sont français.

DIALOGUE

Activité 12. Amis. In your lab manual you will see pictures of various French people. Your friend Stéphanie asks you about them. Answer her questions in the negative, and then give the proper description. *Écoutez le modèle.*

Modèle: Tiens, Caroline est brune, n'est-ce pas? Mais non, elle n'est pas brune. Elle est blonde.

Commençons.

1. Tiens, Madame Guérin est petite, n'est-ce pas? Mais non, elle n'est pas petite. Elle est grande.
2. Dis, Jacques est triste, n'est-ce pas? Mais non, il n'est pas triste. Il est heureux.
3. Dis, Albert est faible, n'est-ce pas? Mais non, il n'est pas faible. Il est fort.
4. Dis, Jeannette est américaine, n'est-ce pas? Mais non, elle n'est pas américaine. Elle est anglaise.
5. Dis, Suzanne est française, n'est-ce pas? Mais non, elle n'est pas française. Elle est canadienne.
6. Tiens, l'étudiant est mexicain, n'est-ce pas? Mais non, il n'est pas mexicain. Il est japonais.

DICTÉE

Activité 13. Suzanne. You will hear a short paragraph. First, listen! Do not write!

Suzanne est une grande fille brune. Elle habite à Paris, mais elle n'est pas française. Elle est américaine. Elle a un copain. C'est un étudiant anglais. Et vous, est-ce que vous avez des amis anglais?

Now write down the sentences in your lab manual as you hear them.

Suzanne est une grande fille brune. / Elle habite à Paris, / mais elle n'est pas française. / Elle est américaine. / Elle a un copain. / C'est un étudiant anglais. / Et vous, / est-ce que vous avez / des amis anglais?

Listen again and check what you wrote.

(Text is reread without pauses.)

Fin de la Leçon 5.
End of Lesson 5.
(music)

LEÇON 6. LE TEMPS LIBRE

PRÉSENTATION

Activité 1. Lecture. *Ouvrez votre livre à la page 88. Écoutez.* Open your textbook to p. 88.

(See textbook page 88.)

Activité 2. Compréhension du texte. You will hear several questions about the text you have just heard. Indicate the correct response by writing in the appropriate space in your lab manual.

Commençons.

1. Qui aime le sport à la télé?
2. Qui va voir un film d'aventure?
3. Qui adore la musique classique?
4. Qui n'est pas un intellectuel?
5. Qui joue au tennis?

Maintenant vérifiez vos réponses. Now check your answers. You should have written:
1. Patrice 2. Michèle 3. Henri 4. Jean-François 5. Nathalie

If you got any wrong, listen to the **Présentation** once more, and do these questions again.

PHONÉTIQUE

Activité 3. Les voyelles /o/ et /ɔ/.

(a) *La voyelle /o/.* The vowel /o/ is different from its English counterpart because there is no glide in French.
Compare: au OH beau BOW

Répétez: au vélo radio métro drôle à bientôt
Margot va au château en vélo.
Léo reste à l'hôtel de Bordeaux.

(b) *La voyelle /ɔ/.* The vowel /ɔ/ is somewhat similar to the "u" in the English word "up." However, the lips are more rounded in French.

Répétez: école joli poli téléphone homme moderne
Nicole téléphone à Monique.
Nous sommes d'accord avec Caroline.

STRUCTURE ET VOCABULAIRE

A. L'usage de l'article défini dans le sens général

Vocabulaire: Les loisirs

Activité 4. Prononciation. *Ouvrez votre livre à la page 91*. Open your textbook to p. 91. Repeat the following nouns.

le tennis
le football
le volleyball
le basketball
le cinéma
le théâtre
la télévision
la cuisine
la danse
la photo
la musique
la peinture
le bridge
le poker
les dames
les échecs
les cartes

Activité 5. Situation: Préférences. You will hear a series of leisure-time activities and hobbies. Say that you like each of them. Be sure to provide the appropriate definite article in your response. *Écoutez le modèle.*

Modèle: musique	J'aime la musique.

Commençons.

cinéma	J'aime le cinéma.
photo	J'aime la photo.
danse	J'aime la danse.
danse moderne	J'aime la danse moderne.
tennis	J'aime le tennis.

Now say that you don't like the following activities. *Écoutez le modèle.*

Modèle: poker	Je n'aime pas le poker.

Commençons.

peinture	Je n'aime pas la peinture.
volleyball	Je n'aime pas le volleyball.
théâtre	Je n'aime pas le théâtre.
dames	Je n'aime pas les dames.
échecs	Je n'aime pas les échecs.

B. Les contractions de l'article défini avec ***à*** *et* ***de***

Activité 6. Situation: Nous parlons. You will hear a series of nouns designating people. Say that you are speaking to these people. *Écoutez le modèle.*

Modèle: le professeur	Nous parlons au professeur.

Commençons.

la jeune fille	Nous parlons à la jeune fille.
le garçon américain	Nous parlons au garçon américain.
l'étudiant français	Nous parlons à l'étudiant français.
les jolies filles	Nous parlons aux jolies filles.
les étudiants japonais	Nous parlons aux étudiants japonais.

Now you say that you are talking ABOUT the following people. *Écoutez le modèle.*

Modèle: le professeur — Nous parlons du professeur.

Commençons.

la fille anglaise	Nous parlons de la fille anglaise.
le garçon espagnol	Nous parlons du garçon espagnol.
les personnes là-bas	Nous parlons des personnes là-bas.
les étudiants américains	Nous parlons des étudiants américains.
l'homme là-bas	Nous parlons de l'homme là-bas.

Activité 7. Situation: Loisirs. You will hear the names of sports and musical instruments. Ask a friend if he plays them. Be careful to use **à** or **de** as appropriate. *Écoutez les modèles.*

Modèles: le piano? — Est-ce que tu joues du piano?
le football? — Est-ce que tu joues au football?

Commençons.

la flûte?	Est-ce que tu joues de la flûte?
le tennis?	Est-ce que tu joues au tennis?
la guitare?	Est-ce que tu joues de la guitare?
le golf?	Est-ce que tu joues au golf?
le violon?	Est-ce que tu joues du violon?
le baseball?	Est-ce que tu joues au baseball?

*C. Le verbe **aller**; le futur proche avec **aller** + infinitif*

Activité 8. Prononciation. *Ouvrez votre livre à la page 95.* Open your textbook to p. 95. The verb **aller** is the only irregular verb in **-er.** Repeat the verb forms and then repeat the sentences.

Commençons.

je vais	Je vais à Paris.
tu vas	Tu vas à l'université.
il va elle va on va	Anne va à Québec.
nous allons	Nous allons à Nice.
vous allez	Vous allez au restaurant.
ils vont elles vont	Elles vont au musée.

Activité 9. Pratique. Now practice the verb **aller** with some substitution exercises. Repeat the key sentence. Then formulate new sentences using the suggested subject.

Commençons.

Nous allons à Paris.
Vous — Vous allez à Paris.
Alice — Alice va à Paris.
Pierre et Nathalie — Pierre et Nathalie vont à Paris.
Tu — Tu vas à Paris.

Marie ne va pas à Québec.
Nous — Nous n'allons pas à Québec.
Paul et Suzanne — Paul et Suzanne ne vont pas à Québec.
Je — Je ne vais pas à Québec.

Vous allez rester ici.
Tu — Tu vas rester ici.
Nicole — Nicole va rester ici.
Claire et Alain — Claire et Alain vont rester ici.

Activité 10. Identification de structures. Listen to the following sentences. Can you determine whether the speaker is talking about an event that is already taking place, or about an event that will occur in the future? Listen carefully to the verb. If the present tense is used, mark the first row **présent** in your lab manual. If the construction used is a form of the verb **aller** followed by an infinitive, mark the second row **futur.**

Commençons.

1. Vous allez visiter Montréal, n'est-ce pas?
2. Michèle visite Québec avec un ami.
3. Henri va travailler à Paris.
4. Nathalie joue au tennis.
5. Je vais téléphoner à des amis.
6. Quand vas-tu téléphoner à Sylvie?
7. Nous voyageons en France.
8. Où allez-vous voyager?

Maintenant vérifiez vos réponses. Now check your answers. You should have marked **futur** for sentences 1, 3, 5, 6, and 8; and **présent** for sentences 2, 4, and 7. If you got any wrong, listen to this activity once more, and do these questions again.

Activité 11. Conversation: Demain. Georges is asking you whether you are doing certain things today. Say that you are going to do them tomorrow. *Écoutez le modèle.*

<u>Modèle</u>: Tu joues au tennis aujourd'hui? — Non, je vais jouer au tennis demain.

Commençons.

Tu travailles aujourd'hui? — Non, je vais travailler demain.
Tu étudies aujourd'hui? — Non, je vais étudier demain.
Tu nages aujourd'hui? — Non, je vais nager demain.
Tu invites Anne aujourd'hui? — Non, je vais inviter Anne demain.

Vocabulaire: ***Où*** *et* ***comment***

Activité 12. Prononciation. *Ouvrez votre livre à la page 96.* Open your textbook to p. 96. Repeat the following nouns.

un aéroport
un bureau
un café
un cinéma
un hôpital
un laboratoire
un magasin
un musée
un restaurant
un stade
un supermarché
un théâtre

une bibliothèque
une école
une église
une fête
une gare
une maison
une piscine
une plage
une poste
une université

Now listen to the following verbs and repeat the sentences.

entrer: Nous entrons dans le magasin.
passer: Est-ce que vous passez par Paris?
passer: Je passe une heure au café.
rester: Paul et Suzanne restent à Cannes.

Now, repeat the following expressions.

ici
là
là-bas
à pied
à vélo

en voiture
en avion
en train
en bus
en métro

Activité 13. Compréhension orale. You will hear where different people are going and what they are going to do there. Listen carefully to each pair of sentences and determine whether the information is logical or not. If the information is logical, mark the first row **logique** in your lab manual. If it is not logical, mark the second row **illogique.**

Commençons.

1. Robert et Sylvie vont à la piscine. Ils vont nager.
2. Nous allons au restaurant. Nous allons dîner.
3. Je vais à la plage. Je vais regarder la télé.
4. Michèle va à la bibliothèque. Elle va jouer aux cartes.
5. Les étudiants vont au laboratoire. Ils vont écouter des cassettes.
6. Vous allez au musée. Vous allez regarder les peintures.
7. Nathalie va au bureau. Elle va travailler.
8. Tu vas au stade. Tu vas jouer aux échecs.

Maintenant vérifiez vos réponses. Now check your answers. You should have marked **logique** for sentences 1, 2, 5, 6, and 7; and **illogique** for sentences 3, 4, and 8. If you got any wrong, listen to this activity once more, and do these sentences again.

D. La préposition ***chez***

Activité 14. Situation: Qui travaille? *Dites que les personnes suivantes travaillent chez elles.* Say that the following people work at home. *Écoutez le modèle.*

Modèle: Paul — Paul travaille chez lui.

Commençons.

Marie	Marie travaille chez elle.
nous	Nous travaillons chez nous.
je	Je travaille chez moi.
Alain	Alain travaille chez lui.
Robert et François	Robert et François travaillent chez eux.
tu	Tu travailles chez toi.
Christine et Sylvie	Christine et Sylvie travaillent chez elles.
vous	Vous travaillez chez vous.

E. Les questions avec inversion

Activité 15. Conversation: Pardon? Élisabeth is telling you about her friends. You did not understand the last part of each sentence and ask her to repeat. Use the appropriate interrogative expression plus inversion. *Écoutez le modèle.*

Modèle: Nathalie arrive demain. — Quand arrive-t-elle?

Commençons.

1. Jérôme rentre à minuit.	À quelle heure rentre-t-il?
2. Marie est à la poste.	Où est-elle?
3. Sylvie voyage en train.	Comment voyage-t-elle?
4. Robert étudie avec Michèle.	Avec qui étudie-t-il?
5. Claire téléphone à Sophie.	À qui téléphone-t-elle?

DIALOGUE

Activité 16. Où? Guy is asking you where certain people are. Answer him according to the pictures in your lab manual. *Écoutez le modèle.*

Modèle: Où est Philippe? — Il est à la piscine.

Commençons.

1. Où est Mlle Rémi?	Elle est au bureau.
2. Où sont les étudiants?	Ils sont à la bibliothèque.
3. Où est M. Thibault?	Il est à l'église.
4. Où est Catherine?	Elle est au cinéma.
5. Où sont les touristes?	Ils sont à l'aéroport.
6. Où est Mme Martin?	Elle est à la gare.

DICTÉE

Activité 17. Temps libre. You will hear a short paragraph. First, listen! Do not write!

Où allez-vous? Moi, je vais à la piscine avec Jean-Michel. Nous allons nager et jouer au volley. À quatre heures, nous allons aller chez lui et nous allons jouer aux cartes. Aimez-vous le bridge?

Now write the sentences in your lab manual as you hear them.

Où / allez-vous? / Moi, je vais / à la piscine avec Jean-Michel. / Nous allons nager / et jouer au volley. / À quatre heures, / nous allons aller / chez lui / et nous allons jouer aux cartes. / Aimez-vous / le bridge? /

Listen again and check what you wrote.

(Text is reread without pauses.)

Fin de la Leçon 6.
End of Lesson 6.
(music)

VIVRE EN FRANCE 2. EN VILLE

Activité 1. La bonne réponse. You will hear people asking you for directions. In your lab manual you will see three possible responses for each question. Select the logical response by circling the corresponding letter.

Commençons.

1. Est-ce que c'est tout droit?
2. Est-ce que c'est loin?
3. Pardon, Mademoiselle, où se trouve l'arrêt d'autobus?
4. Excusez-moi, Monsieur. Savez-vous où est l'hôtel des Anglais?
5. S'il vous plaît, pouvez-vous me dire comment aller à la poste?
6. Dans quelle direction est l'avenue de Toulouse?
7. Est-ce qu'il y a un commissariat de police près d'ici?
8. Excusez-moi, Monsieur. Pouvez-vous me dire où est la librairie Chauvin?

Now listen to the complete exchanges and correct your work. *Écoutez.*

1. Est-ce que c'est tout droit?	Non, vous tournez à gauche.
2. Est-ce que c'est loin?	Non, c'est tout près.
3. Pardon, Mademoiselle, où se trouve l'arrêt d'autobus?	Il se trouve à côté de la pharmacie.
4. Excusez-moi, Monsieur. Savez-vous où est l'hôtel des Anglais?	Il se trouve avenue des Acacias.
5. S'il vous plaît, pouvez-vous me dire comment aller à la poste?	Vous devez traverser la rue Jacob et continuer tout droit.
6. Dans quelle direction est l'avenue de Toulouse?	C'est au sud.
7. Est-ce qu'il y a un commissariat de police près d'ici?	Oui, il y a un commissariat dans l'avenue de la Libération.
8. Excusez-moi, Monsieur. Pouvez-vous me dire où est la librairie Chauvin?	Oui, continuez tout droit. C'est à cent mètres à gauche.

Activité 2. En France. You will hear a conversation between Pierre and Christine. Pierre had invited Christine to dinner at his apartment. She took the bus, but after she got off, she realized that she had forgotten to take along the directions on how to get to Pierre's apartment. Fortunately, there is a phone at the bus stop. Christine calls Pierre to ask for directions. You will hear their conversation twice. First, just listen. The second time, take a pencil and trace Christine's itinerary from the bus stop, which is marked with an "X," to Pierre's apartment.

Although you may not understand every word, you should be able to understand the essential elements of the conversation.

Commençons. Écoutez.

—Allô, Pierre.
—Allô, Christine. Mais, où es-tu?
—Je suis à l'arrêt d'autobus. Dis donc, est-ce que tu peux me dire comment aller chez toi?
—Mais oui, c'est simple. L'arrêt d'autobus est dans l'avenue Victor Hugo. Eh bien, tu vas à gauche pendant 200 mètres.
—Je vais à gauche dans l'avenue Victor Hugo pendant 200 mètres.
—Tu tournes à droite dans la rue de la Victoire.
—Je tourne à droite dans la rue de la Victoire.
—C'est ça! Tu traverses la rue du Général de Gaulle et tu continues tout droit pendant 100 mètres.
—Bon, d'accord. Et après?
—Après tu tournes à gauche dans la rue Voltaire.
—À gauche dans la rue Voltaire.
—Et puis à droite dans le boulevard Carnot.
—Bon.
—À cinquante mètres il y a un hôpital.
—D'accord.
—J'habite en face de l'hôpital.
—C'est simple! J'ai compris! À bientôt.
—Au revoir, à bientôt.

Listen again and draw a path showing how Christine will get to Pierre's house. Mark Pierre's place with an "X."

Écoutez.

(Text is repeated.)

Fin de Vivre en France 2.
End of Vivre en France 2.
(music)

UNITÉ 3: PROBLÈMES D'ARGENT

LEÇON 7. LE BUDGET DE PHILIPPE

PRÉSENTATION

Activité 1. Lecture. *Ouvrez votre livre à la page 108.* Open your textbook to p. 108.

(See textbook page 108.)

Activité 2. Compréhension du texte. You will hear a series of statements about the text you have just heard. Listen carefully to each statement to determine whether it is true or false. If it is true, mark **vrai** in your lab manual. If it is false, mark **faux.**

Commençons.

1. Philippe étudie les sciences économiques.
2. Philippe va à l'Université de Strasbourg.
3. Philippe habite chez ses parents.
4. Philippe habite à la Cité Universitaire.
5. Philippe ne paie pas de scolarité.
6. Philippe travaille dans une banque.

Maintenant vérifiez vos réponses. Now check your answers. You should have marked **vrai** for sentences 1, 4, and 5; and **faux** for sentences 2, 3, and 6.

PHONÉTIQUE

Activité 3. La semi-voyelle /j/

(a) *La combinaison /j/ + voyelle.* The semi-vowel /j/ is similar to the initial sound of the English word *yes.* The French counterpart, however, is shorter and more tense.

Compare: piano PIANO

Répétez: piano bien canadien hier premier juillet brillant payer nettoyer
Vous étudiez l'italien.
Nous payons le loyer le premier janvier.

(b) *La combinaison voyelle + /j/.* The combination vowel + /j/ can occur at the end of a word. In this position the /j/ is pronounced very distinctly.

Répétez: travaille fille Marseille
Les filles travaillent à Marseille.

STRUCTURE ET VOCABULAIRE

Vocabulaire: Les finances personnelles

Activité 4. Prononciation. *Ouvrez votre livre à la page 109*. Open your textbook to p. 109. *Répétez les noms.*

l'argent
le logement
les loisirs
le loyer
un prix
un projet
un repas
les transports
une bourse
une dépense
la scolarité
les vacances

Maintenant répétez les verbes et les expressions. Puis répétez les phrases.

coûter
dépenser
gagner

par jour
par semaine
par mois
combien
combien de + noun

L'appartement coûte 600 dollars par mois.
Combien dépensez-vous pour les repas?
Combien d'argent gagnez-vous?
Qui va gagner ce match de tennis?
Je dépense 10 dollars par jour pour les repas.
Je gagne mille francs par semaine.
Combien dépenses-tu par mois pour ton logement?
Combien coûtent les cassettes?
Combien d'argent as-tu?
Combien de copains vas-tu inviter?

A. Les nombres de 100 à l'infini

Activité 5. Prononciation. *Ouvrez votre livre à la page 110*. Open your textbook to p. 110. Repeat the following numbers.

Commençons.

cent
cent un
cent deux
cent trois
cent dix
cent cinquante
deux cents
deux cent un
deux cent deux
trois cents
trois cent un
quatre cents
neuf cents
mille
mille un
mille cent
mille deux cents
mille trois cents
deux mille
deux mille cent
deux mille deux cents
dix mille
cent mille
un million
deux millions

Activité 6. Compréhension orale. You will hear Philippe telling you how much money his friends have. Listen carefully to each sentence. In your lab manual, there are three choices for each sentence. Circle the number you hear.

Commençons.

1. Paul a 1.000 dollars.
2. Annette a 120 francs.
3. Sylvie a 300 francs.
4. Nous avons 150 dollars.
5. Henri a 10.000 lires.
6. Gilbert a 8.000 marks.
7. Marc a 500 pesetas.
8. Suzanne a 2.000 francs.

Maintenant vérifiez vos réponses. Now check your answers. You should have circled the following answers.

1. mille/second column
2. cent vingt/second column
3. trois cents/first column
4. cent cinquante/second column
5. dix mille/third column
6. huit mille/first column
7. cinq cents/second column
8. deux mille/second column

B. *Le verbe* ***payer***

Activité 7. Prononciation. *Ouvrez votre livre à la page 112.* Open your textbook to p. 112. Listen to the verbs. Then repeat the sentences.

je paie
tu paies
il paie
nous payons
vous payez
ils paient

Je paie le restaurant.
Tu paies le logement.
Christine paie la scolarité.
Comment payons-nous?
Vous payez en francs.
Les Américains paient en dollars.

Activité 8. Pratique. Now practice the verbs **envoyer** and **nettoyer** in a substitution exercise. Repeat the key sentence. Then formulate new sentences using the suggested subjects.

Nous envoyons un télégramme.

vous	Vous envoyez un télégramme.
les touristes	Les touristes envoient un télégramme.
tu	Tu envoies un télégramme.
je	J'envoie un télégramme.

Nous nettoyons l'appartement.

Michèle	Michèle nettoie l'appartement.
les étudiants	Les étudiants nettoient l'appartement.
tu	Tu nettoies l'appartement.
vous	Vous nettoyez l'appartement.

C. *L'expression* ***être à***

D. *La possession avec* ***de***

Activité 9. Conversation: À qui est-ce? Nadine is asking whether certain items belong to certain people. Answer her in the affirmative, using **de** as in the model. *Écoutez le modèle.*

Modèle: La moto est à Pierre? — Oui, c'est la moto de Pierre.

Commençons.

La radio est à Caroline? Oui, c'est la radio de Caroline.
Le vélomoteur est à Jacques? Oui, c'est le vélomoteur de Jacques.
La caméra est à Sylvie? Oui, c'est la caméra de Sylvie.
Les cassettes sont à Robert? Oui, ce sont les cassettes de Robert.
Les livres sont à Jacqueline? Oui, ce sont les livres de Jacqueline.
La voiture est au professeur? Oui, c'est la voiture du professeur.
Les stylos sont aux étudiants? Oui, ce sont les stylos des étudiants.

E. *Les adjectifs possessifs*

Activité 10. Prononciation. *Ouvrez votre livre à la page 116.* Open your textbook to p. 116. To indicate possession or relationship, we often use possessive adjectives. In French, possessive adjectives agree with the nouns they introduce. Repeat after the speaker.

mon vélo
ma moto
mes disques

ton vélo
ta moto
tes disques

son vélo
sa moto
ses disques

notre vélo
notre moto
nos disques

votre vélo
votre moto
vos disques

leur vélo
leur moto
leurs disques

Activité 11. Conversation: Possessions. Danièle is asking whether certain items belong to her friends. Say yes, using the appropriate possessive adjectives. *Écoutez le modèle.*

Modèle: C'est la voiture de Jacques? Oui, c'est sa voiture!

Commençons.

C'est la mobylette de Georges? Oui, c'est sa mobylette!
C'est la chaîne-stéréo de Sylvie? Oui, c'est sa chaîne-stéréo!
C'est l'ordinateur de Marc? Oui, c'est son ordinateur!
Ce sont les disques de Paul? Oui, ce sont ses disques!
Ce sont les cartes de Christine? Oui, ce sont ses cartes!
Ce sont les livres d'Antoine? Oui, ce sont ses livres!
C'est la guitare de Thomas? Oui, c'est sa guitare!
Ce sont les crayons d'Isabelle? Oui, ce sont ses crayons!

Activité 12. Conversation: La famille. You are at a party and M. Jacob wants to know if certain guests are relatives or acquaintances of yours. Answer his questions in the affirmative or in the negative as indicated in your lab manual. *Écoutez le modèle.*

Modèle: Est-ce que Jacqueline est votre sœur? Non, ce n'est pas ma sœur.

Commençons.

1. Est-ce que Philippe est votre frère? Oui, c'est mon frère.
2. Est-ce que Sylvie est votre sœur? Oui, c'est ma sœur.
3. Est-ce que M. Mercier est votre oncle? Non, ce n'est pas mon oncle.
4. Est-ce que Jacques est votre copain? Oui, c'est mon copain.
5. Est-ce que Lucie et Yvette sont vos voisines? Oui, ce sont mes voisines.
6. Est-ce que M. Lebrun est votre grand-père? Non, ce n'est pas mon grand-père.
7. Est-ce que Mme Lenoir est votre tante? Non, ce n'est pas ma tante.

Activité 13. Conversation: La famille Dupont. Look at the family tree shown in your lab manual. You can see that Éric and Stéphanie Dupont are brother and sister. Martine will ask you certain questions about other members of the Dupont family. Identify these people in relation to Éric and Stéphanie. *Écoutez les deux modèles.*

Modèles: Qui est Michel Dupont? C'est leur cousin.
Qui sont Maurice et Colette Charron? Ce sont leurs grands-parents.

Commençons.

Qui est Marc Dupont? C'est leur cousin.
Qui sont Pierre et Joséphine Dupont? Ce sont leurs grands-parents.
Qui est Jean Dupont? C'est leur père.
Qui est Monique Dupont? C'est leur tante.
Qui est Charlotte Dupont? C'est leur cousine.
Qui est François Dupont? C'est leur oncle.

DIALOGUE

Activité 14. Le budget de Christine. In your lab manual look at Christine's budget. Answer the following questions according to the information you see. *Écoutez le modèle.*

Modèle: Combien est-ce que Christine dépense pour le logement? Elle dépense 2.000 francs.

Commençons.

Combien est-ce que Christine dépense pour les repas? Elle dépense 500 francs.
Combien est-ce qu'elle dépense pour les vêtements? Elle dépense 600 francs.
Combien est-ce qu'elle dépense pour ses livres? Elle dépense 230 francs.
Combien est-ce qu'elle dépense pour les transports? Elle dépense 220 francs.
Combien est-ce qu'elle dépense pour les loisirs? Elle dépense 200 francs.
Combien est-ce qu'elle dépense par mois? Elle dépense 3.750 francs.

DICTÉE

Activité 15. Mes voisins. You will hear a short paragraph. First listen! Do not write!

Mes voisins ont deux enfants. Leur fils Robert est étudiant. C'est mon copain. Leur fille Alice est mariée. Son mari travaille au laboratoire de l'université.

Now write the sentences in your lab manual as you hear them.

Mes voisins / ont deux enfants. / Leur fils Robert / est étudiant. / C'est mon copain. / Leur fille Alice / est mariée. / Son mari travaille / au laboratoire / de l'université. /

Listen again and check what you wrote.

(Text is reread without pauses.)

LECTURE CULTURELLE

Activité 16. Lecture. *Ouvrez votre livre à la page 109.* Open your textbook to p. 109. *Écoutez.*

(See textbook page 109.)

Activité 17. Compréhension du texte. You will hear several statements about the text you have just heard. Listen carefully to each statement. If it is true, mark **vrai** in your lab manual. If it is false, mark **faux.**

Commençons.

1. En France, il n'y a pas d'universités publiques.
2. En France, les études sont généralement bon marché.
3. Un petit nombre d'étudiants reçoivent des bourses.
4. Quand ils vont au musée ou au théâtre, les étudiants français ont souvent des réductions.
5. Les étudiants français ne vont pas souvent à l'hôpital parce que les frais médicaux sont très chers.

Maintenant vérifiez vos réponses. Now check your answers. You should have marked **vrai** for sentences 2 and 4; and **faux** for sentences 1, 3, and 5.

Fin de la Leçon 7.
End of Lesson 7.
(music)

LEÇON 8. UN TEE-SHIRT QUI COÛTE CHER

PRÉSENTATION

Activité 1. Lecture. *Ouvrez votre livre à la page 120.* Open your textbook to p. 120. *Écoutez.*

(See textbook page 120.)

Activité 2. Compréhension du texte. You will hear several statements about the text you have just heard. Listen carefully to each statement to determine whether it is true or false. In your lab manual, mark **vrai** for true and **faux** for false.

Commençons.

1. Le grand magasin où sont Carole et Monique s'appelle «Au bon marché.»
2. Carole et Monique regardent des vêtements.
3. Monique achète le tee-shirt rouge parce qu'il n'est pas cher.
4. Le tee-shirt bleu coûte cinquante francs.
5. L'agent de police est un ami de Monique.
6. La contravention coûte deux cents francs.

Maintenant vérifiez vos réponses. Now check your answers. You should have marked **vrai** for statements 2, 4, and 6; and **faux** for statements 1, 3, and 5.

PHONÉTIQUE

Activité 3. La lettre "e." The letter "e" represents several sounds in French.

(a) The letter **é** and the verb endings **-er** and **-ez** represent the sound /e/.

Répétez: café école église aller dansez
René va visiter l'université.

(b) The letters è and ê represent the sound /ɛ/.

Répétez: père mère frère fête être vêtements
Mon père achète des vêtements.

(c) The letter **e** followed by a single consonant and a vowel represents the sound /ə/.

Répétez: chemise chemisier repas
Denise aime la chemise de Renée.

In the middle of a word, the mute **e** is often dropped entirely.

Répétez: sam~~e~~di maint~~e~~nant ach~~e~~ter am~~e~~ner
Nous am~~e~~nons Cath~~e~~rine à la fête sam~~e~~di.

(d) The letter **e** followed by two consonants and a vowel represents the sound /ɛ/.

Répétez: veste lunettes verte cette merci
Quelle veste est-ce qu'Annette va porter?

STRUCTURE ET VOCABULAIRE

Vocabulaire: Quelques vêtements

Activité 4. Prononciation. *Ouvrez votre livre à la page 122.* Open your textbook to p. 122. Repeat the items of clothing.

un anorak
des bas
un chapeau
un chemisier
un costume
un imperméable
un jean
un maillot de bain
un manteau
un pantalon
un pull (un pull-over)
un short
un sweat
un tailleur
un tee-shirt
un vêtement
des bottes
une chemise
des chaussettes
des chaussures
une cravate
une jupe
des lunettes
des lunettes de soleil
une robe
une veste

Now repeat the names of the colors.

noir
bleu
rose
orange
gris
vert
rouge
marron
blanc, blanche
jaune
violet, violette

Activité 5. Pratique. Now practice this new vocabulary in a substitution exercise. First repeat the key sentence. Then formulate new sentences using the suggested items of clothing. Be sure to use the appropriate article.

Commençons.

Je porte un **chemisier** jaune.

pantalon	Je porte un pantalon jaune.
robe	Je porte une robe jaune.
veste	Je porte une veste jaune.

Paul va porter un **costume** bleu.

pull	Paul va porter un pull bleu.
cravate	Paul va porter une cravate bleue.
tee-shirt	Paul va porter un tee-shirt bleu.

Now substitute the color suggested.

Marie a une jupe **marron.**

blanc	Marie a une jupe blanche.
vert	Marie a une jupe verte.
gris	Marie a une jupe grise.

Activité 6. Compréhension orale. You will hear nine sentences, each one containing the name of an item of clothing. Write that word with the corresponding article **un, une,** or **des** in the blanks provided in your lab manual. Don't worry if you do not understand everything that is said. Are you ready? *Êtes-vous prêts?*

Commençons.

1. Marie porte un joli manteau.
2. Je n'aime pas cette cravate-là.
3. Voilà la chemise que je veux acheter.
4. Cet anorak est trop grand.
5. Robert a un très beau costume gris.
6. Ta robe noire est très élégante.
7. Aimez-vous mes nouvelles chaussures?
8. Je déteste ce chemisier rouge et violet.
9. Oh là là! Regarde ce pantalon rose et vert!

Maintenant vérifiez vos réponses. Now check your answers.

1. un manteau
2. une cravate
3. une chemise
4. un anorak
5. un costume
6. une robe
7. des chaussures
8. un chemisier
9. un pantalon

*A. Les verbes comme **acheter** et **préférer***

Activité 7. Prononciation. *Ouvrez votre livre à la page 124.* Open your textbook to p. 124.

Répétez les formes du verbe **acheter.**

j'achète	nous achetons
tu achètes	vous achetez
il achète	elles achètent

Maintenant répétez les formes du verbe **préférer.**

je préfère	nous préférons
tu préfères	vous préférez
on préfère	ils préfèrent

Activité 8. Narration: Préférences. *Les personnes suivantes n'achètent pas de vêtements rouges. Dites qu'elles préfèrent les vêtements bleus.* The following people do not buy red items of clothing. Say that they prefer blue items. *Écoutez le modèle.*

Modèle: Jean n'achète pas la veste rouge. Il préfère la veste bleue.

Commençons.

Nous n'achetons pas le manteau rouge.	Nous préférons le manteau bleu.
Alain et Marc n'achètent pas le pantalon rouge.	Ils préfèrent le pantalon bleu.
Tu n'achètes pas l'anorak rouge.	Tu préfères l'anorak bleu.
Vous n'achetez pas les chaussettes rouges.	Vous préférez les chaussettes bleues.
Je n'achète pas le pull rouge.	Je préfère le pull bleu.
Charlotte n'achète pas le tailleur rouge.	Elle préfère le tailleur bleu.

*B. L'adjectif interrogatif **quel***

Activité 9. Conversation: Caroline. You will hear Caroline talking about her activities. Ask her to be more specific. Begin your questions with the appropriate form of **quel.** *Écoutez le modèle.*

Modèle: J'achète des lunettes. — Quelles lunettes achètes-tu?

Commençons.

J'achète une montre. — Quelle montre achètes-tu?
Je regarde des chaussures. — Quelles chaussures regardes-tu?
J'écoute un disque. — Quel disque écoutes-tu?
Je possède des cassettes. — Quelles cassettes possèdes-tu?

C. L'adjectif démonstratif ***ce***

Activité 10. Conversation: Au grand magasin. You and Raoul are in a department store. Each time he comments on something, you say that there are similar items a little farther away. *Écoutez le modèle.*

Modèle: Cette veste-ci est jolie. — Cette veste-là est jolie aussi.

Commençons.

Cet anorak-ci est cher. — Cet anorak-là est cher aussi.
Ces pantalons-ci sont bon marché. — Ces pantalons-là sont bon marché aussi.
Cette cravate-ci est jolie. — Cette cravate-là est jolie aussi.
Ces chaussures-ci sont très confortables. — Ces chaussures-là sont très confortables aussi.

D. Le comparatif des adjectifs

Activité 11. Prononciation. *Ouvrez votre livre à la page 128.* Open your textbook to p. 128. *Répétez les phrases.*

La robe est plus chère que la jupe.
La veste est plus jolie que le pull.
Pauline est moins riche qu'Éric.
Mais elle est moins égoïste que lui.
Je suis aussi sérieux que toi.
Tu n'es pas aussi brillant que moi.

Activité 12. Situation: Comparaisons. You will hear descriptions of people and things in relation to others. Make comparisons according to the models. *Écoutez le premier modèle.*

Modèle: Pierre est très grand. Jacques est grand. — Pierre est plus grand que Jacques.

Commençons.

Françoise est très intelligente. Son frère est intelligent. — Françoise est plus intelligente que son frère.
Philippe est très amusant. Son cousin est amusant. — Philippe est plus amusant que son cousin.
La chemise rouge est très chère. La chemise bleue est chère. — La chemise rouge est plus chère que la chemise bleue.
Cette voiture-ci est très confortable. Cette voiture-là est confortable. — Cette voiture-ci est plus confortable que cette voiture-là.
Cet ordinateur-ci est très bon. Cet ordinateur-là est bon. — Cet ordinateur-ci est meilleur que cet ordinateur-là.
Ces cassettes-ci sont très bonnes. Ces cassettes-là sont bonnes. — Ces cassettes-ci sont meilleures que ces cassettes-là.

Écoutez le deuxième modèle.

Modèle: Ces chaussures-ci ne sont pas très confortables. Ces chaussures-là sont confortables.	Ces chaussures-ci sont moins confortables que ces chaussures-là.

Commençons.

La cravate jaune n'est pas très jolie. La cravate verte est jolie.	La cravate jaune est moins jolie que la cravate verte.
La veste blanche n'est pas très chère. La veste marron est chère.	La veste blanche est moins chère que la veste marron.
Les Ford ne sont pas très rapides. Les Ferrari sont rapides.	Les Ford sont moins rapides que les Ferrari.
Ces disques-ci ne sont pas très bons. Ces disques-là sont bons.	Ces disques-ci sont moins bons que ces disques-là.

DIALOGUE

Activité 13. En ville. You and Nathalie are in town shopping and talking about clothes. Answer her questions according to the illustrations in your lab manual. *Écoutez le modèle.*

Modèle: Qu'est-ce que tu achètes?	J'achète ce pantalon.

Commençons.

1. Qu'est-ce que tu achètes?	J'achète ces chaussures.
2. Qu'est-ce que tu préfères?	Je préfère cette cravate.
3. Qu'est-ce que tu aimes?	J'aime cette veste.
4. Qu'est-ce que tu regardes?	Je regarde ce chapeau.
5. Qu'est-ce que tu vas acheter?	Je vais acheter ces lunettes de soleil.
6. Qu'est-ce que tu vas porter?	Je vais porter ce manteau.

DICTÉE

Activité 14. Au magasin. You will hear a short paragraph. First listen! Do not write!

Je vais acheter cette cravate rouge. Elle coûte soixante-dix francs. Elle n'est pas très bon marché, mais elle est jolie. Je vais aussi acheter cette chemise bleue et ces chaussures noires. Et toi, quelles chaussures préfères-tu?

Now write the sentences in your lab manual as you hear them.

Je vais acheter / cette cravate rouge. / Elle coûte / soixante-dix francs. / Elle n'est pas / très bon marché, / mais elle est jolie. / Je vais aussi acheter / cette chemise bleue / et ces chaussures noires. / Et toi, / quelles chaussures / préfères-tu? /

Listen again, and check what you wrote.

(Text is reread without pauses.)

LECTURE CULTURELLE

Activité 15. Lecture. *Ouvrez votre livre à la page 121.* Open your textbook to p. 121. *Écoutez.*

(See textbook page 121.)

Activité 16. Compréhension du texte. You will hear several statements about the text you have just heard. Listen carefully to each statement. If it is true, mark **vrai.** If it is false, mark **faux.**

Commençons.

1. Les Français détestent le shopping.
2. Une boutique est un petit magasin.
3. Les grands magasins sont spécialisés dans une catégorie de vêtements.
4. Les Galeries Lafayette et le Printemps sont de grands magasins à Paris.
5. Généralement, les grandes surfaces sont situées dans le centre des grandes villes.
6. Les gens achètent beaucoup de choses différentes dans les grandes surfaces.

Maintenant vérifiez vos réponses. Now check your answers. You should have marked **vrai** for statements 2, 4, and 6; and **faux** for statements 1, 3, and 5.

Fin de la Leçon 8.
End of Lesson 8.
(music)

LEÇON 9. LE RÊVE ET LA RÉALITÉ

PRÉSENTATION

Activité 1. Lecture. Ouvrez votre livre à la page 132. Écoutez.

(See textbook page 132.)

Activité 2. Compréhension du texte. You will hear several statements about the text you have just heard. Listen carefully to each statement. If it is true, mark **vrai** in your lab manual. If it is false, mark **faux.**

Commençons.

1. Michèle habite chez ses parents.
2. La chambre de Michèle est très petite.
3. Michèle pense que le studio au Quartier latin n'est pas cher.
4. Le studio coûte 4.000 francs par mois.
5. Michèle va rester chez ses parents.

Maintenant vérifiez vos réponses. Now check your answers. You should have marked **vrai** for statements 1 and 5; and **faux** for statements 2, 3, and 4.

PHONÉTIQUE

Activité 3. Liaison. Many words in French end in a silent final consonant. In some instances, this consonant is pronounced with the next word when the next word begins with a vowel sound. The two words are then connected by LIAISON. Within a noun group, liaison is required between the words that introduce the noun.

Répétez: un‿appartement
mon‿ami, ton‿école
les‿enfants, mes‿amis
nos‿amis, vos‿amies
quelles‿étudiantes
aux‿étudiants

un bon‿appartement
mon‿excellent‿ami
mes meilleurs‿amis
nos chers‿amis
quels beaux‿enfants
aux nouveaux‿étudiants

Liaison is required between **plus, moins** + adjective.

Répétez: plus‿amusant plus‿heureux plus‿optimiste
moins‿intelligent moins‿idéaliste moins‿énergique

STRUCTURE ET VOCABULAIRE

A. *Le verbe **faire***

Activité 4. Prononciation. *Ouvrez votre livre à la page 134.* Open your textbook to p. 134.
The verb **faire** is irregular.

Repeat the forms of **faire,** and then repeat the sentences.

je fais
tu fais
il fait elle fait on fait
nous faisons
vous faites
ils font elles font

Je fais des projets.
Qu'est-ce que tu fais ici?
Philippe fait son budget.
Nous ne faisons pas de projets.
Faites-vous des projets pour les vacances?
Qu'est-ce qu'ils font à l'université?

The verb **faire** is used in many expressions. Repeat the following sentences.

Je fais attention.
Je fais le ménage.
Je fais la vaisselle.
Je fais mes devoirs.

Je fais des économies.
Je fais un voyage.
Je fais une promenade.
Je fais un match.

Activité 5. Pratique. Now practice the forms of **faire** in some substitution exercises. Repeat the key sentence. Then formulate new sentences using the suggested subjects.

Commençons.

Je fais des projets.

nous	Nous faisons des projets.
tu	Tu fais des projets.
les étudiants	Les étudiants font des projets.
le professeur	Le professeur fait des projets.

Qu'est-ce que **tu** fais ici?

vous — Qu'est-ce que vous faites ici?
Georges — Qu'est-ce que Georges fait ici?
les filles — Qu'est-ce que les filles font ici?

Nous ne faisons pas d'économies.

Marie — Marie ne fait pas d'économies.
vous — Vous ne faites pas d'économies.
Monique et Michèle — Monique et Michèle ne font pas d'économies.
je — Je ne fais pas d'économies.

Activité 6. Situation: Occupations. Say what the following people are doing. Use the verb **faire** and the expressions you will hear. *Écoutez le modèle.*

Modèle: André / la vaisselle — André fait la vaisselle.

Commençons.

Thomas / le ménage — Thomas fait le ménage.
nous / nos devoirs — Nous faisons nos devoirs.
vous / une promenade — Vous faites une promenade.
les voisins / une promenade en auto — Les voisins font une promenade en auto.
tu / un match de tennis — Tu fais un match de tennis.

Vocabulaire: Le logement

Activité 7. Prononciation. *Ouvrez votre livre à la page 136.* Open your textbook to p. 136.

Repeat the nouns after the speaker.

un appartement
un studio
un cabinet de toilette
un garage
le jardin
un mur
un salon
les WC
une maison
une résidence
une chambre
une cuisine
une fenêtre
une pièce
une porte
une salle à manger
une salle de séjour
une salle de bains
les toilettes
un bureau
un fauteuil
un lit
un meuble
un sofa
une chaise
une lampe
une table

Activité 8. Compréhension orale. You will hear a series of sentences in which specific parts of the house are mentioned. Listen carefully to each sentence and, in the space provided in your lab manual, write the part of the house you hear. Be sure to write the corresponding definite articles: **le** or **la.**

Commençons.

1. Ma chambre est confortable mais elle n'est pas très grande.
2. Paul regarde la télé au salon.
3. Nous dînons souvent dans la cuisine.
4. Où est la salle de bains?
5. Catherine n'est pas ici. Elle est dans la salle à manger.
6. Mon père est dans le jardin avec mon frère.

Maintenant vérifiez vos réponses. Now check your answers. You should have written the following words:

1. la chambre
2. le salon
3. la cuisine
4. la salle de bains
5. la salle à manger
6. le jardin

Vocabulaire: Les prépositions de lieu

Activité 9. Prononciation. *Ouvrez votre livre à la page 138.* Open your textbook to p. 138. *Répétez les prépositions et les phrases.*

Commençons.

dans — Le téléviseur est dans la salle de séjour.
par — Je passe par la cuisine pour aller au garage.
entre — Lyon est entre Paris et Nice.

sur — Il y a une lampe sur mon bureau.
sous — Mes chaussettes sont sous le lit.

devant — La chaise est devant le bureau.
derrière — Le jardin est derrière la maison.

près de — J'habite près de l'université.
loin de — Habitez-vous loin du campus?

à côté de — Il y a un café à côté du cinéma.
en face de — En face du cinéma, il y a un restaurant.

à droite de — La salle de bains est à droite de la chambre.
à gauche de — La cuisine est à gauche du salon.

*B. Les adjectifs **beau, nouveau, vieux***

Activité 10. Prononciation. *Ouvrez votre livre à la page 140.* Open your textbook to p. 140.

Répétez:

un beau costume	un nouveau vélo	un vieux livre
un bel homme	un nouvel ami	un vieil ami
une belle robe	une nouvelle moto	une vieille dame
les beaux meubles	les nouveaux pulls	les vieux lits
les belles jupes	les nouvelles robes	les vieilles lampes

Activité 11. Situation: Description. You will hear a series of sentences. Repeat these sentences, using the suggested adjectives. In the first set of sentences, use the appropriate form of the adjective **beau.** *Écoutez le modèle.*

Modèle: Paul a une voiture. — Paul a une belle voiture.

Commençons.

Pierre achète un manteau. — Pierre achète un beau manteau.
Jacqueline loue un appartement. — Jacqueline loue un bel appartement.
J'habite dans une maison. — J'habite dans une belle maison.
François porte un anorak. — François porte un bel anorak.

Now, use the appropriate form of the adjective **nouveau.**
J'ai une auto. — J'ai une nouvelle auto.
Sylvie a un ami. — Sylvie a un nouvel ami.
J'achète ces disques. — J'achète ces nouveaux disques.
Tu cherches un bureau. — Tu cherches un nouveau bureau.

Now, use the appropriate form of the adjective **vieux.**
Pierre porte une chemise. — Pierre porte une vieille chemise.
Est-ce que tu as mes disques? — Est-ce que tu as mes vieux disques?
Henri habite dans un appartement. — Henri habite dans un vieil appartement.
Je vais chez mes amis. — Je vais chez mes vieux amis.

C. Le superlatif

Activité 12. Prononciation. Ouvrez votre livre à la page 141. Répétez les phrases.

C'est la chambre la plus confortable de la maison.
Voici les robes les plus chères du magasin.

Où est l'hôtel le moins cher de la ville?
Vous êtes les étudiants les moins sérieux de la classe.

Vous êtes les meilleures étudiantes de la classe.

Activité 13. Conversation: Ce sont les meilleurs! Michèle will ask you about certain people or things. Say that they are the best in their categories, as indicated in your lab manual. *Écoutez le modèle.*

Modèle: C'est une fille intelligente, n'est-ce pas? — Oui, c'est la fille la plus intelligente de la classe.

Commençons.

1. C'est un étudiant sympathique, n'est-ce pas? — Oui, c'est l'étudiant le plus sympathique de la classe de français.
2. C'est une belle maison, n'est-ce pas? — Oui, c'est la plus belle maison de la ville.
3. C'est un livre intéressant, n'est-ce pas? — Oui, c'est le livre le plus intéressant de la bibliothèque.
4. C'est une veste chère, n'est-ce pas? — Oui, c'est la veste la plus chère du magasin.
5. C'est un bon restaurant, n'est-ce pas? — Oui, c'est le meilleur restaurant de la région.
6. C'est une chambre confortable, n'est-ce pas? — Oui, c'est la chambre la plus confortable de la maison.

D. Le temps

Activité 14. Prononciation. *Ouvrez votre livre à la page 143.* Open your textbook to p. 143.

Répétez les expressions de temps. Repeat the weather expressions.

Quel temps fait-il?

Il fait beau.
Il fait mauvais.
Il fait chaud.
Il fait bon.
Il fait froid.
Il fait du vent.
Il fait un temps épouvantable.
Il pleut.
Il neige.

DIALOGUE

Activité 15. Une question de temps. Michèle will ask you if you are going to do certain things. Tell her that you are not doing those things because of the weather. Base your responses on the illustrations in your lab manual. *Écoutez le modèle.*

Modèle: Est-ce que tu vas nager? — Non, je ne nage pas quand il fait mauvais.

Commençons.

1. Est-ce que tu vas faire une promenade? — Non, je ne fais pas de promenade quand il pleut.
2. Est-ce que tu vas porter un pull? — Non, je ne porte pas de pull quand il fait chaud.
3. Est-ce que tu vas rester chez toi? — Non, je ne reste pas chez moi quand il fait beau.
4. Est-ce que tu vas voyager? — Non, je ne voyage pas quand il neige.

DICTÉE

Activité 16. Le week-end. You will hear a short passage. First listen! Do not write!

Qu'est-ce que vous faites le week-end?
Quand il pleut, je fais le ménage. Mais quand il fait beau, je ne reste pas chez moi. Ce week-end je vais faire une promenade à bicyclette. Je vais aller chez Roger, mon nouvel ami. Il habite un bel appartement dans une vieille maison.

Now write the sentences in your lab manual as you hear them.

Qu'est-ce que vous faites / le week-end? /
Quand il pleut, / je fais le ménage. / Mais quand il fait beau, / je ne reste pas / chez moi. / Ce week-end / je vais faire / une promenade à bicyclette. / Je vais aller / chez Roger, / mon nouvel ami. / Il habite un bel appartement / dans une vieille maison. /

Listen once more and check what you wrote.

(Text is reread without pauses.)

LECTURE CULTURELLE

Activité 17. Lecture. Ouvrez votre livre à la page 133. Écoutez.

(See textbook page 133.)

Activité 18. Compréhension du texte. You will hear several statements about the text you have just heard. Listen carefully to each statement. If it is true, mark **vrai** in your lab manual. If it is false, mark **faux.**

Commençons.

1. Les étudiants français ont souvent des problèmes à trouver un bon logement.
2. En général, les universités françaises sont situées dans les grandes villes.
3. Dans les grandes villes, les appartements ne sont pas bon marché.
4. Les chambres d'étudiant sont très confortables, mais elles sont très chères.
5. En général, les étudiants n'aiment pas habiter à la Cité Universitaire.

Maintenant vérifiez vos réponses. Now check your answers. You should have marked **vrai** for statements 1, 2, and 3; and **faux** for statements 4 and 5.

Fin de la Leçon 9.
End of Lesson 9.
(music)

VIVRE EN FRANCE 3. L'ARGENT FRANÇAIS

Activité 1. La bonne réponse. You will hear a series of questions. In your lab manual you will see three possible responses for each question. Select the logical response by circling the corresponding letter.

Commençons.

1. Je vous dois combien?
2. À combien est le dollar canadien?
3. Vous avez une pièce d'identité?
4. Est-ce que je peux changer mon argent ici?
5. Tu as de la monnaie?
6. Où est-ce que je dois payer?
7. Comment allez-vous payer?
8. En quelles devises voulez-vous votre argent?

Now listen to the complete exchanges and correct your work. *Écoutez.*

1. Je vous dois combien?
   Deux cents francs, s'il vous plaît.
2. À combien est le dollar canadien?
   Il est à 5 francs 10.
3. Vous avez une pièce d'identité?
   Oui, voilà mon passeport.
4. Est-ce que je peux changer mon argent ici?
   Non, mais il y a une banque dans l'avenue du Maine.
5. Tu as de la monnaie?
   Non, j'ai seulement un billet de 500 francs.

6. Où est-ce que je dois payer?
   Allez à la caisse numéro deux.
7. Comment allez-vous payer?
   En espèces.
8. En quelles devises voulez-vous votre argent?
   En livres sterling, s'il vous plaît.

Activité 2. En France. Now you will hear a short conversation that takes place at the foreign exchange desk of a French bank. Listen carefully to the dialogue. Although you may not be able to understand every word of the dialogue, you should understand all the information necessary to fill out the exchange slip in your lab manual. You will hear the conversation twice. First, listen carefully. Then listen again and complete the currency exchange form.

Écoutez.

—Bonjour, Monsieur.
—Bonjour, Mademoiselle. Vous désirez?
—Je voudrais changer de l'argent. Est-ce que je peux changer mon argent ici?
—Bien sûr. En quelles devises avez-vous votre argent?
—J'ai des dollars canadiens.
—Bon, très bien. Aujourd'hui le cours du dollar canadien est de 5 francs 80. Combien d'argent voulez-vous changer?
—J'aimerais changer 300 dollars.
—En quelle forme? Avez-vous des billets ou des chèques de voyage?
—J'ai des chèques de voyage. Tenez, voilà 300 dollars en chèques.
—Bien. Je vais vous demander une pièce d'identité.
—Voici mon passeport.
—Parfait. Signez ici, s'il vous plaît. Et maintenant si vous voulez passer à la caisse numéro deux.

Écoutez à nouveau et écrivez. Listen again and write.

Fin de Vivre en France 3.
End of Vivre en France 3.
(music)

UNITÉ 4: CHEZ LES FRANÇAIS

LEÇON 10. LES PROBLÈMES DE L'EXISTENCE

PRÉSENTATION

Activité 1. Lecture. Ouvrez votre livre à la page 152. Écoutez.

(See textbook page 152.)

Activité 2. Compréhension du texte. You will hear a series of statements about the text you have just heard. Listen carefully to each statement. If the statement is true, mark **vrai** in your lab manual. If the statement is false, mark **faux.**

Commençons.

1. Jean-Claude et Carole sont frère et sœur.
2. Jean-Claude habite chez ses parents.
3. Jean-Claude n'est pas souvent d'accord avec son camarade de chambre.
4. Le problème de Jean-Claude n'a pas de solution.
5. Carole va à l'université.
6. Elle étudie beaucoup.
7. Elle réussit toujours à ses examens.
8. Elle parle à Jean-Claude de ses problèmes.

Maintenant vérifiez vos réponses. You should have marked **vrai** for statements 3, 5, and 6. You should have marked **faux** for statements 1, 2, 4, 7, and 8. If you got any wrong, listen once more to the **Présentation,** and do these questions again.

PHONÉTIQUE

Activité 3. Intonation: Les ordres. In French, commands always begin on a high pitch. The voice then falls until the end of the sentence.

Écoutez: Invite Philippe!

Répétez: Entrons!
N'aie pas peur!
Va au café!
Ne sois pas timide!
Réponds au professeur!
Ne vendez pas vos livres!

STRUCTURE ET VOCABULAIRE

A. *Expressions avec **avoir***

Activité 4. Prononciation. Ouvrez votre livre à la page 154. Répétez les expressions et les phrases.

avoir 19 ans — Pierre a dix-neuf ans.

avoir faim/avoir soif — J'ai faim, mais je n'ai pas soif.
avoir chaud/avoir froid — Il n'a pas froid. Il a chaud.
avoir raison/avoir tort — Paul a tort. Marie a raison.
avoir sommeil — Il est une heure du matin. J'ai sommeil.

avoir peur (de) — Pourquoi as-tu peur? As-tu peur de l'examen?
avoir besoin de — J'ai besoin d'une nouvelle veste.
J'ai besoin d'acheter une veste.

avoir envie de — J'ai envie d'un sandwich, mais je n'ai pas envie d'aller au restaurant.

avoir l'intention de — As-tu l'intention de faire un voyage?

Activité 5. Situation: Quel âge ont-ils? In your lab manual, you will see various people and their ages. As you hear each cue, give the corresponding age in a full sentence, using the proper subject pronoun. *Écoutez le modèle.*

Modèle: Moi — Moi, j'ai 18 ans.

Commençons.

1. moi — Moi, j'ai 21 ans.
2. toi — Toi, tu as 16 ans.
3. vous — Vous, vous avez 75 ans.
4. mon grand-père — Mon grand-père, il a 80 ans.
5. mon cousin — Mon cousin, il a 30 ans.
6. nous — Nous, nous avons 25 ans.

Activité 6. Situation: Logique. You will hear a series of descriptions. Comment on each person, using an appropriate expression with **avoir.** *Écoutez le modèle.*

Modèle: Béatrice achète une pizza. — Elle a faim.

Commençons.

Antoine pense que Montréal est la capitale du Canada. — Il a tort.
Marie pense que Washington est la capitale des États-Unis. — Elle a raison.
Robert achète un Coca-Cola. — Il a soif.
Christine habite à la Martinique. Elle est à la plage. — Elle a chaud.
Il neige et Richard n'a pas d'anorak. — Il a froid.

B. Les verbes réguliers en ***-ir***

Activité 7. Prononciation. *Ouvrez votre livre à la page 157. Un certain nombre de verbes français se terminent en* ***-ir.*** Some French verbs end in **-ir.** Many of these verbs are conjugated like **finir.** *Répétez les verbes et les phrases suivantes.*

je finis — Je finis l'examen.
tu finis — Tu finis la leçon.
elle finit — Elle finit le livre.
nous finissons — Nous finissons à cinq heures.
vous finissez — Quand finissez-vous?
ils finissent — Ils finissent le match.

Répétez les verbes et les phrases.

choisir — Qu'est-ce que vous choisissez? Ce livre-ci?
finir — Le programme finit à deux heures.
réfléchir à — Nous réfléchissons à cette question.
réussir — Vas-tu réussir dans tes projets?
réussir à — Les bons étudiants réussissent toujours à leurs examens.
grossir — Je ne grossis pas parce que je fais attention à mon régime.
maigrir — Est-ce que vous maigrissez?

Activité 8. Pratique. *Maintenant nous allons faire quelques exercices de substitution.* We will now do some substitution exercises. *Répétez la première phrase. Puis faites de nouvelles phrases en utilisant les sujets suggérés.* Repeat the key sentence. Then make new sentences using the subjects indicated.

Commençons.

Je réussis à l'examen.
nous — Nous réussissons à l'examen.
ces étudiants — Ces étudiants réussissent à l'examen.
ma cousine — Ma cousine réussit à l'examen.
tu — Tu réussis à l'examen.

Est-ce que **tu** grossis?
vous — Est-ce que vous grossissez?
Philippe — Est-ce que Philippe grossit?
tes frères — Est-ce que tes frères grossissent?

Tu ne maigris pas.
nous — Nous ne maigrissons pas.
je — Je ne maigris pas.
mon père — Mon père ne maigrit pas.

Activité 9. Situation: Au grand magasin. A number of people are in a department store looking at objects. Say that each person is choosing the object at which he or she is looking. Use the appropriate form of the verb **choisir,** *to choose. Écoutez le modèle.*

Modèle: Paul regarde un livre. — Il choisit un livre.

Commençons.

Je regarde un stylo. — Je choisis un stylo.
Tu regardes une machine à écrire. — Tu choisis une machine à écrire.
Suzanne et Hélène regardent des robes. — Elles choisissent des robes.
Nous regardons des tee-shirts. — Nous choisissons des tee-shirts.
Vous regardez des chemises. — Vous choisissez des chemises.

C. *Les verbes réguliers en* ***-re***

Activité 10. Prononciation. *Ouvrez votre livre à la page 158. Un certain nombre de verbes français se terminent en* ***-re.*** Some French verbs end in **-re.** *Un grand nombre de ces verbes sont conjugés comme* ***attendre.*** Many of these verbs are conjugated like **attendre.** *Répétez les verbes et les phrases suivantes.*

Commençons.

j'attends — J'attends le bus.
tu attends — Tu attends tes amis.
il attend — Paul attend Suzanne.
nous attendons — Nous attendons le professeur.
vous attendez — Qui est-ce que vous attendez?
elles attendent — Qu'est-ce qu'elles attendent?

Maintenant tournez à la page 159. Répétez les verbes et les phrases.

attendre — J'attends un ami.
entendre — Entendez-vous le professeur?
perdre — Pourquoi est-ce que vous perdez patience?
perdre son temps — Je n'aime pas perdre mon temps.
rendre — Je rends les disques à Pierre.
rendre visite à — Nous rendons visite à nos amis.
répondre à — Je vais répondre à ta lettre.
vendre — Jacques vend sa guitare à Antoine.

Activité 11. Pratique. *Maintenant nous allons faire quelques exercices de substitution.* We will now do some substitution exercises.

Commençons.

Je réponds au professeur.
vous — Vous répondez au professeur.
les étudiants — Les étudiants répondent au professeur.
tu — Tu réponds au professeur.

Je n'entends pas la question.
nous — Nous n'entendons pas la question.
Paul — Paul n'entend pas la question.
vous — Vous n'entendez pas la question.

Activité 12. Compréhension: Les problèmes de l'existence. *Antoine vous parle de ses problèmes.* Antoine is talking to you about his problems. Indicate in your lab manual whether you, too, have these problems.

Commençons.

1. Je grossis.
2. Je ne maigris pas.
3. Je perds mon temps à l'université.
4. Je ne finis pas ce que je commence.
5. Je ne réfléchis pas à ce que je fais.
6. J'ai peur des examens.
7. J'ai toujours sommeil.
8. Je n'ai pas envie d'étudier.

D. L'impératif

Activité 13. Situation: S'il te plaît! Imagine you are with your friend Jean-Pierre. Ask him to do the following things. *Écoutez le modèle.*

Modèle: jouer au tennis avec moi — Joue au tennis avec moi, s'il te plaît!

Commençons.

téléphoner à Monique — Téléphone à Monique, s'il te plaît!
acheter cette lampe — Achète cette lampe, s'il te plaît!
finir ce livre — Finis ce livre, s'il te plaît!
attendre mon cousin — Attends mon cousin, s'il te plaît!
être chez moi à midi — Sois chez moi à midi, s'il te plaît!

Now tell Jean-Pierre not to do the following things. *Écoutez le modèle.*

Modèle: perdre ton temps — Ne perds pas ton temps!

Commençons.

étudier ce week-end — N'étudie pas ce week-end!
être impatient — Ne sois pas impatient!
avoir peur de l'examen — N'aie pas peur de l'examen!
aller au café — Ne va pas au café!

Now imagine that you are going to spend the weekend with Jean-Pierre. Suggest the following activities, using the **nous**-form of the imperative. *Écoutez le modèle.*

Modèle: aller au cinéma — Allons au cinéma!

Commençons.

aller au stade — Allons au stade!
faire une promenade — Faisons une promenade!
dîner en ville — Dînons en ville!

DIALOGUE

Activité 14. Que font-ils? You will hear where certain people are. Then you will hear Jean-Claude ask you a question about each person. Answer him according to the illustrations in your lab manual. *Écoutez le modèle.*

Modèle: Janine est devant la poste.
Qu'est-ce qu'elle attend? — Elle attend le bus.

Commençons.

1. Philippe est à Paris.
   À qui est-ce qu'il rend visite? — Il rend visite à Sylvie.
2. M. Martin travaille dans un magasin.
   Qu'est-ce qu'il vend? — Il vend des ordinateurs.
3. Les étudiants sont en classe.
   À qui est-ce qu'ils répondent? — Ils répondent au professeur.
4. Albert va aller à la plage.
   De quoi a-t-il besoin? — Il a besoin de lunettes de soleil.
5. Stéphanie est dans un magasin de vêtements.
   Qu'est-ce qu'elle choisit? — Elle choisit un pantalon.

DICTÉE

Activité 15. Sylvestre. You will hear a short paragraph. First listen! Do not write!

Mon cousin Sylvestre a dix-neuf ans. Il a l'intention d'aller en France. Il a besoin d'argent. Voilà pourquoi il vend son auto. Avez-vous envie d'acheter cette auto? Réfléchissez à ma question!

Now write down the sentences in your lab manual as you hear them.

Mon cousin Sylvestre / a dix-neuf ans. / Il a l'intention / d'aller en France. / Il a besoin / d'argent. / Voilà pourquoi / il vend son auto. / Avez-vous envie / d'acheter cette auto? / Réfléchissez / à ma question! /

Maintenant écoutez encore une fois et vérifiez ce que vous avez écrit. Now listen again and check what you wrote.

(Text is reread without pauses.)

LECTURE CULTURELLE

Activité 16. Lecture. Ouvrez votre livre à la page 153. Écoutez.

(See textbook page 153.)

Activité 17. Compréhension du texte. You will hear several statements about the text you have just heard. Listen carefully to each statement. If it is true, mark **vrai** in your lab manual. If it is false, mark **faux.**

Commençons.

1. *L'Express* est un magazine français.
2. Pour les Français, l'argent est absolument essentiel au bonheur.
3. Pour les Français, le succès personnel n'est pas une chose très importante.
4. Les Français considèrent généralement que la famille est une chose importante.

Maintenant vérifiez vos réponses. You should have marked **vrai** for statements 1, 3, and 4; and **faux** for statement 2. If you got any wrong, listen once more to the activity and do these questions again.

Fin de la Leçon 10.
End of Lesson 10.
(music)

LEÇON 11. UN MOIS À PARIS

PRÉSENTATION

Activité 1. Lecture. Ouvrez votre livre à la page 164. Écoutez.

(See textbook page 164.)

Activité 2. Compréhension du texte. You will hear a series of statements about the text you have just heard. Listen carefully to each statement. If the statement is true, mark **vrai** in your lab manual. If the statement is false, mark **faux.**

Commençons.

1. Kevin a passé un mois à Paris.
2. Il a travaillé.
3. Il a parlé français.
4. Jennifer a étudié à l'Alliance Française.
5. Elle a voyagé.
6. Elle a rencontré beaucoup de gens sympathiques.
7. Bob a toujours parlé français.
8. Il a visité des musées.

Maintenant, vérifiez vos réponses. You should have marked **vrai** for sentences 1, 3, 5, 6, and 8 only. If you got any wrong, listen once more to the **Présentation,** and do these questions again.

PHONÉTIQUE

Activité 3. La voyelle nasale /ɔ̃/. The nasal vowel /ɔ̃/ is represented by the letters "on" and "om" when these letters occur at the end of a word or are followed by a consonant other than "n" or "m." Contrast the nasal and nonnasal vowels in the following pairs of words.

Comparez: Simon — Simone
bon — bonne
Japon — japonais
son — sommes

Répétez: on bon son maison salon pantalon oncle content
Bonjour, Simon. Où sont Yvon et Léon?
Mon oncle Simon est très compétent.

STRUCTURE ET VOCABULAIRE

*A. Le passé composé avec **avoir***

Activité 4. Prononciation. Ouvrez votre livre à la page 166. Répétez les phrases au passé composé.

J'ai voyagé.
Tu as voyagé.
Elle a voyagé.
Nous avons voyagé.
Vous avez voyagé.
Ils ont voyagé.

J'ai visité Paris.
Tu as visité Lyon.
Il a visité Nice.
Nous avons visité Marseille.
Vous avez visité Grenoble.
Elles ont visité Bordeaux.

Maintenant répétez les phrases suivantes.

Nous avons voyagé en France.
Louise a acheté ce pull.
Ils ont vendu leur auto.

Activité 5. Pratique. Maintenant nous allons faire quelques exercices de substitution. Répétez la première phrase. Puis faites de nouvelles phrases en utilisant les sujets suggérés.

Commençons.

Hier, **j'ai** dîné au restaurant.

vous — Hier, vous avez dîné au restaurant.
tu — Hier, tu as dîné au restaurant.
nous — Hier, nous avons dîné au restaurant.

Mon frère a fini ce livre.

vous — Vous avez fini ce livre.
mes cousines — Mes cousines ont fini ce livre.
tu — Tu as fini ce livre.
nous — Nous avons fini ce livre.

J'ai attendu le bus.

Pierre — Pierre a attendu le bus.
vous — Vous avez attendu le bus.
mes amis — Mes amis ont attendu le bus.

Activité 6. Identification de structures. You will hear a series of sentences. In some sentences, the action is taking place in the present; in others, the action occurred in the past. Listen carefully to the verb in each sentence. If the verb is in the present tense, mark the first row **présent** in your lab manual. If the verb is in the passé composé, mark the second row **passé composé.**

Commençons.

1. J'ai téléphoné à François.
2. Nous allons chez lui.
3. Pierre a visité Paris.
4. Henri joue au tennis.
5. Il a invité ses amis.
6. Vous regardez la télé.
7. Vous avez écouté ce disque.
8. Vous travaillez dans une banque.
9. J'ai grossi pendant les vacances.
10. Mes amis n'ont pas rendu visite à leurs cousins.
11. Je choisis une nouvelle raquette.
12. Nous attendons votre réponse.

Maintenant vérifiez vos réponses. You should have marked **présent** for sentences 2, 4, 6, 8, 11, and 12; and **passé composé** for sentences 1, 3, 5, 7, 9, and 10. If you got any wrong, listen once more to these sentences, and do these questions again.

Activité 7. Situation: L'été dernier. You will hear a series of activities. Say that Caroline did each of these things last summer. *Écoutez le modèle.*

<u>Modèle</u>: voyager — L'été dernier, Caroline a voyagé.

Commençons.

nager — L'été dernier, Caroline a nagé.
vendre son vélo — L'été dernier, Caroline a vendu son vélo.
répondre à mes lettres — L'été dernier, Caroline a répondu à mes lettres.
grossir — L'été dernier, Caroline a grossi.
gagner mille dollars — L'été dernier, Caroline a gagné mille dollars.

Activité 8. Narration: Hier aussi! You will hear what certain people are doing today. Say that they also did these things yesterday. *Écoutez le modèle.*

Modèle: Aujourd'hui Charles joue au tennis. Hier aussi, il a joué au tennis.

Commençons.

Aujourd'hui, Sylvie invite ses amis. Hier aussi, elle a invité ses amis.
Aujourd'hui, nous écoutons nos disques. Hier aussi, nous avons écouté nos disques.
Aujourd'hui, mes cousins regardent la télé. Hier aussi, ils ont regardé la télé.
Aujourd'hui, tu danses avec Christine. Hier aussi, tu as dansé avec Christine.
Aujourd'hui, vous dînez à 8 heures. Hier aussi, vous avez dîné à 8 heures.
Aujourd'hui, je perds mon temps. Hier aussi, j'ai perdu mon temps.

B. Le passé composé dans les phrases négatives

Activité 9. Narration: Bonnes résolutions. This morning Éric is catching up on certain tasks. As you hear each statement, say that he did not do these things last night. *Écoutez le modèle.*

Modèle: Ce matin, Éric va nettoyer sa chambre. Hier soir il n'a pas nettoyé sa chambre.

Commençons.

Ce matin, Éric va trouver ses notes. Hier soir, il n'a pas trouvé ses notes.
Ce matin, il va chercher ses cahiers. Hier soir, il n'a pas cherché ses cahiers.
Ce matin, il va finir la leçon. Hier soir, il n'a pas fini la leçon.
Ce matin, il va utiliser son ordinateur. Hier soir, il n'a pas utilisé son ordinateur.
Ce matin, il va rendre ces livres. Hier soir, il n'a pas rendu ces livres.

C. Les questions au passé composé

Activité 10. Conversation: Pourquoi? Olivier is telling you what his friends recently did. Ask him why they did these things. Use inversion in your questions. *Écoutez le modèle.*

Modèle: Sophie a maigri. Vraiment? Pourquoi a-t-elle maigri?

Commençons.

Pierre a travaillé hier. Vraiment? Pourquoi a-t-il travaillé hier?
Anne a vendu son ordinateur. Vraiment? Pourquoi a-t-elle vendu son ordinateur?
Marc a acheté une caméra. Vraiment? Pourquoi a-t-il acheté une caméra?
Claire a invité Robert. Vraiment? Pourquoi a-t-elle invité Robert?
Éric a choisi une nouvelle voiture. Vraiment? Pourquoi a-t-il choisi une nouvelle voiture?

Vocabulaire: Quand?

Activité 11. Conversation: Avant. Denise is asking about your future plans. Respond that you did those things in the past. Where she uses an expression with **prochain,** you will reply using the equivalent expression with **dernier.** *Écoutez le modèle.*

Modèle: Tu vas voyager l'été prochain? Non, j'ai voyagé l'été dernier.

Commençons.

Tu vas travailler le week-end prochain?	Non j'ai travaillé le week-end dernier.
Tu vas visiter Paris l'année prochaine?	Non, j'ai visité Paris l'année dernière.
Tu vas inviter des amis mardi prochain?	Non, j'ai invité des amis mardi dernier.
Tu vas payer le loyer la semaine prochaine?	Non, j'ai payé le loyer la semaine dernière.

D. Les participes passés irréguliers

Activité 12. Prononciation. Ouvrez votre livre à la page 174. Écoutez les verbes et répétez les phrases.

avoir	Nous avons eu une bonne surprise.
être	Jacqueline a été en France en juin.
faire	Mes parents ont fait un voyage au Canada.
il neige	Il a neigé en janvier.
il pleut	Hier, il a plu.
il y a	Il y a eu un accident.

Activité 13. Pratique. Maintenant, nous allons faire quelques exercices de substitution.

Commençons.

J'ai eu un accident.

nous	Nous avons eu un accident.
vous	Vous avez eu un accident.
tu	Tu as eu un accident.

Alain a été à Paris.

mes parents	Mes parents ont été à Paris.
je	J'ai été à Paris.
nous	Nous avons été à Paris.

Jean-Paul a fait une promenade.

vous	Vous avez fait une promenade.
tu	Tu as fait une promenade.
mes copains	Mes copains ont fait une promenade.

Activité 14. Narration: Lundi. Listen to what Pierre is doing today. Say that his sisters did these things last Monday. *Utilisez le passé composé. Écoutez le modèle.*

Modèle: Pierre a fait les courses. — Lundi ses sœurs ont fait les courses.

Commençons.

Pierre a un rendez-vous.	Lundi ses sœurs ont eu un rendez-vous.
Pierre fait la vaisselle.	Lundi ses sœurs ont fait la vaisselle.
Pierre est à la piscine.	Lundi ses sœurs ont été à la piscine.

DIALOGUE

Activité 15. Le week-end dernier. Florence is asking you about what you did last weekend. Answer her questions in the negative, and then explain what you did basing your answer on the illustrations in your lab manual. *Écoutez le modèle.*

Modèle: As-tu dîné chez toi le week-end dernier? Non, je n'ai pas dîné chez moi. J'ai dîné au restaurant.

Commençons.

1. As-tu joué au ping-pong? Non, je n'ai pas joué au ping-pong. J'ai joué au tennis.
2. As-tu écouté tes disques? Non, je n'ai pas écouté mes disques. J'ai écouté mes cassettes.
3. As-tu acheté des chaussures? Non, je n'ai pas acheté de chaussures. J'ai acheté un pull.
4. As-tu rendu visite à Catherine? Non, je n'ai pas rendu visite à Catherine. J'ai rendu visite à Suzanne.
5. As-tu téléphoné à Paul? Non, je n'ai pas téléphoné à Paul. J'ai téléphoné à Jacques.
6. As-tu fait une promenade en auto? Non, je n'ai pas fait de promenade en auto. J'ai fait une promenade à pied.

DICTÉE

Activité 16. Samedi dernier. You will hear a short passage. First listen! Do not write!

Qu'est-ce que vous avez fait samedi dernier? Moi, j'ai téléphoné à Julien. L'après-midi, nous avons joué au tennis. Le soir, nous avons dîné dans un restaurant italien. Après, nous avons rendu visite à un copain. Vraiment, nous n'avons pas perdu notre temps!

Now write the sentences in your workbook as you hear them.

Qu'est-ce que / vous avez fait / samedi dernier? / Moi, j'ai téléphoné / à Julien. / L'après-midi, / nous avons joué au tennis. / Le soir, / nous avons dîné / dans un restaurant italien. / Après, / nous avons rendu visite / à un copain. / Vraiment, / nous n'avons pas / perdu notre temps! /

Maintenant, écoutez encore une fois et vérifiez ce que vous avez écrit. Now listen again and check what you wrote.

(Text is reread without pauses.)

LECTURE CULTURELLE

Activité 17. Lecture. Ouvrez votre livre à la page 165. Écoutez.

(See textbook page 165.)

Activité 18. Compréhension du texte. You will hear several statements about the text you have just heard. Listen carefully to each statement. If it is true, mark **vrai** in your lab manual. If it is false, mark **faux.**

Commençons.

1. À Paris, il y a beaucoup de monuments.
2. Le Louvre et Notre Dame sont des monuments de Paris.
3. Montmartre est un musée parisien.
4. La France a une population de cinquante-cinq millions d'habitants.
5. Dix millions de personnes habitent à Paris.
6. L'avantage d'habiter à Paris c'est qu'il n'y a pas de problèmes de logement et pas de problème de transports.
7. Aujourd'hui, Paris est une ville moderne.

Maintenant vérifiez vos réponses. You should have marked **vrai** for statements 1, 2, 4, and 7; and **faux** for statements 3, 5, and 6. If you got any wrong, listen once more to the activity, and do these questions again.

Fin de la Leçon 11.
End of Lesson 11.
(music)

LEÇON 12. SÉJOUR EN FRANCE

PRÉSENTATION

Activité 1. Lecture. Ouvrez votre livre à la page 176. Écoutez.

(See textbook page 176.)

Activité 2. Compréhension du texte. You will hear a series of statements about the text you have just heard. Listen carefully to each statement. If the statement is true, mark **vrai** in your lab manual. If the statement is false, mark **faux.**

Commençons.

1. Pierre a rencontré Linda à Paris.
2. Linda est une étudiante américaine.
3. Linda est allée à l'université de Paris.
4. Elle a eu un accident d'automobile.
5. Elle est allée à l'hôpital.
6. À l'hôpital, elle a rencontré un Français.
7. Le jeune homme a présenté Linda à ses amis.
8. Linda a aimé son séjour en France.

Maintenant vérifiez vos réponses. You should have marked **vrai** for sentences 2, 5, 6, 7, and 8 only. If you got any wrong, listen once more to the **Présentation,** and do these questions again.

PHONÉTIQUE

Activité 3. La voyelle nasale /ã/. The nasal vowel /ã/ is represented by the letters "an," "am," "en," "em" when these letters occur at the end of a word or are followed by a consonant other than "n" or "m." Contrast the nasal and non-nasal vowels in the following pairs of words.

Comparez: an — année
campagne — camarade
attends — tennis
printemps — système

Répétez: an avant vacances lampe chambre
en entrer vendre temps température
Les enfants passent les vacances à l'étranger.

STRUCTURE ET VOCABULAIRE

Vocabulaire: Vive les vacances!

Activité 4. Narration: Les vacances. You will hear what certain people are doing. From these descriptions state whether or not they are on vacation. Use the appropriate form of the expression **être en vacances,** *to be on vacation,* in affirmative or negative sentences. *Écoutez le modèle.*

Modèle: Jacqueline fait du ski. — Elle est en vacances.

Commençons.

Nous allons à l'université. — Nous ne sommes pas en vacances.
Vous voyagez à l'étranger. — Vous êtes en vacances.
Je parle au professeur. — Je ne suis pas en vacances.
Tu fais un séjour au Mexique. — Tu es en vacances.
Mes cousins étudient. — Ils ne sont pas en vacances.
Mes cousines font leurs valises. — Elles sont en vacances.

*A. Les verbes **sortir, partir** et **dormir***

Activité 5. Prononciation. Ouvrez votre livre à la page 179. Les verbes **sortir, partir** et **dormir** sont irréguliers.

Répétez les phrases suivantes avec le verbe **sortir.**
Je sors avec Marc. — Nous sortons ce soir.
Tu sors maintenant. — Vous sortez demain?
Il sort avec Anne. — Ils sortent souvent.

Maintenant répétez les phrases avec le verbe **partir.**
Je pars maintenant. — Nous partons à une heure.
Tu pars avec Paul? — Vous partez en voiture.
On part avant le dîner. — Elles partent à six heures.

Maintenant répétez les phrases avec le verbe **dormir.**
Je dors peu. — Nous dormons mal.
Tu dors trop. — Vous dormez bien.
Elle dort en classe. — Ils dorment.

Activité 6. Pratique. Maintenant nous allons faire quelques exercices de substitution. Répétez la première phrase. Puis faites de nouvelles phrases en utilisant les sujets suggérés.

Commençons.

Michèle sort demain soir.

nous	Nous sortons demain soir.
vous	Vous sortez demain soir.
tu	Tu sors demain soir.
les étudiantes	Les étudiantes sortent demain soir.

Mes amis ne partent pas.

nous	Nous ne partons pas.
je	Je ne pars pas.
vous	Vous ne partez pas.
Philippe	Philippe ne part pas.

Est-ce que **vous** dormez bien?

tu	Est-ce que tu dors bien?
cet enfant	Est-ce que cet enfant dort bien?
ces gens	Est-ce que ces gens dorment bien?

B. Le passé composé avec ***être***

Activité 7. Prononciation. Ouvrez votre livre à la page 181. Répétez le passé composé du verbe **aller.**

Je suis allé	Nous sommes allés
Tu es allé	Vous êtes allés
Il est allé	Ils sont allés
Elle est allée	Elles sont allées
On est allé	

Maintenant répétez la forme **je** des verbes suivants au passé composé.

arriver:	je suis arrivé
partir:	je suis parti
entrer:	je suis entré
sortir:	je suis sorti
monter:	je suis monté
descendre:	je suis descendu
tomber:	je suis tombé
passer:	je suis passé
rester:	je suis resté
rentrer:	je suis rentré
retourner:	je suis retourné
naître:	je suis né
mourir:	je suis mort

Activité 8. Narration: Voyage en France. You will hear which cities certain students visited last year. From this information say whether or not they went to France. Use the passé composé of the expression **aller en France,** *to go to France*, in affirmative or negative sentences. *Écoutez le modèle.*

Modèle: Philippe a visité Québec. — Il n'est pas allé en France.

Commençons.

Mes cousins ont visité Grenoble.	Ils sont allés en France.
Hélène et Françoise ont visité San Francisco.	Elles ne sont pas allées en France.
J'ai visité Marseille.	Je suis allé en France.
Tu as visité Chicago.	Tu n'es pas allé en France.
Thérèse a visité Paris.	Elle est allée en France.
Vous avez visité Paris.	Vous êtes allés en France.
Nous avons visité Philadelphie.	Nous ne sommes pas allés en France.

Activité 9. Identification de structures. You will hear a series of sentences. Some of the sentences refer to a trip that is currently taking place; others refer to a trip that took place in the past. Listen carefully to the verb. If the verb is in the present tense, mark the first row **présent** in your lab manual. If the verb is in the passé composé, mark the second row **passé composé.**

Commençons.

1. Vous oubliez quelque chose.
2. Nous avons oublié notre caméra.
3. Je suis allé en Italie.
4. Vous allez à la montagne.
5. Nous avons fait un séjour à l'étranger.
6. Paul est sorti avec une Américaine.
7. Henri a rencontré ses amis à Toulouse.
8. Nous sommes à Marseille.
9. Nous sommes allés en Normandie.
10. Ils ont leurs appareils-photos.

Maintenant vérifiez vos réponses. You should have marked **présent** for sentences 1, 4, 8, and 10; and **passé composé** for sentences 2, 3, 5, 6, 7, and 9. If you got any wrong, listen once more to the activity, and do these questions again.

Activité 10. Compréhension orale. You will hear a series of sentences in the passé composé. Listen carefully to the verb used in each sentence and write down the infinitive of this verb in the space provided in your lab manual. *Écoutez le modèle.*

Modèle: Hier, Jacqueline est sortie avec un ami canadien. — You would have written **sortir** in your lab manual.

Commençons.

1. Quelqu'un est entré dans ma chambre.
2. Pierre est arrivé à Montréal le 22 juillet.
3. À quelle heure est-ce que vous êtes partis hier soir?
4. En France, mes parents sont descendus dans des hôtels assez bon marché.
5. Je ne suis pas resté à la plage à cause du mauvais temps.
6. L'année dernière, mon ami Philippe est sorti avec une étudiante américaine.

Maintenant vérifiez vos réponses. You should have written the following verbs.
1. entrer 2. arriver 3. partir 4. descendre 5. rester 6. sortir

If you got any wrong, listen once more to the activity, and do these questions again.

Activité 11. Narration: Mata Hari. Imagine you are a detective reporting by radio on the movements of Mata Hari, Junior. You will be told what she is doing. Report on her movements using the passé composé. *Écoutez le modèle.*

Modèle: Mata Hari arrive à l'aéroport d'Orly. Elle est arrivée à l'aéroport d'Orly.

Commençons.

Elle monte dans un taxi. Elle est montée dans un taxi.
Elle descend à l'hôtel Ritz. Elle est descendue à l'hôtel Ritz.
Elle sort du taxi. Elle est sortie du taxi.
Elle tombe. Elle est tombée.
Elle monte dans sa chambre. Elle est montée dans sa chambre.
Elle reste une heure là-bas. Elle est restée une heure là-bas.
Elle part à sept heures. Elle est partie à sept heures.
Elle va aux Champs-Elysées. Elle est allée aux Champs-Elysées.
Elle entre dans un restaurant. Elle est entrée dans un restaurant.
Elle rentre à l'hôtel à minuit. Elle est rentrée à l'hôtel à minuit.

C. La date et l'année

Activité 12. Compréhension: Dates historiques. You will hear about certain historical events. Although you may not understand every word, you should be able to understand the dates of these events. Write these dates in your lab manual. *Écoutez le modèle.*

Modèle: Les Parisiens ont pris la Bastille le 14 juillet 1789. You should have written: le 14 juillet 1789: July 14, 1789.

Commençons.

1. Louis XIV est mort le premier septembre 1715.
2. Napoléon est né le 15 août 1769.
3. L'indépendance américaine a été proclamée le 4 juillet 1776.
4. L'armistice de la première guerre a été signé le 11 novembre 1918.
5. Pearl Harbor a été attaqué par les Japonais le 7 décembre 1941.
6. Paris a été libéré le 25 août 1944.
7. Martin Luther King a été assassiné le 4 avril 1968.

Maintenant vérifiez vos réponses.

1. le premier septembre 1715: September 1, 1715
2. le 15 août 1769: August 15, 1769
3. le 4 juillet 1776: July 4, 1776
4. le 11 novembre 1918: November 11, 1918
5. le 7 décembre 1941: December 7, 1941
6. le 25 août 1944: August 25, 1944
7. le 4 avril 1968: April 4, 1968

If you got any wrong, listen once more to the activity, and do these questions again.

*D. L'usage du passé avec **Il y a***

Activité 13. Narration: Il y a combien de temps? Now you will hear how long various people have been living in certain places. Use this information to say when they arrived there. Use the passé composé of the verb **arriver** and the construction **il y a** plus elapsed time. *Écoutez le modèle.*

Modèle: Jacques habite à Paris depuis trois mois. Il est arrivé à Paris il y a trois mois.

Commençons.

Suzanne habite à Marseille depuis deux ans. Elle est arrivée à Marseille il y a deux ans.
François habite à New York depuis cinq semaines. Il est arrivé à New York il y a cinq semaines.
Nous habitons ici depuis dix ans. Nous sommes arrivés ici il y a dix ans.
Vous habitez dans cette ville depuis deux mois. Vous êtes arrivés dans cette ville il y a deux mois.
J' habite dans cette résidence depuis six semaines. Je suis arrivé dans cette résidence il y a six semaines.

E. La place de l'adverbe au passé composé

Activité 14. Conversation: Hier aussi. Robert is telling you what people are doing today. Say that they did the same things yesterday. Use the passé composé and be sure to put the adverb in the proper position. *Écoutez le modèle.*

Modèle: Philippe joue bien au tennis. Hier aussi, il a bien joué au tennis.

Commençons.

Les étudiants répondent bien. Hier aussi, ils ont bien répondu.
François dort mal. Hier aussi, il a mal dormi.
Madame Dupont travaille beaucoup. Hier aussi, elle a beaucoup travaillé.
Nous étudions peu. Hier aussi, nous avons peu étudié.
Vous mangez trop. Hier aussi, vous avez trop mangé.
Tu ne travailles pas assez. Hier aussi, tu n'as pas assez travaillé.
La secrétaire répond souvent au téléphone. Hier aussi, elle a souvent répondu au téléphone.

DIALOGUE

Activité 15. Voyage en France. Pierre is asking you about a trip you took in France. Answer him according to the illustrations in your lab manual. *Écoutez le modèle.*

Modèle: Quand es-tu arrivé(e) en France? Je suis arrivé(e) en France le 2 juillet.

Commençons.

1. Quelles villes as-tu visitées? J'ai visité Paris et Nice.
2. Comment as-tu voyagé? J'ai voyagé en train.
3. Dans quel hôtel es-tu resté(e)? Je suis resté(e) à l'hôtel Continental.
4. Qui as-tu rencontré à Nice? J'ai rencontré Jean-Claude.
5. Quand es-tu parti(e) de Nice? Je suis parti(e) de Nice le 18 juillet.
6. Quand as-tu quitté Paris? J'ai quitté Paris le 3 août.
7. Quand es-tu rentré(e) chez toi? Je suis rentré(e) chez moi le 10 août.

DICTÉE

Activité 16. Au Canada. You will hear a short paragraph. First listen! Do not write!

L'année dernière, Georges est allé au Canada avec sa cousine Sylvie. Ils sont partis de Paris le dix juillet. Ils ont visité Québec où ils sont restés deux semaines. Là-bas, Georges a rencontré une étudiante canadienne avec qui il est souvent sorti.

Now write the sentences in your lab manual as you hear them.

L'année dernière, / Georges est allé au Canada / avec sa cousine Sylvie. / Ils sont partis de Paris / le dix juillet. / Ils ont visité Québec / où ils sont restés / deux semaines. / Là-bas / Georges a rencontré / une étudiante canadienne / avec qui il est souvent sorti. /

Maintenant écoutez encore une fois et vérifiez ce que vous avez écrit.

(Text is reread without pauses.)

LECTURE CULTURELLE

Activité 17. Lecture. Ouvrez votre livre à la page 177. Écoutez.

(See textbook page 177.)

Activité 18. Compréhension du texte. You will hear several statements about the text you have just heard. Listen carefully to each statement. If it is true, mark **vrai** in your lab manual. If it is false, mark **faux.**

Commençons.

1. Les universités françaises n'acceptent pas les étudiants étrangers.
2. Un million d'étudiants étrangers étudient en France.
3. Il y a beaucoup d'étudiants algériens, tunisiens et marocains en France.
4. Il y a cent mille étudiants américains dans les universités françaises.

Maintenant vérifiez vos réponses. You should have marked **vrai** for statement 3 only; the other statements are false. If you got any wrong, listen once more to the activity and do these questions again.

Fin de la Leçon 12.
End of Lesson 12.
(music)

VIVRE EN FRANCE 4. À L'HÔTEL

Activité 1. La bonne réponse. You will hear a series of questions. In your lab manual you will see three possible responses for each question. Select the logical response by circling the corresponding letter.

Commençons.

1. Pourquoi es-tu allé à l'auberge de la jeunesse?
2. Où êtes-vous restés pendant les vacances?
3. Est-ce que ta chambre est confortable?
4. Quel est le prix des chambres?
5. Est-ce que vous allez payer par chèque?
6. Combien de temps allez-vous rester?
7. À quelle heure servez-vous le petit déjeuner?
8. Quel genre de chambre désirez-vous?

Now listen to the complete exchanges and correct your work. *Écoutez.*

1. Pourquoi es-tu allé à l'auberge de la jeunesse? Parce que c'est moins cher qu'à l'hôtel.
2. Où êtes-vous restés pendant les vacances? Nous sommes restés dans une pension.
3. Est-ce que ta chambre est confortable? Oui, elle a l'air conditionné et la télé.
4. Quel est le prix des chambres? C'est 500 francs par jour.
5. Est-ce que vous allez payer par chèque? Non, je préfère utiliser ma carte de crédit.
6. Combien de temps allez-vous rester? Une semaine.
7. À quelle heure servez-vous le petit déjeuner? À huit heures du matin.
8. Quel genre de chambre désirez-vous? Une chambre avec salle de bains.

Activité 2. En France. You will hear a short conversation that took place at the reception desk of a hotel on the Atlantic coast. Listen carefully to the dialogue. Although you may not be able to understand every word, you should understand all the relevant information you will need to fill out the hotel card in your lab manual. You will hear the conversation twice. First listen carefully. Then listen again and fill out the card. *Écoutez.*

—Bonjour, Mademoiselle.
—Bonjour, Monsieur. Vous désirez?
—Je voudrais une chambre.
—Avez-vous réservé?
—Non, je n'ai pas réservé.
—C'est pour combien de personnes?
—Pour deux personnes.
—Un moment, s'il vous plaît. Bon, j'ai une chambre à deux lits avec la télévision.
—Est-ce qu'il y a une vue sur l'océan?
—Non, la chambre donne sur le parc.
—Bon. Quel est le prix?
—Quatre cent francs par nuit, service et taxes comprises.
—Bien, je vais la prendre.
—Combien de temps avez-vous l'intention de rester à l'hôtel?
—Dix jours.
—Pouvez-vous me dire votre nom?
—Je m'appelle Monsieur Clément.
—Je vous donne la chambre 76. Voici votre clé et bon séjour à l'Hôtel de la Plage.
—Merci, Mademoiselle.

Écoutez à nouveau et écrivez.

Fin de Vivre en France 4.
End of Vivre en France 4.
(music)

UNITÉ 5: DE JOUR EN JOUR

LEÇON 13. POURQUOI LA FRANCE?

PRÉSENTATION

Activité 1. Lecture. Ouvrez votre livre à la page 196. Écoutez.

(See textbook page 196.)

Activité 2. Compréhension du texte. You will hear a series of statements about the people you have just heard speak. Listen carefully to each statement and indicate to whom it applies. Mark the corresponding column on the answer grid in your lab manual. *Écoutez le modèle.*

Modèle: Elle n'est pas étudiante. Elle est photographe et elle habite en Allemagne. You would have marked: Karin Schmidt.

Commençons.

1. Il est étudiant et il habite au Danemark.
2. Il est étudiant et il aime jouer de la guitare.
3. Elle est étudiante. Elle vient en France avec un groupe d'étudiants.
4. Il est marié. Il vient en France avec sa femme.
5. Il n'est pas marié. Sa copine habite en France.
6. Il n'a pas beaucoup d'argent. Le soir il ne va pas à l'hôtel. Il préfère faire du camping sur la plage.
7. Elle ne va pas visiter la France en auto. Avec ses amis, elle va visiter la Normandie à vélo.
8. Elle pense que les Français sont des gens heureux.
9. Il n'a pas peur des gendarmes.
10. Cette personne aime beaucoup la cuisine française.

Maintenant vérifiez vos réponses. Per Eriksen, phrases 1 et 5; Susan Morrison, phrases 3 et 7; Karin Schmidt, phrase 8; Peter de Jong, phrases 4 et 10; Andrew Mitchell, phrases 2, 6 et 9. If you got any wrong, listen once more to the **Présentation,** and do these questions again.

PHONÉTIQUE

Activité 3. Les lettres "gn." In French, the letters "gn" represent the sound /ɲ/. This sound is similar to the "ny" in "canyon," but it is pronounced with more tension.

Répétez: campagne montagne Espagne Allemagne espagnol
Les montagnes en Allemagne sont magnifiques.
Agnès boit du champagne espagnol.

STRUCTURE ET VOCABULAIRE

*A. Le verbe **venir***

Activité 4. Prononciation. Ouvrez votre livre à la page 198. Le verbe **venir** est irrégulier. Répétez les verbes et les phrases suivantes.

je viens
tu viens
elle vient
nous venons
vous venez
elles viennent
je suis venu

Je viens de France.
Tu viens avec nous?
Elle vient chez moi.
Nous venons de chez un ami.
Vous venez à six heures, n'est-ce pas?
Elles viennent au café avec nous.
Elles sont venues avec leurs amis.

Activité 5. Pratique. Maintenant nous allons faire quelques exercices de substitution. Répétez la première phrase. Puis faites de nouvelles phrases en utilisant les sujets suggérés.

Commençons.

Martine vient de la piscine.
nous — Nous venons de la piscine.
tu — Tu viens de la piscine.
les filles — Les filles viennent de la piscine.
vous — Vous venez de la piscine.

Marc ne revient pas à midi.
nous — Nous ne revenons pas à midi.
vous — Vous ne revenez pas à midi.
nos voisins — Nos voisins ne reviennent pas à midi.
je — Je ne reviens pas à midi.

Christine est revenue avant-hier.
je — Je suis revenue avant-hier.
vous — Vous êtes revenues avant-hier.
nous — Nous sommes revenues avant-hier.
mes parents — Mes parents sont revenus avant-hier.

*B. Le passé récent avec **venir de***

Activité 6. Identification de structures. You will hear various speakers talking about either something that happened recently or something that will happen in the future. Listen carefully to the verb constructions. If you hear a form of **venir de** followed by an infinitive, mark the first row **passé** in your lab manual. If you hear a form of the verb **aller** followed by an infinitive, mark the second row **futur.**

Commençons.

1. Je viens de jouer au tennis.
2. Je vais jouer au ping-pong.
3. Paul va inviter Marc.
4. Jeanette vient de téléphoner à Marc.
5. Nous allons faire les courses.
6. Ils vont sortir.
7. Tu viens de faire la vaisselle.
8. Michel vient de finir ses devoirs.
9. Mes frères viennent de nettoyer leur chambre.
10. Ils vont faire une promenade.

Maintenant vérifiez vos réponses. You should have marked **passé** for sentences 1, 4, 7, 8, and 9; and **futur** for sentences 2, 3, 5, 6, and 10. If you got any wrong, listen once more to the sentences and do these questions again.

Activité 7. Narration: Pourquoi pas? You will hear what certain people are not doing now. Say that this is because they have just done these things. *Écoutez le modèle.*

Modèle: Paul n'étudie pas.	Il vient d'étudier.

Commençons.

Henri ne travaille pas.	Il vient de travailler.
Philippe et Jacques ne dînent pas.	Ils viennent de dîner.
Nous ne préparons pas le dîner.	Nous venons de préparer le dîner.
Vous ne nettoyez pas l'appartement.	Vous venez de nottoyer l'appartement.
Je ne joue pas au tennis.	Je viens de jouer au tennis.
Tu ne fais pas les courses.	Tu viens de faire les courses.

C. L'usage de l'article défini avec les noms géographiques

Vocabulaire: Le monde

Activité 8. Prononciation. Ouvrez votre livre à la page 202. Répétez le nom des pays et des nationalités suivantes.

Commençons.

le Brésil	brésilien
le Canada	canadien
les États-Unis	américain
le Japon	japonais
le Mexique	mexicain
le Portugal	portugais
l'Allemagne	allemand
l'Angleterre	anglais
la Belgique	belge
la Chine	chinois
l'Égypte	égyptien
l'Espagne	espagnol
la France	français
la Grèce	grec
l'Irlande	irlandais
l'Italie	italien
la Russie	russe
la Suisse	suisse

Activité 9. Pratique. When a nationality is mentioned, respond with the name of the corresponding country. *Écoutez le modèle.*

Modèle: français	la France

Commençons.

anglais — l'Angleterre
italien — l'Italie
espagnol — l'Espagne
japonais — le Japon
mexicain — le Mexique
chinois — la Chine
américain — les États-Unis
allemand — l'Allemagne
canadien — le Canada

D. *L'usage des prépositions avec les villes et les pays*

Activité 10. Narration: Nationalités. You will be told the nationalities of different people. Say that each person lives in his or her country of origin. *Écoutez le modèle.*

Modèle: Henri est français. — Il habite en France.

Commençons.

Jacques est canadien. — Il habite au Canada.
Mes cousines sont suisses. — Elles habitent en Suisse.
Luisa est mexicaine. — Elle habite au Mexique.
Pedro et Luis sont brésiliens. — Ils habitent au Brésil.
Vous êtes anglaises. — Vous habitez en Angleterre.
Tu es allemand. — Tu habites en Allemagne.
Térésa est espagnole. — Elle habite en Espagne.
Monsieur Katagiri est japonais. — Il habite au Japon.
Madame Tang est chinoise. — Elle habite en Chine.
Je suis américain. — J'habite aux États-Unis.

Activité 11. Narration: Origines. You will again hear the nationalities of different people. Say that each person comes from his or her country of origin. *Écoutez le modèle.*

Modèle: Paul est français. — Il vient de France.

Commençons.

Françoise est belge. — Elle vient de Belgique.
Miko est japonais. — Il vient du Japon.
Maria est mexicaine. — Elle vient du Mexique.
Karin est allemande. — Elle vient d'Allemagne.
Ma cousine est portugaise. — Elle vient du Portugal.

E. *L'usage du présent avec* **depuis**

Activité 12. Conversation: Depuis quand? Monsieur Leclerc is asking how long you have been doing certain things. Answer him using the time expressions in your lab manual. *Écoutez le modèle.*

Modèle: Depuis quand habitez-vous ici? — J'habite ici depuis janvier.

Commençons.

1. Depuis quand étudiez-vous le français?	J'étudie le français depuis septembre.
2. Depuis quand étudiez-vous?	J'étudie depuis midi.
3. Depuis quand regardez-vous ce programme?	Je regarde ce programme depuis sept heures.
4. Depuis combien de temps êtes-vous à l'université?	Je suis à l'université depuis deux ans.
5. Depuis combien de temps travaillez-vous ici?	Je travaille ici depuis un mois.
6. Depuis combien de temps faites-vous cet exercice?	Je fais cet exercice depuis cinq minutes.

DIALOGUE

Activité 13. Quel pays? Pierre is asking you various questions. Answer him using the names of the countries illustrated in your lab manual. Be sure to use the appropriate preposition and/or article. *Écoutez les deux modèles.*

Modèles: Où vas-tu passer l'été?	Je vais passer l'été au Japon.
Quel pays veux-tu visiter?	Je veux visiter la Grèce.

Commençons.

1. Où habitent tes cousins?	Ils habitent au Canada.
2. Quel pays vas-tu visiter cet été?	Je vais visiter le Mexique.
3. De quel pays venez-vous?	Nous venons du Brésil.
4. Où avez-vous passé les vacances?	Nous avons passé les vacances en Espagne.
5. Quel pays préfères-tu visiter?	Je préfère visiter l'Irlande.
6. De quel pays arrivent ces touristes?	Ils arrivent du Portugal.

DICTÉE

Activité 14. Catherine. You will hear a short paragraph. First listen! Do not write!

Je viens de téléphoner à Catherine. Elle vient de passer une semaine à Québec. Maintenant, elle est à Montréal. Elle est là-bas depuis samedi. Elle revient aux États-Unis le premier juillet.

Now write the sentences in your lab manual as you hear them.

Je viens de téléphoner à Catherine. / Elle vient de passer / une semaine à Québec. / Maintenant, elle est à Montréal. / Elle est là-bas / depuis samedi. / Elle revient / aux États-Unis / le premier juillet. /

Écoutez encore une fois et vérifiez ce que vous avez écrit.

(Text is reread without pauses.)

LECTURE CULTURELLE

Activité 15. Lecture. Ouvrez votre livre à la page 197. Écoutez.

(See textbook page 197.)

Activité 16. Compréhension du texte. You will hear several statements concerning the text you have just heard. Listen carefully to each statement. If it is true, mark **vrai** in your lab manual. If it is false, mark **faux.**

Commençons.

1. La France est un pays très touristique.
2. En général, les touristes allemands et anglais n'aiment pas visiter la France.
3. Les touristes visitent la France pour des raisons différentes.
4. L'avantage des voyages organisés c'est la possibilité de rencontrer beaucoup de jeunes Français.
5. Certaines universités françaises ont des cours d'été.
6. Les étudiants qui visitent la France en auto-stop ne dépensent pas beaucoup d'argent pour les transports.
7. Certains étudiants sportifs visitent la France à bicyclette.

Maintenant vérifiez vos réponses. You should have marked **vrai** for statements 1, 3, 5, 6, and 7; and **faux** for statements 2 and 4. If you got any wrong, listen once more to the activity, and do these questions again.

Fin de la Leçon 13.
End of Lesson 13.
(music)

LEÇON 14. POUR GARDER LA LIGNE

PRÉSENTATION

Activité 1. Lecture. Ouvrez votre livre à la page 208. Écoutez.

(See textbook page 208.)

Activité 2. Compréhension du texte. You will now be asked a few questions about the four opinions you have just heard. Listen carefully and mark **oui** or **non** for each question in your lab manual.

Commençons.

Marie-Noëlle est étudiante et elle n'a pas de problème avec sa ligne.

1. Est-ce qu'elle mange beaucoup?
2. Est-ce qu'elle boit du thé?

Jean-Philippe est technicien et il a tendance à grossir.

3. Est-ce qu'il mange de la viande?
4. Est-ce qu'il boit de la bière?

Évelyne est vendeuse et elle n'a pas de régime spécial.

5. Est-ce qu'elle boit de la bière?
6. Est-ce qu'elle grossit?

Raymond Lucas est retraité.

7. Est-ce qu'il mange beaucoup?
8. Est-ce qu'il boit de l'alcool?

Maintenant vérifiez vos réponses. You should have marked **oui** for questions 2, 3, 5, 7, and 8. You should have marked **non** for questions 1, 4, and 6. If you got any wrong, listen once more to the **Présentation,** and do these questions again.

PHONÉTIQUE

Activité 3. La lettre "h." In French, unlike English, the letter "h" is always silent.

Le *«h» muet.* Most words that begin with "h" are treated as if they began with the vowel sound. Before a mute "h," elision and liaison are required.

Répétez: l'homme un‿homme j'habite vous‿habitez l'heure
En‿hiver, ces‿hommes partent à six‿heures.

Le *«h» aspiré.* Some words that begin with "h" are treated as if they began with a consonant sound. These words are marked with an asterisk in the dictionary. Before an aspirate "h" there is never elision or liaison.

Répétez: un hors- d'œuvre des haricots le hockey le huit
Nous jouons au hockey le huit octobre.

STRUCTURE ET VOCABULAIRE

*A. Le verbe **prendre***

Activité 4. Prononciation. Ouvrez votre livre à la page 210. Le verbe **prendre** est irrégulier. Répétez les verbes et les phrases suivantes.

je prends — Je prends mes disques.
tu prends — Prends-tu ta bicyclette?
il prend — Jacques ne prend pas sa voiture.
nous prenons — Nous prenons nos livres.
vous prenez — Est-ce que vous prenez votre caméra?
ils prennent — Mes cousins prennent leur appareil-photo.
j'ai pris — Est-ce que tu as pris tes cassettes?

Activité 5. Pratique. Maintenant nous allons faire quelques exercices de substitution. Répétez la première phrase. Puis faites de nouvelles phrases en utilisant les sujets suggérés.

Commençons.

Marie prend une pizza.
nous — Nous prenons une pizza.
vous — Vous prenez une pizza.
je — Je prends une pizza.
mes amis — Mes amis prennent une pizza.

Apprenez-**vous** l'espagnol?

tu	Apprends-tu l'espagnol?
vous	Apprenez-vous l'espagnol?
Marie	Marie apprend-elle l'espagnol?
Marc et Paul	Marc et Paul apprennent-ils l'espagnol?

Je n'ai pas compris la leçon.

nous	Nous n'avons pas compris la leçon.
tu	Tu n'as pas compris la leçon.
les étudiants	Les étudiants n'ont pas compris la leçon.

B. L'article partitif

Vocabulaire: Au menu

Activité 6. Prononciation. Regardez votre livre à la page 213. Répétez les mots suivants.

les hors d'œuvre
le jambon
le saucisson
le poisson
le saumon
le thon
la sole
la viande
le bœuf
le porc
le poulet
le rosbif
le fromage
la salade
le dessert
le gâteau
le yaourt
la crème
la glace
la tarte
les autres produits
le beurre
un œuf
le pain
le poivre
le sel
le sucre
la confiture
la crème
la mayonnaise
la moutarde

manger
Qu'est-ce que vous mangez?

Activité 7. Narration: À la cafétéria. You will hear what foods certain people like. Say that they will get these foods as they go through the cafeteria line. Use the verb **prendre** and the appropriate partitive article. *Écoutez le modèle.*

Modèle: François aime la salade. — Il va prendre de la salade.

Commençons.

Isabelle aime le jambon.	Elle va prendre du jambon.
Jacqueline aime la confiture.	Elle va prendre de la confiture.
Henri aime le poulet.	Il va prendre du poulet.
Éric aime les spaghetti.	Il va prendre des spaghetti.
Sylvie aime le saucisson.	Elle va prendre du saucisson.
Monique aime le poisson.	Elle va prendre du poisson.
Thérèse aime le pain.	Elle va prendre du pain.

Nathalie aime le porc. — Elle va prendre du porc.
Pierre aime le bœuf. — Il va prendre du bœuf.

C. L' article partitif dans les phrases négatives

Activité 8. Situation: Au régime. Philippe is on a special diet and does not eat any meat products. You will hear the names of various foods. Say whether or not Philippe is buying these foods. *Écoutez le modèle.*

<u>Modèle</u>: le rosbif? — Il n'achète pas de rosbif.

Commençons.

le yaourt? — Il achète du yaourt.
le porc? — Il n'achète pas de porc.
la crème? — Il achète de la crème.
la salade? — Il achète de la salade.
le poulet? — Il n'achète pas de poulet.
la viande? — Il n'achète pas de viande.

D. Le verbe ***boire***

Activité 9. Prononciation. Ouvrez votre livre à la page 216. Le verbe **boire** est irrégulier. Répétez les verbes et les phrases suivantes.

Commençons.

je bois — Moi, je bois du café.
tu bois — Tu bois de la limonade?
il boit — Jacques boit toujours de la bière.
nous buvons — Nous ne buvons pas de vin.
vous buvez — Buvez-vous du thé?
ils boivent — Mes parents boivent du champagne.
j'ai bu — Mes amis ont bu du café ce matin.

Activité 10. Pratique. Maintenant nous allons faire quelques exercices de substitution. Répétez la première phrase. Puis faites de nouvelles phrases en utilisant les sujets suggérés.

Marc ne boit pas de vin.
nous — Nous ne buvons pas de vin.
tu — Tu ne bois pas de vin.
mes grands-parents — Mes grands-parents ne boivent pas de vin.
vous — Vous ne buvez pas de vin.

J'ai bu du café.
nous — Nous avons bu du café.
tu — Tu as bu du café.
Caroline — Caroline a bu du café.

Vocabulaire: Boissons

Activité 11. Prononciation. Ouvrez votre livre à la page 216. Répétez les noms des boissons.

le café
le jus d'orange
le lait
le thé
le vin
la bière
la boisson
l'eau
l'eau minérale
la limonade

Activité 12. Situation: Que boivent-ils? François and Caroline avoid caffeine and alcohol. Indicate whether or not they drink the following beverages. *Écoutez le modèle.*

Modèle: la limonade? Oui, ils boivent de la limonade.

Commençons.

l'eau? Oui, ils boivent de l'eau.
le café? Non, ils ne boivent pas de café.
le lait? Oui, ils boivent du lait.
la bière? Non, ils ne boivent pas de bière.
le vin? Non, ils ne boivent pas de vin.
le jus d'orange? Oui, ils boivent du jus d'orange.

Activité 13. Compréhension. You will hear some sentences, each one containing the name of a food or beverage. In the space provided in your lab manual, write the name of that food or beverage with the appropriate definite article. Don't worry if you do not understand everything that is said. Concentrate on the name of the food or beverage. *Êtes-vous prêts?* Are you ready?

Commençons.

1. Prenez-vous du fromage?
2. Si tu vas chez le boulanger, achète un gâteau!
3. En effet, le sucre est sur la table.
4. Non merci, je ne prends pas de pain!
5. Passe-moi la glace, s'il te plaît!
6. Je ne mange pas de beurre parce que je ne veux pas grossir.
7. Je n'aime pas le poisson. Et toi?
8. Où est la bière?
9. Au dîner, nous buvons du vin.

Maintenant vérifiez vos réponses.

1. le fromage
2. le gâteau
3. le sucre
4. le pain
5. la glace
6. le beurre
7. le poisson
8. la bière
9. le vin

If you got any wrong, listen once more to the activity, and do these questions again.

E. L'emploi idiomatique de ***faire***

Activité 14. Conversation: Vos activités. Vincent is asking you about whether you like certain school and leisure activities. Answer in the affirmative, saying you engage in these activities. *Écoutez le modèle.*

Modèle: Tu aimes la photo?	Oui, je fais de la photo.

Commençons.

Tu aimes le ski?	Oui, je fais du ski.
Tu aimes la biologie?	Oui, je fais de la biologie.
Tu aimes le sport?	Oui, je fais du sport.

Now say that you do not engage in these activities.

Modèle: Tu aimes le jogging?	Non, je ne fais pas de jogging.

Commençons.

Tu aimes la gymnastique?	Non, je ne fais pas de gymnastique.
Tu aimes la danse?	Non, je ne fais pas de danse.
Tu aimes l'aérobic?	Non, je ne fais pas d'aérobic.

DIALOGUE

Activité 15. Nourriture et boissons. Marie-Noëlle is going to ask you several questions. Answer her according to the illustrations in your lab manual. Be sure to use the appropriate partitive articles. *Écoutez le modèle.*

Modèle: Qu'est-ce que tu bois?	Je bois du café.

Commençons.

1. Qu'est-ce que tu manges?	Je mange du pain.
2. Qu'est-ce que tu as bu hier soir?	J'ai bu de la bière.
3. Qu'est-ce que tu vas prendre au dessert?	Je vais prendre de la glace.
4. Qu'est-ce que tu as mangé au restaurant?	J'ai mangé du poulet.
5. Qu'est-ce que tu veux?	Je veux du fromage.
6. Qu'est-ce que tu vas acheter?	Je vais acheter du vin.
7. Qu'est-ce qu'il y a dans le réfrigérateur?	Il y a du lait.
8. Qu'est-ce que tu prends?	Je prends de la salade.
9. Qu'est-ce que tu as mangé hier?	J'ai mangé du poisson.
10. Qu'est-ce que tu vas prendre maintenant?	Je vais prendre de l'eau.

DICTÉE

Activité 16. Au restaurant. You will hear a short passage. First listen! Do not write!

Guillaume et Suzanne sont au restaurant. Guillaume regarde le menu. Il va prendre du poulet et de la salade. Il va boire du vin. Suzanne va prendre de la salade, mais elle ne va pas prendre de poulet. Elle va prendre du jambon et boire de l'eau minérale.

Now write the sentences in your lab manual as you hear them.

Commençons.

Guillaume et Suzanne sont au restaurant. / Guillaume regarde le menu. / Il va prendre du poulet / et de la salade. / Il va boire du vin. / Suzanne va prendre de la salade, / mais elle ne va pas / prendre de poulet. / Elle va prendre / du jambon / et boire / de l'eau minérale. /

Now listen again and check what you wrote.

(Text is reread without pauses.)

LECTURE CULTURELLE

Activité 17. Lecture. Ouvrez votre livre à la page 209. Écoutez.

(See textbook page 209.)

Activité 18. Compréhension du texte. You will hear several statements about the text you have just heard. Listen carefully to each statement. If it is true, mark **vrai** in your lab manual. If it is false, mark **faux.**

Commençons.

1. En général, les Français ne dépensent pas beaucoup d'argent pour leur nourriture.
2. En général, les Français aiment les bons vins.
3. Les Français d'aujourd'hui mangent plus de pain et boivent plus de vin qu'avant.
4. Les Français d'aujourd'hui sont plus sportifs et physiquement plus actifs qu'avant.
5. Les Français ne pratiquent pas le jogging.

Maintenant vérifiez vos réponses. You should have marked **vrai** for statements 2 and 4. You should have marked **faux** for statements 1, 3, and 5. If you got any wrong, listen once more to the activity, and do these questions again.

Fin de la Leçon 14.
End of Lesson 14.
(music)

LEÇON 15. BON APPÉTIT!

PRÉSENTATION.

Activité 1. Lecture. Ouvrez votre livre à la page 220. Écoutez.

(See textbook page 220.)

Activité 2. Compréhension du texte. You will hear a series of statements about the text you have just heard. Listen carefully to each statement and in your lab manual mark **vrai** or **faux.**

Commençons.

1. Philippe a invité Corinne au restaurant.
2. Comme hors d'œuvre Corinne commande du saumon.
3. Philippe veut commander du vin ordinaire.
4. Philippe est malade parce qu'il a trop mangé.
5. C'est Corinne que paie le repas.

Maintenant vérifiez vos réponses. You should have marked **vrai** for statements 1, 2, and 5; and **faux** for statements 3 and 4.

PHONÉTIQUE

Activité 3. Les voyelles /ø/ et /œ/. The French vowels /ø/ and /œ/ have no counterparts in English.

(a) *La voyelle /ø/.* To pronounce the vowel /ø/, round your lips tensely as you say the sound /e/.

Répétez: eux deux heureux Eugène serveuse il pleut
Eugène n'est pas heureux quand il pleut.
Monsieur Lebleu dîne avec eux.

(b) *La voyelle /œ/.* To pronounce the vowel /œ/, round your lips as you say the sound /ɛ/.

Répétez: sœur heure œuf beurre peur meuble
Le professeur déjeune à une heure.
Ma sœur prend du beurre avec son œuf.

STRUCTURE ET VOCABULAIRE

Vocabulaire: Les repas

Activité 4. Prononciation. Ouvrez votre livre à la page 222. Répétez le nom des repas.

un petit déjeuner un déjeuner un dîner

Maintenant répétez la forme-**je** des verbes suivants et écoutez les phrases qui utilisent ces verbes.

Commençons.

apporter	j'apporte	Jean-Claude a apporté un gâteau.
commander	je commande	Qu'est-ce que tu vas commander pour le dîner?
déjeuner	je déjeune	Nous avons déjeuné à midi.
dîner	je dîne	Nous dînons à huit heures.
fumer	je fume	Je ne fume pas et je déteste les gens qui fument.
garder	je garde	Je veux garder la ligne.
préparer	je prépare	Qui a préparé ce repas?
servir	je sers	Le garçon sert le repas.
être au régime	je suis au régime	Je suis au régime parce que je veux maigrir.
faire les courses	je fais les courses	Si tu fais les courses, achète du pain.
faire la cuisine	je fais la cuisine	Robert adore faire la cuisine.

Activité 5. Questions personnelles. You will hear some questions about your meals and your eating habits. Answer these questions by checking the appropriate response **oui** or **non** in your lab manual.

Commençons.

1. Êtes-vous au régime?
2. Prenez-vous le petit déjeuner à la cantine de votre université?
3. Déjeunez-vous chez vous?
4. Dînez-vous souvent au restaurant?
5. Chez vous, est-ce que vous faites la cuisine?
6. Est-ce que vous mangez beaucoup au petit déjeuner?
7. Est-ce que vous aimez la cuisine italienne?
8. Est-ce que vous fumez?

Now you will hear the questions again. This time, answer in full sentences according to what you marked in your lab manual. For example, listen to question one: **Êtes-vous au régime?** If you are now on a diet and marked **oui,** you would say: **Oui, je suis au régime.** If you are not on a diet and marked **non,** you would say: **Non, je ne suis pas au régime.** You will not hear a confirmation of your responses. Let's continue with question 2.

Commençons.

A. *Le verbe* ***mettre***

Activité 6. Prononciation. *Ouvrez votre livre à la page 224. Le verbe* ***mettre*** *est irrégulier.* The verb **mettre,** *to put,* is irregular. *Répétez les phrases suivantes.* Repeat the following sentences.

Je mets ma veste.
Tu mets ton pull.
Elle met un tee-shirt.
Nous mettons un disque de jazz.
Vous mettez de la musique classique.
Ils mettent du rock.
Vous avez mis la radio.

Activité 7. Pratique. Maintenant nous allons faire quelques exercices de substitution. Répétez la première phrase. Puis faites de nouvelles phrases en utilisant les sujets suggérés.

Commençons.

Martine met la table.

nous	Nous mettons la table.
je	Je mets la table.
mes frères	Mes frères mettent la table.
tu	Tu mets la table.

Où est-ce que **tu** as mis la voiture?

Jacques	Où est-ce que Jacques a mis la voiture?
vous	Où est-ce que vous avez mis la voiture?
tes parents	Où est-ce que tes parents ont mis la voiture?

B. *L'usage de l'article partitif, de l'article défini et de l'article indéfini*

Activité 8. Conversation: Préférences. Paul et Michèle are asking you about your eating preferences. Answer their questions in the affirmative. *Écoutez les modèles.*

Modèles:		
	Aimes-tu le caviar?	Oui, j'aime le caviar.
	Manges-tu du caviar?	Oui, je mange du caviar.

Commençons.

Aimes-tu la glace? Oui, j'aime la glace.
Manges-tu de la glace? Oui, je mange de la glace.
Aimes-tu l'eau minérale? Oui, j'aime l'eau minérale.
Bois-tu de l'eau minérale? Oui, je bois de l'eau minérale.
Aimes-tu les œufs? Oui, j'aime les œufs.
Manges-tu des œufs? Oui, je mange des œufs.
Aimes-tu les hors d'œuvre? Oui, j'aime les hors d'œuvre.
Manges-tu des hors d'œuvre? Oui, je mange des hors d'œuvre.
Aimes-tu le lait? Oui, j'aime le lait.
Bois-tu du lait? Oui, je bois du lait.

Vocabulaire: Fruits et légumes

Activité 9. Prononciation. Ouvrez votre livre à la page 230. Répétez le nom des fruits et des légumes.

les fruits
- un pamplemousse
- une banane
- une orange
- une pomme
- une poire
- une fraise
- une cerise

les légumes
- des haricots
- des petits pois
- une pomme de terre
- des frites
- une carotte
- une tomate

Activité 10. Pratique. *Maintenant faites un exercice de substitution.* Repeat the key sentences. Then replace the first part of the sentence with the expression suggested. Be sure to use the appropriate article with the fruit or vegetable.

Répétez:

J'aime les fruits.
Est-ce qu'il y a — Est-ce qu'il y a des fruits?
Nous prenons — Nous prenons des fruits.
Paul ne mange pas — Paul ne mange pas de fruits.
Monique déteste — Monique déteste les fruits.

J'aime les fraises.
Qui va prendre — Qui va prendre des fraises?
Où sont — Où sont les fraises?
Comme dessert, il y a — Comme dessert, il y a des fraises.
Roger ne mange pas — Roger ne mange pas de fraises.

Activité 11. Compréhension: Au restaurant. You will hear several customers giving their orders. Listen carefully. In your lab manual, write what each customer orders. Use the appropriate partitive article.

Commençons.

J'aime les légumes. Je vais prendre des carottes.
Vous n'avez pas d'eau minérale. Bon, alors, je vais prendre de la bière.
J'aime la viande, mais je suis au régime. Vous avez du poisson? Bon, je vais prendre de la sole. Non merci, je ne vais pas prendre des frites avec la sole.
Qu'est-ce que vous avez comme dessert? De la glace et des fruits. Eh bien, je vais prendre une poire. Non merci, pas de fromage aujourd'hui!

Maintenant vérifiez vos réponses. You should have written the following: 1. des carottes 2. de la bière 3. de la sole 4. une poire.

C. Expressions de quantité

Activité 12. Prononciation. Ouvrez votre livre à la page 231. Répétez les expressions de quantité et les phrases suivantes.

Commençons.

combien...?	Combien coûtent ces disques?
combien de...?	Combien de disques as-tu?
peu	Je travaille peu.
peu de	J'ai peu d'argent.
un peu	J'ai mangé un peu.
un peu de	J'ai mangé un peu de jambon.
assez	Tu ne voyages pas assez.
assez de	Tu n'as pas assez de vacances.
beaucoup	Marc aime beaucoup le jazz.
beaucoup de	Il a beaucoup de disques de jazz.
trop	Vous jouez trop.
trop de	Vous avez trop de loisirs.
beaucoup trop	Nous étudions beaucoup trop.
beaucoup trop de	Nous avons beaucoup trop d'examens.
plus de	Nous avons plus de travail que toi.
moins de	J'ai moins d'argent que mes amis.
autant de	Simon n'a pas autant d'ambition que sa sœur.

Activité 13. Conversation: D'autres quantités. Marc is asking you some questions. Answer in the affirmative or in the negative, using the expression of quantity indicated in your lab manual. *Écoutez le modèle.*

<u>Modèle</u>: Est-ce que Paul a de l'argent? Non, il n'a pas beaucoup d'argent.

Commençons.

1. Est-ce que Jacqueline a de la patience? Oui, elle a beaucoup de patience.
2. Est-ce que Charles gagne de l'argent? Non, il ne gagne pas assez d'argent.
3. Est-ce que Philippe mange du pain? Oui, il mange trop de pain.
4. Est-ce qu'Alice boit du café? Non, elle ne boit pas beaucoup de café.
5. Est-ce que Suzanne fait du sport? Oui, elle fait beaucoup de sport.

DIALOGUE

Activité 14. Nourriture et boissons. Nathalie is going to ask you several questions. Answer her according to the illustrations in your lab manual. Be sure to use the appropriate partitive articles. *Écoutez le modèle.*

Modèle: Qu'est-ce que tu as commandé? J'ai commandé du poisson.

Commençons.

1. Qu'est-ce que tu as commandé avec le repas? J'ai commandé du vin.
2. Qu'est-ce que tu as mis sur ton pain? J'ai mis du beurre.
3. Qu'est-ce que tu as mis dans ton café? J'ai mis du sucre.
4. Qu'est-ce que tu vas servir au dîner? Je vais servir du poulet.
5. Qu'est-ce que tu as préparé? J'ai préparé des frites.
6. Qu'est-ce qu'il y a dans cette tarte? Il y a des fraises.
7. Qu'est-ce que tu as apporté? J'ai apporté des poires.
8. Qu'est-ce que tu as acheté au supermarché? J'ai acheté des cerises.

DICTÉE

Activité 15. Au restaurant. You will hear a short passage. First listen! Do not write!

Nous déjeunons souvent dans ce restaurant. La viande et les légumes sont toujours très bons. François va commander du poulet avec des frites. Moi, je vais prendre de la sole parce que je suis au régime.

Now write the sentences in your lab manual as you hear them.

Nous déjeunons souvent / dans ce restaurant. / La viande et les légumes / sont toujours très bons. / François va commander / du poulet avec des frites. / Moi, / je vais prendre de la sole / parce que je suis au régime. /

Écoutez encore une fois et vérifiez ce que vous avez écrit.

(Text is reread without pauses.)

LECTURE CULTURELLE

Activité 16. Lecture. Ouvrez votre livre à la page 221. Écoutez.

(See textbook page 221.)

Activité 17. Compréhension du texte. You will hear several statements about the text you have just heard. Listen carefully to each statement. If it is true, mark **vrai** in your lab manual. If it is false, mark **faux.**

Commençons.

1. Le petit déjeuner est le premier repas de la journée.
2. Au petit déjeuner, les Français mangent du pain et du beurre.
3. On mange la salade avant le plat principal.
4. Le dîner est généralement plus léger que le déjeuner.
5. Avec les repas, les Français boivent généralement du café.

Maintenant vérifiez vos réponses. You should have marked **vrai** for statements 1, 2, and 4; and **faux** for statements 3 and 5.

Fin de la Leçon 15.
End of Lesson 15.
(music)

VIVRE EN FRANCE 5. AU CAFÉ

Activité 1. La bonne réponse. You will hear a series of questions. In your lab manual you will see three possible responses for each question. Select the logical response by circling the corresponding letter.

Commençons.

1. Je n'ai pas très faim. Est-ce que vous avez quelque chose de léger?
2. Garçon, s'il vous plaît. Pouvez-vous m'apporter l'addition?
3. Qu'est-ce que vous allez prendre comme plat principal?
4. Est-ce que vous voulez un dessert?
5. Qu'est-ce qu'il y a comme hors d'œuvre?
6. Est-ce que tu veux du saucisson?
7. Vous allez prendre une boisson?
8. Je vous dois combien?

Now listen to the complete exchanges and correct your work. *Écoutez.*

1. Je n'ai pas très faim. Est-ce que vous avez quelque chose de léger?
   Bien sûr. Voulez-vous un croque-monsieur?
2. Garçon, s'il vous plaît. Pouvez-vous m'apporter l'addition?
   Voilà! Ça fait 48 francs.
3. Qu'est-ce que vous allez prendre comme plat principal?
   Je vais prendre le lapin farci.
4. Est-ce que vous voulez un dessert?
   Donnez-moi une crème caramel.
5. Qu'est-ce qu'il y a comme hors d'œuvre?
   Il y a des œufs mayonnaise.
6. Est-ce que tu veux du saucisson?
   Non, je vais prendre du jambon.
7. Vous allez prendre une boisson?
   Oui, donnez-moi de l'eau minérale, s'il vous plaît.
8. Je vous dois combien?
   Attendez une seconde. Je vais préparer l'addition.

Activité 2. En France. You will hear a short conversation in a restaurant. The waiter is taking the client's order. Listen carefully to the dialogue. Although you may not be able to understand every word, you should be able to understand all the information you need to fill out the order form in your lab manual. You will hear the conversation twice. First, listen carefully. Then as you hear the conversation the second time, fill out the client's order.

Commençons. Écoutez.

—Bonjour, Mademoiselle.
—Bonjour, Monsieur.
—Est-ce que vous avez choisi?
—Oui, j'ai choisi.
—Très bien, qu'est-ce que vous allez prendre comme hors d'œuvre?
—Je vais prendre la salade de tomates.
—Et comme plat principal?
—Je vais prendre le lapin farci.
—Ah, je suis désolé, Mademoiselle, mais nous n'avons plus de lapin farci.
—Bon, qu'est-ce que vous me recommandez alors?
—Je vous recommande le poulet rôti. C'est la spécialité de la maison.
—Très bien. Je vais prendre le poulet rôti.
—Et avec ça, haricots verts ou petits pois?
—Donnez-moi les petits pois.
—Et après cela, une salade verte?
—Oui, donnez-moi une salade verte.
—Un fromage?
—Non, pas de fromage.
—Bon. . . . Alors, comme dessert?
—Quelles tartes avez-vous?
—Voyons, nous avons des tartes aux fraises, des tartes aux pommes, des tartes aux cerises. Personnellement, je vous recommande la tarte aux cerises.
—Bon, d'accord pour la tarte aux cerises.
—Et comme boisson? Vin blanc? Vin rouge?
—Non, je vais prendre de l'eau minérale.
—Merci beaucoup, Mademoiselle!

Écoutez à nouveau et écrivez.

Fin de Vivre en France 5.
End of Vivre en France 5.
(music)

UNITÉ 6: À L'UNIVERSITÉ

LEÇON 16. LA COURSE AUX DIPLÔMES

PRÉSENTATION

Activité 1. Lecture. Ouvrez votre livre à la page 240. Écoutez.

(See textbook page 240.)

Activité 2. Compréhension du texte. You will hear several statements about the text you have just heard. Listen carefully to each statement. If the statement is true, mark **vrai** in your lab manual. If the statement is false, mark **faux.**

Commençons.

1. Brigitte prépare une licence de chimie.
2. Avec cette licence Brigitte peut enseigner dans un lycée.
3. Avec cette licence Brigitte peut travailler dans un laboratoire.
4. Brigitte préfère enseigner.

Maintenant vérifiez vos réponses. Toutes les phrases sont vraies. All the statements are true.

PHONÉTIQUE

Activité 3. Les semi-voyelles /w/ et /ɥ/. When the vowel sounds /w/ and /ɥ/ are followed by another vowel in the same syllable, they are pronounced rapidly as semi-vowels.

(a) *La semi-voyelle /w/.* The semi-vowel /w/ usually occurs together with the vowel /a/. In this combination, it is represented by the letters "oi."

Répétez: moi voici toi vouloir devoir chinois soir
Moi, je nettoie ma chambre ce soir.
Voilà la voiture de François.

The semi-vowel /w/ also occurs in the combinations "oui" and "oin."

Répétez: oui Louis Louise besoin moins
Mais oui, Louise a besoin de Louis.

(b) *La semi-voyelle /ɥ/.* The semi-vowel /ɥ/ usually occurs before the vowel /i/. It is similar to the vowel /y/, but it is pronounced more rapidly and with greater tension. Keep your lips rounded and your tongue against the lower front teeth when pronouncing /ɥ/.

Répétez: lui huit suis nuit cuisine Suisse minuit
Le huit juillet nous allons en Suisse.
Je suis chez lui.

STRUCTURE ET VOCABULAIRE

Vocabulaire: Les études

Activité 4. Prononciation. Ouvrez votre livre à la page 242.

Répétez les noms.

un conseil
un cours
un devoir
un diplôme
une classe
des études
une note
des notes

Maintenant répétez les adjectifs.

facile
difficile
utile
inutile
gratuit
seul

Maintenant répétez la forme **-je** des verbes que vous allez entendre.

enseigner: j'enseigne
faire des études: je fais des études
suivre un cours: je suis un cours
commencer: je commence
faire des progrès: je fais des progrès
obtenir: j'obtiens
réussir: je réussis
préparer un examen: je prépare un examen
passer un examen: je passe un examen
être reçu à un examen: je suis reçu à mon examen
rater un examen: je rate mon examen

Maintenant répétez les adverbes.

ensemble seulement vite

Activité 5. Pratique. Maintenant nous allons faire quelques exercices de substitution. Répétez la première phrase. Puis faites de nouvelles phrases en utilisant les sujets suggérés.

Commençons.

Marc obtient de très bonnes notes.

nous	Nous obtenons de très bonnes notes.
je	J'obtiens de très bonnes notes.
vous	Vous obtenez de très bonnes notes.
mes sœurs	Mes sœurs obtiennent de très bonnes notes.

Anne et Marie **préparent** leur examen.

rater — Anne et Marie ratent leur examen.
passer — Anne et Marie passent leur examen.
réussir à — Anne et Marie réussissent à leur examen.
être reçu à — Anne et Marie sont reçues à leur examen.

Activité 6. Compréhension orale. You will hear several general statements. Listen carefully to each statement and decide whether it is logical or not. If the statement is logical, mark the first row **logique** in your lab manual. If it's not logical, mark the second row **illogique.**

Commençons.

1. Quand on étudie, on fait des progrès.
2. Quand on prépare bien un examen, on rate cet examen.
3. Quand on rate un examen facile, on obtient une bonne note.
4. Quand on réussit à un examen, on est heureux.
5. Quand on est professeur, on enseigne.
6. Quand les cours sont gratuits, on ne paie pas de scolarité.

Maintenant vérifiez vos réponses. You should have marked **logique** for sentences 1, 4, 5, and 6 only. If you got any wrong, listen once more to this activity and do these questions again.

A. *Le verbe **suivre***

Activité 7. Prononciation. Ouvrez votre livre à la page 245. Le verbe **suivre** est irrégulier. Répétez les phrases suivantes.

Je suis un cours d'anglais.
Tu suis un cours de maths.
Elle suit un cours de chimie.
Nous suivons un régime.
Vous suivez la politique.
Elles suivent nos conseils.
J'ai suivi un cours de français.

Activité 8. Pratique. Maintenant nous allons faire quelques exercices de substitution. Répétez la phrase. Puis faites de nouvelles phrases en utilisant les sujets suggérés.

Commençons.

Tu suis un régime.

nous — Nous suivons un régime.
je — Je suis un régime.
vous — Vous suivez un régime.
mes cousines — Mes cousines suivent un régime.

Quel cours suis-**tu**?

vous — Quel cours suivez-vous?
nous — Quel cours suivons-nous?
Roger — Roger, quel cours suit-il?
Anne et Sylvie — Anne et Sylvie, quel cours suivent-elles?

B. *Les verbes* ***vouloir*** *et* ***pouvoir***

Activité 9. Prononciation. Ouvrez votre livre à la page 246. Les verbes **vouloir** et **pouvoir** sont irréguliers. Répétez les formes du verbe **vouloir** et écoutez les phrases.

Commençons.

je veux	Je veux un livre.
tu veux	Tu veux aller en France.
on veut	On veut gagner de l'argent.
nous voulons	Nous voulons voyager.
vous voulez	Vous voulez aller en ville.
ils veulent	Ils veulent parler français.
j'ai voulu	J'ai voulu voyager.

Maintenant, répétez les formes du verbe **pouvoir.**

je peux	Je peux prendre ce livre?
tu peux	Tu peux travailler pour Air France.
il peut	Il peut travailler cet été.
nous pouvons	Nous pouvons aller au Canada.
vous pouvez	Vous pouvez prendre mon auto.
elles peuvent	Elles peuvent parler avec Jacques.
j'ai pu	J'ai pu visiter la Suisse.

Activité 10. Narration: Mais non! Nothing is going right today. You will hear what certain people want to do. Say that they cannot do these things. *Écoutez le modèle.*

Modèle: Georges veut sortir. — Mais non, il ne peut pas sortir!

Commençons.

Tu veux fumer.	Mais non, tu ne peux pas fumer!
Nous voulons déjeuner maintenant.	Mais non, nous ne pouvons pas déjeuner maintenant!
Mes copains veulent faire la cuisine.	Mais non, ils ne peuvent pas faire la cuisine!
Vous voulez mettre la télé.	Mais non, vous ne pouvez pas mettre la télé!

Activité 11. Narration: Ce soir. You will hear what certain students are doing tonight. From this information, decide whether or not they want to go out. Use the appropriate form of **vouloir sortir** in affirmative or negative sentences. *Écoutez le modèle.*

Modèle: Thérèse regarde la télé. — Elle ne veut pas sortir.

Commençons.

Thomas a un rendez-vous avec Janine.	Il veut sortir.
Nous avons un examen demain matin.	Nous ne voulons pas sortir.
Vous préparez vos leçons.	Vous ne voulez pas sortir.
Je voudrais aller au cinéma.	Je veux sortir.
Tu vas dîner au restaurant.	Tu veux sortir.
Mes amis ont envie d'aller au concert.	Ils veulent sortir.
Annie et Hélène ont envie d'écouter leurs disques.	Elles ne veulent pas sortir.

C. *Le verbe* ***devoir***

Activité 12. Prononciation. Ouvrez votre livre à la page 248.

Le verbe **devoir** est irrégulier. Répétez les phrases suivantes.

Je dois étudier.
Tu dois préparer tes examens.
On doit passer un examen.
Nous devons rentrer chez nous.
Vous devez acheter ce livre.
Elles doivent prendre de l'argent.
J'ai dû téléphoner à mon père.

Activité 13. Narration: Obligations. You will hear what certain people are doing. Say that they have to do these things. Use the appropriate form of **devoir** and the infinitive of the verb you hear. *Écoutez le modèle.*

<u>Modèle</u>: Mon cousin travaille. — Il doit travailler.

Commençons.

Ma sœur étudie l'espagnol. — Elle doit étudier l'espagnol.
Nous préparons l'examen. — Nous devons préparer l'examen.
Les étudiants réussissent à l'examen. — Ils doivent réussir à l'examen.
Nous parlons français en classe. — Nous devons parler français en classe.
Je pars à deux heures. — Je dois partir à deux heures.
Tu attends. — Tu dois attendre.
Vous prenez vos cahiers. — Vous devez prendre vos cahiers.

Activité 14. Situation: Jean-Michel. You will hear what Jean-Michel did. Say that he wanted to, was able to, or had to do these things. Use the passé composé of the verb suggested in your lab manual. *Écoutez les deux modèles.*

<u>Modèles</u>: Jean-Michel est parti. — Il a dû partir.
Jean-Michel a voyagé. — Il a voulu voyager.

Commençons.

1. Jean-Michel est allé en France. — Il a voulu aller en France.
2. Jean-Michel a réussi à son examen. — Il a pu réussir à son examen.
3. Jean-Michel est rentré hier. — Il a dû rentrer hier.
4. Jean-Michel a gagné mille dollars. — Il a pu gagner mille dollars.

D. *L'expression impersonnelle* ***il faut***

Activité 15. Narration: Il faut. You will hear someone making certain suggestions to a friend. Make a general suggestion on the same theme, using the expression **il faut.** *Écoutez le modèle.*

<u>Modèle</u>: Travaille! — Il faut travailler!

Commençons.

Écoute le professeur! — Il faut écouter le professeur!
Fais des progrès! — Il faut faire des progrès!
Fais du sport! — Il faut faire du sport!
Va à la bibliothèque! — Il faut aller à la bibliothèque!
Finis l'examen! — Il faut finir l'examen!
Maigris! — Il faut maigrir!
Suis mes conseils! — Il faut suivre mes conseils!

Now, use **il faut** in negative sentences. *Écoutez le modèle.*

Modèle: Ne rate pas l'examen! — Il ne faut pas rater l'examen!

Commençons.

Ne quitte pas l'université! — Il ne faut pas quitter l'université!
N'oublie pas tes amis! — Il ne faut pas oublier tes amis!
Ne sors pas ce soir! — Il ne faut pas sortir ce soir!
Ne perds pas ton temps! — Il ne faut pas perdre ton temps!
Ne mets pas la télé! — Il ne faut pas mettre la télé!
Ne fume pas! — Il ne faut pas fumer!

Vocabulaire: Expressions indéfinies de quantité

Activité 16. Prononciation. Ouvrez votre livre à la page 252. Répétez les expressions et les phrases.

autre
L'autre jour je suis allé au parc.
Les autres étudiants ne sont pas venus.
Je cherche un autre appartement.
Voulez-vous visiter d'autres appartements?

certain
J'ai besoin d'un certain livre.
Certains problèmes n'ont pas de solution.

chaque
Chaque banlieue est différente.

plusieurs
Notre ville a plusieurs parcs.

quelques
Marc a quelques magazines français chez lui.

de nombreux
J'ai de nombreuses amies à Paris.

tout
Je comprends tout.
Est-ce que toute la classe comprend la leçon?
Tous les hommes sont égaux.
Nous allons au cinéma toutes les semaines.

tout le monde
Est-ce que tout le monde a compris?

Activité 17. Conversation: Que cherches-tu? Jeanne is asking you whether you are looking for certain things. Reply that you are looking for others. *Écoutez le modèle.*

Modèle: Cherches-tu ce stylo? — Non, je cherche un autre stylo.

Commençons.

Cherches-tu ces cahiers? — Non, je cherche d'autres cahiers.
Cherches-tu ce livre? — Non, je cherche un autre livre.
Cherches-tu cette cassette? — Non, je cherche une autre cassette.
Cherches-tu ces examens? — Non, je cherche d'autres examens.

Activité 18. Jouons un rôle: La ville de Toulouse. Whenever Christine makes observations about Toulouse, Pierre agrees completely. Play the role of Pierre, using the appropriate form of **tout** in your replies. *Écoutez le modèle.*

Modèle: La ville est jolie, n'est-ce pas? Oui, toute la ville est jolie.

Commençons.

Les habitants sont sympathiques, n'est-ce pas?	Oui, tous les habitants sont sympathiques.
Le centre est très propre, n'est-ce pas?	Oui, tout le centre est très propre.
La banlieue est agréable, n'est-ce pas?	Oui, toute la banlieue est agréable.
Nos voisins sont sympathiques, n'est-ce pas?	Oui, tous nos voisins sont sympathiques.
Les parcs sont beaux, n'est-ce pas?	Oui, tous les parcs sont beaux.
Les rues sont belles, n'est-ce pas?	Oui, toutes les rues sont belles.

DIALOGUE

Activité 19. Activités. Françoise is asking you about various activities. Answer her according to the illustrations in your lab manual. *Écoutez le modèle.*

Modèle: Qu'est-ce que tu veux faire ce soir? Je veux regarder la télé.

Commençons.

1. Qu'est-ce que tu dois faire avant l'examen?	Je dois étudier.
2. Qu'est-ce que tes copains veulent faire ce week-end?	Ils veulent aller à la piscine.
3. Qu'est-ce qu'on peut faire ce soir?	On peut dîner au restaurant.
4. Qu'est-ce que vous devez faire après le dîner?	Nous devons faire la vaisselle.
5. Qu'est-ce que vous devez faire demain?	Nous devons nettoyer l'appartement.
6. Qu'est-ce qu'on peut faire à Paris?	On peut visiter la Tour Eiffel.

DICTÉE

Activité 20. Ce soir. You will hear a short passage. First listen! Do not write!

Ce soir, mes amis veulent aller au cinéma. Je veux sortir avec eux, mais je ne peux pas. Demain, j'ai un examen très difficile. Je dois rester chez moi. À mon université, il faut beaucoup étudier si on ne veut pas rater ses examens.

Now write the sentences in your lab manual as you hear them.

Ce soir, mes amis / veulent aller au cinéma. / Je veux sortir / avec eux, / mais je ne peux pas. / Demain, / j'ai un examen / très difficile. / Je dois rester / chez moi. / À mon université, / il faut / beaucoup étudier / si on ne veut pas / rater ses examens. /

Écoutez encore une fois et vérifiez ce que vous avez écrit.

(Text is reread without pauses.)

LECTURE CULTURELLE

Activité 21. Lecture. Ouvrez votre livre à la page 241. Écoutez.

(See textbook page 241.)

Activité 22. Compréhension du texte. You will hear several statements about the text you have just heard. Listen carefully to each statement. If it is true, mark **vrai** in your lab manual. If it is false, mark **faux.**

Commençons.

1. En général, les diplômes français et les diplômes américains sont équivalents.
2. Les étudiants français passent le baccalauréat après quatre années d'université.
3. Trente pour cent des étudiants qui passent le bac ratent cet examen.
4. La licence et la maîtrise sont des diplômes universitaires.
5. Les deux premières années d'université sont généralement très faciles.
6. Les étudiants français obtiennent la maîtrise après un minimum de quatre ans d'université.

Maintenant vérifiez vos réponses. You should have marked **vrai** for statements 3, 4, and 6; and **faux** for statements 1, 2, and 5.

Fin de la Leçon 16.
End of Lesson 16.
(music)

LEÇON 17. DES NOTES IMPORTANTES

PRÉSENTATION

Activité 1. Lecture. Ouvrez votre livre à la page 254. Écoutez.

(See textbook page 254.)

Activité 2. Compréhension du texte. *Vous allez entendre des phrases du texte que vous avez écouté. Indiquez dans votre manuel de laboratoire si ces phrases sont vraies ou fausses.* You will hear several sentences about the text you have just heard. Indicate in your lab manual if these sentences are true or false.

Commençons.

1. Michèle et Béatrice habitent ensemble.
2. Béatrice cherche son livre de physique.
3. Béatrice suit un cours de biologie.
4. Béatrice cherche son livre parce qu'elle veut étudier.
5. Jean-Pierre Marin est le copain de Michèle.
6. Béatrice a pris beaucoup de notes pendant la classe.

Maintenant vérifiez vos réponses. You should have marked **vrai** for sentences 1 and 3; and **faux** for sentences 2, 4, 5, and 6.

PHONÉTIQUE

Activité 3. La consonne /l/. The French consonant /l/ is a delicate or "light" L-sound.

Écoutez: il belle l'eau

The English consonant /l/ is often much thicker or darker.

Comparez: il EEL l'eau LOW

In French, the consonant /l/ is pronounced with the tip of the tongue touching the upper front teeth.

Répétez: elle il quel belle Paul lui leur utile facile
Il s'appelle Paul Laval.
Lucile lui téléphone lundi.

STRUCTURE ET VOCABULAIRE

Vocabulaire: Les études supérieures

Activité 4. Prononciation. Ouvrez votre livre à la page 256. Répétez les noms suivants.

les lettres:
- la littérature
- la philosophie
- l'histoire
- les langues

les beaux arts:
- la peinture
- la sculpture
- l'architecture

les sciences humaines et sociales:
- l'anthropologie
- la psychologie
- les sciences politiques
- les sciences économiques

les sciences:
- la chimie
- la biologie
- la physique
- les mathématiques

les études d'ingénieur:
- l'électronique
- l'informatique

les études commerciales:
- la gestion
- la publicité
- le marketing
- l'administration des affaires

la médecine
la pharmacie
le droit

Activité 5. Compréhension orale. You will hear pairs of sentences. Listen to each pair carefully. If the second sentence is a logical continuation of the first sentence, mark the first row **logique** in your lab manual. If it is not logical, mark the second row **illogique.**

Commençons.

1. Mélanie a fait des études commerciales. C'est une spécialiste de la gestion des entreprises.
2. Christine aime les sciences sociales. Elle étudie la chimie et la physique.
3. Michèle est une étudiante en lettres. Elle étudie la littérature française.
4. Thomas est un étudiant en médecine. Il étudie la biologie.
5. Raymond fait des études d'ingénieur. Il étudie la psychologie.
6. Isabelle fait des études de droit. Elle étudie la législation commerciale.

7. Les ingénieurs d'IBM sont des spécialistes en informatique.
8. À la Business School de Harvard, on étudie l'administration des affaires.

Maintenant vérifiez vos réponses. You should have marked **illogique** for sentences 2 and 5 only. If you made any mistakes, listen once more to these sentences and do these questions again.

A. *Le verbe* ***voir***

Activité 6. Prononciation. Ouvrez votre livre à la page 257. Répétez les phrases avec le verbe **voir.**

Je vais voir un film.
Je vois mes amis le samedi soir.
Vois-tu souvent tes grands-parents?
Éric voit souvent ses copains.
Nous voyons François ce soir.
Est-ce que vous voyez bien avec ces lunettes?
Ils voient un film d'aventures.
Quel film as-tu vu?

Activité 7. Pratique. Maintenant nous allons faire quelques exercices de substitution. Répétez la phrase. Puis faites de nouvelles phrases en utilisant les sujets suggérés.

Répétez:

Je vois souvent mes parents.
nous — Nous voyons souvent nos parents.
vous — Vous voyez souvent vos parents.
Alice et Marie — Alice et Marie voient souvent leurs parents.

Je n'ai pas vu l'accident.
Thomas — Thomas n'a pas vu l'accident.
ces gens — Ces gens n'ont pas vu l'accident.
vous — Vous n'avez pas vu l'accident.

B. *Le verbe* ***connaître***

Activité 8. Prononciation. Ouvrez votre livre à la page 258. Répétez les phrases avec le verbe **connaître.**

Je dois connaître ta tante.
Je connais Marc.
Tu connais Martine.
On connaît le professeur.
Nous connaissons des Français.
Vous connaissez un restaurant.
Elles connaissent quelqu'un d'intéressant.
J'ai connu ton grand-père.

Activité 9. Pratique. Maintenant nous allons faire un exercice de substitution. Répétez la première phrase. Puis faites de nouvelles phrases en utilisant les sujets suggérés.

Commençons.

Georges connaît un bon restaurant.
nous — Nous connaissons un bon restaurant.
tu — Tu connais un bon restaurant.
mes parents — Mes parents connaissent un bon restaurant.
je — Je connais un bon restaurant.

C. *Les pronoms **le, la, les***

Activité 10. Identification de structures. You will hear Florence commenting about several people. Is she talking about her boyfriend, her sister, or her cousins? Listen carefully to the object pronoun in each sentence. If it is **le,** she is talking about her boyfriend *Philippe.* Mark the first row in your lab manual. If the object pronoun is **la,** she is referring to her sister *Annie.* Mark the second row. If the pronoun is **les,** she is talking about her cousins *Jacques et Pierre.* Mark the third row.

Commençons.

1. Je ne les trouve pas très amusants.
2. Je la trouve très remarquable.
3. Je les invite rarement.
4. Je vais le chercher à son bureau.
5. Je ne la comprends pas toujours.
6. Je le préfère à mes autres amis.
7. Je le trouve très sympathique.
8. Bien sûr, je les connais très bien.

Maintenant vérifiez vos réponses. You should have marked *Philippe* for sentences 4, 6, and 7; *Annie* for sentences 2 and 5; and *Jacques et Pierre* for sentences 1, 3, and 8. If you got any wrong, listen once more to this activity and do these questions again.

Activité 11. Situation: Moi aussi. Béatrice is talking about things she does. Say that you do the same things, using direct object pronouns in your statements. *Écoutez le modèle.*

Modèle: Je comprends mes parents. — Moi aussi, je les comprends.

Commençons.

Je comprends mon père. — Moi aussi, je le comprends.
Je comprends ma mère. — Moi aussi, je la comprends.
J'invite mes amis. — Moi aussi, je les invite.
J'invite mon meilleur ami. — Moi aussi, je l'invite.
J'écoute le professeur. — Moi aussi, je l'écoute.
Je prends le métro. — Moi aussi, je le prends.
Je choisis cette cassette. — Moi aussi, je la choisis.
Je vends mes disques. — Moi aussi, je les vends.
Je suis le cours de français. — Moi aussi, je le suis.

Activité 12. Conversation: Les garçons, non. Les filles, oui. You have been invited to a party, and Jean-Michel is asking whether you know certain people. Answer that you know all the girls, but not the boys. *Écoutez le modèle.*

Modèle: Tu connais Paul? — Non, je ne le connais pas.

Commençons.

Tu connais Sylvie? — Oui, je la connais.
Tu connais Jacqueline et Anne-Marie? — Oui, je les connais.
Tu connais Thomas? — Non, je ne le connais pas.
Tu connais Georges et Robert? — Non, je ne les connais pas.
Tu connais Roger? — Non, je ne le connais pas.
Tu connais Isabelle? — Oui, je la connais.
Tu connais Catherine? — Oui, je la connais.
Tu connais Jacques? — Non, je ne le connais pas.
Tu connais Louis et Henri? — Non, je ne les connais pas.

Vocabulaire: Quelques verbes utilisés avec un complément d'objet direct

Activité 13. Prononciation. Ouvrez votre livre à la page 260. Répétez les mini-dialogues.

Aides-tu tes amis?
Bien sûr, je les aide.

Aimes-tu tes cours?
Non, je ne les aime pas.

Attends-tu le professeur?
Non, je ne l'attends pas.

Cherches-tu ton livre?
Oui, je le cherche.

Écoutes-tu souvent tes disques?
Oui, je les écoute souvent.

Regardes-tu la télé?
Oui, je la regarde.

Comment trouves-tu ce livre?
Je le trouve assez intéressant.

Quand est-ce que tu vois tes cousins?
Je les vois le week-end.

*D. Les pronoms **le, la, les** à l'infinitif*

Activité 14. Conversation: Oui, bien sûr! Imagine you are in a good mood. Answer *yes* to Nathalie's questions. Use the appropriate direct object pronouns. *Écoutez le modèle.*

Modèle: Vas-tu écouter le professeur? — Oui, bien sûr je vais l'écouter.

Commençons.

Vas-tu aider tes amis? — Oui, bien sûr, je vais les aider.
Vas-tu chercher mon cahier? — Oui, bien sûr, je vais le chercher.
Vas-tu regarder ces notes? — Oui, bien sûr, je vais les regarder.
Vas-tu trouver ma montre? — Oui, bien sûr, je vais la trouver.
Vas-tu attendre Charlotte? — Oui, bien sûr, je vais l'attendre.

E. Passé composé: L'accord du participe passé

Activité 15. Conversation: Oui et non. Éric is asking you a series of questions in the passé composé. Answer him using direct object pronouns. Answer the first group of questions in the affirmative. *Écoutez le modèle.*

Modèle: Tu as invité Pierre? — Oui, je l'ai invité.

Commençons.

Tu as invité Jacqueline? — Oui, je l'ai invitée.
Tu as acheté ces cassettes? — Oui, je les ai achetées.
Tu as fini ce livre? — Oui, je l'ai fini.
Tu as compris la leçon? — Oui, je l'ai comprise.
Tu as compris le professeur? — Oui, je l'ai compris.

Now answer his next set of questions in the negative. *Écoutez le modèle.*

Modèle: Tu as invité Marie? — Non, je ne l'ai pas invitée.

Commençons.

Tu as écouté ce disque? Non, je ne l'ai pas écouté.
Tu as regardé ces livres? Non, je ne les ai pas regardés.
Tu as fait ton lit? Non, je ne l'ai pas fait.
Tu as mis la table? Non, je ne l'ai pas mise.
Tu as pris mes cahiers? Non, je ne les ai pas pris.

DIALOGUE

Activité 16. Où et quand? Béatrice will ask you a series of questions about when and where things happened in the past. Answer her using the suggestions in your lab manual. *Écoutez le modèle.*

Modèle: Où as-tu acheté cette montre? Je l'ai achetée en Suisse.

Commençons.

1. Où as-tu rencontré Bernard? Je l'ai rencontré dans la rue.
2. Quand as-tu vu Janine? Je l'ai vue pendant la classe de français.
3. Où as-tu trouvé ces livres? Je les ai trouvés au salon.
4. Où as-tu attendu tes copains? Je les ai attendus au café.
5. À quelle heure as-tu vu le film? Je l'ai vu à huit heures.
6. Quand as-tu pris ces photos? Je les ai prises pendant les vacances.
7. Quand as-tu fait les courses? Je les ai faites hier soir.
8. Où as-tu appris le français? Je l'ai appris à Montréal.

DICTÉE

Activité 17. Monique et Henri. You will hear a short paragraph. First listen! Do not write!

Connais-tu Monique? Moi, je la connais bien. Je l'ai rencontrée l'année dernière à Paris. Je vais l'inviter à la fête. Elle va venir avec son cousin Henri. Je ne le connais pas, mais ses amis le trouvent très sympathique. Il fait des études d'ingénieur à l'Université de Grenoble.

Now, write the sentences in your lab manual as you hear them.

Connais-tu Monique? / Moi, je la connais bien. / Je l'ai rencontrée / l'année dernière à Paris. / Je vais l'inviter à la fête. / Elle va venir / avec son cousin Henri. / Je ne le connais pas, / mais ses amis / le trouvent très sympathique. / Il fait / des études d'ingénieur / à l'Université de Grenoble. /

Écoutez encore une fois et vérifiez ce que vous avez écrit.

(Text is reread without pauses.)

LECTURE CULTURELLE

Activité 18. Lecture. Ouvrez votre livre à la page 255. Écoutez.

(See textbook page 255.)

Activité 19. Compréhension du texte. *Vous allez entendre des phrases concernant le texte que vous avez écouté. Indiquez dans votre manuel de laboratoire si ces phrases sont vraies ou fausses.* You will hear several statements about the text you have just heard. Listen carefully to each statement. If it is true, mark **vrai** in your lab manual. If it is false, mark **faux.**

Commençons.

1. Quatre-vingts pour cent des jeunes Français ne font pas d'études supérieures.
2. On va à l'université pour passer le baccalauréat.
3. Quand on n'a pas le bac, on peut continuer ses études dans une grande école.
4. Il y a soixante-sept universités dans la région parisienne.
5. Les universités françaises sont divisées en UER qui sont des Unités spécialisées d'enseignement et de recherche.
6. Polytechnique et Centrale sont de grandes écoles scientifiques et techniques.
7. À HEC, on peut étudier le marketing.

Maintenant vérifiez vos réponses. You should have marked **vrai** for statements 1, 5, 6, and 7; and **faux** for statements 2, 3, and 4.

Fin de la Leçon 17.
End of Lesson 17.
(music)

LEÇON 18. UN CONTESTATAIRE

PRÉSENTATION

Activité 1. Lecture. Ouvrez votre livre à la page 268. Écoutez.

(See textbook page 268.)

Activité 2: Compréhension du texte. *Vous allez entendre des phrases du texte que vous avez écouté. Indiquez dans votre manuel de laboratoire si ces phrases sont vraies ou fausses.* You will hear several sentences about the text you have just heard. Indicate in your lab manual if these statements are true or false.

Commençons.

1. Thomas et Jacqueline vont à l'université.
2. Thomas étudie les sciences politiques.
3. Jacqueline fait des études d'ingénieur.
4. Thomas critique le système universitaire français.
5. Thomas demande souvent des conseils à ses professeurs.
6. Thomas n'aime pas sortir avec ses copains.
7. Thomas prépare le baccalauréat.
8. Thomas espère être professeur.

Maintenant vérifiez vos réponses. You should have marked **vrai** for statements 1, 2, 4, and 8; and **faux** for statements 3, 5, 6, and 7.

PHONÉTIQUE

Activité 3. La liaison: Le groupe verbal. As you recall, liaison is required between the subject pronoun and verb. Liaison is also required between object pronouns and the verb.

Répétez: Nous les‿envoyons.
Vous nous‿écrivez.
Mes cousins nous‿invitent.
Nous voulons les‿obtenir.
Je vais vous‿aider.

STRUCTURE ET VOCABULAIRE

A. Les verbes ***dire, lire, écrire***

Activité 4. Prononciation. Ouvrez votre livre à la page 270. Les verbes **dire, lire** et **écrire** sont irréguliers.

Répétez les phrases suivantes.

dire
Je dis que j'ai raison.
Tu dis une chose stupide.
On dit que c'est vrai.
Nous disons la vérité.
Vous dites que c'est facile.
Ils disent que j'ai tort.
J'ai dit la vérité.

lire
Je lis un magazine.
Tu lis une annonce.
Il lit un article.
Nous lisons un livre.
Vous lisez le journal.
Ils lisent une lettre.
J'ai lu ce journal.

écrire
J'écris une lettre.
Tu écris à un ami.
Elle écrit à une amie.
Nous écrivons un poème.
Vous écrivez un roman.
Elles écrivent à un ami.
J'ai écrit à un ami.

Activité 5. Pratique. Maintenant nous allons faire quelques exercices de substitution. Répétez la phrase. Puis faites de nouvelles phrases en utilisant les sujets suggérés.

Commençons.

Henri dit des mensonges.

vous	Vous dites des mensonges.
tu	Tu dis des mensonges.
tes frères	Tes frères disent des mensonges.
nous	Nous disons des mensonges.

Marie lit des bandes dessinées.

nous	Nous lisons des bandes dessinées.
tu	Tu lis des bandes dessinées.
vous	Vous lisez des bandes dessinées.
vos cousines	Vos cousines lisent des bandes dessinées.

J'écris un article.

tes parents	Tes parents écrivent un article.
nous	Nous écrivons un article.
vous	Vous écrivez un article.
Pierre	Pierre écrit un article.

*B. La conjonction **que***

Activité 6. Situation: Ils étudient trop! *Les étudiants suivants pensent qu'ils étudient trop. Exprimez leur opinion en complétant les phrases avec l'expression **étudier trop**.* The following students think that they are studying too much. Express their opinions by completing the sentences with the appropriate form of **étudier trop.** *Écoutez le modèle.*

Modèle: Nous pensons — Nous pensons que nous étudions trop.

Commençons.

Marc dit	Marc dit qu'il étudie trop.
Je trouve	Je trouve que j'étudie trop.
Vous pensez	Vous pensez que vous étudiez trop.
Alice écrit à sa famille	Alice écrit à sa famille qu'elle étudie trop.

*C. Les pronoms **lui, leur***

Activité 7. Prononciation. *Ouvrez votre livre à la page 273.* Pierre is asking questions. Jacqueline answers him, using the indirect object pronouns **lui** and **leur.** Listen to the questions and answers and repeat only the answers.

Commençons.

Tu parles souvent à Thomas?	Oui, je lui parle souvent.
Tu as téléphoné au professeur?	Oui, je lui ai téléphoné.
Tu parles souvent à Marie?	Non, je ne lui parle pas souvent.
Tu as téléphoné souvent à sa mère?	Non, je ne lui ai pas téléphoné.
Tu téléphones souvent à tes cousines?	Oui, je leur téléphone souvent.
Tu as répondu à nos camarades?	Oui, je leur ai répondu.

Activité 8. Identification de structures. You will hear Jacqueline speaking. Can you tell whether she is referring to her sister Sylvie or to her cousins Marc and Éric? Listen carefully to the pronouns. If you hear **lui,** the speaker is talking about one person. Mark the first row, *Sylvie,* in your lab manual. If you hear **leur,** she is talking about more than one person. Mark the second row, *Marc et Éric.*

Commençons.

1. Je leur téléphone souvent.
2. Je ne lui parle pas de mes problèmes personnels.
3. Je lui ai demandé l'adresse de ses amis américains.
4. Je leur rends visite assez souvent.
5. Je lui ai vendu ma caméra.
6. Je leur ai montré mes photos de vacances.
7. Je ne veux pas lui répondre.
8. D'accord! Je vais leur poser cette question.

Maintenant vérifiez vos réponses. You should have marked *Sylvie* for sentences 2, 3, 5, and 7; and *Marc et Éric* for sentences 1, 4, 6, and 8. If you made any mistakes, listen once more to this activity and do these questions again.

Vocabulaire: Quelques verbes utilisés avec un complement d'objet indirect

Activité 9. Prononciation. Ouvrez votre livre à la page 274. Écoutez les verbes et répétez les phrases.

Commençons.

parler à — Qui a parlé à Henri?
poser une question à — As-tu posé la question au professeur?
rendre visite à — Hier, j'ai rendu visite à un ami.
répondre à — Réponds à Pierre.
téléphoner à — Téléphonez à vos amis.
demander quelque chose à — Demande des conseils à ton père.
dire quelque chose à — As-tu dit la vérité à tes parents?
donner quelque chose à — Je donne un livre à Paul.
écrire quelque chose à — J'ai écrit une lettre à Anne.
envoyer quelque chose à — As-tu envoyé la carte à Éric?
montrer quelque chose à — J'ai montré mes photos à Albert.
prêter quelque chose à — Je prête mes disques à Albert.
rendre quelque chose à — Je dois rendre ce disque à Pierre.

Activité 10. Pratique. Maintenant nous allons faire un exercice de substitution. Répétez la première phrase. Puis faites de nouvelles phrases en utilisant les verbes suggérés.

Commençons.

Est-ce que vous **parlez** à Jacqueline?
téléphoner — Est-ce que vous téléphonez à Jacqueline?
répondre — Est-ce que vous répondez à Jacqueline?
rendre visite — Est-ce que vous rendez visite à Jacqueline?

Marc **demande** de l'argent à Nathalie.
donner — Marc donne de l'argent à Nathalie.
prêter — Marc prête de l'argent à Nathalie.
rendre — Marc rend de l'argent à Nathalie.
envoyer — Marc envoie de l'argent à Nathalie.

Activité 11. Conversation: Hier. Martine will ask you if you did certain things yesterday. First answer her questions in the affirmative, using indirect object pronouns. *Écoutez le modèle.*

Modèle: Avez-vous téléphoné à vos parents? — Oui, je leur ai téléphoné.

Commençons.

Avez-vous parlé à votre professeur de français? Oui, je lui ai parlé.
Avez-vous prêté vos notes à vos amis? Oui, je leur ai prêté mes notes.
Avez-vous montré vos photos à votre meilleur ami? Oui, je lui ai montré mes photos.

Now answer in the negative. *Écoutez le modèle.*

Modèle: Avez-vous téléphoné à votre cousine? Non, je ne lui ai pas téléphoné.

Commençons.

Avez-vous rendu visite à vos grands-parents? Non, je ne leur ai pas rendu visite.
Avez-vous donné votre cahier au professeur? Non, je ne lui ai pas donné mon cahier.
Avez-vous parlé au président de l'université? Non, je ne lui ai pas parlé.

*D. Les pronoms **me, te, nous, vous***

Activité 12. Jouons un rôle: Mais oui! Thérèse is asking Richard various things. Richard says *yes* to everything. Play the role of Richard as in the model. *Écoutez.*

Modèle: Tu me téléphones? Mais oui, je te téléphone.

Commençons.

Tu me trouves sympathique? Mais oui, je te trouve sympathique.
Tu m'attends après la classe? Mais oui, je t'attends après la classe.
Tu m'aides avec mes devoirs? Mais oui, je t'aide avec tes devoirs.

Now Thérèse is asking Thomas questions about herself and her sister Lucie. *Écoutez le modèle.*

Modèle: Tu nous donnes cinq dollars? Mais oui, je vous donne cinq dollars.

Commençons.

Tu nous trouves intelligentes? Mais oui, je vous trouve intelligentes.
Tu nous prêtes ta voiture? Mais oui, je vous prête ma voiture.
Tu nous rends visite cet été? Mais oui, je vous rends visite cet été.

E. La place des pronoms à l'impératif

Activité 13. Situation: S'il te plaît! Ask a French friend to do the following things for you. *Écoutez le modèle.*

Modèle: téléphoner ce soir Téléphone-moi ce soir!

Commençons.

inviter à la fête Invite-moi à la fête!
aider avec le devoir de français Aide-moi avec le devoir de français!
donner des conseils Donne-moi des conseils!
donner ton adresse en France Donne-moi ton adresse en France!
prêter ton vélo Prête-moi ton vélo!

Activité 14. Conversation: Fais-le toi-même! Albert will ask you to do certain things. Tell him to do these things himself. Be sure to use the appropriate direct or indirect object pronouns. Use the expression **toi-même,** which means *yourself. Écoutez le modèle.*

Modèle: Invite Jacqueline! — Invite-la toi-même!

Commençons.

Invite Henri! — Invite-le toi-même!
Invite ces garçons! — Invite-les toi-même!
Téléphone à M. Lambert! — Téléphone-lui toi-même!
Téléphone à Mme Rochette! — Téléphone-lui toi-même!
Achète le journal! — Achète-le toi-même!
Fais tes devoirs! — Fais-les toi-même!

DIALOGUE

Activité 15. Qu'est-ce que tu fais? Thomas is asking you several questions. Answer him according to the illustrations in your lab manual. *Écoutez le modèle.*

Modèle: Qu'est-ce que tu écris à Jacqueline? — Je lui écris une lettre.

Commençons.

1. Qu'est-ce que tu écris à tes grands-parents? — Je leur écris une carte postale.
2. Qu'est-ce que tu envoies à ta cousine? — Je lui envoie un magazine.
3. Qu'est-ce que tu montres à tes copains? — Je leur montre des photos.
4. Qu'est-ce que tu prêtes à Denise? — Je lui prête un disque.
5. Qu'est-ce que tu vas donner à ton père pour son anniversaire? — Je vais lui donner une cravate.
6. Qu'est-ce que tu vas donner à tes cousins pour leur anniversaire? — Je vais leur donner des cassettes.

DICTÉE

Activité 16. J'ai besoin de mon livre. You will hear a short paragraph. First listen! Do not write!

Tu connais Christine, n'est-ce pas? Elle m'a parlé de toi quand je lui ai rendu visite hier. Je lui ai prêté un livre, et maintenant j'ai besoin de ce livre. Je veux lui téléphoner. Donne-moi son numéro de téléphone, s'il te plaît!

Now write the sentences in your lab manual as you hear them.

Tu connais Christine / n'est-ce pas? / Elle m'a parlé de toi / quand je lui ai rendu visite hier. / Je lui ai prêté / un livre, / et maintenant / j'ai besoin / de ce livre. / Je veux / lui téléphoner. / Donne-moi / son numéro de téléphone, s'il te plaît! /

Écoutez encore une fois et vérifiez ce que vous avez écrit.

(Text is reread without pauses.)

LECTURE CULTURELLE

Activité 17. Lecture. Ouvrez votre livre à la page 269. Écoutez.

(See textbook page 269.)

Activité 18. Compréhension du texte. *Vous allez entendre des phrases concernant le texte que vous avez écouté. Indiquez dans votre manuel de laboratoire si ces phrases sont vraies ou fausses.* You will hear several sentences about the text you have just heard. Indicate in your lab manual if these sentences are true or false.

Commençons.

1. Les étudiants français prennent une part très active dans les campagnes électorales.
2. Ils militent pour certaines grandes causes.
3. Les étudiants français considèrent que la lutte contre le racisme est une cause importante.
4. En mai 1968, ils ont participé à une grande manifestation contre l'énergie nucléaire.
5. La mini-révolution de 1968 a eu des conséquences sur les structures universitaires.
6. Les étudiants français n'ont pas d'influence politique.

Maintenant vérifiez vos réponses. Les phrases suivantes sont vraies: 2, 3, et 5, et les phrases suivantes sont fausses: 1, 4, et 6.

Fin de la Leçon 18.
End of Lesson 18.
(music)

VIVRE EN FRANCE 6. LE COURRIER

Activité 1. La bonne réponse. You will hear a series of questions. In your lab manual there are three possible responses for each question. Select the logical response by circling the corresponding letter.

Commençons.

1. Qu'est-ce qu'il y a dans ce paquet?
2. Pourquoi est-ce que tu vas à la poste?
3. Comment voulez-vous envoyer cette lettre?
4. Est-ce que le courrier est arrivé?
5. Pourquoi est-ce que tu vas à la poste restante?
6. Dis, Paul! Est-ce que tu as un timbre à 2 francs 20?
7. Pourquoi est-ce que tu achètes des aérogrammes?
8. Où est-ce que je mets le code postal?

Now listen to the complete exchanges and correct your work. *Écoutez.*

1. Qu'est-ce qu'il y a dans ce paquet?
   Il y a un livre.
2. Pourquoi est-ce que tu vas à la poste?
   Je dois envoyer un télégramme.
3. Comment voulez-vous envoyer cette lettre?
   Je voudrais l'envoyer en recommandé.
4. Est-ce que le courrier est arrivé?
   Oui! Tiens, ces cartes postales sont pour toi.

5. Pourquoi est-ce que tu vas à la poste restante?
   J'attends une lettre de mon copain Pierre.
6. Dis, Paul! Est-ce que tu as un timbre à 2 francs 20?
   Bien sûr, mais dis-moi, à qui est-ce que tu écris?
7. Pourquoi est-ce que tu achètes des aérogrammes?
   J'ai l'intention d'écrire à ma cousine qui habite au Canada.
8. Où est-ce que je mets le code postal?
   Mets-le ici, à côté du nom de la ville.

Activité 2. En France. You will now hear a short conversation that took place at the window of a French post office. Listen carefully to the dialogue between the postal clerk and the customer. In your lab manual, you will be asked to calculate the amount of money the customer owes. Although you may not be able to understand every word, you should be able to understand all the information necessary to do your calculation. You will hear the conversation twice. First listen carefully. Then listen again and write down the necessary information in your lab manual.

Commençons. Écoutez.

—Bonjour, Monsieur.
—Bonjour, Mademoiselle. Vous désirez?
—Je voudrais envoyer cette lettre aux États-Unis.
—Voyons. Votre lettre pèse 12 grammes. Ça fait quatre francs 50. Tenez, voici un timbre à 4 francs et un timbre à 50 centimes.
—Je voudrais aussi envoyer ces deux lettres.
—C'est pour les États-Unis aussi?
—Non, c'est pour la France.
—Bon, pour la France c'est 2 francs 20. Tenez, voilà deux timbres à 2 francs 20. Ce sera tout?
—Non, j'ai aussi besoin d'aérogrammes. Combien coûtent-ils?
—C'est 3 francs 70 l'aérogramme.
—Bon, donnez-moi trois aérogrammes, s'il vous plaît.
—Voilà trois aérogrammes à 3 francs 70.
—Je vous dois combien?
—Attendez une petite seconde. Je dois faire mon calcul.

Écoutez à nouveau et écrivez.

(Dialogue is reread.)

Fin de Vivre en France 6.
End of Vivre en France 6.
(music)

UNITÉ 7: HIER ET AUJOURD'HUI

LEÇON 19. LA VIE URBAINE: POUR OU CONTRE?

PRÉSENTATION

Activité 1. Lecture. Ouvrez votre livre à la page 288. Écoutez.

(See textbook page 288.)

Activité 2. Compréhension du texte. Vous allez entendre des phrases concernant les personnes que vous avez entendues. Indiquez dans votre manuel de laboratoire si ces phrases sont vraies ou fausses.

Commençons.

1. Dominique Bellamy habite à Paris.
2. Elle apprécie les avantages culturels de grandes villes.
3. Nelly Chollet aime son travail.
4. Elle est née dans la ville où elle habite aujourd'hui.
5. Pierre Barthe est une personne indépendante.
6. Ses voisins le connaissent bien.
7. Christophe Lemaire trouve que la vie dans une grande ville peut être dangereuse.
8. Il pense que la vie en ville est bon marché.
9. Christine Leroi a beaucoup de travail et peu de loisirs.
10. Le week-end elle sort souvent.
11. Sylviane Dumoulin a beaucoup d'amis.
12. L'appartement où elle habite est ancien et il n'est pas confortable.

Maintenant vérifiez vos réponses. Les phrases suivantes sont vraies: 2, 3, 5, 7 et 9. Les phrases suivantes sont fausses: 1, 4, 6, 8, 10, 11 et 12.

PHONÉTIQUE

Activité 3. Les lettres «qu». The letters "qu" almost always represent the sound /k/.

Répétez: qui Québec quand quartier politique physique
Quand as-tu quitté Québec?
Monique a répondu à la question.
Dominique adore la musique classique.

STRUCTURE ET VOCABULAIRE

Vocabulaire: La ville

Activité 4. Prononciation. Ouvrez votre livre à la page 290. Répétez les noms.

la ville
un bâtiment
un boulevard
un bureau
le centre
un centre commercial
un habitant
un immeuble

un parc
un quartier
une avenue
la banlieue
une rue
une usine
une ville

la vie urbaine
le bruit
le crime
un problème
la circulation
la pollution
la vie

Répétez les adjectifs et les expressions:

agréable
désagréable
ancien
moderne
propre

sale
gagner sa vie
à la campagne
en ville

pour
contre
au contraire
au moins

Activité 5. Pratique. Maintenant nous allons faire quelques exercices de substitution. Répétez la première phrase. Puis faites de nouvelles phrases en utilisant les noms suggérés. Faites attention à la forme de l'adjectif **beau.**

Commençons.

Voici un beau **quartier.**

rue	Voici une belle rue.
bâtiment	Voici un beau bâtiment.
avenue	Voici une belle avenue.
bureau	Voici un beau bureau.

Ce **quartier** est ancien.

ville	Cette ville est ancienne.
usine	Cette usine est ancienne.
immeuble	Cet immeuble est ancien.

A. Le verbe ***savoir***

Activité 6. Prononciation. Ouvrez votre livre à la page 292. Le verbe **savoir** est irrégulier. Répétez les formes de **savoir** dans les phrases suivantes.

Je sais parler français.
Tu sais parler espagnol.
On sait jouer au tennis.
Nous savons jouer de la guitare.
Vous savez faire du ski.
Elles savent piloter un avion.
J'ai su la réponse à cette question.

Activité 7. Pratique. Maintenant nous allons faire quelques exercices de substitution. Répétez la première phrase. Puis faites de nouvelles phrases en utilisant les sujets suggérés.

Commençons.

Marie sait faire du ski.

nous	Nous savons faire du ski.
je	Je sais faire du ski.
mes frères	Mes frères savent faire du ski.

Sais-**tu** nager?

vous	Savez-vous nager?
Anne	Anne sait-elle nager?
Richard et Marc	Richard et Marc savent-ils nager?

Activité 8. Situation: Le savoir. You will hear what various people do. Say they know how to do these things. To do this, use the appropriate form of **savoir** plus the infinitive. *Écoutez le modèle.*

<u>Modèle</u>: Henri joue au tennis. Il sait jouer au tennis.

Commençons.

Suzanne danse le tango.	Elle sait danser le tango.
Paul et Denis nagent.	Ils savent nager.
Nous parlons français.	Nous savons parler français.
Mon cousin parle japonais.	Il sait parler japonais.
Vous jouez du piano.	Vous savez jouer du piano.
Tu joues de la guitare électrique.	Tu sais jouer de la guitare électrique.

B. ***Connaître*** *vs.* ***savoir***

Activité 9. Situation: Bien sûr! You will hear certain names and certain facts. Say that you know the corresponding people, places, or facts, using **je connais** or **je sais,** as appropriate.

<u>Modèle</u>: le président de l'université Bien sûr! Je connais le président de l'université.

Commençons.

mes voisins	Bien sûr! Je connais mes voisins.
où travaillent mes voisins	Bien sûr! Je sais où travaillent mes voisins.
où habite le professeur	Bien sûr! Je sais où habite le professeur.
la maison du professeur	Bien sûr! Je connais la maison du professeur.
un bon restaurant français	Bien sûr! Je connais un bon restaurant français.
qui est le président de la France	Bien sûr! Je sais qui est le président de la France.
New York	Bien sûr! Je connais New York.
Paris	Bien sûr! Je connais Paris.
des Parisiens	Bien sûr! Je connais des Parisiens.

C. *Le pronom relatif* ***qui***

Activité 10. Situation: C'est vrai! You will hear a series of statements. Agree with them according to the model. *Écoutez le modèle.*

Modèle: New York est une ville intéressante. — C'est vrai! C'est une ville qui est intéressante.

Commençons.

Boston est une ville ancienne. — C'est vrai! C'est une ville qui est ancienne.
Avignon est une ville agréable. — C'est vrai! C'est une ville qui est agréable.
La pollution est un problème important. — C'est vrai! C'est un problème qui est important.
Le football est un sport dangereux. — C'est vrai! C'est un sport qui est dangereux.
Le champagne est un vin excellent. — C'est vrai! C'est un vin qui est excellent.

D. *Le pronom relatif* ***que***

Activité 11. Conversation: Oui, c'est ça! Sylviane will ask you a series of questions. Answer her in the affirmative according to the model. *Écoutez le modèle.*

Modèle: Tu achètes ce livre? — Oui, c'est le livre que j'achète.

Commençons.

Tu écoutes cette cassette? — Oui, c'est la cassette que j'écoute.
Tu invites ce garçon? — Oui, c'est le garçon que j'invite.
Tu invites cette fille? — Oui, c'est la fille que j'invite.
Tu regardes ce magazine? — Oui, c'est le magazine que je regarde.
Tu aides cet étudiant? — Oui, c'est l'étudiant que j'aide.
Tu cherches ce disque? — Oui, c'est le disque que je cherche.

Activité 12. Situation: Comment s'appelle-t-elle? Bernard wants to know the names of various girls he notices. Formulate his questions, using **qui** or **que** as appropriate. *Écoutez les deux modèles.*

Modèles: Une fille passe dans la rue. — Comment s'appelle la fille qui passe dans la rue?
Paul connaît une fille. — Comment s'appelle la fille que Paul connaît?

Commençons.

Pierre regarde une fille. — Comment s'appelle la fille que Pierre regarde?
Une fille travaille là-bas. — Comment s'appelle la fille qui travaille là-bas?
Une fille vient. — Comment s'appelle la fille qui vient?
Marc attend une fille. — Comment s'appelle la fille que Marc attend?
Paul trouve une fille très jolie. — Comment s'appelle la fille que Paul trouve très jolie?
Une fille me regarde. — Comment s'appelle la fille qui me regarde?

E. *Les expressions* ***quelqu'un, quelque chose*** *et leurs contraires*

Activité 13. Conversation: Non! Florence is asking you several questions. Answer these questions in the negative. Use the expressions **ne . . . personne** or **ne . . . rien** as appropriate. *Écoutez le modèle.*

Modèle: Vous invitez quelqu'un ce soir? — Non, je n'invite personne.

Commençons.

Vous attendez quelqu'un?	Non, je n'attends personne.
Vous sortez avec quelqu'un demain?	Non, je ne sors avec personne.
Vous parlez à quelqu'un?	Non, je ne parle à personne.
Vous faites quelque chose?	Non, je ne fais rien.
Vous achetez quelque chose?	Non, je n'achète rien.
Vous voulez quelque chose?	Non, je ne veux rien.
Vous mangez quelque chose?	Non, je ne mange rien.

DIALOGUE

Activité 14. Où habites-tu? Pierre va vous poser des questions sur l'endroit où vous habitez. Répondez-lui. Puis indiquez vos réponses dans votre manuel de laboratoire. Il n'y a pas de confirmations parce que les réponses vont varier.

Commençons.

1. Est-ce que tu habites dans une ville ou à la campagne?
2. Est-ce que tu habites dans le centre ou dans la banlieue?
3. Est-ce que tu habites dans un immeuble ou dans une maison individuelle?
4. Est-ce qu'il y a beaucoup de circulation dans la rue où tu habites?
5. Est-ce qu'il y a beaucoup de bruit dans ton quartier?
6. Est-ce qu'il y a beaucoup de pollution dans ta ville?
7. Combien d'habitants y a-t-il dans ta ville?

DICTÉE

Activité 15. Ma voisine. *Vous allez entendre un court paragraphe. Écoutez d'abord! N'écrivez pas!* You will hear a short paragraph. First listen! Do not write!

J'habite dans un immeuble qui n'est pas très moderne mais que je trouve confortable. Je connais tous mes voisins. J'ai une voisine qui est très sympathique et que j'invite souvent chez moi. C'est une étudiante qui a passé plusieurs années dans une université américaine.

Maintenant écrivez les phrases dans votre manuel de laboratoire. Now write the sentences in your lab manual.

J'habite dans un immeuble / qui n'est pas très moderne / mais que je trouve confortable. / Je connais tous mes voisins. / J'ai une voisine / qui est très sympathique / et que j'invite / souvent chez moi. / C'est une étudiante / qui a passé / plusieurs années / dans une université américaine. /

Écoutez encore une fois et vérifiez ce que vous avez écrit.

(Text is reread without pauses.)

LECTURE CULTURELLE

Activité 16. Lecture. Ouvrez votre livre à la page 289. Écoutez.

(See textbook page 289.)

Activité 17. Compréhension du texte. Vous allez entendre des phrases concernant le texte que vous avez écouté. Indiquez dans votre manuel de laboratoire si ces phrases sont vraies ou fausses.

1. En 1900, la majorité des Français habitaient dans des grandes villes.
2. Aujourd'hui, la population française est une population essentiellement urbaine.
3. Lyon et Marseille sont des villes très anciennes.
4. Marseille est un grand port situé sur l'océan Atlantique.
5. À Toulouse, il y a une industrie spécialisée dans la construction d'avions.
6. Strasbourg est située au centre géographique de l'Europe.

Maintenant vérifiez vos réponses. Les phrases suivantes sont vraies: 2, 3 et 5. Les phrases suivantes sont fausses: 1, 4 et 6.

Fin de la Leçon 19.
End of Lesson 19.
(music)

LEÇON 20. LA TÉLÉVISION: UN BIEN OU UN MAL?

PRÉSENTATION

Activité 1. Lecture. Ouvrez votre livre à la page 302. Écoutez.

(See textbook page 302.)

Activité 2. Compréhension du texte. Vous allez entendre des phrases concernant le texte que vous avez écouté. Indiquez dans votre manuel de laboratoire si ces phrases sont vraies ou fausses.

Commençons.

1. Maurice Pécoul et Louis Juéry habitent dans un petit village.
2. Ils ont une opinion différente des avantages de la télévision.
3. Avant la télévision, les jeunes allaient souvent au cinéma.
4. Avant la télévision, les gens du village rencontraient leurs amis au café.

5. Maintenant les gens ne sortent pas souvent.
6. Le soir, ils regardent la télévision.

Maintenant vérifiez vos réponses. Les phrases suivantes sont vraies: 1, 2, 4, 5 et 6, et la phrase 3 est fausse.

PHONÉTIQUE

Activité 3. Les terminaisons -tion et -sion. Many French words end in **-tion** and **-sion.** These endings are usually pronounced /sjɔ̃/ and /zjɔ̃/. The ending **-stion,** as in **question,** is pronounced /stjɔ̃/. In practicing these endings, pronounce the /j/ rapidly with great tension. Avoid the "sh" or "zh" sounds that characterize the corresponding English endings.

Comparez:	
station	STATION
mission	MISSION
télévision	TELEVISION

Répétez: nation attention émission émotion exception télévision décision occasion
À la télévision, j'aime les émissions sportives.
Faites attention aux exceptions!

STRUCTURE ET VOCABULAIRE

Vocabulaire: La télévision

Activité 4. Situation: La télévision. Maurice only watches "serious" programs on television. You will hear a list of programs; say whether he watches them or not. *Écoutez le modèle.*

<u>Modèle</u>: les informations? — Oui, il regarde les informations.

Commençons.

les variétés?	Non, il ne regarde pas les variétés.
les jeux télévisés?	Non, il ne regarde pas les jeux télévisés.
les nouvelles?	Oui, il regarde les nouvelles.
les films?	Oui, il regarde les films.
la publicité?	Non, il ne regarde pas la publicité.
les documentaires?	Oui, il regarde les documentaires.
les dessins animés?	Non, il ne regarde pas les dessins animés.

A. Le verbe ***vivre***

Activité 5. Prononciation. Ouvrez votre livre à la page 305. Le verbe **vivre** est irrégulier. Répétez les phrases suivantes.

Je vis en France.
Tu vis à Paris.
Il vit en Italie.
Nous vivons bien.
Vous vivez mal.
Elles vivent confortablement.
J'ai vécu trois ans en France.

Activité 6. Pratique. Maintenant nous allons faire un exercice de substitution. Répétez la phrase. Puis faites de nouvelles phrases en utilisant les sujets suggérés.

Commençons.

Nous vivons aux États-Unis.

je	Je vis aux États-Unis.
vous	Vous vivez aux États-Unis.
tu	Tu vis aux États-Unis.
tes parents	Tes parents vivent aux États-Unis.
Julie	Julie vit aux États-Unis.

B. Quelques expressions négatives

Activité 7. Pratique. Nous allons faire quelques exercices de substitution avec **ne . . . jamais** et **ne . . . plus.** Répétez la première phrase. Puis faites de nouvelles phrases en utilisant les sujets suggérés.

Commençons.

Brigitte ne regarde jamais la télé.

vous	Vous ne regardez jamais la télé.
tu	Tu ne regardes jamais la télé.
je	Je ne regarde jamais la télé.

Maintenant changez les verbes.

Commençons.

Monique ne **fume** plus.

travailler	Monique ne travaille plus.
faire des recherches	Monique ne fait plus de recherches.
faire des économies	Monique ne fait plus d'économies.
voyager	Monique ne voyage plus.

Activité 8. Narration: Jamais! You are going to listen to what certain people do not like to do. Say that they never do these things. Use the negative construction **ne . . . jamais.** *Écoutez le modèle.*

Modèle: Paul déteste étudier. — Il n'étudie jamais.

Commençons.

Henri déteste perdre son temps.	Il ne perd jamais son temps.
Sylvie déteste téléphoner à ses cousins.	Elle ne téléphone jamais à ses cousins.
Vous détestez écouter la météo.	Vous n'écoutez jamais la météo.
Je déteste regarder les dessins animés.	Je ne regarde jamais les dessins animés.
Nous détestons nettoyer l'appartement.	Nous ne nettoyons jamais l'appartement.

C. L'imparfait

Activité 9. Prononciation. Ouvrez votre livre à la page 308. L'imparfait est un temps de passé.

Répétez les formes de l'imparfait du verbe **parler.**

je parlais	nous parlions
tu parlais	vous parliez
il parlait	ils parlaient

Maintenant répétez les formes de l'imparfait du verbe **finir.**

je finissais	nous finissions
tu finissais	vous finissiez
il finissait	ils finissaient

Répétez les formes de l'imparfait du verbe **vendre.**

je vendais	nous vendions
tu vendais	vous vendiez
il vendait	ils vendaient

Only the verb **être** has an irregular imperfect stem. ***Répétez les formes de l'imparfait du verbe être.***

j'étais	nous étions
tu étais	vous étiez
il était	ils étaient

Activité 10. Pratique. Maintenant nous allons faire quelques exercices de substitution. Répétez la phrase. Puis faites de nouvelles phrases en utilisant les sujets suggérés.

Commençons.

Je regardais un dessin animé.

tu	Tu regardais un dessin animé.
nous	Nous regardions un dessin animé.
vous	Vous regardiez un dessin animé.
les enfants	Les enfants regardaient un dessin animé.

Je n'étais pas en classe hier.

vous	Vous n'étiez pas en classe hier.
nous	Nous n'étions pas en classe hier.
le professeur	Le professeur n'était pas en classe hier.
tu	Tu n'étais pas en classe hier.

Maintenant changez les verbes.

Commençons.

Marc **finissait** le livre.

choisir	Marc choisissait le livre.
regarder	Marc regardait le livre.
comprendre	Marc comprenait le livre.
acheter	Marc achetait le livre.
prendre	Marc prenait le livre.
vouloir	Marc voulait le livre.
avoir	Marc avait le livre.
rendre	Marc rendait le livre.

Activité 11. Narration: Avant! You will hear what certain people are doing now. Say what they were doing before. Use the imperfect tense and the expressions suggested in your lab manual. *Écoutez le modèle.*

Modèle: Philippe habite à Paris. — Avant, il habitait à Québec.

Commençons.

1. Mademoiselle Arnaud travaille à Genève. — Avant, elle travaillait à Marseille.
2. Tu étudies l'allemand. — Avant, tu étudiais l'italien.
3. Mes copains jouent au tennis. — Avant, ils jouaient au football.
4. Vous habitez à la campagne. — Avant, vous habitiez en ville.
5. Je regarde le feuilleton. — Avant, je regardais les nouvelles.
6. Nous écoutons du jazz. — Avant, nous écoutions de la musique classique.
7. Tu lis un roman. — Avant, tu lisais les bandes dessinées.
8. Vous sortez le dimanche. — Avant, vous sortiez le samedi.

D. *L'imparfait et le passé composé: conditions habituelles et événements spécifiques*

Activité 12. Identification de structures. You will hear a series of sentences. The action in each sentence takes place in the past. Was the event isolated and specific, or did it take place on a regular basis? Listen carefully to the tense of the verb. If the verb is in the passé composé, the action was specific. Mark the first row **événement spécifique** in your lab manual. If the verb is in the imperfect, the event occurred on a regular basis. Mark the second row **événement habituel.**

Commençons.

1. Nous sommes allés en vacances en Espagne.
2. Avant, nous allions en Italie.
3. Je voyageais avec mes parents.
4. J'ai voyagé avec un ami.
5. Tu as passé tes vacances chez nous.
6. Tu passais tes vacances en famille.
7. J'ai joué au golf.
8. Je jouais au tennis.

Maintenant vérifiez vos réponses. You should have marked **événement habituel** for sentences 2, 3, 6, and 8 only. If you made any mistakes, listen once more to these sentences and do these questions again.

Vocabulaire: Expressions de temps

Activité 13. Prononciation. Ouvrez votre livre à la page 312. Répétez les expressions de temps.

(1) Description d'événements spécifiques

lundi	une fois
un lundi	deux fois
un jour	plusieurs fois
le 3 juin	

(2) Description de conditions et d'actions habituelles

le lundi	d'habitude
tous les lundis	habituellement
chaque jour	autrefois
tous les jours	

(3) Description d'événements spécifiques ou d'actions habituelles

souvent	parfois
rarement	quelquefois
longtemps	
tout le temps	
de temps en temps	

Activité 14. Jouons un rôle: Questions. Yves pose quelques questions à Guy. Jouez le rôle de Guy en utilisant les informations de votre manuel de laboratoire. Écoutez les modèles.

<u>Modèles</u>: Combien de temps as-tu habité à Québec? — J'ai habité un an à Québec.
Et avant, où habitais-tu? — J'habitais à Paris.

Commençons.

1. Où est-ce que tu as travaillé cet été? — J'ai travaillé dans une pharmacie.
2. Et avant, où est-ce que tu travaillais? — Je travaillais dans un magasin de vêtements.
3. Avec qui es-tu sorti lundi dernier? — Je suis sorti avec Denise.
4. Et pendant les vacances avec qui sortais-tu? — Je sortais avec Monique.
5. Combien de fois es-tu allé au Mexique? — Je suis allé deux fois au Mexique.
6. Avec qui est-ce que tu allais en vacances quand tu étais jeune? — J'allais en vacances avec mes parents.
7. Où est-ce que tu as rencontré Henri? — Je l'ai rencontré dans la rue.
8. Où est-ce que tu rencontrais tes copains quand tu étais à l'université? — Je les rencontrais au café.

DIALOGUE

Activité 15. Pendant les vacances. Marie va vous poser des questions sur ce que vous faisiez pendant les vacances. Répondez-lui en utilisant les informations de votre manuel de laboratoire. Écoutez le modèle.

<u>Modèle</u>: Qu'est-ce que tu faisais le lundi soir? — Je suivais un cours de judo.

Commençons.

1. Qu'est-ce que tu faisais le dimanche matin? Je dormais.
2. Qu'est-ce que tu faisais le vendredi soir? J'allais à la discothèque.
3. Qu'est-ce que tu faisais le mercredi après-midi? Je jouais au tennis.
4. Qu'est-ce que tu faisais le jeudi après-midi? Je déjeunais au restaurant.
5. Qu'est-ce que tu faisais le lundi matin? Je travaillais au supermarché.
6. Qu'est-ce que tu faisais le mardi soir? Je sortais avec mes copains.
7. Qu'est-ce que tu faisais le dimanche après-midi? Je regardais la télé.
8. Qu'est-ce que tu faisais le samedi après-midi? J'allais à la piscine.

DICTÉE

Activité 16. Le fils des voisins. *Vous allez entendre un court paragraphe. Écoutez d'abord! N'écrivez pas!* You will hear a short paragraph. First listen! Do not write!

Quand j'avais douze ans, j'habitais dans un petit village. Je passais tous mes week-ends avec Henri, le fils des voisins. C'était mon meilleur ami. Nous allions souvent à la plage et parfois nous faisions des promenades à bicyclette.

Maintenant écrivez les phrases dans votre manuel de laboratoire. Now write these sentences in your lab manual.

Quand j'avais douze ans, / j'habitais dans un petit village. / Je passais tous mes week-ends / avec Henri, / le fils des voisins. / C'était mon meilleur ami. / Nous allions souvent à la plage / et parfois / nous faisions des promenades / à bicyclette. /

Écoutez encore une fois et vérifiez ce que vous avez écrit.

(Text is reread without pauses.)

LECTURE CULTURELLE

Activité 17. Lecture. Ouvrez votre livre à la page 303. Écoutez.

(See textbook page 303.)

Activité 18. Compréhension du texte. Vous allez entendre des phrases concernant le texte que vous avez écouté. Indiquez dans votre manuel de laboratoire si ces phrases sont vraies ou fausses.

Commençons.

1. En 1953, la majorité des Français avait la télévision.
2. Autrefois, le gouvernement français contrôlait la télévision.
3. TF 1, Antenne 2 et FR 3 sont le nom de plusieurs chaînes de télévision française.
4. Il y a six chaînes de télévision en France.
5. Les Français ne regardent pas souvent la télévision.
6. Les feuilletons américains sont populaires en France.
7. *Apostrophes* est le nom d'un jeu télévisé.
8. Alain Delon et Yves Montand sont des journalistes de télévision.

Maintenant vérifiez vos réponses. Les phrases suivantes sont vraies: 2, 3, 4 et 6. Les phrases suivantes sont fausses: 1, 5, 7 et 8.

Fin de la Leçon 20.
End of Lesson 20.
(music)

LEÇON 21. UN CAMBRIOLAGE

PRÉSENTATION

Activité 1. Lecture. Ouvrez votre livre à la page 316. Écoutez.

(See textbook page 316.)

Activité 2. Compréhension du texte. Vous allez entendre des phrases concernant le texte que vous avez écouté. Indiquez dans votre manuel de laboratoire si ces phrases sont vraies ou fausses.

Commençons.

1. Le cambriolage a eu lieu hier soir.
2. Un témoin a assisté au cambriolage.
3. Ce témoin a décrit le cambriolage à la police.
4. Le cambriolage a eu lieu à neuf heures du matin.
5. Ce jour-là, il faisait mauvais.
6. Le cambrioleur était un homme assez jeune.
7. Il avait une complice.
8. Cette complice est entrée dans la galerie d'art.
9. Le témoin a eu peur et il est parti à toute vitesse.
10. Les cambrioleurs sont partis en voiture.

Maintenant vérifiez vos réponses. Les phrases suivantes sont vraies: 2, 3, 5, 6, 7 et 10. Les phrases suivantes sont fausses: 1, 4, 8 et 9.

PHONÉTIQUE

Activité 3. Les lettres «ai». At the end of a word, the letters "ai" represent the sound /e/. When followed by a silent final consonant, they also usually are pronounced /e/. However, when followed by a pronounced consonant, they represent the sound /ɛ/.

Comparez:	j'ai	j'aime
	français	française
	fait	faire

Répétez: j'ai le lait le fait anglais français j'aide semaine anniversaire fraise urbaine
Je n'ai pas pris de lait.
Tu m'aides la semaine prochaine?

NOTE: The letters "ain" and "aim" represent the nasal vowel /ɛ̃/.

Répétez: pain faim demain bain soudain
Soudain Alain avait très faim.

STRUCTURE ET VOCABULAIRE

Vocabulaire: Événements

Activité 4. Prononciation. Ouvrez votre livre à la page 318. Répétez les noms.

un accident
un cambriolage
un événement
un fait
un siècle
un témoin
une époque
une histoire
une scène

Maintenant répétez les verbes et les expressions. Écoutez les phrases.

arriver	Qu'est-ce qui est arrivé ce jour-là?
assister à	Vas-tu assister au match de football? Hier, j'ai assisté à un accident.
avoir lieu	Quand a eu lieu le cambriolage?
expliquer	Peux-tu m'expliquer cette histoire?
raconter	Aimez-vous raconter des histoires drôles?
remarquer	Je n'ai rien remarqué.
d'abord	D'abord, nous sommes allés au cinéma.
puis	Puis, nous sommes allés au café.
ensuite	Ensuite, nous avons joué aux cartes.
enfin	Enfin, nous sommes rentrés chez nous.
finalement	Finalement, je suis allé au lit.
pendant	Nous avons raconté des histoires pendant deux heures.
pendant que	Pendant que tu parlais, Paul a pris une photo.
soudain	Soudain, j'ai entendu un grand bruit.
tout à coup	Tout à coup, j'ai vu l'accident.
tout de suite	Nous avons tout de suite téléphoné à la police.

A. Le passé composé et l'imparfait: événement spécifique et circonstances de l'événement

Activité 5. Identification de structures. You will hear someone talking about an accident he witnessed. Can you tell which sentences describe the circumstances of the accident, and which sentences report the principal events? Listen carefully to the tense of the verb. If the verb is in the imperfect, a circumstance is being described. Mark the first row **circonstance** in your lab manual. If the verb is in the passé composé a specific event is being reported. Mark the second row **événement spécifique.**

Commençons.

1. Il était neuf heures du soir.
2. Je rentrais chez moi.
3. Il faisait noir.
4. La visibilité était mauvaise.
5. J'ai vu une voiture.
6. Cette voiture venait de l'avenue de Strasbourg.
7. C'était une Peugeot.
8. Le chauffeur n'a pas vu le «stop».
9. Il n'a pas fait attention.
10. Il est entré dans une autre voiture.
11. Il y a eu un choc violent.
12. La police est arrivée.
13. Une ambulance est arrivée.
14. Cette ambulance a transporté une personne à l'hôpital.

Vérifiez vos réponses. You should have marked **circonstance** for sentences 1, 2, 3, 4, 6, and 7 only. If you made any mistakes, listen once more to these sentences, and do these questions again.

Activité 6. Jouons un rôle: Au commissariat de police. Éric a été témoin d'un cambriolage hier soir. Maintenant il répond aux questions de l'inspecteur de police. Jouez le rôle d'Éric en utilisant les informations dans votre manuel de laboratoire. Écoutez le modèle.

Modèle: Où étiez-vous hier soir à huit heures? J'étais dans la rue Carnot.

Commençons.

1. Qu'est-ce que vous faisiez? Je faisais une promenade.
2. Quel temps faisait-il? Il faisait mauvais.
3. Qui avez-vous vu dans la rue? J'ai vu un homme assez grand.
4. D'où sortait-il? Il sortait de la Banque Nationale.
5. Quels vêtements portait-il? Il portait un costume beige.
6. Qu'est-ce qu'il avait avec lui? Il avait un grand sac.
7. Qu'est-ce qu'il a fait? Il a appelé un taxi.
8. De quelle couleur était le taxi? C'était un taxi jaune.

B. L'imparfait et le passé composé: actions progressives et événements spécifiques

Activité 7. Narration: Hier. You will hear what certain people do at certain hours. Say that at the same hour yesterday, these people were doing the same thing. *Écoutez le modèle.*

Modèle: Jacques dîne à six heures. Hier, à six heures, il dînait.

Commençons.

Suzanne déjeune à midi. Hier, à midi, elle déjeunait.
Nous déjeunons à une heure. Hier, à une heure, nous déjeunions.
Philippe travaille à trois heures. Hier, à trois heures, il travaillait.
Tu travailles à cinq heures. Hier, à cinq heures, tu travaillais.
Isabelle fait les courses à huit heures. Hier, à huit heures, elle faisait les courses.
Je bois un café après le dîner. Hier, après le dîner, je buvais un café.
Vous lisez le journal avant le dîner. Hier, avant le dîner, vous lisiez le journal.

Activité 8. Narration: La résidence. You will hear what various people are doing. Say that they were doing these things yesterday when Robert returned to the dorm. *Écoutez le modèle.*

Modèle: Je fais mes devoirs. Je faisais mes devoirs quand Robert est rentré.

Commençons.

Anne étudie. Anne étudiait quand Robert est rentré.
Claire raconte une histoire. Claire racontait une histoire quand Robert est rentré.
Nous nous disputons. Nous nous disputions quand Robert est rentré.
Tu fais le ménage. Tu faisais le ménage quand Robert est rentré.
Paul écrit à sa cousine. Paul écrivait à sa cousine quand Robert est rentré.
Je prépare un sandwich. Je préparais un sandwich quand Robert est rentré.
Pierre et Roger boivent une bière. Pierre et Roger buvaient une bière quand Robert est rentré.
Vous fumez une cigarette. Vous fumiez une cigarette quand Robert est rentré.
Quatre étudiants jouent au bridge. Quatre étudiants jouaient au bridge quand Robert est rentré.

C. *L'imparfait et le passé composé dans la même phrase*

Activité 9. Narration: Pourquoi pas? You will hear what certain people are doing. Say that they did not go out this morning because of these activities. Use the passé composé of **sortir** and the imperfect of the verb you will hear. *Écoutez le modèle.*

Modèle: Nicole attend un ami.	Nicole n'est pas sortie parce qu'elle attendait un ami.

Commençons.

Henri attend sa cousine.	Henri n'est pas sorti parce qu'il attendait sa cousine.
Suzanne a envie de dormir.	Suzanne n'est pas sortie parce qu'elle avait envie de dormir.
Thomas a du travail.	Thomas n'est pas sorti parce qu'il avait du travail.
François veut regarder la télé.	François n'est pas sorti parce qu'il voulait regarder la télé.
Jeannette veut préparer l'examen.	Jeannette n'est pas sortie parce qu'elle voulait préparer l'examen.

Activité 10. Jouons un rôle: Pourquoi? Olivier demande à Nicole pourquoi elle a fait certaines choses. Jouez le rôle de Nicole. Répondez aux questions d'Olivier en utilisant les informations qui se trouvent dans votre manuel de laboratoire. Écoutez le modèle.

Modèle: Pourquoi es-tu allée au restaurant?	Je suis allé au restaurant parce que j'avais faim.

Commençons.

1. Pourquoi es-tu allée au café?	Je suis allée au café parce que j'avais soif.
2. Pourquoi es-tu allée à la campagne?	Je suis allée à la campagne parce que je voulais faire une promenade.
3. Pourquoi es-tu allée à Madrid?	Je suis allée à Madrid parce que je voulais apprendre l'espagnol.
4. Pourquoi as-tu téléphoné à Charles?	J'ai téléphoné à Charles parce que j'avais envie de lui parler.
5. Pourquoi es-tu restée chez toi?	Je suis restée chez moi parce que j'avais l'intention d'étudier.

D. *Le plus-que-parfait*

Activité 11. Prononciation. Ouvrez votre livre à la page 328. Répétez les formes du plus-que-parfait.

étudier	sortir
j'avais étudié	j'étais sorti(e)
tu avais étudié	tu étais sorti(e)
il avait étudié	elle était sortie
nous avions étudié	nous étions sorti(e)s
vous aviez étudié	vous étiez sorti(e)(s)
elles avaient étudié	ils étaient sortis
je n'avais pas étudié	je n'étais pas sorti(e)
est-ce que tu avais étudié?	est-ce que tu étais sorti(e)?
avais-tu étudié?	étais-tu sorti(e)?

DIALOGUE

Activité 12. Alibis. Un inspecteur de police vérifie l'alibi de certaines personnes. Répondez à ses questions. Pour cela, dites où étaient les personnes et ce qu'elles faisaient en utilisant les informations dans votre manuel de laboratoire. Écoutez le modèle.

Modèle: Où était Monsieur Arnaud à dix heures? Il était chez lui. Il regardait la télé.

Commençons.

1. Où était Mlle Chevalier à trois heures de l'après-midi? Elle était au bureau. Elle travaillait.
2. Où était Jacques Verdier à deux heures du matin? Il était dans sa chambre. Il dormait.
3. Où étaient vos voisins à midi? Ils étaient au restaurant. Ils déjeunaient.
4. Où étaient ces étudiants à neuf heures du soir? Ils étaient à la bibliothèque. Ils étudiaient.
5. Où étiez-vous à sept heures? J'étais dans la rue. Je faisais du jogging.

DICTÉE

Activité 13. Hier soir. Vous allez entendre un court paragraphe. Écoutez d'abord! N'écrivez pas!

Hier soir, je suis sorti avant le dîner. Il faisait un temps épouvantable. Il neigeait et la visibilité était très mauvaise. Quand je suis rentré, j'ai vu quelqu'un qui attendait un taxi, mais il n'y avait pas de taxi. J'ai reconnu mon ami Jean-Claude. Je l'ai invité chez moi et nous avons dîné ensemble.

Maintenant écrivez les phrases dans votre manuel de laboratoire.

Hier soir, / je suis sorti avant le dîner. / Il faisait un temps épouvantable. / Il neigeait / et la visibilité était très mauvaise. / Quand je suis rentré, / j'ai vu quelqu'un / qui attendait un taxi, / mais il n'y avait pas de taxi. / J'ai reconnu / mon ami Jean-Claude. / Je l'ai invité chez moi / et nous avons dîné ensemble.

Écoutez encore une fois et vérifiez ce que vous avez écrit.

(Text is reread without pauses.)

LECTURE CULTURELLE

Activité 14. Lecture. Ouvrez votre livre à la page 317. Écoutez.

(See textbook page 317.)

Activité 15. Compréhension du texte. Vous allez entendre des phrases concernant le texte que vous avez écouté. Indiquez dans votre manuel de laboratoire si ces phrases sont vraies ou fausses.

Commençons.

1. Les uniformes français sont différents.
2. Quand un touriste a besoin d'un renseignement, il peut le demander à un agent de police.
3. Quand on est stationné illégalement, on peut avoir une contravention.
4. Les gendarmes portent un uniforme différent en hiver et en été.
5. Les gardes républicains sont des agents de police qui portent des vêtements civils.

Maintenant vérifiez vos réponses. Les phrases suivantes sont vraies: 1, 2, 3 et 4. La phrase 5 est fausse.

Fin de la Leçon 21.
End of Lesson 21.
(music)

VIVRE EN FRANCE 7. LES SORTIES

Activité 1. La bonne réponse. *Vous allez entendre une série de questions. Dans votre manuel de laboratoire, il y a trois réponses possibles pour chaque question. Indiquez quelle est la réponse logique. Faites un cercle autour de la lettre qui correspond à cette réponse.* You will hear a series of questions. In your lab manual there are three possible responses for each question. Select the logical response. Circle the corresponding letter.

Commençons.

1. Qu'est-ce qu'on joue au théâtre de l'Odéon cette semaine?
2. Quand est-ce que tu veux voir le film?
3. Qu'est-ce que tu as vu hier soir à la télé?
4. Il y a une nouvelle exposition au Centre Pompidou. Est-ce que tu veux y aller avec moi?
5. Tu es libre ce soir?
6. On va prendre un verre?
7. Alors, on se retrouve au Café de l'Univers demain soir à sept heures?
8. Tu as des projects pour le week-end?

Maintenant écoutez les questions et les réponses correspondantes. Écoutez.

1. Qu'est-ce qu'on joue au théâtre de l'Odéon cette semaine?
   Je pense que c'est une pièce de Pirandello.
2. Quand est-ce que tu veux voir le film?
   On peut aller à la séance de vingt heures.
3. Qu'est-ce que tu as vu hier soir à la télé?
   Un excellent spectacle de variétés.
4. Il y a une nouvelle exposition au Centre Pompidou. Est-ce que tu veux y aller avec moi?
   Oh, tu sais, moi, je ne connais rien à l'art moderne.
5. Tu es libre ce soir?
   Non, je dois étudier.
6. On va prendre un verre?
   Volontiers, est-ce qu'il y a un café près d'ici?
7. Alors, on se retrouve au Café de l'Univers demain soir à sept heures?
   C'est entendu!
8. Tu as des projets pour le week-end?
   Oui, je vais aller à un concert avec mes copains.

Activité 2. En France. Vous allez entendre une conversation entre Jean-Claude et Jacqueline. Dans cette conversation, Jean-Claude veut inviter Jacqueline. Écoutez bien le dialogue. Même si vous ne comprenez pas tous les mots, vous pouvez comprendre les éléments essentiels de ce dialogue. Utilisez ces éléments pour compléter le carnet de rendez-vous de Jacqueline qui se trouve dans votre manual de laboratoire. D'abord, écoutez le dialogue.

—Allô, Jacqueline?
—Allô! Ah, c'est toi, Jean-Claude. Comment vas-tu?
—Ça va, ça va! Dis, donc, j'ai deux billets pour le concert des Chats Sauvages. Ça t'intéresse?
—Ça dépend. Quand est-ce?
—Vendredi prochain.
—Attends une seconde. Voyons, vendredi prochain, c'est le 21 mai. Ah, vraiment, ça n'est pas de chance. Ce jour-là je dois aller à la fête d'anniversaire de ma cousine Caroline.
—Et dimanche, tu es libre?
—Dimanche le 23 mai. Oui, je suis libre.
—On peut aller au théâtre!
—Qu'est-ce tu as envie de voir?
—On joue une pièce de Beckett au Quartier latin.
—Ah, oui, je sais! *En attendant Godot!* Je l'ai vue le mois dernier. C'est formidable!
—Bon alors, on peut aller au cinéma. On joue un film de Woody Allen à l'Odéon: «Hannah et ses sœurs». Tu l'as vu?
—«Hannah et ses sœurs»? Non, je ne l'ai pas vu. . . . On dit que c'est bien! Écoute, d'accord! Allons au cinéma.
—À quelle séance veux-tu aller? Il y a une séance à 20 heures et une autre à 22 heures.
—Allons à la séance de 22 heures. Ensuite, je t'invite à prendre quelque chose dans un café.
—Bon, d'accord! Où est-ce qu'on se retrouve?
—Eh bien, devant le cinéma, dix minutes avant le film.
—Parfait! Alors je te retrouve devant l'Odeon dimanche prochain à dix heures moins dix.
—D'accord!
—À dimanche prochain.
—À dimanche et merci!
—Au revoir, Jacqueline.
—Au revoir, Jean-Claude.

Écoutez à nouveau et écrivez.

Fin de Vivre en France 7.
End of Vivre en France 7.
(music)

UNITÉ 8: IMAGES DE LA VIE

LEÇON 22. VIVE LES LOISIRS!

PRÉSENTATION

Activité 1. Lecture. Ouvrez votre livre à la page 338. Écoutez.

(See textbook page 338.)

Activité 2. Compréhension du texte. Vous allez entendre une série de phrases concernant le texte que vous avez écouté. Indiquez dans votre manuel de laboratoire à qui chaque phrase s'applique. Écoutez le modèle.

Modèle: La lecture et la musique sont ses loisirs favoris. You should have marked "Henri."

Commençons.

1. Cette personne est mariée et a des enfants.
2. C'est quelqu'un qui aime beaucoup les sports.
3. Il n'a pas beaucoup d'argent. Quand il en a, il va voir un film.
4. C'est un étudiant.
5. Avant, il faisait du théâtre mais aujourd'hui il n'en fait plus.
6. Elle fait du jogging.
7. C'est une personne active qui aime l'exercice physique.
8. Elle a trop de travail et pas assez de loisirs. Le week-end elle reste chez elle.
9. Il joue d'un instrument de musique.
10. Le mari de cette personne rencontre ses amis au café.

Maintenant vérifiez vos réponses. Anne-Marie: phrases 2, 6 et 7. François: phrase 5. Henri: phrases 3, 4 et 9. Josiane: phrases 1, 8 et 10.

PHONÉTIQUE

Activité 3. Les sons /ʒ/ et /g/.
(a) La consonne /ʒ/.
The consonant /ʒ/ is similar to the sound represented by the letter "g" in the English word *mirage*. Do not pronounce a /d/ before /ʒ/, unless there is a "d" in the written form of the word, as in **budget.**

Répétez: je Jean âge argent régime logement gymnastique
Quel âge a Gigi?
Jacques fait du patinage avec Roger.

(b) La consonne /g/.
The French consonant /g/ is pronounced with greater tension than the corresponding sound in English.

Répétez: grand grippe guitare garçon glace langue
Guy va garder la guitare de Margot.
Guillaume est un grand garçon.

STRUCTURE ET VOCABULAIRE

Vocabulaire: La santé, les sports et les loisirs

Activité 4. Prononciation. Ouvrez votre livre à la page 340. Répétez les noms suivants.

un loisir
un rhume
un sport
le temps libre
la forme
la grippe
une maladie
la santé

Répétez les noms des sports et des loisirs.

l'alpinisme
le camping
le jogging
le patinage
le ski
le ski nautique
la gymnastique
la lecture
la marche à pied
la natation
la planche à voile
la voile

Maintenant répétez les adjectifs.

bien portant
malade
fatigué
en forme
gros
mince

Maintenant écoutez les verbes et les expressions et répétez les phrases.

pratiquer — Quels sports pratiques-tu?
avoir l'air — Vous avez l'air fatigué.
être en bonne santé — Je suis en bonne santé parce que je fais du sport.
être en mauvaise santé — Vous êtes pâle! Etes-vous en mauvaise santé?
être en forme — M. Renaud grossit. Il n'est pas en forme.
faire des exercices — Quand fais-tu tes exercices?

Activité 5. Compréhension orale. You will hear statements about health, sports, and leisure time activities. Are these statements logical or not? Listen carefully to each statement. If it is a logical statement, mark the first row **logique** in your lab manual. If it is not logical, mark the second row **illogique.**

Commençons.

1. Je vais souvent à la piscine. La natation est mon sport favori.
2. Henri fait attention à sa santé. Il fait du sport et il ne fume pas.
3. S'il neige cet hiver, nous pouvons faire du ski nautique.
4. Pour son anniversaire, j'ai donné un livre à ma mère. Elle adore la lecture.
5. Marc n'est pas en forme. Il doit avoir la grippe.
6. Nous n'allons pas rester à l'hôtel pendant les vacances. Nous allons faire du camping.
7. François va passer l'été à Miami. Là-bas, il va faire du patinage tous les jours.
8. Monique aime beaucoup l'alpinisme. Voilà pourquoi elle va à la montagne tous les étés.

Vérifiez vos réponses. You should have marked **logique** for sentences 1, 2, 4, 5, 6, and 8. If you made any mistakes, listen once more to this activity, and do these questions again.

*A. Le verbe **courir***

Activité 6. Prononciation. Ouvrez votre livre à la page 342. Le verbe **courir** est irrégulier. Répétez les formes suivantes.

je cours
tu cours
il court

nous courons
vous courez
elles courent

j'ai couru

Activité 7. Pratique. Maintenant nous allons faire quelques exercices de substitution. Répétez la première phrase. Puis faites de nouvelles phrases en utilisant les sujets suggérés.

Commençons.

Nous courons tous les jours.

Paul	Paul court tous les jours.
ces étudiants	Ces étudiants courent tous les jours.
tu	Tu cours tous les jours.

Tu n'as pas couru très vite.

nous	Nous n'avons pas couru très vite.
je	Je n'ai pas couru très vite.
cette personne	Cette personne n'a pas couru très vite.

*B. Le pronom **y***

Activité 8. Conversation: Où allez-vous? M. Durand is asking you several questions. Answer them in the affirmative using the pronoun **y.** *Écoutez le modèle.*

Modèle: Allez-vous souvent au cinéma? Oui, j'y vais souvent.

Commençons.

Allez-vous souvent chez votre meilleur ami?	Oui, j'y vais souvent.
Travaillez-vous à la bibliothèque?	Oui, j'y travaille.
Êtes-vous allé(e) à New York?	Oui, j'y suis allé(e).

Now answer in the negative. *Écoutez le modèle.*

Modèle: Allez-vous souvent chez le dentiste? Non, je n'y vais pas souvent.

Commençons.

Dînez-vous souvent au restaurant? Non, je n'y dîne pas souvent.
Êtes-vous allé(e) à Montréal? Non, je n'y suis pas allé(e).
Êtes-vous resté(e) à la maison ce week-end? Non, je n'y suis pas resté(e).

Activité 9. Conversation: Que fait Bernard? Charlotte is asking you questions about Bernard. Answer them in the affirmative, using pronouns. Use **lui** or **leur** if the sentence refers to a person and **y** if the sentence refers to a thing. *Écoutez les deux modèles.*

Modèles: Est-ce que Bernard joue au tennis? Oui, il y joue.
Est-ce qu'il téléphone à ses amis? Oui, il leur téléphone.

Commençons.

Est-ce qu'il pense à ses études? Oui, il y pense.
Est-ce qu'il réussit à ses examens? Oui, il y réussit.
Est-ce qu'il téléphone à sa mère? Oui, il lui téléphone.
Est-ce qu'il répond au téléphone? Oui, il y répond.
Est-ce qu'il répond à ses copains? Oui, il leur répond.
Est-ce qu'il fait attention à sa santé? Oui, il y fait attention.
Est-ce qu'il écrit à son oncle? Oui, il lui écrit.

*C. Le pronom **en***

Activité 10. Conversation: Un végétarien! Jacques is a vegetarian. He does not eat meat, but he eats everything else. You will hear Anne asking you questions about Jacques' eating habits. Answer her, using the pronoun **en,** in affirmative or negative sentences. *Écoutez le modèle.*

Modèle: Est-ce qu'il mange du rosbif? Non, il n'en mange pas.

Commençons.

Est-ce qu'il mange du fromage? Oui, il en mange.
Est-ce qu'il commande de la glace? Oui, il en commande.
Est-ce qu'il prend de la salade? Oui, il en prend.
Est-ce qu'il prend du jambon? Non, il n'en prend pas.
Est-ce qu'il veut des fruits? Oui, il en veut.
Est-ce qu'il veut du porc? Non, il n'en veut pas.

Activité 11. Conversation: Conseils. Monique is asking you whether she should do certain things. Tell her yes, using the affirmative imperative and the pronoun **en.** *Écoutez le modèle.*

Modèle: Est-ce que je dois faire de l'athlétisme? Oui, fais-en!

Commençons.

Est-ce que je dois faire de la gymnastique?	Oui, fais-en!
Est-ce que je dois acheter des disques?	Oui, achètes-en!
Est-ce que je dois acheter de la bière?	Oui, achètes-en!
Est-ce que je peux prendre de la salade?	Oui, prends-en!
Est-ce que je peux boire du thé?	Oui, bois-en!
Est-ce que je peux manger du pain?	Oui, manges-en!

*D. Le pronom **en** avec les expressions de quantité*

Activité 12. Conversation: Nous aussi! Alain is talking about how things are in France. Say that the situation is the same in the United States. *Écoutez le modèle.*

Modèle: En France, nous avons beaucoup de travail. Nous aussi, nous en avons beaucoup.

Commençons.

En France, nous avons trop d'examens.	Nous aussi, nous en avons trop.
En France, nous suivons plusieurs cours.	Nous aussi, nous en suivons plusieurs.
En France, nous lisons beaucoup de livres.	Nous aussi, nous en lisons beaucoup.
En France, nous avons assez de loisirs.	Nous aussi, nous en avons assez.

DIALOGUE

Activité 13. Activités. Annie va vous demander ce que font certaines personnes et où elles font ces choses. Répondez-lui en utilisant les informations de votre manuel de laboratoire. Écoutez le modèle.

Modèle: Qu'est-ce que Jacques fait en été?	Il fait de la voile.
Ah bon, et où est-ce qu'il en fait?	Il en fait à Toulon.

Commençons.

1. Qu'est-ce que Nadine fait en hiver?	Elle fait du ski.
Ah bon, et où est-ce qu'elle en fait?	Elle en fait en Suisse.
2. Qu'est-ce que tes copains font pendant les vacances?	Ils font de la planche à voile.
Ah bon, et où est-ce qu'ils en font?	Ils en font à la Martinique.
3. Qu'est-ce que Jacqueline a fait l'été dernier?	Elle a fait du camping.
Ah bon, et où est-ce qu'elle en a fait?	Elle en a fait en Normandie.
4. Qu'est-ce que tu as fait pendant les vacances?	J'ai fait du ski nautique.
Ah bon, et où est-ce que tu en as fait?	J'en ai fait à Biarritz.
5. Qu'est-ce que tu vas faire ce soir?	Je vais faire du jogging.
Ah bon, et où est-ce que tu vas en faire?	Je vais en faire au parc Monceau.

DICTÉE

Activité 14. À la mer. Vous allez entendre un court paragraphe. Écoutez d'abord! N'écrivez pas!

Allez-vous souvent à la mer? Quand j'étais jeune, j'y allais tous les étés. C'est là que j'ai appris à faire de la voile. J'en faisais très souvent. Maintenant je n'en fais plus parce que je n'ai pas de bateau. Si j'ai de l'argent, je vais en acheter un cet été.

Maintenant écrivez les phrases dans votre manuel de laboratoire.

Allez-vous souvent à la mer? / Quand j'étais jeune, / j'y allais / tous les étés. / C'est là / que j'ai appris / à faire de la voile. / J'en faisais très souvent. / Maintenant / je n'en fais plus / parce que je n'ai pas de bateau. / Si j'ai de l'argent, / je vais en acheter un / cet été. /

Écoutez encore une fois et vérifiez ce que vous avez écrit.

(Text is reread without pauses.)

LECTURE CULTURELLE

Activité 15. Lecture. Ouvrez votre livre à la page 339. Écoutez.

(See textbook page 339.)

Activité 16. Compréhension du texte. Vous allez entendre des phrases concernant le texte que vous avez écouté. Indiquez dans votre manuel de laboratoire si ces phrases sont vraies ou fausses.

Commençons.

1. Entre le temps libre et l'argent, les Français préfèrent l'argent.
2. Pour les Français, les loisirs sont un élément très important de l'existence.
3. Les Français aiment le cinéma et la musique, mais ils détestent les sports.
4. Le ski et le tennis sont des sports populaires en France.
5. Le gouvernement français encourage directement la pratique du sport.

Maintenant vérifiez vos réponses. Les phrases suivantes sont vraies: 2, 4 et 5. Les phrases suivantes sont fausses: 1 et 3.

Fin de la Leçon 22.
End of Lesson 22.
(music)

LEÇON 23. UNE JOURNÉE COMMENCE

PRÉSENTATION

Activité 1. Lecture. Ouvrez votre livre à la page 352. Écoutez.

(See textbook page 352.)

Activité 2. Compréhension du texte. Vous allez entendre une série de phrases concernant le texte que vous avez écouté. Indiquez dans votre manuel de laboratoire si ces phrases sont vraies ou fausses.

Commençons.

1. Le texte décrit les avantages d'habiter à la campagne.
2. L'un des problèmes modernes est le bruit.
3. Mlle Legrand se réveille à huit heures du matin.
4. Quand elle prépare son petit déjeuner, elle écoute de la musique.
5. M. Charron est le voisin de Mlle Legrand.
6. Il se rase avec un rasoir mécanique.
7. M. Dumas se réveille quand il entend Mme Dupont chanter dans la salle de bains.
8. Tous les matins M. Imbert entend M. Dumas faire de la gymnastique.

Maintenant vérifiez vos réponses. Les phrases suivantes sont vraies: 2, 4 et 5. Les phrases suivantes sont fausses: 1, 3, 6, 7 et 8.

PHONÉTIQUE

Activité 3. La chute de la voyelle /ə/. The mute "e" of the reflexive pronouns **me, te,** and **se** is dropped in rapid conversation when the preceding word ends in a vowel sound.

Répétez:		
	je me lève	je me lève
	tu te rases	tu te rases
	je me réveille	je me réveille
	tu te couches	tu te couches

When the preceding word ends in a consonant sound, the mute "e" is pronounced. Compare the following examples of rapid speech. In the first group of words in each pair, the reflexive pronoun is preceded by a consonant sound: the vowel /ə/ is prounced.

Répétez:		
	il se rase	Jean s~~e~~ rase
	elle se réveille	Marie s~~e~~ réveille
	Paul se promène	Guy s~~e~~ promène

STRUCTURE ET VOCABULAIRE

Vocabulaire: Quelques activités

Activité 4. Prononciation. Ouvrez votre livre à la page 354. Répétez les mots suivants et les phrases.

appeler — Je vais t'appeler demain.
casser — Attention! Ne casse pas le vase!
couper — Coupez le pain, s'il vous plaît.
fermer — Fermez vos livres!
laver — Je lave ma voiture assez souvent.
réveiller — Il est huit heures. Réveille ton frère!
prêt — Êtes-vous prêts? Je vous attends!
jusqu'à — Nous travaillons jusqu'à midi.
tôt — Nous partons tôt.
tard — Nous rentrons tard.

A. L'usage de l'article défini avec les parties du corps

Vocabulaire: Les parties du corps

Activité 5. Prononciation. Ouvrez votre livre à la page 355. Répétez les parties du corps.

la tête
les cheveux
le cou
le nez
l'œil
les yeux
la bouche
les dents
la figure
la gorge
l'oreille

le corps
le cœur
le doigt
le dos
le genou
le pied
le ventre
la jambe
la main

Activité 6. Compréhension orale. You will hear several sentences. In each sentence, a part of the body will be mentioned. Listen carefully and write the name of this part of the body in the space provided in your lab manual. Be sure to use the correct definite article.

Commençons.

1. Paul a les yeux bleus.
2. Connais-tu Isabelle? C'est la fille qui a les cheveux courts.
3. Si vous ne voulez pas avoir froid aux oreilles, mettez votre chapeau.
4. S'il te plaît, ne mets pas les pieds sur la table.
5. Quand j'ai mal à la tête, je prends de l'aspirine.
6. Qu'est-ce que vous avez dans la bouche?

Maintenant vérifiez vos réponses. You should have written the following words: 1. les yeux 2. les cheveux 3. les oreilles 4. les pieds 5. la tête 6. la bouche

B. Les verbes pronominaux: formation et sens réfléchi

Activité 7. Prononciation. Ouvrez votre livre à la page 358. Répétez les formes du verbe **se laver** au présent.

Je me lave.
Tu te laves.
Il se lave.
Nous nous lavons.
Vous vous lavez.
Elles se lavent.
Je ne me lave pas.
Est-ce que tu te laves?

Maintenant répétez les phrases suivantes avec le verbe **s'acheter.**

Je m'achète des disques.
Tu t'achètes un téléviseur.
Il s'achète un appareil-photo.
Nous nous achetons des vêtements.
Vous vous achetez un ordinateur.
Elles s'achètent une voiture.
Je ne m'achète pas de cigarettes.
Est-ce que tu t'achètes des livres?

Activité 8. Pratique. Maintenant nous allons faire quelques exercices de substitution. Répétez la phrase. Puis faites de nouvelles phrases en utilisant les sujets suggérés.

Commençons.

Pierre se regarde dans la glace.

je	Je me regarde dans la glace.
nous	Nous nous regardons dans la glace.
ces garçons	Ces garçons se regardent dans la glace.
tu	Tu te regardes dans la glace.

Je ne me coupe jamais.

tu	Tu ne te coupes jamais.
nous	Nous ne nous coupons jamais.
Sophie	Sophie ne se coupe jamais.
vous	Vous ne vous coupez jamais.

Est-ce que **Paul** s'achète des disques?

tu	Est-ce que tu t'achètes des disques?
vous	Est-ce que vous vous achetez des disques?
Alice et Suzanne	Est-ce qu'Alice et Suzanne s'achètent des disques?

Vocabulaire: Quelques occupations de la journée

Activité 9. Prononciation. Ouvrez votre livre à la page 360. Répétez la forme **-je** des verbes et écoutez les phrases.

se réveiller:	Je me réveille	À quelle heure est-ce que tu te réveilles?
se lever:	Je me lève	Je me lève à huit heures et demie.
se brosser:	Je me brosse	Tu te brosses les dents.
se laver:	Je me lave	Nous nous lavons dans la salle de bains.
se raser:	Je me rase	Paul se rase avec un rasoir électrique.
s'habiller:	Je m'habille	Anne s'habille toujours bien.
se peigner:	Je me peigne	Vous vous peignez souvent.
se promener:	Je me promène	Je me promène après la classe.
se coucher:	Je me couche	Je ne me couche pas avant minuit.
se reposer:	Je me repose	Je me repose après le dîner.

Activité 10. Pratique. Maintenant nous allons faire quelques exercices de substitution. Répétez la première phrase. Puis faites de nouvelles phrases en utilisant les verbes suggérés.

Commençons.

Nous **nous reposons** maintenant.

s'habiller	Nous nous habillons maintenant.
se lever	Nous nous levons maintenant.
se coucher	Nous nous couchons maintenant.

Tu ne **te rases** pas?

se laver	Tu ne te laves pas?
se peigner	Tu ne te peignes pas?
se réveiller	Tu ne te réveilles pas?

Activité 11. Jouons un rôle: Mme Charron est curieuse. Mme Charron pose des questions à Philippe. Jouez le rôle de Philippe. Utilisez les réponses suggérées dans votre manuel de laboratoire. Écoutez le modèle.

Modèle: À quelle heure est-ce que vous vous réveillez? — Je me réveille à sept heures.

Commençons.

1. À quelle heure est-ce que vous vous levez? — Je me lève à sept heures et quart.
2. Où est-ce que vous vous lavez? — Je me lave dans la salle de bains.
3. Comment est-ce que vous vous rasez? — Je me rase avec un rasoir électrique.
4. Où est-ce que vous vous habillez? — Je m'habille dans ma chambre.
5. Comment est-ce que vous vous promenez? — Je me promène en voiture.
6. Quand est-ce que vous vous reposez? — Je me repose après le déjeuner.
7. À quelle heure est-ce que vous vous couchez? — Je me couche à onze heures et demie.

C. L'infinitif des verbes pronominaux

Activité 12. Narration: Demain aussi. You will hear what certain people are doing today. Say that they are going to do the same things tomorrow. Use the construction **aller** plus the infinitive of the reflexive verb you hear. *Écoutez le modèle.*

Modèle: Charles se promène. — Demain aussi, il va se promener.

Commençons.

Charles se promène.	Demain aussi, il va se promener.
Nous nous promenons.	Demain aussi, nous allons nous promener.
Tu te promènes.	Demain aussi, tu vas te promener.
Philippe se repose.	Demain aussi, il va se reposer.
Vous vous reposez.	Demain aussi, vous allez vous reposer.
Jacqueline se couche tard.	Demain aussi, elle va se coucher tard.
Robert se lève tôt.	Demain aussi, il va se lever tôt.
Hélène et Louis se promènent dans le parc.	Demain aussi, ils vont se promener dans le parc.

D. *Le verbe* ***ouvrir***

Activité 13. Prononciation. Ouvrez votre livre à la page 364. Répétez le verbe **ouvrir** dans les phrases suivantes.

J'ouvre la porte.
Tu ouvres le cahier.
On ouvre le livre.
Nous ouvrons la fenêtre.
Vous ouvrez le magazine.
Elles ouvrent le journal.
J'ai ouvert votre lettre.

Maintenant répétez la forme **-je** des verbes suivants et écoutez les phrases.

découvrir:	je découvre	Les médecins vont découvrir une cure contre le cancer.
offrir:	j'offre	Mes parents m'ont offert une nouvelle voiture.
ouvrir:	j'ouvre	Ouvrez la fenêtre, s'il vous plaît.
souffrir:	je souffre	As tu souffert quand tu es allé chez le dentiste?

DIALOGUE

Activité 14. Qu'est-ce que tu cherches? Véronique vous demande quels objets vous cherchez. Répondez-lui sur la base des illustrations de votre manuel de laboratoire. Ensuite elle va vous demander pourquoi vous en avez besoin. Répondez-lui d'une manière logique. Écoutez le modèle.

Modèle: Qu'est-ce que tu cherches? — Je cherche la brosse à dents.
Ah bon? Pourquoi est-ce que tu en as besoin? — Je vais me brosser les dents.

Commençons.

1. Qu'est-ce que tu cherches? — Je cherche le savon.
   Ah bon? Pourquoi est-ce que tu en as besoin? — Je vais me laver.
2. Qu'est-ce que tu veux? — Je veux le peigne.
   Ah bon? Pourquoi est-ce que tu en as besoin? — Je vais me peigner.
3. Qu'est-ce que tu cherches? — Je cherche le dentifrice.
   Ah bon? Pourquoi est-ce que tu en as besoin? — Je vais me brosser les dents.
4. Qu'est-ce que tu veux? — Je veux le rasoir.
   Ah bon? Pourquoi est-ce que tu en as besoin? — Je vais me raser.
5. Qu'est-ce que tu cherches? — Je cherche la brosse.
   Ah bon? Pourquoi est-ce que tu en as besoin? — Je vais me brosser les cheveux.

DICTÉE

Activité 15. Le dimanche. Vous allez entendre un court paragraphe. Écoutez d'abord! N'écrivez pas!

À quelle heure est-ce que vous vous levez le dimanche? Moi, je ne me lève jamais avant dix heures. Je me rase, je me lave, je m'habille et j'écoute la radio. L'après-midi, je me promène avec mon amie Marie-Laure. Nous nous promenons souvent à la campagne. Et vous, est-ce que vous vous promenez avec vos amis?

Maintenant écrivez les phrases dans votre manuel de laboratoire.

À quelle heure / est-ce que vous vous levez / le dimanche? / Moi, je ne me lève jamais / avant dix heures. / Je me rase, / je me lave, / je m'habille / et j'écoute la radio. / L'après-midi, je me promène / avec mon amie Marie-Laure. / Nous nous promenons souvent / à la campagne. / Et vous, / est-ce que vous vous promenez / avec vos amis? /

Écoutez encore une fois et vérifiez ce que vous avez écrit.

(Text is reread without pauses.)

LECTURE CULTURELLE

Activité 16. Lecture. Ouvrez votre livre à la page 353. Écoutez.

(See textbook page 353.)

Activité 17. Compréhension du texte. Vous allez entendre des phrases concernant le texte que vous avez écouté. Indiquez dans votre manuel de laboratoire si ces phrases sont vraies ou fausses.

Commençons.

1. Dans les grandes villes, la majorité des gens habitent dans des maisons individuelles.
2. Les HLM sont des habitations où le loyer est bon marché.
3. C'est le gouvernement français qui a donné l'argent nécessaire à la construction des HLM.
4. La majorité des HLM sont situés à la campagne.
5. La pollution, le bruit, l'absence d'espaces verts sont des problèmes communs aux villes industrielles.
6. En général, quand on a beaucoup d'argent on n'habite pas dans une HLM.

Maintenant vérifiez vos réponses. Les phrases suivantes sont vraies: 2, 3, 5 et 6. Les phrases suivantes sont fausses: 1 et 4.

Fin de la Leçon 23.
End of Lesson 23.
(music)

LEÇON 24. QUELLE BONNE SURPRISE!

PRÉSENTATION

Activité 1. Lecture. Ouvrez votre livre à la page 366. Écoutez.

(See textbook page 366.)

Activité 2. Compréhension du texte. Vous allez entendre des phrases concernant le texte que vous avez écouté. Indiquez dans votre manuel de laboratoire si ces phrases sont vraies ou fausses.

Commençons.

1. Jean-Marc a rendez-vous avec la jeune fille.
2. La jeune fille s'appelle Catherine.
3. L'été dernier, elle est allée dans une soirée chez des gens qui s'appellent Launay.
4. À cette soirée, elle a rencontré Jean-Marc.
5. Les Launay sont des cousins de Jean-Marc.
6. Jean-Marc pense que la jeune fille est sympathique.
7. Il l'invite à rester au café.
8. La jeune fille accepte l'invitation.

Maintenant vérifiez vos réponses. Les phrases suivantes sont vraies: 2, 3, 6, 7 et 8. Les phrases suivantes sont fausses: 1, 4 et 5.

PHONÉTIQUE

Activité 3. Les consonnes /p/, /t/ et /k/. The French consonants /p/, /t/, and /k/ are pronounced differently from their English counterparts. To understand this difference more clearly, perform the following experiment. Hold a piece of paper in front of your mouth as you say the English words: "pot," "top," and "cot." The paper will move somewhat because you release a puff of air when you pronounce the initial English consonants "p," "t," and "k." Now try the same experiment with the English words "spot," "stop," and "Scot." The paper hardly moves because the consonants are pronounced without a puff of air when they follow an "s." In French the consonants /p/, /t/, and /k/ in initial position are always pronounced *without* a puff of air.

Répétez: pied peigne patinage parc problème
tête temps trop tard tôt
cou corps cœur couper casser courir
Pierre est plus pessimiste que Paul.
Thomas a téléphoné trop tard.
Catherine a cassé la caméra de Kiki.

STRUCTURE ET VOCABULAIRE

Vocabulaire: Entre amis

Activité 4. Prononciation. Ouvrez votre livre à la page 368. Répétez les noms:

un rendez-vous une fête une rencontre une réunion une soirée

Maintenant répétez les verbes et écoutez les phrases.

avoir rendez-vous — J'ai rendez-vous chez le dentiste.
donner rendez-vous à — Alice donne rendez-vous à Marc.
Je vous donne rendez-vous à midi.

s'entendre bien avec — Je m'entends bien avec mes amis.
se disputer avec — Je me dispute avec mon frère.
se rencontrer — Où est-ce que nous allons nous rencontrer?

A. Les verbes pronominaux: sens idiomatique

Activité 5. Prononciation. Ouvrez votre livre à la page 369. Répétez la forme **je** des verbes suivants. Puis écoutez les phrases.

s'approcher de:	je m'approche	Je ne t'entends pas. Peux-tu t'approcher?
s'arrêter:	je m'arrête	Est-ce que l'autobus s'arrête ici?
s'asseoir:	je m'assieds	Je vais m'asseoir à cette table.
se dépêcher:	je me dépêche	Pourquoi est-ce que tu te dépêches?
s'énerver:	je m'énerve	Pourquoi est-ce qu'il s'énerve?
s'impatienter:	je m'impatiente	Je m'impatiente quand tu n'es pas prêt.
s'intéresser à:	je m'intéresse à	Les étudiants s'intéressent à la politique.
se mettre en colère:	je me mets en colère	Éric se mettait souvent en colère.
se préoccuper de:	je me préoccupe de	Sylvie se préoccupe des problèmes de ses amis.
se préparer:	je me prépare	Nous nous préparons pour la fête.
s'amuser:	je m'amuse	J'espère que nous allons nous amuser.
s'appeler:	je m'appelle	Comment s'appelle ce restaurant?
s'excuser:	je m'excuse	Quand j'ai tort, je m'excuse.
s'occuper de:	je m'occupe de	Nous nous occupons d'un club sportif. Je m'occupe de ce problème.
se rendre compte de:	je me rends compte de	Est-ce que tu te rends compte de ton erreur?
se souvenir de:	je me souviens de	Je me souviens de la date du rendez-vous.
se tromper:	je me trompe	Ce n'est pas vrai. Tu te trompes.

Activité 6. Pratique. Maintenant nous allons faire quelques exercices de substitution. Répétez la première phrase. Puis, faites de nouvelles phrases en utilisant les sujets et les verbes suggérés.

Commençons.

Bernard se souvient de ce restaurant.

nous	Nous nous souvenons de ce restaurant.
vos cousins	Vos cousins se souviennent de ce restaurant.
je	Je me souviens de ce restaurant.

Nous **nous dépêchons.**

s'énerver	Nous nous énervons.
se mettre en colère	Nous nous mettons en colère.
s'impatienter	Nous nous impatientons.
s'amuser	Nous nous amusons.

Activité 7. Compréhension orale. You will hear a series of sentences. Some are logical; others are not. Listen carefully to each sentence. If it is logical, mark the first row **logique** in your lab manual. If it is not logical, mark the second row **illogique.**

Commençons.

1. Je suis poli. Je m'excuse toujours quand j'ai tort.
2. Nous venons de courir. Maintenant nous nous arrêtons parce que nous sommes fatigués.
3. J'ai oublié le nom de votre ami. Je ne me souviens pas comment il s'appelle.
4. Alice ne peut pas sortir avec nous ce soir. Elle doit s'occuper de son petit frère.
5. Je me dépêche parce que j'ai une classe dans vingt minutes.
6. Thomas est un garçon heureux. Il ne s'amuse jamais.

7. Nathalie est une fille très calme. Elle ne se met jamais en colère.
8. Je déteste attendre. Je ne m'impatiente jamais.

Vérifiez vos réponses. You should have marked **illogique** for sentences 6 and 8 only. If you got any wrong, listen once more to this activity, and do these questions again.

B. L'impératif des verbes pronominaux

Activité 8. Situation: S'il te plaît! Tell your friend Jean-Pierre to do certain things. Use the verbs you hear in affirmative commands. *Écoutez le modèle.*

Modèle: se préparer pour le concert — Prépare-toi pour le concert!

Commençons.

se raser — Rase-toi!
se dépêcher — Dépêche-toi!
s'amuser — Amuse-toi!
se reposer — Repose-toi!

Now tell your friend not to do the following things. *Écoutez le modèle.*

Modèle: s'impatienter — Ne t'impatiente pas!

Commençons.

se mettre en colère — Ne te mets pas en colère!
se disputer avec ses amis — Ne te dispute pas avec tes amis!
se disputer avec ses parents — Ne te dispute pas avec tes parents!
s'énerver — Ne t'énerve pas!

Activité 9. Situation: Bons conseils. Tell your friends to do what they are not presently doing. *Écoutez le modèle.*

Modèle: Vos amis ne se dépêchent pas. — Dépêchez-vous!

Commençons.

Vos amis ne se reposent pas. — Reposez-vous!
Vos amis ne se lèvent pas. — Levez-vous!
Vos amis ne s'amusent pas. — Amusez-vous!

Now tell your friends not to do what they are presently doing. *Écoutez le modèle.*

Modèle: Vos amis se disputent. — Ne vous disputez pas!

Commençons.

Vos amis s'énervent. — Ne vous énervez pas!
Vos amis se mettent en colère. — Ne vous mettez pas en colère.
Vos amis s'impatientent. — Ne vous impatientez pas!

C. Les verbes pronominaux: sens réciproque

Activité 10. Prononciation. Ouvrez votre livre à la page 373. Écoutez les situations et répétez les verbes réciproques.

Charles aime Monique. Monique aime Charles. — Ils s'aiment.
Robert rencontre Anne. Anne rencontre Robert. — Ils se rencontrent.
Je téléphonais à mes amis. Mes amis me téléphonaient. — Nous nous téléphonions.

D. Le passé composé des verbes pronominaux

Activité 11. Prononciation. Ouvrez votre livre à la page 374. Le passé composé des verbes pronominaux est formé avec le verbe **être.** Répétez les formes du passé composé du verbe **s'amuser.**

je me suis amusé(e)
tu t'es amusé(e)
il s'est amusé
nous nous sommes amusé(e)s
vous vous êtes amusé(e)(s)
elles se sont amusées

Maintenant répétez les formes négatives.

je ne me suis pas amusé(e)
tu ne t'es pas amusé(e)
il ne s'est pas amusé
nous ne nous sommes pas amusé(e)s
vous ne vous êtes pas amusé(e)(s)
elles ne se sont pas amusées

Activité 12. Identification de structures. You will hear a series of sentences. In some sentences, the action is taking place in the present; in others, the action occurred in the past. Listen carefully to the verb in each sentence. If the verb is in the present tense, mark the first row, **présent,** in your lab manual. If the verb is in the passé composé, mark the second row, **passé.**

Commençons.

1. Ils se sont disputés.
2. Le professeur s'est énervé.
3. Je m'achète un livre.
4. Nous nous préparons pour l'examen.
5. Vous vous êtes promenés en ville.
6. Je me promène avec un ami.
7. Jacqueline ne s'amuse pas.
8. Est-ce que tes parents se sont impatientés?
9. Tu ne t'es pas assez reposé.
10. Henri se repose dans sa chambre.

Maintenant vérifiez vos réponses. You should have marked **passé** for sentences 1, 2, 5, 8, and 9 only. If you made any mistakes, you may want to listen once more to these sentences, and do these questions again.

Activité 13. Narration: Hier. You will hear what certain people are doing. Say that they also did these things yesterday. *Écoutez le modèle.*

Modèle: Nathalie se repose. — Hier aussi, elle s'est reposée.

Commençons.

Nous nous disputons. — Hier aussi, nous nous sommes disputé(e)s.
Vous vous couchez tard. — Hier aussi, vous vous êtes couché(e)(s) tard.
Tu t'achètes une glace. — Hier aussi, tu t'es acheté une glace.
Mes parents se lèvent tôt. — Hier aussi, mes parents se sont levés tôt.
Philippe se promène. — Hier aussi, il s'est promené.

Now you will hear what people are not doing. Say that they didn't do these things yesterday either. *Écoutez le modèle.*

Modèle: Marie ne s'amuse pas. — Hier non plus, elle ne s'est pas amusée.

Commençons.

Vous ne vous réveillez pas tôt. — Hier non plus, vous ne vous êtes pas réveillé(e)(s) tôt.
Laurent ne se mets pas en colère. — Hier non plus, Laurent ne s'est pas mis en colère.
Nous ne nous couchons pas avant minuit. — Hier non plus, nous ne nous sommes pas couché(e)s avant minuit.

Activité 14. Conversation: Samedi dernier. Élisabeth is asking whether you did certain things last Saturday. Answer her in the affirmative. *Écoutez le modèle.*

Modèle: Est-ce que tu t'es levé(e) tôt? — Oui, je me suis levé(e) tôt.

Commençons.

Est-ce que tu t'es promené(e)? — Oui, je me suis promené(e).
Est-ce que tu t'es amusé(e)? — Oui, je me suis amusé(e).
Est-ce que tu t'es couché(e) tard? — Oui, je me suis couché(e) tard.

Now answer in the negative. *Écoutez le modèle.*

Modèle:
Est-ce que tu t'es reposé(e)? — Non, je ne me suis pas reposé(e).

Commençons.

Est-ce que tu t'es impatienté(e)? — Non, je ne me suis pas impatienté(e).
Est-ce que tu t'es disputé(e) avec tes amis? — Non, je ne me suis pas disputé(e) avec mes amis.
Est-ce que tu t'es couché(e) tôt? — Non, je ne me suis pas couché(e) tôt.

DIALOGUE

Activité 15. Le week-end dernier. Sylvie va vous poser certaines questions sur votre week-end. Répondez-lui en utilisant les informations de votre manuel de laboratoire. *Écoutez le modèle.*

Modèle: À quelle heure est-ce que tu t'es levé(e)? — Je me suis levé(e) à dix heures.

Commençons.

1. À qui as-tu téléphoné? J'ai téléphoné à un copain.
2. À quelle heure est-ce que vous vous êtes rencontrés? Nous nous sommes rencontrés à deux heures.
3. Qu'est-ce que vous avez fait? Nous avons fait une promenade en ville.
4. Où est-ce que vous vous êtes arrêtés? Nous nous sommes arrêtés dans un café.
5. Où est-ce que vous vous êtes assis? Nous nous sommes assis à la terrasse.
6. Qu'est-ce que vous avez commandé? Nous avons commandé des glaces.
7. Où est-ce que vous êtes allés ensuite? Nous sommes allés au cinéma.
8. Qu'est-ce que vous avez vu? Nous avons vu un film d'Hitchcock.
9. À quelle heure es-tu rentré chez toi? Je suis rentré chez moi à sept heures.

DICTÉE

Activité 16. Guy et Suzanne. Vous allez entendre un court paragraphe. Écoutez d'abord! N'écrivez pas!

Aujourd'hui, Guy s'est levé tôt. Il s'est rasé et il s'est habillé. Après il a téléphoné à Suzanne. Ils se sont donné rendez-vous au café de l'université pour trois heures. Guy est arrivé un peu en retard, mais Suzanne ne s'est pas impatientée. Guy et Suzanne se sont promenés jusqu'à sept heures. Est-ce qu'ils s'aiment? C'est possible.

Maintenant écrivez les phrases dans votre manuel de laboratoire.

Aujourd'hui, / Guy s'est levé tôt. / Il s'est rasé / et il s'est habillé. / Après il a téléphoné / à Suzanne. / Ils se sont donné rendez-vous / au café de l'université / pour trois heures. / Guy est arrivé / un peu en retard, / mais Suzanne ne s'est pas impatientée. / Guy et Suzanne se sont promenés / jusqu'à sept heures. / Est-ce qu'ils s'aiment? / C'est possible. /

Écoutez encore une fois et vérifiez ce que vous avez écrit.

(Text is reread without pauses.)

LECTURE CULTURELLE

Activité 17. Lecture. Ouvrez votre livre à la page 367. Écoutez.

(See textbook page 367.)

Activité 18. Compréhension du texte. Vous allez entendre des phrases concernant le texte que vous avez écouté. Indiquez dans votre manuel de laboratoire si ces phrases sont vraies ou fausses.

Commençons.

1. Autrefois, les filles et les garçons allaient à des écoles différentes.
2. À l'université, les filles et les garçons avaient des classes séparées.
3. Aujourd'hui, la majorité des lycées sont mixtes.
4. Aujourd'hui, les jeunes ont beaucoup plus d'occasions de se rencontrer qu'autrefois.
5. Une «boum» est une fête où l'on invite ses copains et ses copines.
6. Les boums ont généralement lieu dans des clubs privés.
7. Une fête est une réunion où il n'y a pas de buffet.
8. En général, on s'habille bien pour aller à une soirée.

Maintenant vérifiez vos réponses. Les phrases suivantes sont vraies: 1, 3, 4, 5 et 8. Les phrases suivantes sont fausses: 2, 6 et 7.

Fin de la Leçon 24.
End of Lesson 24.
(music)

VIVRE EN FRANCE 8. LE SPORT ET LA SANTÉ

Activité 1. La bonne réponse. Vous allez entendre une série de questions. Pour chaque question, indiquez dans votre manuel de laboratoire quelle est la réponse logique. Pour cela, faites un cercle autour de la lettre qui correspond à cette réponse.

Commençons.

1. Qu'est-ce que tu as fait à la piscine? Tu t'es baigné?
2. Où est-ce que tu t'entraînes?
3. Vous avez été à la campagne ce week-end?
4. Quel sport pratiquais-tu quand tu étais à l'université?
5. Tu veux faire de la plongée sous-marine avec nous?
6. Tu es malade?
7. Tu as mal à l'estomac?
8. Comment est-ce que tu t'es fait mal au genou?
9. Qu'est-ce que tu fais pour rester en bonne santé?
10. Tu es fatigué! Qu'est-ce que tu as fait?
11. Tu as fait beaucoup de ski pendant les vacances d'hiver?
12. Où est-ce que tu t'es fait mal?

Maintenant écoutez les questions et les réponses correspondantes.

1. Qu'est-ce que tu as fait à la piscine? Tu t'es baigné?
   Non, mais j'ai pris un bon bain de soleil.
2. Où est-ce que tu t'entraînes?
   Je vais tous les soirs au Stade Municipal.
3. Vous avez été à la campagne ce week-end?
   Oui, et nous avons fait plusieurs longues randonnées à pied.
4. Quel sport pratiquais-tu quand tu étais à l'université?
   Je faisais de l'aviron.
5. Tu veux faire de la plongée sous-marine avec nous?
   Écoute, j'aimerais bien ... mais je ne sais pas nager!
6. Tu es malade?
   Oui, je crois que j'ai la grippe.
7. Tu as mal à l'estomac?
   Oui, je crois que j'ai trop mangé.
8. Comment est-ce que tu t'es fait mal au genou?
   Je suis tombé de vélo.
9. Qu'est-ce que tu fais pour rester en bonne santé?
   Je mange modérément et je fais du jogging tous les jours.
10. Tu es fatigué! Qu'est-ce que tu as fait?
    J'ai couru pendant 15 kilomètres.
11. Tu as fait beaucoup de ski pendant les vacances d'hiver?
    Hélas, non! Je me suis cassé la jambe le jour de mon arrivée.
12. Où est-ce que tu t'es fait mal?
    Je me suis foulé le poignet.

Activité 2. En France. Vous allez entendre une conversation qui a lieu dans un club de sport. Dans ce dialogue, un employé du club pose certaines questions à une personne qui désire devenir membre du club. Écoutez attentivement cette conversation. Même si vous ne comprenez pas tous les mots du dialogue, vous pouvez comprendre les éléments essentiels. Sur la base de ces éléments, complétez le questionnaire qui se trouve dans votre manuel de laboratoire. Vous allez entendre deux fois la conversation. D'abord écoutez.

Commençons.

—Bonjour, Mademoiselle. Qu'est-ce que je peux faire pour vous?
—Bonjour, Monsieur. J'ai lu votre annonce dans *la Nouvelle République* et j'aimerais m'inscrire à votre club de sport.
—C'est très facile, mais d'abord si vous le voulez bien, je vais vous poser quelques questions sur vos aptitudes sportives. Ce questionnaire nous permet de mieux servir notre clientèle.
—Bon, d'accord!
—Bien, dites-moi donc quels sont les sports que vous pratiquez?
—Eh bien, je fais du jogging.
—Vous en faites régulièrement?
—Oui! J'en fais tous les jours. Je cours 8 à 10 kilomètres par jour.
—Est-ce que vous faites de la natation?
—Non, je ne nage pas très souvent. Il n'y a pas de piscine dans le quartier où j'habite.
—Est-ce que vous jouez au tennis?
—Oui, un peu, surtout en été. Je ne suis pas une championne!
—Est-ce que vous jouez au basket ou au volley?
—Non, je ne fais pas de sport d'équipe.
—Bon. . . . Est-ce qu'il y a d'autres sports que vous pratiquez?
—Ah oui, j'oubliais. Je fais du judo!
—Quel est votre niveau?
—Eh bien, je suis ceinture noire.
—Très bien. Parlons un peu de votre santé. Comment vous sentez-vous?
—Je suis en excellente forme.
—Est-ce que vous avez eu des accidents?
—Attendez, oui. . . . Je me suis cassé la jambe quand j'étais jeune. Je faisais de l'équitation, et hop, je suis tombée de cheval.
—Bon. . . . Je pense que vous allez trouver notre club à votre goût. Au fait, j'ai oublié de vous demander votre nom.
—Je m'appelle Sylvie Lambert.
—Eh bien, soyez la bienvenue au Club du gymnaute.

Écoutez à nouveau et écrivez.

Fin de Vivre en France 8.
End of Vivre en France 8.
(music)

UNITÉ 9: PERSPECTIVES D'AVENIR

LEÇON 25. À QUAND LE MARIAGE?

PRÉSENTATION

Activité 1. Lecture. Ouvrez votre livre à la page 384. Écoutez.

(See textbook page 384.)

Activité 2. Compréhension du texte. Vous allez entendre des phrases concernant le texte que vous avez écouté. Indiquez dans votre manuel de laboratoire si ces phrases sont vraies ou fausses.

Commençons.

1. Xavier et sa copine sont étudiants.
2. Ils ne veulent pas se marier.
3. Corinne est fiancée.
4. Elle ne veut pas avoir d'enfants.
5. Delphine sort avec beaucoup de garçons.
6. Le copain de Delphine veut se marier.
7. Alain pense que le mariage n'est pas nécessaire.
8. Jean-Pierre a une copine avec qui il va se marier.

Maintenant vérifiez vos réponses. Les phrases suivantes sont vraies: 1, 6 et 7. Les phrases suivantes sont fausses: 2, 3, 4, 5 et 8.

PHONÉTIQUE

Activité 3. Consonnes finales. When the last syllable of a word or group of words in French ends in a consonant sound, that consonant is strongly released, that is, it is very distinctly pronounced. In English, on the other hand, final consonants are often not released or they are pronounced with very little tension. As you practice the following words, release the final consonants very clearly.

Répétez: robe douce stade actif longue gentille
grec cruel dame personne préoccupe
chère rousse nette sportive heureuse

STRUCTURE ET VOCABULAIRE

Vocabulaire: L'amitié, l'amour et le mariage

Activité 4. Prononciation. Ouvrez votre livre à la page 386. Répétez la forme **-je** des verbes et écoutez les phrases.

aimer:	j'aime	Tu m'aimes?
aimer bien:	j'aime bien	Je t'aime bien.
se fiancer avec:	je me fiance avec	Henri va se fiancer avec Louise.
épouser:	j'épouse	Jean va épouser Éliane.
se marier avec:	je me marie avec	Alice va se marier avec André.
divorcer:	je divorce	Mon oncle vient de divorcer.

Activité 5. Compréhension orale. You will hear a series of opinions about love, friendship, and marriage. Listen carefully to each opinion and decide whether or not you agree with it. If you agree with the opinion, check the first row, **d'accord,** in your lab manual. If you do not agree with it, check the second row, **pas d'accord.**

Commençons.

1. Le mariage est une institution archaïque.
2. L'amitié est plus importante que l'amour.
3. Quand un homme et une femme s'aiment, ils doivent se marier.
4. Quand on se marie, on perd son indépendance.
5. Quand on ne veut pas avoir d'enfants, il est inutile de se marier.
6. Le divorce est dangereux pour la société.

Answers will vary.

A. Adjectifs irréguliers

Activité 6. Prononciation. Ouvrez votre livre à la page 387. Répétez le masculin et le féminin des adjectifs suivants.

sérieux	sérieuse
actif	active
cruel	cruelle
bon	bonne
canadien	canadienne
cher	chère
discret	discrète
travailleur	travailleuse
créateur	créatrice

Les adjectifs masculins en **-al** ont leur pluriel en **-aux.** Répétez.

original	originaux
loyal	loyaux
libéral	libéraux

Maintenant tournez à la page 389. Répétez les adjectifs suivants.

gros	grosse
gentil	gentille
faux	fausse
roux	rousse
doux	douce
jaloux	jalouse
net	nette
sot	sotte
blanc	blanche
franc	franche
long	longue
favori	favorite
fou	folle

Activité 7. Identification de structures. You will hear a series of sentences describing different people whose names can be given to men or women. Can you tell from the form of the adjectives whether these phrases describe a man or a woman? If the adjective is masculine, mark the first row in your lab manual. If it is feminine, mark the second row.

Commençons.

1. Dominique est assez travailleur.
2. Claude est trop impulsive.
3. André n'est pas assez sérieux.
4. René est généralement attentif.
5. Dominique est un peu fou.
6. Renée est très franche.
7. Claude est assez gentille.
8. Andrée est trop conservatrice.
9. Renée est hyperactive.
10. Dominique est indiscret.

Maintenant vérifiez vos réponses. Les adjectifs suivants sont masculins: 1, 3, 4, 5 et 10. Les adjectifs suivants sont féminins: 2, 6, 7, 8 et 9.

Activité 8. Conversation: Eux aussi! Alain is describing certain people and objects. Each description is followed by a question. Answer his questions using the same adjectives. *Écoutez le modèle.*

Modèle: Alice est sérieuse. Et ses frères? — Ils sont sérieux aussi.

Commençons.

1. M. Moreau est conservateur. Et Mme Moreau? — Elle est conservatrice aussi.
2. Ces filles sont sportives. Et ces garçons? — Ils sont sportifs aussi.
3. Gisèle est originale. Et ses cousins? — Ils sont originaux aussi.
4. Ce jeune assistant est travailleur. Et la nouvelle secrétaire? — Elle est travailleuse aussi.
5. Paul est ponctuel. Et Béatrice? — Elle est ponctuelle aussi.
6. Cette jeune fille est italienne. Et ce jeune homme? — Il est italien aussi.
7. Marie est rousse. Et Jacques? — Il est roux aussi.
8. Cette robe est longue. Et ce pantalon? — Il est long aussi.
9. Le vin est frais. Et la bière? — Elle est fraîche aussi.
10. Le bureau est blanc. Et la table? — Elle est blanche aussi.

Activité 9. Situations: Est-ce que c'est vrai? You will hear descriptions of several people. After each description you will hear a second sentence. State whether this second sentence is true or not. *Écoutez les deux modèles.*

Modèles:	Henri n'aime pas travailler. Il est paresseux.	C'est vrai! Il est paresseux.
	Louis déteste jouer au tennis. Il est très sportif.	C'est faux! Il n'est pas très sportif.

Commençons.

Jacqueline regarde souvent son horoscope. Elle est superstitieuse.	C'est vrai! Elle est superstitieuse.
Catherine ne prépare pas ses examens. Elle est consciencieuse.	C'est faux! Elle n'est pas consciencieuse.
Philippe est un garçon brillant. Il est génial.	C'est vrai! Il est génial.
Thérèse dit toujours la vérité. Elle est franche.	C'est vrai! Elle est franche.
Sophie n'est jamais à l'heure. Elle est ponctuelle.	C'est faux! Elle n'est pas ponctuelle.
Sylvie est toujours contente. Elle est heureuse.	C'est vrai! Elle est heureuse.
François aide ses amis. Il est loyal.	C'est vrai! Il est loyal.
Nicole ne parle jamais de ses amies. Elle est discrète.	C'est vrai! Elle est discrète.
Marc n'a pas peur de l'examen. Il est inquiet.	C'est faux! Il n'est pas inquiet.
Ce professeur donne des examens difficiles. Il est gentil.	C'est faux! Il n'est pas gentil.

B. Les adverbes en ***-ment***

Activité 10. Conversation: Comment? Listen to the adjective used to describe each of the following people. Then answer Paul's question about how each acts or reacts by using the corresponding adverb. *Écoutez le modèle.*

Modèle: Georges est sérieux. Comment étudie-t-il?	Il étudie sérieusement.

Commençons.

Marc est consciencieux. Comment travaille-t-il?	Il travaille consciencieusement.
Philippe est énergique. Comment parle-t-il?	Il parle énergiquement.
Charles est prudent. Comment vit-il?	Il vit prudemment.
Olivier est impulsif. Comment joue-t-il au tennis?	Il joue impulsivement.
Jacques est patient. Comment répond-il?	Il répond patiemment.

C. Les nombres ordinaux

Activité 11. Pratique. You will hear a series of numbers. Give the corresponding ordinal numbers. *Écoutez le modèle.*

Modèle: cinq	cinquième

Commençons.

quatre	quatrième
onze	onzième
douze	douzième
quinze	quinzième
trois	troisième
six	sixième
un	premier
vingt et un	vingt et unième
trente-trois	trente-troisième
cinquante-sept	cinquante-septième
soixante	soixantième
cent	centième

D. La construction verbe + infinitif

Vocabulaire: Verbes suivis de l'infinitif

Activité 12. Prononciation. *Maintenant ouvrez votre livre à la page 395.* Here is a list of verbs followed by **à** or **de** plus infinitive. Listen to the verbs, and repeat the sentences.

apprendre à	Nous apprenons à jouer de la guitare.
chercher à	Je n'ai pas cherché à gagner de l'argent.
commencer à	J'ai commencé à travailler lundi.
continuer à	Continuez-vous à étudier le français?
hésiter à	N'hésitez pas à parler.
réussir à	J'ai réussi à réparer ma voiture.
s'arrêter de	Quand est-ce que tu t'arrêtes d'étudier?
cesser de	J'ai cessé de fumer.
choisir de	J'ai choisi de dire la vérité.
décider de	Nous avons décidé de faire plus de sport.
essayer de	Essayez de jouer mieux!
finir de	J'ai fini d'étudier.
oublier de	As-tu oublié de fermer la porte?
refuser de	Nous refusons de répondre à la question.
regretter de	Je ne regrette pas d'apprendre le français.
rêver de	Caroline rêve d'acheter une voiture.
se souvenir de	Est-ce que tu t'es souvenu de téléphoner à Paul?

Activité 13. Pratique. Maintenant nous allons faire quelques exercices de substitution. Répétez la première phrase. Puis faites de nouvelles phrases en utilisant les verbes suggérés.

Commençons.

J'apprends à faire du ski.

commencer	Je commence à faire du ski.
hésiter	J'hésite à faire du ski.

Tu **décides** de travailler.

cesser	Tu cesses de travailler.
essayer	Tu essaies de travailler.
finir	Tu finis de travailler.
oublier	Tu oublies de travailler.
refuser	Tu refuses de travailler.

Be sure to use **à** or **de** in your new sentence if needed.

Commençons.

Claire **va** étudier.

commencer	Claire commence à étudier.
refuser	Claire refuse d'étudier.
oublier	Claire oublie d'étudier.
hésiter	Claire hésite à étudier.
décider	Claire décide d'étudier.
essayer	Claire essaie d'étudier.

Activité 14. Réactions personnelles. Listen carefully to the following statements and determine whether or not you do the same things. If you do, mark the first row **moi aussi** in your lab manual. If you do not do the same thing, mark the second row **pas moi.**

Commençons.

1. J'apprends à jouer de la guitare.
2. Je commence à parler français assez bien.
3. J'hésite à parler français en classe.
4. J'ai cessé de fumer.
5. J'ai décidé de passer une année en France.
6. J'essaie de faire des économies.
7. Je refuse d'aider mes amis.
8. Je rêve d'être président des États-Unis.

Answers will vary.

DIALOGUE

Activité 15. Concierge. Imaginez que vous êtes concierge dans un immeuble parisien. Quelqu'un vous demande à quel étage habitent certaines personnes. Répondez en utilisant les indications de votre manuel de laboratoire. Notez que le mot **étage** signifie *floor.* Écoutez le modèle.

<u>Modèle</u>: Où habite Mlle Dupuis? — Elle habite au cinquième étage.

Commençons.

Où habite Mme Guignard?	Elle habite au 16e étage.
Où habite le docteur Charron?	Il habite au 21e étage.
Où habite M. Lévy?	Il habite au 10e étage.
Où habite Mlle Henri?	Elle habite au 2e étage.
Où habite M. Pascal?	Il habite au premier étage.
Où habite Mme Fabre?	Elle habite au 9e étage.

DICTÉE

Activité 16. Étienne et ses sœurs. Vous allez entendre un court paragraphe. Écoutez d'abord! N'écrivez pas!

Connais-tu Étienne? C'est un garçon très travailleur et très ambitieux. Ses sœurs sont assez différentes. Christine est une fille très sportive mais elle n'est pas très intellectuelle. Catherine est une fille très idéaliste et très généreuse. Voilà pourquoi elle a beaucoup d'amis loyaux.

Maintenant écrivez les phrases dans votre manuel de laboratoire.

Connais-tu Étienne? / C'est un garçon / très travailleur / et très ambitieux. / Ses sœurs / sont assez différentes. / Christine est une fille / très sportive / mais elle n'est pas / très intellectuelle. / Catherine est une fille / très idéaliste et très généreuse. / Voilà pourquoi / elle a beaucoup / d'amis loyaux. /

Écoutez encore une fois et vérifiez ce que vous avez écrit.

(Text is reread without pauses.)

LECTURE CULTURELLE

Activité 17. Lecture. Ouvrez votre livre à la page 385. Écoutez.

(See textbook page 385.)

Activité 18. Compréhension du texte. Vous allez entendre des phrases concernant le texte que vous avez écouté. Indiquez dans votre manuel de laboratoire si ces phrases sont vraies ou fausses.

Commençons.

1. Pour la majorité des Français, le mariage est une chose très sérieuse.
2. Les jeunes qui se marient ont généralement la même origine socio-économique.
3. Quand on se marie, on va d'abord à l'église. Après, on va, si on veut, à la mairie.
4. À la mairie, les jeunes mariés reçoivent un livret de famille.
5. En France, il es illégal de vivre en couple sans être marié.

Maintenant vérifiez vos réponses. Les phrases suivantes sont vraies: 1, 2 et 4. Les phrases 3 et 5 sont fausses.

Fin de la Leçon 25.
End of Lesson 25.
(music)

LEÇON 26. DANS DIX ANS

PRÉSENTATION

Activité 1. Lecture. Ouvrez votre livre à la page 398. Écoutez.

(See textbook page 398.)

Activité 2. Compréhension du texte. Vous allez entendre une série de phrases concernant le texte que vous avez entendu. Indiquez dans votre manuel de laboratoire à qui chaque phrase s'applique.

Commençons.

1. Il n'est pas satisfait du travail qu'il fait maintenant.
2. Aujourd'hui, elle est étudiante. Dans dix ans, elle sera dans la profession qu'elle prépare maintenant.
3. Elle ne sait pas quelle sera sa profession future mais elle sait qu'elle changera de profession.
4. Aujourd'hui il est assez idéaliste. Il est certainement plus idéaliste qu'il ne sera dans dix ans.
5. Elle s'occupera de personnes qui ont des problèmes de santé.
6. Il aura une existence confortable. En été, il prendra des vacances et il voyagera à l'étranger.
7. Elle aura une bonne situation mais elle n'est pas sûre d'être plus heureuse qu'aujourd'hui.
8. Il n'est pas étudiant mais il suit des cours qui lui permettront d'avoir un meilleur travail.

Maintenant vérifiez vos réponses: Michèle: phrases 2, 5 et 7. Anne-Marie: phrase 3. Jacques: phrases 1 et 8. Martin: phrases 4 et 6.

PHONÉTIQUE

Activité 3. La consonne /r/. The French letter "r" never represents the sound of the English "r." The French "r" is a soft sound pronounced at the back of the throat. To learn to pronounce the French /r/, say "ah" and clear your throat at the same time: /a/ + (forced /r/).

Répétez: a-ra a-ra a-ra

Now practice the following words and sentences using the French /r/.

Répétez: Paris Robert reçoit regrette
j'irai je ferai je saurai je voudrai je recevrai
Roger devra rester à Rome.
René arrivera à Rouen mercredi.

STRUCTURE ET VOCABULAIRE

*A. Le verbe **recevoir***

Activité 4. Prononciation. Ouvrez votre livre à la page 401. Répétez les formes du verbe **recevoir** et écoutez les phrases.

je reçois — Je reçois une lettre.
tu reçois — Tu reçois un télégramme.
on reçoit — On reçoit son diplôme.
nous recevons — Nous recevons cette revue.
vous recevez — Vous recevez un bon salaire.
elles reçoivent — Elles reçoivent de l'argent de leurs parents.
j'ai reçu — J'ai reçu une bonne note à l'examen.

Maintenant répétez les formes **je** des verbes suivants et écoutez les phrases.

décevoir:	je déçois	Ne décevez pas vos amis.
apercevoir:	j'aperçois	Avez-vous aperçu votre cousin ce matin?
s'apercevoir:	je m'aperçois	Je me suis aperçu de mon erreur.

Activité 5. Pratique. Maintenant faites un exercice de transformation. Mettez les phrases suivantes au passé composé. Écoutez le modèle.

Modèle: Je reçois mon diplôme. — J'ai reçu mon diplôme.

Commençons.

Vous recevez un bon salaire. — Vous avez reçu un bon salaire.
Tu déçois tes amis. — Tu as déçu tes amis.
Nous nous apercevons des difficultés. — Nous nous sommes aperçus des difficultés.

B. Le futur: formation régulière

Activité 6. Prononciation. Ouvrez votre livre à la page 402.

Répétez les formes du futur du verbe **habiter.**

j'habiterai
tu habiteras
il habitera
nous habiterons
vous habiterez
elles habiteront

Maintenant répétez les formes du futur du verbe **finir.**

je finirai
tu finiras
il finira
nous finirons
vous finirez
elles finiront

Maintenant répétez les formes du futur du verbe **vendre.**

je vendrai
tu vendras
il vendra
nous vendrons
vous vendrez
elles vendront

Activité 7. Pratique. Nous allons faire quelques exercices de substitution. Répétez la première phrase. Puis faites de nouvelles phrases en utilisant les sujets suggérés.

Commençons.

Je dînerai à huit heures.
nous — Nous dînerons à huit heures.
tu — Tu dîneras à huit heures.
vous — Vous dînerez à huit heures.

Je réussirai à mon examen.
Jean — Jean réussira à son examen.
nous — Nous réussirons à notre examen.
les étudiants — Les étudiants réussiront à leur examen.

Je ne répondrai jamais à cette lettre.
mon oncle — Mon oncle ne répondra jamais à cette lettre.
vous — Vous ne répondrez jamais à cette lettre.
mes cousins — Mes cousins ne répondront jamais à cette lettre.

Activité 8. Conversation: Les vacances. Stéphanie is asking about your summer plans. Answer her questions in the affirmative. *Écoutez le modèle.*

Modèle: Est-ce que tu vas travailler? — Oui, je travaillerai.

Commençons.

Est-ce que tu vas jouer au tennis? — Oui, je jouerai au tennis.
Est-ce que tu vas sortir souvent? — Oui, je sortirai souvent.
Est-ce que tu vas prendre des photos? — Oui, je prendrai des photos.
Est-ce que tu vas te reposer? — Oui, je me reposerai.

Now say that you will not do the following activities. *Écoutez le modèle.*

Modèle: Est-ce que tu vas écrire un roman? — Non, je n'écrirai pas de roman.

Commençons.

Est-ce que tu vas voyager? — Non, je ne voyagerai pas.
Est-ce que tu vas partir en vacances? — Non, je ne partirai pas en vacances.
Est-ce que tu vas grossir? — Non, je ne grossirai pas.
Est-ce que tu vas rendre visite à mes cousins? — Non, je ne rendrai pas visite à tes cousins.
Est-ce que tu vas te lever tôt? — Non, je ne me lèverai pas tôt.

C. *Futurs irréguliers*

Activité 9. Prononciation. Ouvrez votre livre à la page 406. Répétez la forme **-je** des verbes suivants. Puis répétez les phrases.

être:	je serai	Nous serons à l'heure.
avoir:	j'aurai	Éric aura vingt ans en juin.
aller:	j'irai	J'irai au Sénégal l'été prochain.
faire:	je ferai	Est-ce qu'il fera beau ce week-end?
courir:	je courrai	Est-ce que tu courras dans le marathon?
devoir:	je devrai	Tu devras prendre des photos.
envoyer:	j'enverrai	Est-ce que tu m'enverras des cartes postales?
obtenir:	j'obtiendrai	Anne obtiendra son passeport demain.
pouvoir:	je pourrai	Vous pourrez visiter le Louvre.
recevoir:	je recevrai	Nous recevrons notre diplôme en juin.
savoir:	je saurai	Je ne saurai jamais bien jouer au tennis.
venir:	je viendrai	Viendrez-vous avec nous?
voir:	je verrai	Nous verrons mes amies.
vouloir:	je voudrai	Mes cousins ne voudront pas venir avec nous.

Maintenant répétez le futur des expressions suivantes. *Écoutez les phrases.*

il y a	il y aura	Il y aura un concert dimanche.
il faut	il faudra	Il faudra acheter des billets.
il pleut	il pleuvra	J'espère qu'il ne pleuvra pas.

Activité 10. Conversation: Le week-end. Robert is asking you about your weekend plans. Answer him in the affirmative, using the future tense. *Écoutez le modèle.*

Modèle: Est-ce que tu vas aller à la piscine? — Oui, j'irai à la piscine.

Commençons.

Est-ce que tu vas faire du jogging?	Oui, je ferai du jogging.
Est-ce que tu vas pouvoir sortir?	Oui, je pourrai sortir.
Est-ce que tu vas venir à notre fête?	Oui, je viendrai à votre fête.
Est-ce que tu vas obtenir la voiture de ton père?	Oui, j'obtiendrai la voiture de mon père.

Now say that you will *not* do the following things. *Écoutez le modèle.*

Modèle: Est-ce que tu vas aller à la bibliothèque? — Non, je n'irai pas à la bibliothèque.

Commençons.

Est-ce que tu vas être en classe?	Non, je ne serai pas en classe.
Est-ce que tu vas avoir des devoirs?	Non, je n'aurai pas de devoirs.
Est-ce que tu vas aller en ville?	Non, je n'irai pas en ville.
Est-ce que tu vas faire du camping?	Non, je ne ferai pas de camping.
Est-ce que tu vas voir tes cousins?	Non, je ne verrai pas mes cousins.
Est-ce que tu vas devoir étudier?	Non, je ne devrai pas étudier.
Est-ce que tu vas vouloir te lever à six heures?	Non, je ne voudrai pas me lever à six heures.

Activité 11. Narration: Demain. Listen to what the following people are not doing today. Say that they will do these things tomorrow. *Écoutez le modèle.*

Modèle: Jean-Paul ne fait pas les courses. Il fera les courses demain.

Commençons.

Monique ne fait pas ses devoirs. Elle fera ses devoirs demain.
Michèle n'a pas de travail. Elle aura du travail demain.
Paul n'est pas à la plage. Il sera à la plage demain.
Marc et Anne ne peuvent pas venir. Ils pourront venir demain.
Stéphanie et Alice ne voient pas Robert. Elles verront Robert demain.
Tu ne vas pas à la bibliothèque. Tu iras à la bibliothèque demain.
Vous ne savez pas la leçon. Vous saurez la leçon demain.
Claire ne vient pas. Elle viendra demain.
Nous ne voulons pas sortir. Nous voudrons sortir demain.
Tu ne veux pas courir. Tu courras demain.
Je ne veux pas envoyer cette lettre. J'enverrai cette lettre demain.

Vocabulaire: Quelques professions

Activité 12. Prononciation. Ouvrez votre livre à la page 408. Répétez les noms des professions.

un architecte une architecte
un avocat une avocate
un employé une employée
un fonctionnaire une fonctionnaire
un homme d'affaires une femme d'affaires
un infirmier une infirmière
un informaticien une informaticienne
un journaliste une journaliste
un ouvrier une ouvrière
un patron une patronne
un secrétaire une secrétaire
un vendeur une vendeuse
un cadre
un écrivain
un ingénieur
un médecin

Activité 13. Compréhension orale. You will hear a series of statements describing what different people will be doing. Look at the two professions suggested in your lab manual and circle the appropriate future profession. *Écoutez le modèle.*

Modèle: Catherine travaillera à l'hôpital Pasteur. You should have marked **infirmière.**

Commençons.

1. Pierre s'occupera des personnes malades.
2. Philippe travaillera dans une usine d'automobiles.
3. Marie-Thérèse étudie la chimie et la physique.
4. Antoine travaillera dans un magasin de vêtements.
5. Hélène écrira de nombreux articles pour un magazine français.
6. Albert espère qu'il aura un patron sympathique.
7. Henriette aura des responsabilités importantes dans l'usine où elle travaillera.
8. Thomas écrira des romans.

Maintenant vérifiez vos réponses. After each person's name is stated, say what you have decided his or her profession will be. *Écoutez le modèle.*

Modèle: Catherine — Elle sera infirmière.

Commençons.

Pierre	Il sera médecin.
Philippe	Il sera ouvrier.
Marie-Thérèse	Elle sera ingénieur.
Antoine	Il sera vendeur.
Hélène	Elle sera journaliste.
Albert	Il sera employé.
Henriette	Elle sera cadre.
Thomas	Il sera écrivain.

If you made any mistakes, listen once more to these sentences and do these questions again.

D. La construction ***si*** *+ présent*

Activité 14. Narration: À Paris. You will hear what several people want to do when they are in Paris. Say that if they go to Paris they will do these things. *Écoutez le modèle.*

Modèle: Paul veut visiter le Louvre. — Si Paul va à Paris, il visitera le Louvre.

Commençons.

Je veux voir Notre Dame.	Si je vais à Paris, je verrai Notre Dame.
Tu veux monter à la Tour Eiffel.	Si tu vas à Paris, tu monteras à la Tour Eiffel.
Nous voulons aller à l'Opéra.	Si nous allons à Paris, nous irons à l'Opéra.
Pierre et Nathalie veulent prendre des photos.	Si Pierre et Nathalie vont à Paris, ils prendront des photos.
Vous voulez suivre des cours à la Sorbonne.	Si vous allez à Paris, vous suivrez des cours à la Sorbonne.

E. L'usage des temps après ***quand***

Activité 15. Narration: Quand? Say what things must happen before the following people go to Paris. *Écoutez le modèle.*

Modèle: Marie doit avoir son passeport. — Quand Marie aura son passeport, elle ira à Paris.

Commençons.

Pierre doit avoir son diplôme. — Quand Pierre aura son diplôme, il ira à Paris.
Nathalie doit avoir de l'argent. — Quand Nathalie aura de l'argent, elle ira à Paris.
Catherine doit gagner mille dollars. — Quand Catherine gagnera mille dollars, elle ira à Paris.
Philippe doit faire des économies. — Quand Philippe fera des économies, il ira à Paris.

DIALOGUE

Activité 16. D'accord! Anne-Marie va vous demander de faire certaines choses. Exprimez votre accord et dites quand vous ferez ces choses. Utilisez les informations de votre manuel de laboratoire. Écoutez le modèle.

Modèle: Va à la poste! — D'accord, j'irai à la poste à deux heures.

Commençons.

1. Téléphone à Jean-Claude! — D'accord, je téléphonerai à Jean-Claude avant le dîner.
2. Achète le journal! — D'accord, j'acheterai le journal après la classe.
3. Finis ce livre! — D'accord, je finirai ce livre avant le week-end.
4. Sois à l'heure! — D'accord, je serai à l'heure pour le rendez-vous.
5. Aie tes notes! — D'accord, j'aurai mes notes pour la classe d'histoire.
6. Viens chez moi! — D'accord, je viendrai chez toi demain.
7. Va au cinéma! — D'accord, j'irai au cinéma dimanche soir.
8. Envoie cette lettre! — D'accord, j'enverrai cette lettre avant jeudi.

DICTÉE

Activité 17. Voyage en Italie. Vous allez entendre un court paragraphe. Écoutez d'abord! N'écrivez pas!

Si j'ai de l'argent cet été, je ferai un voyage en Italie avec mon ami Charles. Nous irons d'abord à Rome. Quand nous serons là-bas, nous verrons mes cousins. J'espère qu'ils pourront nous trouver un hôtel bon marché. Je leur enverrai un télégramme quand je saurai la date de notre départ.

Maintenant écrivez les phrases dans votre manuel de laboratoire.

Si j'ai de l'argent / cet été, / je ferai un voyage en Italie / avec mon ami Charles. / Nous irons / d'abord à Rome. / Quand nous serons là-bas, / nous verrons / mes cousins. / J'espère / qu'ils pourront nous trouver / un hôtel bon marché. / Je leur enverrai un télégramme / quand je saurai / la date / de notre départ. /

Écoutez les phrases encore une fois et vérifiez ce que vous avez écrit.

(Text is reread without pauses.)

LECTURE CULTURELLE

Activité 18. Lecture. Ouvrez votre livre à la page 399. Écoutez.

(See textbook page 399.)

Activité 19. Compréhension du texte. Vous allez entendre des phrases concernant le texte que vous avez écouté. Indiquez dans votre manuel de laboratoire si ces phrases sont vraies ou fausses.

Commençons.

1. Aujourd'hui, la société française est plus stable qu'autrefois.
2. Autrefois, les gens voyageaient rarement.
3. Autrefois, les enfants avaient souvent la même profession que leurs parents.
4. Aujourd'hui, les Français changent plus souvent de résidence qu'autrefois.
5. Aujourd'hui, les Français changent de profession plus souvent que les Américains.
6. Aujourd'hui, il est très difficile de prédire son avenir professionnel.

Maintenant vérifiez vos réponses. Les phrases suivantes sont vraies: 2, 3 et 4. Les phrases suivantes sont fausses: 1, 5 et 6.

Fin de la Leçon 26.
End of Lesson 26.
(music)

LEÇON 27. SI VOUS AVIEZ PLUS D'ARGENT. . . ?

PRÉSENTATION

Activité 1. Lecture. Ouvrez votre livre à la page 414. Écoutez.

(See textbook page 414.)

Activité 2. Compréhension du texte. Vous allez entendre plusieurs phrases concernant le texte que vous avez entendu. Indiquez dans votre manuel de laboratoire à quelles personnes ces phrases s'appliquent.

Commençons.

1. Elle s'est mariée il n'y a pas très longtemps.
2. Il aime les pays exotiques.
3. S'il avait plus d'argent, il cesserait de travailler.
4. Elle est mariée et elle a une vie confortable.
5. Il aime passer les week-ends à la campagne.
6. Selon cette personne, l'argent ne rend pas nécessairement les gens heureux.
7. Cette personne ne sait pas comment elle dépenserait son argent.
8. Cette personne resterait dans son appartement qu'elle rendrait plus confortable.

Maintenant vérifiez vos réponses. Paul: phrase 5. Jacqueline: phrases 1 et 8. Robert: phrases 2 et 3. Marie-France: phrases 4, 6 et 7.

PHONÉTIQUE

Activité 3. Intonation à l'intérieur de la phrase. Within a longer declarative French sentence, the voice rises at the end of each group of words. In English, on the contrary, the voice drops at the end of each group of words.

Comparez: Si j'avais le temps, j'apprendrais le chinois.

If I had the time, I would learn Chinese.

Répétez: Si je pouvais conduire, je louerais une voiture.
Si tu partais plus tôt, tu serais à l'heure.
Si nous avions de l'argent, nous irions en France.

STRUCTURE ET VOCABULAIRE

Vocabulaire: Projets de vacances

Activité 4. Prononciation. Ouvrez votre livre à la page 416. Répétez les noms suivants.

un départ
le commencement
le hasard
l'avenir
un jour de congé

une arrivée
la fin
une occasion
la chance
une fête

Maintenant répétez les verbes et les expressions suivantes et écoutez les phrases.

avoir l'occasion — As-tu eu l'occasion de voir ce film sur Tahiti?
durer — Les grandes vacances durent trois mois.
réaliser — Je voulais aller au Japon cet été, mais je n'ai pas réalisé ce projet.

chacun — Est-ce que chacun a acheté son billet d'avion?
ailleurs — L'année dernière, je suis allé au Canada. Cette année je vais aller ailleurs.
vers — Il est allé vers la plage.
Il rentrera vers midi.
à cause de — J'ai étudié à cause de l'examen.
cependant — J'ai raté mon examen.
Cependant j'avais beaucoup travaillé.
pourtant — Anne réussit toujours à ses examens. Pourtant elle ne travaille pas beaucoup.

A. Le conditionnel: formation

Activité 5. Prononciation. Ouvrez votre livre à la page 418. Répétez les formes du conditionnel du verbe **habiter** dans l'expression **habiter en France.**

J'habiterais en France.
Tu habiterais en France.
Il habiterait en France.

Nous habiterions en France.
Vous habiteriez en France.
Ils habiteraient en France.

Activité 6. Pratique. Maintenant nous allons faire quelques exercices de substitution. Répétez la première phrase. Puis faites de nouvelles phrases en utilisant les sujets suggérés.

Commençons.

Henri achèterait une voiture.

nous	Nous achèterions une voiture.
vous	Vous achèteriez une voiture.
mes amis	Mes amis achèteraient une voiture.

Bernard ne fumerait plus.

je	Je ne fumerais plus.
nous	Nous ne fumerions plus.
tu	Tu ne fumerais plus.
vous	Vous ne fumeriez plus.

Où irais-**tu**?

vous	Où iriez-vous?
on	Où irait-on?
nous	Où irions-nous?

Activité 7. Identification de structures. You will hear a series of sentences. Is the speaker stating a definite plan, or is he merely talking about a hypothetical project? Listen carefully to the tense of the verb. If the verb is in the future tense, the plan is definite. Mark the first row **certitude** in your lab manual. If the verb is in the conditional, the project is hypothetical. Mark the second row **hypothèse.**

Commençons.

1. Paul voyagera.
2. Marie-Luce visiterait la Grèce.
3. Nous achèterions une voiture.
4. Tu irais au Portugal.
5. Michèle verra ses amis.
6. Vous habiteriez à Paris.
7. Jacques pourra voyager.
8. Mes cousins étudieront l'anglais.
9. Vous suivriez des cours.
10. Ma sœur apprendra l'anglais.
11. Nous nous marierons.
12. Ils partiraient en vacances.

Maintenant vérifiez vos réponses. You should have marked **hypothèse** for sentences 2, 3, 4, 6, 9, and 12 only. If you made any mistakes, listen once more to this activity, and do these questions again.

B. Le conditionnel: usage

Activité 8. Situation: En France. Imagine that you are planning to spend some time in France. You are going to hear a series of activities. Say that you would do these things if you were going to France. *Écoutez le modèle.*

<u>Modèle</u>: aller à Paris	Oui, j'irais à Paris.

Commençons.

aller dans une université française	Oui, j'irais dans une université française.
avoir des amis français	Oui, j'aurais des amis français.
faire du camping	Oui, je ferais du camping.
voir les musées	Oui, je verrais les musées.

Now say you would not do the following things. *Écoutez le modèle.*

Modèle: aller dans les Alpes — Non, je n'irais pas dans les Alpes.

Commençons.

aller en Provence — Non, je n'irais pas en Provence.
faire du ski — Non, je ne ferais pas de ski.
avoir une auto — Non, je n'aurais pas d'auto.
être timide — Non, je ne serais pas timide.
voir la Normandie — Non, je ne verrais pas la Normandie.

Activité 9. Narration: Avec mille dollars. You will hear what various people would like to do. Say that with one thousand dollars, they would do these things. *Écoutez le modèle.*

Modèle: Je voudrais aller en Espagne. — Avec mille dollars, j'irais en Espagne.

Commençons.

Marc voudrait venir avec moi. — Avec mille dollars, il viendrait avec moi.
Nous voudrions boire du champagne tous les jours. — Avec mille dollars, nous boirions du champagne tous les jours.
Tu voudrais visiter l'Italie. — Avec mille dollars, tu visiterais l'Italie.
Vous voudriez voyager. — Avec mille dollars, vous voyageriez.
Mes parents voudraient achèter un nouveau téléviseur. — Avec mille dollars, ils achèteraient un nouveau téléviseur.

Activité 10. Narration: Qu'est-ce qu'il a dit? You will hear Jean-Philippe make certain statements about future events. Report on what he said. *Écoutez le modèle.*

Modèle: Élisabeth écrira un roman. — Il a dit qu'Élisabeth écrirait un roman.

Commençons.

Paul et Lucie se marieront. — Il a dit que Paul et Lucie se marieraient.
Nous partirons à midi. — Il a dit que nous partirions à midi.
Vous saurez la réponse demain. — Il a dit que vous sauriez la réponse demain.
Il faudra travailler dimanche. — Il a dit qu'il faudrait travailler dimanche.

*C. Résumé: L'usage des temps après **si***

Activité 11. Narration: Si nous avions le temps. . . . You will hear what various people like to do. Say that they would do these things if they had the time. *Écoutez le modèle.*

Modèle: Tu voudrais écrire des poèmes. — Si tu avais le temps, tu écrirais des poèmes.

Commençons.

Anne voudrait apprendre l'anglais. — Si elle avait le temps, elle apprendrait l'anglais.
Nous voudrions visiter Québec. — Si nous avions le temps, nous visiterions Québec.
Vous voudriez lire le journal. — Si vous aviez le temps, vous liriez le journal.
Mes parents voudraient aller au cinéma. — S'ils avaient le temps, ils iraient au cinéma.
Je voudrais faire une promenade. — Si j'avais le temps, je ferais une promenade.

D. Le verbe ***conduire***

Activité 12. Prononciation. Ouvrez votre livre à la page 423. Le verbe **conduire** est irrégulier. Répétez les phrases suivantes.

Je conduis bien.
Tu conduis mal.
On conduit vite.

Nous conduisons une Renault.
Vous conduisez une Ferrari.
Elles conduisent une Citroën.
J'ai conduit la voiture de mon grand-père.

Un certain nombre de verbes sont conjugués comme **conduire.** Répétez la forme **je** de ces verbes, et écoutez les phrases.

construire:	je construis	Qui a construit la Tour Eiffel?
détruire:	je détruis	Un cyclone a détruit cette maison.
produire:	je produis	On produit beaucoup de vin en France.
traduire:	je traduis	Je traduirai cet article en français.
se conduire bien:	je me conduis bien	En classe, nous nous conduisons bien.
se conduire mal:	je me conduis mal	Pourquoi est-ce que Pierre se conduit mal?

DIALOGUE

Activité 13. Conditions. Robert va vous demander ce que vous feriez dans certaines conditions. Répondez-lui sur la base des illustrations de votre manuel de laboratoire. Écoutez le modèle.

Modèle: Qu'est-ce que tu achèterais si tu avais mille dollars? — J'achèterais un ordinateur.

Commençons.

1. Qu'est-ce que tu achèterais si tu gagnais à la loterie? — J'achèterais une voiture.
2. Qu'est-ce que tu boirais si tu avais soif? — Je boirais de la bière.
3. Qu'est-ce que tu commanderais si tu allais au restaurant? — Je commanderais du poulet.
4. Où irais-tu si tu étais en vacances? — J'irais à Paris.
5. Qu'est-ce que tu ferais si tu allais à la plage? — Je ferais de la planche à voile.
6. Comment voyagerais-tu si tu allais au Canada? — Je voyagerais en avion.

DICTÉE

Activité 14. Après l'université. Vous allez entendre un court paragraphe. Écoutez d'abord! N'écrivez pas!

Qu'est-ce que je ferais si je n'étais pas étudiant? Je ne resterais pas ici. Si j'avais de l'argent, je ferais un grand voyage. Je verrais de nouveaux pays. J'irais au Japon ou en Chine. Je reviendrais en France après deux ou trois ans.

Maintenant, écrivez les phrases dans votre manuel de laboratoire.

Qu'est-ce que je ferais / si je n'étais pas étudiant? / Je ne resterais pas ici. / Si j'avais de l'argent, / je ferais / un grand voyage. / Je verrais / de nouveaux pays. / J'irais au Japon / ou en Chine. / Je reviendrais en France / après deux ou trois ans. /

Écoutez les phrases encore une fois et vérifiez ce que vous avez écrit.

(Text is reread without pauses.)

LECTURE CULTURELLE

Activité 15. Lecture. Ouvrez votre livre à la page 415. Écoutez.

(See textbook page 415.)

Activité 16. Compréhension du texte. Vous allez entendre des phrases concernant le texte que vous avez écouté. Indiquez dans votre manuel de laboratoire si ces phrases sont vraies ou fausses.

Commençons.

1. En général, les Français prennent plus de vacances que les Américains.
2. Quand ils prennent des vacances, les Français ne sont pas payés.
3. Pendant les vacances, la majorité des Français ne restent pas chez eux.
4. Quand ils vont en vacances à l'étranger, les Français vont généralement dans un pays méditerranéen.
5. Les Français attachent beaucoup d'importance aux vacances.
6. Les médias donnent une place très minime aux vacances.

Maintenant vérifiez vos réponses. Les phrases suivantes sont vraies: 1, 3, 4 et 5. Les phrases suivantes sont fausses: 2 et 6.

Fin de la Leçon 27.
End of Lesson 27.

VIVRE EN FRANCE 9. EN VOYAGE

Activité 1. La bonne réponse. Vous allez entendre une série de questions. Pour chaque question, indiquez dans votre manuel de laboratoire quelle est la réponse logique. Pour cela, faites un cercle autour de la lettre qui correspond à cette réponse.

Commençons.

1. Pardon Monsieur, est-ce que ce siège est libre?
2. Pouvez-vous me dire d'où part l'avion pour Fort-de-France?
3. Il y a une escale à Genève, n'est-ce pas?
4. Pouvez-vous me dire où je peux obtenir ma carte d'embarquement?
5. Voulez-vous un aller et retour?
6. Est-ce que le train est direct?
7. Est-ce que l'avion de Londres est à l'heure?

8. Où est-ce qu'on vend les billets de train pour Marseille?
9. À quelle heure est-ce qu'il y a des trains pour Toulouse dans l'après-midi?
10. Est-ce que tu vas enregistrer tes bagages?

Maintenant écoutez les questions et les réponses correspondantes.

1. Pardon Monsieur, est-ce que ce siège est libre?
   Non, il est occupé.
2. Pouvez-vous me dire d'où part l'avion pour Fort-de-France?
   Bien sûr, allez à la porte F.
3. Il y a une escale à Genève, n'est-ce pas?
   Je ne pense pas. On m'a dit que l'avion était direct.
4. Pouvez-vous me dire où je peux obtenir ma carte d'embarquement?
   Mais oui! Allez au comptoir d'Air Maroc.
5. Voulez-vous un aller et retour?
   Non, donnez-moi un aller simple.
6. Est-ce que le train est direct?
   Non, il y a une correspondance à Saint-Pierre-des-Corps.
7. Est-ce que l'avion de Londres est à l'heure?
   Non, il a une demi-heure de retard.
8. Où est-ce qu'on vend les billets de train pour Marseille?
   Allez au guichet 2.
9. À quelle heure est-ce qu'il y a des trains pour Toulouse dans l'après-midi?
   Je ne sais pas. Vous pouvez demander au bureau de renseignements.
10. Est-ce que tu vas enregistrer tes bagages?
    Non, je vais les garder avec moi.

Activité 2. En France. Vous allez entendre une conversation qui a lieu dans une agence de voyages. Dans cette conversation, quelqu'un veut réserver un billet d'avion. Écoutez bien la conversation entre cette personne et l'employé de l'agence de voyages. Sur la base des informations que vous allez entendre, complétez la fiche de réservation qui se trouve dans votre manuel de laboratoire. D'abord, écoutez.

Commençons.

—Bonjour, Madame. Vous désirez?
—Bonjour, Monsieur. Je voudrais aller à Chicago samedi prochain.
—Voyons, samedi prochain, c'est le 2 septembre. Préférez-vous voyager dans la matinée ou dans la soirée?
—Je préfère la matinée.
—Très bien. Il y a un vol Air France qui part à 10 heures 30. Est-ce que cela vous va?
—Cela me convient très bien. C'est le vol Air France numéro 102.
—Est-ce que je prépare votre billet?
—Oui, s'il vous plaît.
—Je vais vous demander votre nom.
—Je m'appelle Janine Thomas.
—Très bien. Ce sera un aller simple ou un aller et retour?
—Un aller et retour.
—Bon, vous partez le 2 septembre, et quand est-ce que vous allez rentrer?
—Je vais rentrer le 8 septembre.
—Vous voyagez en classe touriste?
—Non, non, en première classe.
—Très bien. Et comment allez-vous payer? Par chèque ou avec une carte de crédit?
—Avec une carte de crédit. La voilà.
—Merci. . . . Si vous voulez attendre un petit instant. . . . Je vais préparer votre billet et votre carte d'embarquement.

Maintenant écoutez et écrivez.

End of Vivre en France 9.
Fin de Vivre en France 9.

UNITÉ 10: NOTRE MONDE

LEÇON 28. LA RÉUSSITE

PRÉSENTATION

Activité 1. Lecture. Ouvrez votre livre à la page 432.

(See textbook page 432.)

Activité 2. Compréhension du texte. Vous allez entendre des phrases concernant le texte que vous avez écouté. Indiquez dans votre manuel de laboratoire si ces phrases sont vraies ou fausses.

Commençons.

1. Christine Thévenet est étudiante en médecine.
2. Elle n'a pas l'intention de se marier immédiatement.
3. Jean-François Fournier travaille dans une banque.
4. Il voudrait avoir un travail avec beaucoup de responsabilités.
5. Thérèse Maury ne s'intéresse pas particulièrement à la réussite matérielle.
6. Elle aimerait changer de profession.
7. Élisabeth Raynal travaille beaucoup.
8. Elle aime son travail parce qu'il lui permet d'avoir beaucoup de loisirs.
9. Antoine Verdier pense que les jeunes sont très travailleurs.

Maintenant vérifiez vos réponses. Les phrases suivantes sont vraies: 2, 3, 5 et 7. Les phrases suivantes sont fausses: 1, 4, 6, 8 et 9.

PHONÉTIQUE

Activité 3. Autres liaisons. Liaison is required after one-syllable prepositions and adverbs.

Répétez: en‿aidant en‿invitant en‿oubliant en‿Espagne
dans‿un moment dans‿une heure
sans‿étudier sans‿aimer sans‿attendre
très‿amusant très‿intéressant
plus‿actif plus‿original plus‿utile
moins‿important moins‿intelligent

Liaison is also required in certain fixed phrases.

Répétez: les‿États‿Unis de temps‿en temps
Comment‿allez-vous?

STRUCTURE ET VOCABULAIRE

Vocabulaire: Le travail et la vie économique

Activité 4. Prononciation. Ouvrez votre livre à la page 435. Répétez les noms.

un chef
un domaine
l'esprit
le sens des affaires
le travail
un travail
les affaires
une compagnie
une entreprise
une firme
la réussite

Maintenant répétez l'adjectif et les verbes. Puis répétez les phrases.

propre — J'aimerais être mon propre patron.
créer — Cette personne a créé sa propre entreprise.
entreprendre — Avez-vous le désir d'entreprendre?
établir — Cette entreprise a établi des relations commerciales avec la Chine.
réussir — Selon vous, est-il important de réussir financièrement?

A. L'infinitif

Activité 5. Conversation: Préférences. Sophie is telling you what certain people do not do. Say that you prefer to do these things. Use the infinitive of the verbs you will hear. *Écoutez le modèle.*

Modèle: Philippe ne travaille pas. — Moi, je préfère travailler.

Commençons.

Anne n'étudie pas. — Moi, je préfère étudier.
Sylvie ne voyage pas. — Moi, je préfère voyager.
Marc ne maigrit pas. — Moi, je préfère maigrir.
Robert ne va pas en classe. — Moi, je préfère aller en classe.
Michel n'est pas à l'heure. — Moi, je préfère être à l'heure.
Claire ne sort pas souvent. — Moi, je préfère sortir souvent.
Éric ne fait pas d'économies. — Moi, je préfère faire des économies.

*B. La construction adjectif/nom + **de** + infinitif*

Activité 6. Narration: Sentiments. You will hear about the feelings of different people and why they feel that way. Rephrase the sentences, using the construction adjective plus infinitive. *Écoutez le modèle.*

Modèle: Robert est heureux parce qu'il voyage. — Robert est heureux de voyager.

Commençons.

Nous sommes heureux parce que nous réussissons à l'examen. — Nous sommes heureux de réussir à l'examen.
Suzanne est triste parce qu'elle part. — Suzanne est triste de partir.
Henri est fatigué parce qu'il travaille. — Henri est fatigué de travailler.
Vous êtes fatigué parce que vous attendez. — Vous êtes fatigué d'attendre.
Charles est furieux parce qu'il perd son match. — Charles est furieux de perdre son match.

Activité 7. Conversation: La vie à l'université. Alain is asking you about life at your university. Tell him it is necessary to do the things he mentions. *Écoutez le modèle.*

Modèle: Est-ce qu'on étudie beaucoup? — Ah oui! Il est nécessaire d'étudier beaucoup.

Commençons.

Est-ce qu'on achète beaucoup de livres? — Ah oui! Il est nécessaire d'acheter beaucoup de livres.
Est-ce qu'on lit ces livres? — Ah oui! Il est nécessaire de lire ces livres.
Est-ce qu'on prend des notes? — Ah oui! Il est nécessaire de prendre des notes.
Est-ce qu'on fait des devoirs? — Ah oui! Il est nécessaire de faire des devoirs.
Est-ce qu'on prépare des examens? — Ah oui! Il est nécessaire de préparer des examens.
Est-ce qu'on s'amuse de temps en temps? — Ah oui! Il est nécessaire de s'amuser de temps en temps.

C. La construction préposition + infinitif

Activité 8. Prononciation. Ouvrez votre livre à la page 439. Répétez les prépositions et les phrases.

pour — J'apprends le français pour aller en France.
sans — Sans étudier, vous ne réussirez pas à l'examen.
avant de — Nous avons dîné avant de partir.
au lieu de — Au lieu d'étudier, Jacques est sorti.
après — Qu'est-ce que tu vas faire après avoir obtenu ton diplôme?

Activité 9. Pratique. Maintenant nous allons faire quelques exercices de substitution. Répétez la première phrase. Puis faites de nouvelles phrases en utilisant les infinitifs suggérés.

Commençons.

Nous avons déjeuné avant de **partir.**
aller en classe — Nous avons déjeuné avant d'aller en classe.
jouer au tennis — Nous avons déjeuné avant de jouer au tennis.
faire de la voile — Nous avons déjeuné avant de faire de la voile.

Vous ne pouvez pas réussir sans **étudier.**
travailler — Vous ne pouvez pas réussir sans travailler.
être ambitieux — Vous ne pouvez pas réussir sans être ambitieux.
parler anglais et français — Vous ne pouvez pas réussir sans parler anglais et français.

Jacques doit travailler au lieu de **se reposer.**
dormir — Jacques doit travailler au lieu de dormir.
lire un roman policier — Jacques doit travailler au lieu de lire un roman policier.
sortir avec ses copains — Jacques doit travailler au lieu de sortir avec ses copains.

D. Le participe présent

Activité 10. Narration: À l'université. Say what the following students do while they study. *Écoutez le modèle.*

Modèle: Monique écoute la radio. — Monique étudie en écoutant la radio.

Commençons.

Roger regarde la télé. — Roger étudie en regardant la télé.
Claire écoute ses cassettes. — Claire étudie en écoutant ses cassettes.
Charles boit du café. — Charles étudie en buvant du café.
Marie mange du chocolat. — Marie étudie en mangeant du chocolat.

Now say what the following students do to stay in shape. *Écoutez le modèle.*

Modèle: Richard nage. — Richard reste en forme en nageant.

Commençons.

Béatrice fait du jogging. — Béatrice reste en forme en faisant du jogging.
Nathalie danse. — Nathalie reste en forme en dansant.
Pierre se promène à vélo. — Pierre reste en forme en se promenant à vélo.

Now say how the following students prepare for exams. *Écoutez le modèle.*

Modèle: Robert lit ses notes. — Robert prépare ses examens en lisant ses notes.

Commençons.

Thomas regarde ses livres. — Thomas prépare ses examens en regardant ses livres.
Marc copie ses notes. — Marc prépare ses examens en copiant ses notes.
Anne-Marie dort. — Anne-Marie prépare ses examens en dormant.

DIALOGUE

Activité 11. Comment? Christine va vous demander comment vous faites certaines choses. Répondez-lui en mentionnant les activités indiquées par les illustrations dans votre manuel de laboratoire. Écoutez le modèle.

Modèle: Comment est-ce que tu te reposes? — Je me repose en lisant.

Commençons.

1. Comment est-ce que tu restes en forme? — Je reste en forme en faisant du jogging.
2. Comment est-ce que tu apprends les nouvelles? — J'apprends les nouvelles en regardant la télé.
3. Comment est-ce que tu vas gagner de l'argent cet été? — Je vais gagner de l'argent en travaillant dans un restaurant.
4. Comment est-ce que tu vas réussir à l'examen? — Je vais réussir à l'examen en étudiant.
5. Quand tu voyages pendant les vacances, comment fais-tu des économies? — Je fais des économies en faisant du camping.

DICTÉE

Activité 12. Pour apprendre l'anglais. Vous allez entendre un court paragraphe. Écoutez d'abord! N'écrivez pas!

Au lieu d'aller en vacances cet été, je vais travailler. Je veux gagner de l'argent pour passer deux mois en Angleterre. C'est en travaillant à Madrid que j'ai appris l'espagnol. C'est en allant en Angleterre que j'apprendrai l'anglais.

Maintenant écrivez les phrases dans votre manuel de laboratoire.

Au lieu d'aller / en vacances cet été, / je vais travailler. / Je veux / gagner de l'argent / pour passer / deux mois en Angleterre. / C'est en travaillant à Madrid / que j'ai appris l'espagnol. / C'est en allant en Angleterre / que j'apprendrai l'anglais. /

Écoutez les phrases encore une fois et vérifiez ce que vous avez écrit.

(Text is reread without pauses.)

LECTURE CULTURELLE

Activité 13. Lecture. Ouvrez votre livre à la page 434. Écoutez.

(See textbook page 434.)

Activité 14. Compréhension du texte. Vous allez entendre plusieurs phrases concernant le texte que vous avez écouté. Indiquez dans votre manuel de laboratoire si ces phrases sont vraies ou fausses.

Commençons.

1. Molière et Victor Hugo sont des écrivains français.
2. Les Français admirent l'esprit d'entreprise des Américains.
3. L'état joue un rôle très important dans l'économie française.
4. Beaucoup d'entreprises françaises sont nationalisées.
5. La majorité des Français travaillent pour le gouvernement.
6. Autrefois les Français avaient une attitude très positive vis-à-vis du capitalisme.
7. François Mitterand est un artiste français.
8. Aujourd'hui, beaucoup de jeunes Français ont le désir d'entreprendre.

Maintenant vérifiez vos réponses. Les phrases suivantes sont vraies: 1, 2, 3, 4 et 8. Les phrases suivantes sont fausses: 5, 6 et 7.

Fin de la Leçon 28.
End of Lesson 28.
(music)

LEÇON 29. CONVERSATION AVEC UN QUÉBÉCOIS

PRÉSENTATION

Activité 1. Lecture. Ouvrez votre livre à la page 446. Écoutez.

(See textbook page 446.)

Activité 2. Compréhension du texte. Vous allez entendre une série de phrases concernant le texte que vous avez écouté. Indiquez dans votre manuel de laboratoire si ces phrases sont vraies ou fausses.

Commençons.

1. Approximativement 30 pour cent de la population canadienne parle français.
2. L'étudiant canadien s'appelle Denis Thibodeau.
3. Il est né à Montréal.
4. Il parle français et anglais, mais il préfère parler français.
5. En 1980, le Québec est devenu indépendant.
6. Denis Thibodeau veut être ingénieur.
7. Les parents de Denis sont d'accord avec les projets professionnels de leur fils.

Maintenant vérifiez vos réponses. Les phrases suivantes sont vraies: 1, 2, 4 et 7. Les phrases suivantes sont fausses: 3, 5 et 6.

PHONÉTIQUE

Activité 3. Les lettres «in» et «im». The letters "in" and "im" represent the nasal vowel / $\tilde{\varepsilon}$ / when followed by a consonant sound.

Contrastez:	inutile	inviter
	imaginatif	impulsif
	immeuble	impatient

Répétez: imperméable impulsif indiscret infirmier inquiet
informatique ingénieur instant intéressant
Madame Imbert s'intéresse à l'informatique.

STRUCTURE ET VOCABULAIRE

Vocabulaire: Traditions

Activité 4. Prononciation. Ouvrez votre livre à la page 448. Répétez les noms.

un échange un rapport une langue une tradition

Maintenant répétez les adjectifs, les verbes et les expressions. Écoutez les phrases.

actuel — Quelle est la population actuelle du Canada?
réel — Est-ce que l'inflation est un problème réel aujourd'hui?
seul — Est-ce que le français est la seule langue officielle du Québec?
véritable — Est-ce qu'il y a une véritable solution à ce problème?

conserver — Conservez vos notes: elles peuvent être utiles plus tard.
garder — Allez-vous garder votre livre de français?
organiser — Il faut organiser des échanges entre les deux pays.
maintenir — Est-ce que les Américains maintiennent leurs traditions?

à l'heure actuelle — À l'heure actuelle, je n'ai pas de projets.
absolument — Vous devez absolument lire ce livre.
actuellement — Actuellement, mes cousins habitent à Montréal.

A. La formation du subjonctif: verbes à un radical

Activité 5. Prononciation. Ouvrez votre livre à la page 450. Répétez les formes du subjonctif des verbes **parler, finir** et **attendre.**

Il faut que je parle.
Il faut que tu parles.
Il faut qu'il parle.
Il faut que nous parlions.
Il faut que vous parliez.
Il faut qu'elles parlent.

Il faut que je finisse.
Il faut que tu finisses.
Il faut qu'elle finisse.
Il faut que nous finissions.
Il faut que vous finissiez.
Il faut qu'ils finissent.

Il faut que j'attende.
Il faut que tu attendes.
Il faut qu'on attende.
Il faut que nous attendions.
Il faut que vous attendiez.
Il faut qu'elles attendent.

Activité 6. Pratique. Maintenant nous allons faire quelques exercices de substitution. Répétez la première phrase. Puis faites de nouvelles phrases en utilisant les sujets suggérés.

Commençons.

Il faut que **mes amis** réussissent.
je — Il faut que je réussisse.
ma sœur — Il faut que ma sœur réussisse.
vous — Il faut que vous réussissiez.

Il faut que **mes parents** répondent.
tu — Il faut que tu répondes.
nous — Il faut que nous répondions.
votre amie — Il faut que votre amie réponde.

Il faut que **tu** partes.

mon père	Il faut que mon père parte.
vous	Il faut que vous partiez.
vos amis	Il faut que vos amis partent.

Activité 7. Jouons un rôle: Le contraire. Yves mentions what certain people are not doing. Marie says they should do these things. Play the role of Marie. *Écoutez le modèle.*

Modèle: Philippe ne sort pas. — Il faut qu'il sorte.

Commençons.

Jacqueline n'étudie pas.	Il faut qu'elle étudie.
Sylvie ne maigrit pas.	Il faut qu'elle maigrisse.
Paul n'attend pas.	Il faut qu'il attende.
Charles ne répond pas.	Il faut qu'il réponde.
Caroline ne dort pas.	Il faut qu'elle dorme.
Alice ne met pas ses lunettes.	Il faut qu'elle mette ses lunettes.

B. La formation du subjonctif: verbes à deux radicaux

Activité 8. Prononciation. Ouvrez votre livre à la page 452. Répétez le subjonctif du verbe **venir.**

Commençons.

Il faut que je vienne.	Il faut que nous venions.
Il faut que tu viennes.	Il faut que vous veniez.
Il faut qu'il vienne.	Il faut qu'elles viennent.

Activité 9. Conversation: Obligations scolaires. Denis will ask you if you are doing certain things. Answer that you have to do them, using the expression **il faut que** and the subjunctive. *Écoutez le modèle.*

Modèle: Est-ce que vous achetez beaucoup de livres? — Oui, il faut que j'achète beaucoup de livres.

Commençons.

Est-ce que vous prenez beaucoup de notes?	Oui, il faut que je prenne beaucoup de notes.
Est-ce que vous buvez du café quand vous étudiez?	Oui, il faut que je boive du café.
Est-ce que vous recevez de bonnes notes?	Oui, il faut que je reçoive de bonnes notes.
Est-ce que vous payez le loyer?	Oui, il faut que je paie le loyer.

C. L'usage du subjonctif après certaines expressions d'obligation et d'opinion

Activité 10. Vocabulaire: Prononciation. Ouvrez votre livre à la page 456. Répétez les expressions d'opinion suivantes.

Il est bon
Il est essentiel
Il est important
Il est indispensable
Il est inutile
Il est juste
Il est nécessaire
Il est normal
Il est possible
Il est préférable
Il est utile
Il est dommage
Il vaut mieux

*D. Le subjonctif d'**être** et d'**avoir***

Activité 11. Prononciation. Ouvrez votre livre à la page 457. Les verbes **être** et **avoir** ont un subjonctif irrégulier. Répétez les phrases suivantes.

Il faut que je sois énergique.
Il faut que tu sois patient.
Il faut qu'il soit riche.
Il faut que nous soyons ambitieux.
Il faut que vous soyez courageux.
Il faut qu'ils soient persévérants.

Il faut que j'aie de l'énergie.
Il faut que tu aies de la patience.
Il faut qu'il ait de l'argent.
Il faut que nous ayons de l'ambition.
Il faut que vous ayez du courage.
Il faut qu'ils aient de la persévérance.

Activité 12. Pratique. Maintenant nous allons faire quelques exercices de substitution. Répétez la première phrase. Puis faites de nouvelles phrases en utilisant les sujets suggérés.

Commençons.

Il est dommage que **je** sois en retard.
vous — Il est dommage que vous soyez en retard.
tu — Il est dommage que tu sois en retard.
nous — Il est dommage que nous soyons en retard.
nos cousins — Il est dommage que nos cousins soient en retard.

Il est dommage que **vous** n'ayez pas d'argent.
tu — Il est dommage que tu n'aies pas d'argent.
tes copains — Il est dommage que tes copains n'aient pas d'argent.
nous — Il est dommage que nous n'ayons pas d'argent.
je — Il est dommage que je n'aie pas d'argent.

E. L'usage du subjonctif après les verbes de volonté

Activité 13. Identification de structures. In the sentences you will hear, wishes are expressed. Can you tell whether the wish concerns the subject of the sentence or someone else? Listen carefully to the second verb in each sentence. If the verb is in the infinitive form, mark the first row **le sujet** in your lab manual. If the verb is in the subjunctive, mark the second row **une personne différente.**

Commençons.

1. Stéphanie souhaite visiter le Canada.
2. Je souhaite qu'elle prenne des photos de Québec.
3. Nous préférons que vous ne partiez pas avec lui.
4. Vous voulez venir aussi, n'est-ce pas?
5. Paul désire connaître Hélène.
6. Il veut qu'elle sorte avec lui.
7. Henri souhaite téléphoner à ses amis.
8. Il préfère que vous leur téléphoniez après dix heures.

Maintenant vérifiez vos réponses. You should have marked **le sujet** for sentences 1, 4, 5, and 7 only. If you made any mistakes, listen once more to these sentences, and do the questions again.

Activité 14. Jouons un rôle: Révolte! Nicole's mother is telling her to do certain things, but Nicole says she does not want to do them. Play the role of Nicole. *Écoutez le modèle.*

Modèle: Je veux que tu mettes la table. — Je ne veux pas mettre la table.

Commençons.

Je veux que tu apprennes tes leçons. — Je ne veux pas apprendre mes leçons.
Je veux que tu ouvres la fenêtre. — Je ne veux pas ouvrir la fenêtre.
Je veux que tu dises la vérité. — Je ne veux pas dire la vérité.
Je veux que tu sois patiente. — Je ne veux pas être patiente.
Je veux que tu aies de bonnes notes. — Je ne veux pas avoir de bonnes notes.

Activité 15. Conversation: Non! Your cousin is asking your permission to do certain things. Tell him no. *Écoutez le modèle.*

Modèle: Est-ce que je peux fumer dans ta chambre? — Non, je ne veux pas que tu fumes dans ma chambre.

Commençons.

1. Est-ce que je peux regarder tes photos? — Non, je ne veux pas que tu regardes mes photos.
2. Est-ce que je peux utiliser ton vélo? — Non, je ne veux pas que tu utilises mon vélo.
3. Est-ce que je peux prendre tes cassettes? — Non, je ne veux pas que tu prennes mes cassettes.
4. Est-ce que je peux finir la bière? — Non, je ne veux pas que tu finisses la bière.
5. Est-ce que je peux sortir avec toi? — Non, je ne veux pas que tu sortes avec moi.

DIALOGUE

Activité 16. Désolé! Daniel va vous proposer certaines choses. Excusez-vous et dites que vous avez d'autres obligations. Décrivez ces obligations en utilisant le calendrier de votre manuel de laboratoire. Écoutez le modèle.

Modèle: Est-ce que tu veux sortir avec moi jeudi? — Désolé, mais il faut que je passe à la bibliothèque.

Commençons.

1. Est-ce que je peux t'inviter au restaurant mardi? — Désolé, mais il faut que je nettoie mon appartement.
2. Est-ce que tu veux aller au cinéma dimanche? — Désolé, mais il faut que je rende visite à mes grands-parents.
3. J'ai deux billets pour le concert de vendredi. Est-ce que tu veux venir avec moi? — Désolé, mais il faut que je finisse le devoir de maths.
4. J'organise une fête lundi. Est-ce que tu veux venir chez moi? — Désolé, mais il faut que je conduise Michèle à l'aéroport.
5. Mercredi je vais faire du jogging. Est-ce que tu veux faire du jogging avec moi? — Désolé, mais il faut que je suive le cours de l'Alliance Française.

DICTÉE

Activité 17. Les courses. Vous allez entendre un court paragraphe. Écoutez d'abord! N'écrivez pas!

Je vais aller au supermarché. Il faut que j'achète de la bière. Ensuite, je veux passer à la bibliothèque. Il faut que je prenne un livre. Non, il n'est pas nécessaire que vous veniez avec moi. Mais, j'aimerais bien que vous me prêtiez votre voiture.

Maintenant, écrivez les phrases dans votre manuel de laboratoire.

Je vais aller / au supermarché. / Il faut que j'achète / de la bière. / Ensuite, / je veux passer / à la bibliothèque. / Il faut que je prenne / un livre. / Non, il n'est pas nécesaire / que vous veniez / avec moi. / Mais, j'aimerais bien / que vous me prêtiez / votre voiture. /

Écoutez le texte encore une fois et vérifiez ce que vous avez écrit.

(Text is reread without pauses.)

LECTURE CULTURELLE

Activité 18. Lecture. Ouvrez votre livre à la page 447. Écoutez.

(See textbook page 447.)

Activité 19. Compréhension du texte. Vous allez entendre des phrases concernant le texte que vous avez écouté. Indiquez dans votre manuel de laboratoire si ces phrases sont vraies ou fausses.

Commençons.

1. Québec est la deuxième ville d'expression française dans le monde.
2. Il y a douze millions de francophones au Canada.
3. Jacques Cartier est un explorateur français.
4. C'est Samuel de Champlain qui a découvert le Saint Laurent.
5. La «Nouvelle France» est l'ancien nom du Canada français.
6. Les Acadiens de la Louisiane sont d'origine canadienne.
7. Le mot «acadien» est une déformation du mot «canadien».
8. En 1980, les Québécois ont voté sur la question de l'indépendance de leur province.

Maintenant vérifiez vos réponses. Les phrases suivantes sont vraies: 3, 5, 6 et 8. Les phrases suivantes sont fausses: 1, 2, 4 et 7.

Fin de la Leçon 29.
End of Lesson 29.
(music)

LEÇON 30. FRANÇAIS OU EUROPÉENS?

PRÉSENTATION

Activité 1. Lecture. Ouvrez votre livre à la page 462. Écoutez.

(See textbook page 462.)

Activité 2. Compréhension du texte. Vous allez entendre des phrases concernant le texte que vous avez écouté. Indiquez dans votre manuel de laboratoire si ces phrases sont vraies ou fausses.

Commençons.

1. Jean-Louis Laroche croit à l'existence de l'Europe.
2. Il souhaite l'unification politique de l'Europe.
3. Brigitte Garcia est une étudiante espagnole.
4. Pour elle, les différents pays d'Europe ont une histoire commune qui les unit.
5. Pour Philippe Saint Martin, la question de nationalité n'a pas beaucoup d'importance.
6. Il n'est pas spécialement attaché à l'idée d'une Europe unie.
7. Monique Lescure fait beaucoup de voyages professionnels.
8. Elle ne croit pas à l'avenir de l'Europe.
9. Aujourd'hui, Antoine Guérin est très anti-allemand.
10. Pour lui, le danger d'une guerre entre les pays d'Europe est très réel.

Maintenant vérifiez vos réponses. Les phrases suivantes sont vraies: 1, 2, 5, 6 et 7. Les phrases suivantes sont fausses: 3, 4, 8, 9 et 10.

PHONÉTIQUE

Activité 3. Les lettres «s», «c» et «ç».

(a) *La lettre «s».* Between two vowels, the letter "s" represents the sound /z/.

Écoutez: rose musique

In other positions, the letter "s" represents the sound /s/.

Écoutez: souvent reste

Répétez: hasard entreprise réaliser chose épouser
santé esprit impossible conserver sûr
Isabelle est sûre de réussir dans son entreprise.

(b) *La lettre «c»*. Before the letters "e," "i," and "y," the letter "c" represents the sound /s/.

Écoutez: certain citoyen cyclone exercice

Before the letters "a," "o," and "u," before a consonant, and in final position, the letter represents the sound /k/.

Écoutez: cadre cœur curieux crème avec

Répétez: nécessaire médecin bicyclette douce
avocat congé chacun croire parc
Caroline et Cécile se rencontrent au cinéma.

(c) *La lettre «ç»*. The letter always represents the sound /s/. It occurs only before "a," "o," and "u."

Répétez: ça français garçon commençons reçu
François est reçu à son examen de français.

STRUCTURE ET VOCABULAIRE

Vocabulaire: La politique internationale

Activité 4. Vocabulaire: Prononciation. Ouvrez votre livre à la page 465. Répétez les noms.

un citoyen	une citoyenne
un allié	la douane
un ennemi	la frontière
un gouvernement	la guerre
un traité	la loi
	la paix

Maintenant répétez les formes **-je** des verbes et écoutez les phrases.

Commençons.

menacer:	je menace	L'inflation menace la stabilité économique.
partager:	je partage	Les gens égoïstes ne partagent rien.
protéger:	je protège	Les lois protègent les citoyens.

A. *Le verbe* ***croire***

Activité 5. Prononciation. Ouvrez votre livre à la page 466. Le verbe **croire** est irrégulier. Répétez les formes suivantes.

je crois
tu crois
il croit

nous croyons
vous croyez
elles croient

j'ai cru

Activité 6. Pratique. Maintenant nous allons faire un exercice de substitution. Répétez la première phrase. Puis faites de nouvelles phrases en utilisant les sujets suggérés. Répétez.

Marthe ne croit pas au progrès.
nous — Nous ne croyons pas au progrès.
je — Je ne crois pas au progrès.
vous — Vous ne croyez pas au progrès.
mes parents — Mes parents ne croient pas au progrès.

B. *Subjonctifs irréguliers*

Activité 7. Prononciation. Ouvrez votre livre à la page 467. Les verbes **faire, pouvoir, savoir, aller** et **vouloir** ont un subjonctif irrégulier. Répétez la forme **-je** et la forme **-nous** de ces verbes.

Il faut que je fasse
Il faut que nous fassions
Il faut que je puisse
Il faut que nous puissions
Il faut que je sache
Il faut que nous sachions
Il faut que j'aille
Il faut que nous allions
Il faut que je veuille
Il faut que nous voulions

Activité 8. Pratique. Maintenant nous allons faire quelques exercices de substitution. Répétez la phrase. Puis faites de nouvelles phrases en utilisant les sujets suggérés.

Commençons.

Maman veut que **je** fasse les courses.
nous — Maman veut que nous fassions les courses.
tu — Maman veut que tu fasses les courses.
vous — Maman veut que vous fassiez les courses.

Il est dommage que **tu** ne puisses pas venir.
nous — Il est dommage que nous ne puissions pas venir.
ton oncle — Il est dommage que ton oncle ne puisse pas venir.
vous — Il est dommage que vous ne puissiez pas venir.

Il vaut mieux que **je** sache la vérité.
Papa — Il vaut mieux que Papa sache la vérité.
tu — Il vaut mieux que tu saches la vérité.
mes sœurs — Il vaut mieux que mes sœurs sachent la vérité.
vous — Il vaut mieux que vous sachiez la vérité.

Il est normal que **tu** veuilles être médecin.

Georges — Il est normal que Georges veuille être médecin.
je — Il est normal que je veuille être médecin.
mes cousins — Il est normal que mes cousins veuillent être médecins.
nous — Il est normal que nous voulions être médecins.

Il faut qu'**Éric** aille en Espagne.

mes cousines — Il faut que mes cousines aillent en Espagne.
je — Il faut que j'aille en Espagne.
nous — Il faut que nous allions en Espagne.

C. L'usage du subjonctif après les expressions de doute

Activité 9. Identification de structures. You will hear a series of clauses. Each clause represents the second half of a sentence. Can you tell whether the beginning of the sentence expressed a certainty or a doubt? Listen carefully to the tense of the verb in each clause. If the verb is in the indicative, a certainty is being expressed. Mark the first row **je sais** in your lab manual. If the verb is in the subjunctive, a doubt is being expressed. Mark the second row **je doute. . . .**

Commençons.

1. . . . que tu fais beaucoup de sport.
2. . . . que tu fasses des progrès en français.
3. . . . que Paul va en Espagne cet été.
4. . . . qu'il aille aussi au Portugal.
5. . . . que vous alliez en Allemagne.
6. . . . que vous voulez aller à Francfort.
7. . . . que tu veuilles sérieusement apprendre le français.
8. . . . que vous puissiez voyager sans passeport.
9. . . . que Michel peut aller en France sans visa.
10. . . . que tu sais parler allemand.

Maintenant, vérifiez vos réponses. You should have marked **je doute** for sentences 2, 4, 5, 7, and 8 only. If you made any mistakes, listen once more to this activity, and do these questions again.

Activité 10. Conversation: Je le doute. . . . Georges is making a number of statements. Express your doubts about these statements. *Écoutez le modèle.*

<u>Modèle</u>: Le français est difficile. — Je doute que le français soit difficile.

Commençons.

Les étudiants sont paresseux. — Je doute que les étudiants soient paresseux.
Jacqueline a beaucoup de patience. — Je doute que Jacqueline ait beaucoup de patience.
Suzanne fait des progrès en anglais. — Je doute que Suzanne fasse des progrès en anglais.
Il fera beau demain. — Je doute qu'il fasse beau demain.
Monique sait notre adresse. — Je doute que Monique sache notre adresse.
Vous pouvez travailler ce week-end. — Je doute que vous puissiez travailler ce week-end.

Activité 11. Situation: Opinions. Is French a useful language? People have different opinions about this. Express these, and be sure to use the indicative or the subjunctive as appropriate. *Écoutez les modèles.*

<u>Modèles</u>: Jacques est sûr . . . — Jacques est sûr que le français est utile.
Vous doutez . . . — Vous doutez que le français soit utile.

Commençons.

Claire pense . . . — Claire pense que le français est utile.
Je crois . . . — Je crois que le français est utile.
Anne ne pense pas . . . — Anne ne pense pas que le français soit utile.
Il est vrai . . . — Il est vrai que le français est utile.
Mes parents ne sont pas sûrs . . . — Mes parents ne sont pas sûrs que le français soit utile.
Tu es certain . . . — Tu es certain que le français est utile.

D. L'usage du subjonctif après les expressions d'émotion

Activité 12. Prononciation. Ouvrez votre livre à la page 470. Répétez les expressions d'émotion et écoutez les phrases.

être content — Je suis content que tu ailles en France cet été.
être heureux — Êtes-vous heureux que vos amis aillent à Paris?
être désolé — Je suis désolé que vous ne veniez pas avec nous.
être triste — Jacques est triste que Sylvie ne lui écrive pas.
regretter — Paul regrette que ses amis ne puissent pas voyager.
déplorer — Je déplore que vous ayez cette attitude absurde.
être surpris — Jean est surpris que tu ne viennes pas avec nous.
avoir peur — J'ai peur qu'il fasse mauvais ce week-end.
être fier — M. Durand est fier que sa fille soit médecin.
être furieux — Philippe est furieux que tu ne l'attendes jamais.

Activité 13. Pratique. Maintenant nous allons faire quelques exercices de substitution. Répétez la première phrase. Puis faites de nouvelles phrases en utilisant les expressions suggérées.

Commençons.

Je regrette que tu ne puisses pas venir.
j'ai peur — J'ai peur que tu ne puisses pas venir.
je suis désolée — Je suis désolée que tu ne puisses pas venir.
je suis furieuse — Je suis furieuse que tu ne puisses pas venir.
je suis triste — Je suis triste que tu ne puisses pas venir.

Je suis heureuse que tu reçoives ton diplôme.
je suis fier — Je suis fier que tu reçoives ton diplôme.
je suis surpris — Je suis surpris que tu reçoives ton diplôme.

Activité 14. Narration: Réactions. You will hear how certain people react to various situations. Express this in a single sentence. *Écoutez le modèle.*

<u>Modèle</u>: Paul est content. Marie va en France. — Paul est content que Marie aille en France.

Commençons.

Nous sommes fiers. Notre fille est médecin. — Nous sommes fiers que notre fille soit médecin.
Monique est heureuse. Il fait beau. — Monique est heureuse qu'il fasse beau.
Christine est triste. Philippe n'écrit pas. — Christine est triste que Philippe n'écrive pas.
Nous avons peur. L'examen est difficile. — Nous avons peur que l'examen soit difficile.
Je suis désolé. Vous ne pouvez pas dormir. — Je suis désolé que vous ne puissiez pas dormir.

E. L'usage du subjonctif après certaines conjonctions

Activité 15. Prononciation. Ouvrez votre livre à la page 472. Répétez les conjonctions et écoutez les phrases.

parce que	Je me repose parce que je suis fatigué.
pendant que	Allez à la plage pendant qu'il fait beau.
depuis que	Charles cherche du travail depuis qu'il a son diplôme.
à condition que	Charles ira en France à condition qu'il ait de l'argent.
avant que	Je lui téléphonerai avant qu'il parte.
jusqu'à ce que	Je resterai chez moi jusqu'à ce que vous téléphoniez.
pour que	Je te prête le journal pour que tu lises cet article.
sans que	Alice est partie sans que je lui dise au revoir.

Activité 16. Pratique. Maintenant nous allons faire quelques exercices de substitution. Répétez la première phrase. Puis faites de nouvelles phrases en utilisant les sujets suggérés.

Commençons.

Je resterai ici jusqu'à ce que Marc vienne.

nous	Nous resterons ici jusqu'à ce que Marc vienne.
Marie	Marie restera ici jusqu'à ce que Marc vienne.

Marc part pour que **je** puisse être seul.

Anne	Marc part pour qu'Anne puisse être seule.
vous	Marc part pour que vous puissiez être seul.
ses camarades	Marc part pour que ses camarades puissent être seuls.

Activité 17. Conversation: Au téléphone. Nicole is telling you what certain people are going to do. Say that you will phone them before that. Use **avant que,** and the subjunctive of the verbs mentioned. *Écoutez le modèle.*

Modèle: Nathalie va partir en voyage.	Je téléphonerai à Nathalie avant qu'elle parte en voyage.

Commençons.

Vos cousins vont partir au Mexique.	Je téléphonerai à mes cousins avant qu'ils partent au Mexique.
Thérèse va dîner.	Je téléphonerai à Thérèse avant qu'elle dîne.
Charles va aller au concert.	Je téléphonerai à Charles avant qu'il aille au concert.
Caroline et Jeanne vont aller au cinéma.	Je téléphonerai à Caroline et à Jeanne avant qu'elles aillent au cinéma.
Paul va faire les courses.	Je téléphonerai à Paul avant qu'il fasse les courses.

F. Résumé: Les principaux usages du subjonctif

Activité 18. Compréhension orale. *Est-ce que j'ai raison?* Am I right? You will hear what various people think. If their statement uses the indicative, mark the top row **indicatif** in your lab manual. If the statement uses the subjunctive, mark the bottom row **subjonctif.** Since the expression **J'ai(e) raison** sounds the same in the subjunctive and the indicative, you will have to listen carefully to the first part of each statement.

Commençons.

1. Jean-Paul dit que j'ai raison.
2. Monique doute que j'aie raison.
3. Claire est heureuse que j'aie raison.
4. Le professeur sait que j'ai raison.
5. Mon petit ami est sûr que j'ai raison.
6. Il est essentiel que j'aie raison.
7. Mes camarades pensent que j'ai raison.
8. Henri a peur que j'aie raison.
9. Paul souhaite que j'aie raison.
10. Martine regrette que j'aie raison.
11. Il vaut mieux que j'aie raison.
12. Il faut que j'aie raison.

Maintenant vérifiez vos réponses. You should have marked **subjonctif** for sentences 2, 3, 6, 8, 9, 10, 11, and 12. If you made any mistakes, listen once more to these sentences and do them again.

DIALOGUE

Activité 19. Réactions. Jean-Louis va vous décrire certains événements futurs. Exprimez votre réaction selon l'attitude représentée par l'illustration dans votre manuel de laboratoire. Écoutez le modèle.

Modèle: Je vais gagner à la loterie. — Je doute que tu gagnes à la loterie.

Commençons.

1. Je vais faire un voyage cet été. — Je suis contente que tu fasses un voyage cet été.
2. Je dois aller à l'hôpital. — Je suis triste que tu ailles à l'hôpital.
3. Mes cousins vont pouvoir s'acheter une Rolls Royce. — Je doute que vos cousins puissent s'acheter une Rolls Royce.
4. Monique va venir à ta fête d'anniversaire. — Je suis contente que Monique vienne à ma fête d'anniversaire.
5. Philippe va recevoir une mauvaise note à l'examen. — Je suis triste que Philippe reçoive une mauvaise note à l'examen.
6. Il va faire très mauvais ce week-end. — Je doute qu'il fasse très mauvais ce week-end.

DICTÉE

Activité 20. Visite à Genève. Vous allez entendre un court paragraphe. Écoutez d'abord! N'écrivez pas!

Je suis content que tu ailles à Genève cet été, mais j'ai peur que tu ne puisses pas rencontrer mon frère. Je sais qu'il voyage beaucoup et je doute qu'il soit chez lui en juillet.

Maintenant écrivez les phrases dans votre manuel de laboratoire.

Je suis content / que tu ailles à Genève / cet été, / mais j'ai peur / que tu ne puisses pas / rencontrer mon frère. / Je sais / qu'il voyage beaucoup / et je doute / qu'il soit / chez lui / en juillet. /

Écoutez les phrases encore une fois et vérifiez ce que vous avez écrit.

(Text is reread without pauses.)

LECTURE CULTURELLE

Activité 21. Lecture. Ouvrez votre livre à la page 464. Écoutez.

(See textbook page 464.)

Activité 22. Compréhension du texte. Vous allez entendre des phrases concernant le texte que vous avez écouté. Indiquez dans votre manuel de laboratoire si ces phrases sont vraies ou fausses.

Commençons.

1. Avant 1944, les pays européens étaient souvent en guerre entre eux.
2. Après 1944, ces pays ont décidé d'établir une paix permanente.
3. Le Bénélux est un petit pays d'Europe.
4. C'est Roosevelt qui a suggéré à la France et à l'Allemagne de former une union économique.
5. L'Angleterre, L'Irlande et le Danemark ont formé une union économique rivale du Marché Commun.
6. Le premier président du Parlement Européen était une femme.
7. Aujourd'hui, il y a six pays dans le Marché Commun.
8. La Grèce, l'Espagne et le Portugal sont membres du Marché Commun.

Maintenant vérifiez vos réponses. Les phrases suivantes sont vraies: 1, 2, 6 et 8. Les phrases suivantes sont fausses: 3, 4, 5 et 7.

Fin de la Leçon 30.
End of Lesson 30.
(music)

VIVRE EN FRANCE 10. L'ACHAT DES VÊTEMENTS

Activité 1. La bonne réponse. Vous allez entendre une série de questions. Pour chaque question, indiquez dans votre manuel de laboratoire quelle est la réponse logique, en faisant un cercle autour de la lettre qui correspond.

Commençons.

1. Dis donc, ta nouvelle veste est vraiment bon marché. Où est-ce que tu l'as trouvée?
2. Est-ce que cette chemise est en coton?
3. Quelle sorte de chaussures cherchez-vous?
4. Quelle est ta pointure?
5. Que penses-tu de ce complet gris?
6. Dis donc, Henri, est-ce que tu peux me prêter cent francs?
7. Qu'est-ce que tu vas mettre s'il fait froid ce soir?
8. Est-ce que ce peignoir te va?
9. Est-ce que ta sœur a acheté une voiture neuve?
10. Qu'est-ce que Mireille portait avec sa nouvelle robe noire?

Maintenant écoutez les questions et les réponses correspondantes.

1. Dis donc, ta nouvelle veste est vraiment bon marché. Où est-ce que tu l'as trouvée?
   Je l'ai achetée dans une boutique de soldes rue de Sèvres.
2. Est-ce que cette chemise est en coton?
   Non, elle est en laine!
3. Quelle sorte de chaussures cherchez-vous?
   Je cherche des mocassins.
4. Quelle est ta pointure?
   Je chausse du trente-huit.
5. Que penses-tu de ce complet gris?
   J'aime la veste mais je n'aime pas le pantalon.
6. Dis donc, Henri, est-ce que tu peux me prêter cent francs?
   Désolé, mais je n'ai pas mon portefeuille sur moi.
7. Qu'est-ce que tu vas mettre s'il fait froid ce soir?
   Je vais mettre mon blouson de cuir.
8. Est-ce que ce peignoir te va?
   Non, il est trop serré.
9. Est-ce que ta sœur a acheté une voiture neuve?
   Non, elle a acheté une Toyota d'occasion.
10. Qu'est-ce que Mireille portait avec sa nouvelle robe noire?
    Elle portait une ceinture blanche.

Activité 2. En France. Vous allez entendre une conversation qui a lieu au bureau des réclamations d'un grand magasin. Dans cette conversation, une cliente du magasin déclare la perte de son sac à un employé. Écoutez bien cette conversation. Même si vous ne comprenez pas tous les mots, vous devriez pouvoir en comprendre les éléments essentiels. Sur la base de ces éléments, complétez la déclaration de perte qui se trouve dans votre manuel de laboratoire. D'abord, écoutez la conversation.

—Bonjour, Madame. Qu'est-ce que je peux faire pour vous?
—Ah Monsieur, quelle catastrophe! Je viens de perdre mon sac! C'était un sac. . . .
—Attendez. Je vais prendre des notes. D'abord, pouvez-vous me dire où vous étiez quand vous avez constaté la disparition de votre sac?
—Je sortais du magasin.
—Bon. Est-ce que vous pouvez me décrire ce sac?
—Eh bien, c'était un grand sac en plastique.
—Et qu'est-ce qu'il y avait dans ce sac?
—Eh bien, il y avait ce que je venais d'acheter dans votre magasin.
—Pouvez-vous préciser?
—Eh bien, il y avait des vêtements.
—Quelle sorte de vêtements?
—Il y avait un blouson que j'avais acheté pour mon fils.
—De quelle couleur?
—C'était un blouson de cuir noir.
—Bon. Et quoi d'autre?
—Il y avait deux chemises de coton.
—De quelle couleur?
—Des chemises blanches.
—Manches courtes ou manches longues?
—Manches longues. Il y avait aussi la cravate que j'avais achetée à mon mari pour son anniversaire. C'était une belle cravate de soie bleue unie.
—C'est tout?
—Non, il y avait aussi une paire de chaussures.
—Quel genre de chaussures?
—Des mocassins de cuir rouge.

—Pointure?
—Du 39. Oui, c'est ça: du 39.
—Est-ce qu'il y avait d'autres choses dans votre sac?
—Euh non. . . . Attendez. . . . Si . . . il y avait . . . Mon Dieu! Il y avait mon portefeuille!!

Écoutez à nouveau et écrivez.

Fin de Vivre en France 10.
End of Vivre en France 10.
(music)

UNITÉ 11: POINTS DE VUE

LEÇON 31. LA NOUVELLE TECHNOLOGIE

PRÉSENTATION

Activité 1. Lecture. Ouvrez votre livre à la page 484. Écoutez.

(See textbook page 484.)

Activité 2. Compréhension du texte. Maintenant vous allez entendre des phrases concernant le texte que vous avez écouté. Indiquez dans votre manuel de laboratoire si ces phrases sont vraies ou fausses.

1. Emmanuel vient d'acheter un magnétoscope.
2. Il n'a pas besoin de son ordinateur.
3. Chez elle, Monique a beaucoup de gadgets électroniques.
4. Elle trouve que la technologie a beaucoup d'avantages.
5. Michel travaille dans une usine.
6. Pour lui, la technologie moderne est une des causes du chômage.
7. Anne-Laure est allée à New York pour acheter un ordinateur.
8. À New York, elle a acheté des vases qu'elle a vendus à Paris.

Maintenant vérifiez vos réponses. Les phrases suivantes sont vraies: 3, 4, 5 et 6. Les phrases suivantes sont fausses: 1, 2, 7 et 8.

PHONÉTIQUE

Activité 3. Syllabation. Speakers of French tend to make every syllable end on a vowel sound. In liaison, therefore, the liaison consonant is pronounced as if it were the first sound of the following word. When two consonant sounds come together in a word, there is a tendency to end the first syllable on the vowel sound and begin the next syllable with two consonant sounds. Practice French syllabication by pronouncing the following words and sentences according to the divisions indicated.

Répétez: i•l est im•po•rtant
le•s É•tat•s-U•nis
ju•squ'à -c~~e~~ qu'i•l a•rrive
à l'heu-r~~e~~ a•ctuelle
i•l a•rri•v~~e~~ dan•s u•n in•stant

STRUCTURE ET VOCABULAIRE

Vocabulaire: La technologie

Activité 4. Prononciation. Ouvrez votre livre à la page 487. Répétez les noms.

un appareil
un moyen
un ordinateur
le progrès
un savant
un sujet
un télécopieur
une découverte
l'informatique
une invention
la vitesse

Maintenant écoutez les verbes et répétez les phrases.

faire des progrès	Faites-vous des progrès en français?
se passer de	Je ne peux pas me passer de mon ordinateur.
se servir de	Est-ce que tu te sers d'un ordinateur?

A. *Révision: Les pronoms compléments d'objet direct et indirect*

Activité 5. Conversation: Curiosité. Mme Gasse is asking you various questions. Answer her in the affirmative using the appropriate direct or indirect object pronoun. *Écoutez le modèle.*

<u>Modèle</u>: Vous regardez souvent la télévision? Oui, je la regarde souvent.

Commençons.

Vous achetez le journal?	Oui, je l'achète.
Vous aidez vos parents?	Oui, je les aide.
Vous téléphonez à vos cousins?	Oui, je leur téléphone.
Vous écrivez à votre meilleur ami?	Oui, je lui écris.
Vous connaissez vos voisins?	Oui, je les connais.
Vous avez parlé au professeur aujourd'hui?	Oui, je lui ai parlé.
Vous avez regardé votre horoscope ce matin?	Oui, je l'ai regardé.
Vous avez écouté la radio ce matin?	Oui, je l'ai écoutée.
Vous avez rendu visite à votre meilleur ami ce week-end?	Oui, je lui ai rendu visite.

B. *L'ordre des pronoms compléments*

Activité 6. Prononciation. *L'ordre des pronoms compléments. Ouvrez votre livre à la page 490.* You will hear sentences containing both a direct and an indirect object. Repeat the second sentence in each pair.

Je prête ma moto à Richard.	Je la lui prête.
Alice rend le magnétophone à Éric.	Alice le lui rend.
Anne ne montre pas ses photos à ses parents.	Anne ne les leur montre pas.
Vous ne dites pas la vérité aux étudiants.	Vous ne la leur dites pas.
Je te donne mon numéro de téléphone.	Je te le donne.
Charles ne nous prête pas sa voiture.	Il ne nous la prête pas.

Activité 7. Conversation: La photo. Mireille is asking to whom Anne is giving her photograph. Answer her according to suggestions in your lab manual. *Écoutez le modèle.*

Modèle: Est-ce qu'Anne donne sa photo à son ami Paul? — Oui, elle la lui donne.

Commençons.

1. Est-ce qu'Anne donne sa photo à ses parents? — Oui, elle la leur donne.
2. Est-ce qu'Anne donne sa photo à son oncle? — Oui, elle la lui donne.
3. Est-ce qu'Anne donne sa photo à ses cousins? — Non, elle ne la leur donne pas.
4. Est-ce qu'Anne donne sa photo à la voisine? — Non, elle ne la lui donne pas.

Activité 8. Conversation: La chambre de Philippe. Now Mireille is asking whether or not Philippe is showing Alice the various things in his room. Answer according to the replies in your lab manual. *Écoutez le modèle.*

Modèle: Est-ce que Philippe montre à Alice son nouveau livre? — Oui, il le lui montre.

Commençons.

1. Est-ce que Philippe montre à Alice son ordinateur? — Oui, il le lui montre.
2. Est-ce que Philippe montre à Alice ses disques? — Oui, il les lui montre.
3. Est-ce que Philippe montre à Alice la photo de Nicole? — Non, il ne la lui montre pas.
4. Est-ce que Philippe montre à Alice le poème qu'il a écrit? — Non, il ne le lui montre pas.

Activité 9. Conversation: Prêts. Julien is mentioning that other people have some of your things. Tell him that you know you have lent these things to them. Use the verb **prêter** and two object pronouns. *Écoutez le modèle.*

Modèle: Marc a ta guitare. — Je sais. Je la lui ai prêtée.

Commençons.

Suzanne a tes cassettes.	Je sais. Je les lui ai prêtées.
Claire a ton vélo.	Je sais. Je le lui ai prêté.
Mes cousins ont ta voiture.	Je sais. Je la leur ai prêtée.
Thomas et André ont tes skis.	Je sais. Je les leur ai prêtés.
Annie et Hélène ont ton livre.	Je sais. Je le leur ai prêté.

Activité 10. Jouons un rôle: Oui ou non. Georges' roommate Michel is asking him to do things for him. Georges answers in the affirmative, using object pronouns. *Écoutez le modèle.*

Modèle: Est-ce que tu me prêtes ta voiture? — Oui, je te la prête.

Commençons.

Est-ce que tu me montres tes notes?	Oui, je te les montre.
Est-ce que tu me prêtes dix dollars?	Oui, je te les prête.
Est-ce que tu m'offres cette photo?	Oui, je te l'offre.

Now Alain and Charles, whom Georges does not know very well, are asking him for things. This time Georges answers in the negative. *Écoutez le modèle.*

Modèle: Est-ce que tu nous prêtes ta voiture? — Non, je ne vous la prête pas.

Commençons.

Est-ce que tu nous montres tes notes?	Non, je ne vous les montre pas.
Est-ce que tu nous prêtes dix dollars?	Non, je ne vous les prête pas.
Est-ce que tu nous offres cette photo?	Non, je ne vous l'offre pas.

C. L'ordre des pronoms à la forme affirmative de l'impératif

Activité 11. Situation: S'il te plaît! You will hear François asking certain things of his friends. Rephrase his requests using two object pronouns. *Écoutez le modèle.*

Modèle: Prête-moi ta guitare! — Prête-la-moi, s'il te plaît.

Commençons.

Prête-moi ton livre!	Prête-le-moi, s'il te plaît!
Prête-moi tes disques!	Prête-les-moi, s'il te plaît!
Montre-moi ta photo!	Montre-la-moi, s'il te plaît!
Montre-moi ton ordinateur!	Montre-le-moi, s'il te plaît!
Donne-moi cette adresse!	Donne-la-moi, s'il te plaît!
Vends-moi ta mini-chaîne!	Vends-la-moi, s'il te plaît!
Vends-moi tes cassettes!	Vends-les-moi, s'il te plaît!

*D. L'ordre des pronoms avec **y** et **en***

Activité 12. Narration: Pierre. Pierre gives advice to everyone. Confirm the following statements, using object pronouns. *Écoutez le modèle.*

Modèle: Pierre donne des conseils à son frère. — Oui, il lui en donne.

Commençons.

Pierre nous donne des conseils.	Oui, il nous en donne.
Pierre te donne des conseils.	Oui, il t'en donne.
Pierre donne des conseils à ses camarades.	Oui, il leur en donne.
Pierre me donne des conseils.	Oui, il m'en donne.
Pierre vous donne des conseils.	Oui, il vous en donne.

Pierre, however, never lends anyone any money. Confirm these statements. *Écoutez le modèle.*

Modèle: Pierre ne prête jamais d'argent à sa sœur. — Non, il ne lui en prête jamais.

Commençons.

Pierre ne me prête jamais d'argent.	Non, il ne m'en prête jamais.
Pierre ne vous prête jamais d'argent.	Non, il ne vous en prête jamais.
Pierre ne te prête jamais d'argent.	Non, il ne t'en prête jamais.
Pierre ne prête jamais d'argent à ses frères.	Non, il ne leur en prête jamais.
Pierre ne nous prête jamais d'argent.	Non, il ne nous en prête jamais.

Pierre does like to take his friends to various places. Confirm the following statements. *Écoutez le modèle.*

Modèle: Pierre nous amène au cinéma. — Oui, il nous y amène.

Commençons.

Pierre nous amène au restaurant.	Oui, il nous y amène.
Pierre t'amène au musée.	Oui, il t'y amène.
Pierre amène ses cousins au théâtre.	Oui, il les y amène.

DIALOGUE

Activité 13. Moi et mes copains. Emmanuel va vous demander ce que vous avez fait pour certains copains. Répondez-lui en utilisant le nom de l'objet illustré dans votre manuel de laboratoire. Ensuite il va vous poser une autre question. Répondez-lui en utilisant les informations de votre manuel de laboratoire. Écoutez le modèle.

Modèle: Qu'est-ce que tu as prêté à Jacques?	Je lui ai prêté mon ordinateur.
Pour combien de temps est-ce que tu le lui as prêté?	Je le lui ai prêté pour une semaine.

Commençons.

1. Qu'est-ce que tu as prêté à Philippe?	Je lui ai prêté ma voiture.
Pour combien de temps est-ce que tu la lui as prêtée?	Je la lui ai prêtée pour le week-end.
2. Qu'est-ce que tu as vendu à tes cousins?	Je leur ai vendu mon vélo.
Pour combien d'argent est-ce que tu le leur as vendu?	Je le leur ai vendu pour 500 francs.
3. Qu'est-ce que tu as montré à tes copains?	Je leur ai montré mes photos.
Quand est-ce que tu les leur as montrées?	Je les leur ai montrées hier soir.
4. Qu'est-ce que tu as apporté à Jacqueline?	Je lui ai apporté mes disques.
Quand est-ce que tu les lui as apportés?	Je les lui ai apportés pour sa fête.

DICTÉE

Activité 14. Mon vélo. Vous allez entendre un court paragraphe. Écoutez! N'écrivez pas!

Je n'ai pas mon vélo. Je l'ai prêté à Thomas. Demande-le-lui. S'il ne te le donne pas, dis-lui que je vais le chercher demain.

Maintenant écrivez les phrases dans votre cahier.

Je n'ai pas mon vélo. / Je l'ai prêté à Thomas. / Demande-le-lui. / S'il ne te le donne pas, / dis-lui / que je vais / le chercher / demain. /

Écoutez encore une fois et vérifiez ce que vous avez écrit.

(Text is reread without pauses.)

LECTURE CULTURELLE

Activité 15. Lecture. Ouvrez votre livre à la page 486. Écoutez.

(See textbook page 486.)

Activité 16. Compréhension du texte. Vous allez entendre des phrases concernant le texte que vous avez écouté. Indiquez dans votre cahier si ces phrases sont vraies ou fausses.

Commençons.

1. Le Concorde est un avion très rapide.
2. Le TGV est le nom du métro parisien.
3. On peut prendre le RER pour aller de Paris à Genève.
4. Le Minitel est une invention française.
5. Le Minitel est un petit téléviseur.
6. Avec le Minitel on peut obtenir beaucoup d'informations différentes.

Maintenant vérifiez vos réponses. Les phrases suivantes sont vraies: 1, 4 et 6. Les phrases suivantes sont fausses: 2, 3 et 5.

Fin de la Leçon 31.
End of Lesson 31.
(music)

LEÇON 32. RÉFLEXIONS SUR L'AMÉRIQUE

PRÉSENTATION

Activité 1. Lecture. Ouvrez votre livre à la page 496. Écoutez.

(See textbook page 496.)

Activité 2. Compréhension du texte. Maintenant vous allez entendre des phrases concernant le texte que vous avez écouté. Indiquez dans votre manuel de laboratoire si ces phrases sont vraies ou fausses.

Commençons.

1. Généralement cette étudiante française admire l'Amérique.
2. Cette étudiante aimerait visiter les États-Unis.
3. Elle pense que les Américains sont des gens très égoïstes.
4. Elle pense qu'il n'y a pas assez de compétition aux États-Unis.
5. Elle pense que les Français vivent d'une façon plus modérée que les Américains.
6. Elle admire les géants du jazz.

Maintenant vérifiez vos réponses. Les phrases suivantes sont vraies: 1, 2, 5 et 6. Les phrases suivantes sont fausses: 3 et 4.

PHONÉTIQUE

Activité 3. Les lettres «ch». In French the letters "ch" represent the sound / ʃ / as in the English word *shop*. In French there is no /t/ before / ʃ /, unless there is a "t" in the written form, as in **un match.**

Répétez: chez Charles acheter dépêcher machine
Charlotte cherche sa machine à écrire.
Charles achète une chemise blanche.

STRUCTURE ET VOCABULAIRE

Vocabulaire: Analyse et évaluation

Activité 4. Prononciation. Ouvrez votre livre à la page 498. Répétez les noms.

le pouvoir	une analyse	une méthode
un sondage	une idée	la moitié

Maintenant répétez les verbes et les expressions. Écoutez les phrases.

admirer:	j'admire	Quelle est la personne que vous admirez le plus?
attirer:	j'attire	Je voudrais attirer votre attention sur ce point.
avoir tendance à:	j'ai tendance à	Vous avez tendance à généraliser.
critiquer:	je critique	Pourquoi est-ce que tu critiques tout?
juger:	je juge	Ne jugez pas les gens sur leurs apparences.
en cas de		Que ferais-tu en cas de révolution?
la plupart de		La plupart des Américains sont idéalistes.

A. *Le pronom interrogatif **lequel***

Activité 5. Conversation: Au centre commercial. Several French tourists have spent the afternoon at your shopping center. You will hear them tell you what they bought. Ask them to be more specific, using the appropriate form of **lequel.** *Écoutez le modèle.*

Modèle: J'ai acheté un transistor. — Ah oui? Lequel?

Commençons.

J'ai acheté une caméra. — Ah oui? Laquelle?
J'ai acheté un livre de photos. — Ah oui? Lequel?
J'ai acheté une calculatrice. — Ah oui? Laquelle?
J'ai acheté des disques. — Ah oui? Lesquels?
J'ai acheté des romans policiers. — Ah oui? Lesquels?
J'ai acheté des cassettes. — Ah oui? Lesquelles?
J'ai acheté des lunettes de soleil. — Ah oui? Lesquelles?

B. *Révision: Les pronoms relatifs **qui** et **que***

Activité 6. Situation: Visite en Amérique. You will hear various comments about the United States. Express these in sentences using **qui** or **que** as appropriate. The first set of comments is about New York. *Écoutez les modèles.*

Modèles: New York attire les Français. — New York est une ville qui attire les Français.
Les Français visitent New York. — New York est une ville que les Français visitent.

Commençons.

New York a beaucoup de musées. — New York est une ville qui a beaucoup de musées.
Certaines personnes critiquent New York. — New York est une ville que certaines personnes critiquent.
D'autres personnes adorent New York. — New York est une ville que d'autres personnes adorent.

The second set of comments is about American traditions. *Écoutez le modèle.*

Modèle: Les traditions changent. — Quelles sont les traditions qui changent?

Commençons.

Les traditions vous intéressent. — Quelles sont les traditions qui vous intéressent?
Nous maintenons les traditions. — Quelles sont les traditions que nous maintenons?
Nous conservons les traditions. — Quelles sont les traditions que nous conservons?

C. Le pronom relatif ***lequel***

Activité 7. Pratique. Nous allons faire quelques exercices de substitution. Répétez la première phrase. Puis faites de nouvelles phrases en utilisant les noms suggérés.

Commençons.

Voici **le sondage** avec lequel je travaille.

la méthode	Voici la méthode avec laquelle je travaille.
les idées	Voici les idées avec lesquelles je travaille.
le texte	Voici le texte avec lequel je travaille.

Vous critiquez **les méthodes** avec lesquelles vous n'êtes pas d'accord.

les traditions	Vous critiquez les traditions avec lesquelles vous n'êtes pas d'accord.
la politique	Vous critiquez la politique avec laquelle vous n'êtes pas d'accord.
le sondage	Vous critiquez le sondage avec lequel vous n'êtes pas d'accord.

D. Le pronom ***dont***

Activité 8. Prononciation. Ouvrez votre livre à la page 504. Répétez les phrases.

Voici un jeune homme. Je vous ai parlé de ce jeune homme.
Voici le jeune homme dont je vous ai parlé.
La politique est un sujet. Je ne parle jamais de ce sujet.
La politique est un sujet dont je ne parle jamais.
Avez-vous ces livres? J'ai besoin de ces livres.
Avez-vous les livres dont j'ai besoin?

Activité 9. Pratique. Maintenant nous allons faire quelques exercices de substitution. Répétez la première phrase. Puis faites de nouvelles phrases en utilisant les noms suggérés.

Commençons.

Qui est **le jeune homme** dont vous m'avez parlé?

la jeune fille	Qui est la jeune fille dont vous m'avez parlé?
le professeur	Qui est le professeur dont vous m'avez parlé?
les étudiants	Qui sont les étudiants dont vous m'avez parlé?

Donnez-moi **les livres** dont j'ai besoin.

le journal	Donnez-moi le journal dont j'ai besoin.
la calculatrice	Donnez-moi la calculatrice dont j'ai besoin.
l'argent	Donnez-moi l'argent dont j'ai besoin.

Activité 10. Conversation: Oui! Yvette is asking you various questions. Answer her in the affirmative using the pronoun **dont.** *Écoutez le modèle.*

Modèle: Avez-vous besoin de ce journal? — Oui, c'est le journal dont j'ai besoin.

Commençons.

Avez-vous parlé de ce film? — Oui, c'est le film dont j'ai parlé.
Vous souvenez-vous de ce roman? — Oui, c'est le roman dont je me souviens.
Avez-vous envie de ce disque? — Oui, c'est le disque dont j'ai envie.

*E. Le pronom démonstratif **celui***

Activité 11. Conversation: À la librairie. Imagine that you are working in a French bookstore. You will hear customers asking you for certain things. Give them a choice. *Écoutez le modèle.*

Modèle: Je voudrais un journal. — Lequel? Celui-ci ou celui-là?

Commençons.

Je voudrais une revue. — Laquelle? Celle-ci ou celle-là?
Je voudrais un roman policier. — Lequel? Celui-ci ou celui-là?
Je voudrais des journaux anglais. — Lesquels? Ceux-ci ou ceux-là?
Je voudrais des revues americaines. — Lesquelles? Celles-ci ou celles-là?

Activité 12. Jouons un rôle: Camarades de chambre. Élisabeth and her roommate Michèle are constantly exchanging clothes. Élisabeth is home for the weekend and her mother doesn't recognize many items. Élisabeth explains that they belong to Michèle. Give Élisabeth's replies. *Écoutez les modèles.*

Modèles: Ce n'est pas ta robe? — Non, c'est celle de Michèle.
Ce ne sont pas tes jeans? — Non, ce sont ceux de Michèle.

Commençons.

Ce n'est pas ta jupe? — Non, c'est celle de Michèle.
Ce ne sont pas tes chaussures? — Non, ce sont celles de Michèle.
Ce n'est pas ton tee-shirt? — Non, c'est celui de Michèle.
Ce ne sont pas tes chemisiers? — Non, ce sont ceux de Michèle.

Activité 13. Jouons un rôle: La chambre de Pierre. Frédéric is in Pierre's room. He points out various objects and wants to know what they are. Pierre answers his questions in the affirmative. Play the role of Pierre. *Écoutez le modèle.*

Modèle: C'est le livre que tu lis? — Oui, c'est celui que je lis.

Commençons.

C'est le magazine que tu cherches? — Oui, c'est celui que je cherche.
C'est la machine à écrire que tu utilises? — Oui, c'est celle que j'utilise.
Ce sont les disques que tu as achetés en Espagne? — Oui, ce sont ceux que j'ai achetés en Espagne.
Ce sont les chaussures que tu as mises hier? — Oui, ce sont celles que j'ai mises hier.
C'est la montre que tu avais perdue? — Oui, c'est celle que j'avais perdue.

DIALOGUE

Activité 14. Un choix. Robert va vous offrir un choix entre deux options. Choisissez l'option représentée dans votre manuel de laboratoire. Écoutez bien le modèle.

Modèle: Il y a deux trains qui vont à Lyon. Le premier part à 8 heures 10. Le second part à 9 heures et quart.
Lequel vas-tu prendre?
Je vais prendre celui qui part à 9 heures et quart.

Commençons.

1. Il y a deux avions qui vont à Montréal. Le premier part à 10 heures. Le second part à 11 heures. Lequel vas-tu prendre?
   Je vais prendre celui qui part à 10 heures.
2. Il y a deux bons restaurants dans votre quartier. L'un sert des spécialités vietnamiennes, l'autre sert des spécialités italiennes. Lequel préfères-tu?
   Je préfère celui qui sert des spécialités vietnamiennes.
3. Voici deux appareils-photo. L'un coûte 2.000 francs. L'autre coûte 3.000 francs. Lequel vas-tu acheter?
   Je vais acheter celui qui coûte 3.000 francs.
4. Il y a deux bons hôtels dans cette ville. L'un est situé près de la plage. L'autre est situé près du musée. Dans lequel vas-tu rester?
   Je vais rester dans celui qui est près du musée.

DICTÉE

Activité 15. Mes disques. Vous allez entendre un court paragraphe. Écoutez d'abord! N'écrivez pas!

J'ai plusieurs disques. Lequel veux-tu écouter? Personnellement, je préfère celui qui est sur la petite table. C'est celui que mon frère Julien m'a donné pour mon anniversaire.

Maintenant écrivez les phrases dans votre manuel de laboratoire.

J'ai plusieurs disques. / Lequel / veux-tu écouter? / Personnellement, je préfère / celui qui est / sur la petite table. / C'est celui / que mon frère Julien / m'a donné / pour mon anniversaire. /

Écoutez encore une fois et vérifiez ce que vous avez écrit.

(Text is reread without pauses.)

LECTURE CULTURELLE

Activité 16. Lecture. Ouvrez votre livre à la page 497. Écoutez la première partie de ces renseignements.

(See textbook page 497.)

Activité 17. Compréhension du texte. Vous allez entendre des phrases concernant le texte que vous avez écouté. Indiquez dans votre manuel de laboratoire si ces phrases sont vraies ou fausses.

Commençons.

1. Les Français condamnent le style de vie américain.
2. Les films américains ont généralement beaucoup de succès en France.
3. La majorité des Français sont violemment anti-américains.
4. Les Français pensent qu'aux États-Unis les relations humaines ne sont pas très solides.
5. Les Français admirent les Américains pour leurs traditions culturelles.

Maintenant vérifiez vos réponses. Les phrases suivantes sont vraies: 2 et 4. Les phrases suivantes sont fausses: 1, 3 et 5.

Fin de la Leçon 32.
End of Lesson 32.
(music)

LEÇON 33. VIVE LA LIBERTÉ!

PRÉSENTATION

Activité 1. Lecture. Ouvrez votre livre à la page 510. Écoutez.

(See textbook page 510.)

Activité 2. Compréhension du texte. Vous allez entendre des phrases concernant le texte que vous avez écouté. Indiquez dans votre manuel de laboratoire si ces phrases sont vraies ou fausses.

Commençons.

1. Olivier Leclerc est étudiant en médecine.
2. Il n'aime pas particulièrement nettoyer sa chambre.
3. Florence Arnaud n'est pas d'accord avec le système universitaire.
4. Si elle avait le choix, elle n'étudierait pas les maths.
5. Damien Groult est un militaire de carrière.
6. Il n'aime pas l'armée parce que c'est un pacifiste.
7. Marie-France Granger est journaliste.
8. Elle pense que les journaux français représentent les diverses tendances politiques.
9. Jean-Pierre Garand pense que la liberté crée certaines responsabilités.
10. Il pense que les Français d'aujourd'hui sont très conscients de leurs responsabilités.
11. Marie-Louise Weninger a eu une vie très active.
12. Aujourd'hui elle n'est plus active parce qu'elle est trop âgée.

Maintenant vérifiez vos réponses. Les phrases suivantes sont vraies: 2, 3, 4, 7, 8, 9 et 11. Les phrases suivantes sont fausses: 1, 5, 6, 10 et 12.

PHONÉTIQUE

Activité 3. Les voyelles nasales /ɑ̃/ et /ɔ̃/. It is important to distinguish clearly between the nasal vowels /ɑ̃/ and /ɔ̃/.

Contrastez: dans dont sans sont

Répétez: dans dont sans sont
invention content rencontre se rendre compte
jambon mensonge comprendre compétent
Je me rends compte que je perds mon temps.
On est content de rencontrer de bons amis.

STRUCTURE ET VOCABULAIRE

Vocabulaire: La vie politique

Activité 4. Prononciation. Ouvrez votre livre à la page 513. Répétez les noms et les adjectifs.

un droit
un impôt
un individu

l'égalité
la liberté
la responsabilité

individuel
libre
privé
public
responsable

Maintenant écoutez les verbes et répétez les phrases.

être obligé de — Je ne peux pas sortir ce soir. Je suis obligé de travailler.
exprimer — En votant, nous exprimons nos opinions.
lutter — Luttons pour la justice et contre les inégalités!

A. Les pronoms interrogatifs invariables

Activité 5. Prononciation. Ouvrez votre livre à la page 514. Répétez les questions et écoutez les réponses.

Qui fait ce bruit? — C'est le voisin qui ronfle.
Qui est-ce qui fait ce bruit? — C'est le voisin qui ronfle.
Qu'est-ce qui fait ce bruit? — C'est un avion qui passe.

Qui cherches-tu? — Je cherche le professeur.
Qui est-ce que tu cherches? — Je cherche le professeur.
Que cherches-tu? — Je cherche mon livre de français.
Qu'est-ce que tu cherches? — Je cherche mon livre de français.

Avec qui travailles-tu? — Je travaille avec Paul.
Avec qui est-ce que tu travailles? — Je travaille avec Paul.
Avec quoi travailles-tu? — Je travaille avec un ordinateur.
Avec quoi est-ce que tu travailles? — Je travaille avec un ordinateur.

Activité 6. Identification de structures. You will hear a series of questions. Does each question concern a person or a thing? Listen carefully to the interrogative expression at the beginning of each question. If you hear the expression **qui est-ce qui** or **qui est-ce que,** the question is about a person. Mark the first row **une personne** in your lab manual. If you hear the expression **qu'est-ce qui** or **qu'est-ce que,** the question concerns a thing. Mark the second row **une chose.**

Commençons.

1. Qu'est-ce que tu écoutes maintenant?
2. Qui est-ce que tu regardes en ce moment?
3. Qu'est-ce qui t'inquiète aujourd'hui?
4. Qu'est-ce qui t'amuse?
5. Qui est-ce qui est venu hier matin?
6. Qu'est-ce que vous avez apporté avec vous?
7. Qui est-ce qui t'a donné cette idée absurde?
8. Qu'est-ce qui t'a donné ces idées extraordinaires?
9. Qui est-ce que tu as remarqué au café?
10. Qu'est-ce que tu as remarqué à la fête?

Maintenant vérifiez vos réponses. You should have marked **une personne** for questions 2, 5, 7, and 9 only. If you got any wrong, listen once more to these sentences and do these questions again.

Activité 7. Conversation: Hier. Marc is saying what happened to Daniel yesterday. Ask for more details. In your questions, use the appropriate pronouns: **qui est-ce qui** and **qu'est-ce qui** to refer to subjects, and **qui est-ce que** and **qu'est-ce que** to refer to objects. *Écoutez les modèles.*

Modèles: Quelqu'un a invité Daniel. — Qui est-ce qui a invité Daniel?
Daniel a dit quelque chose. — Qu'est-ce que Daniel a dit?

Commençons.

Daniel a attendu quelqu'un. — Qui est-ce que Daniel a attendu?
Quelqu'un est venu en voiture. — Qui est-ce qui est venu en voiture?
Quelque chose est arrivé. — Qu'est-ce qui est arrivé?
Daniel a vu quelqu'un. — Qui est-ce que Daniel a vu?
Daniel lui a montré quelque chose. — Qu'est-ce que Daniel lui a montré?

Activité 8. Identification de structures. You will hear a series of questions. Are the questions about a person or a thing? Listen carefully to the interrogative pronoun. If you hear the pronoun **qui,** mark the first row **une personne** in your workbook. If you hear **quoi,** mark the second row **une chose.**

Commençons.

1. À qui parles-tu?
2. De qui parlez-vous?
3. À quoi pensez-vous?
4. À qui penses-tu?
5. De quoi parlez-vous maintenant?
6. Avec quoi est-ce que tu joues?
7. Avec qui joues-tu au tennis?
8. Avec quoi fais-tu ça?
9. Avec qui est-ce que vous allez au cinéma?
10. De quoi as-tu besoin pour la fête?

Vérifiez vos réponses. You should have marked **une personne** for sentences 1, 2, 4, 7, and 9 only. If you made any mistakes, listen once more to this activity, and do these questions again.

Activité 9. Conversation: Pardon? Marc is making various statements. Ask him to repeat what he said. Begin your questions with a preposition and the appropriate interrogative pronoun. *Écoutez les modèles.*

Modèles:	Je sors avec une amie anglaise.	Pardon? Avec qui sors-tu?
	Je joue au volleyball.	Pardon? À quoi joues-tu?

Commençons.

Je parle à Paul.	Pardon? À qui parles-tu?
Je parle souvent de mes classes.	Pardon? De quoi parles-tu souvent?
Je parle de Francine.	Pardon? De qui parles-tu?
Je parle des vacances.	Pardon? De quoi parles-tu?
Je vais chez un ami.	Pardon? Chez qui vas-tu?
Je pense aux vacances.	Pardon? À quoi penses-tu?
Je travaille avec Mme Leblanc.	Pardon? Avec qui travailles-tu?

B. Les pronoms ***ce qui, ce que***

Activité 10. Prononciation. Ouvrez votre livre à la page 517. Écoutez les questions et répétez les phrases.

Qu'est-ce qui est arrivé?	Dis-moi ce qui est arrivé.
Qu'est-ce qui vous amuse?	Je vous demande ce qui vous amuse.
Qu-est-ce que tu fais?	Je voudrais savoir ce que tu fais.
Qu'est-ce que Pierre pense de ce livre?	Dites-moi ce que Pierre pense de ce livre.

Maintenant répétez les phrases suivantes avec **ce qui** et **ce que.**

Dites-moi ce qui vous amuse.	Je déteste ce qui est compliqué.
Dites-moi ce que vous voulez.	Ce qui est simple ne m'intéresse pas.
J'aime ce qui est beau.	Ce que tu dis n'est pas vrai.

Activité 11. Pratique. Maintenant nous allons faire quelques exercices de substitution. Répétez la première phrase. Puis faites de nouvelles phrases en utilisant les adjectifs suggérés.

Commençons.

Nous aimons ce qui est **beau.**

simple	Nous aimons ce qui est simple.
intéressant	Nous aimons ce qui est intéressant.
neuf	Nous aimons ce qui est neuf.

Cette fois changez le dernier verbe.

Commençons.

On ne sait pas ce que tu **penses.**

dire	On ne sait pas ce que tu dis.
vouloir	On ne sait pas ce que tu veux.
faire	On ne sait pas ce que tu fais.

Activité 12. Conversation: Discrétion. Marguerite is asking you questions about your best friend Robert. You do not want to answer these questions. Say that you do not know. Begin your responses by **Je ne sais pas.** *Écoutez le modèle.*

<u>Modèle</u>: Qu'est-ce que Robert fait? — Je ne sais pas ce qu'il fait.

Commençons.

Qu'est-ce qu'il va faire cet été?	Je ne sais pas ce qu'il va faire cet été.
Qu'est-ce qu'il regarde à la télé?	Je ne sais pas ce qu'il regarde à la télé.
Qu'est-ce qu'il aime faire?	Je ne sais pas ce qu'il aime faire.

Marguerite persists in asking still more questions about Robert. Begin your responses by **Je ne peux pas vous dire.** *Écoutez le modèle.*

<u>Modèle</u>: Qu'est-ce qui intéresse Robert? — Je ne peux pas vous dire ce qui l'intéresse.

Commençons.

Qu'est-ce qui l'amuse?	Je ne peux pas vous dire ce qui l'amuse.
Qu'est-ce qui l'attire?	Je ne peux pas vous dire ce qui l'attire.

DIALOGUE

Activité 13. Questions indirectes. Olivier va vous poser des questions indirectes sur ce que vous avez fait. Répondez-lui sur la base des illustrations de votre manuel de laboratoire. Écoutez le modèle.

<u>Modèle</u>: Est-ce que tu peux me dire ce que tu as perdu? — J'ai perdu mon livre de français.

Commençons.

1. Est-ce que tu peux me dire ce que tu as mangé hier soir?	J'ai mangé du poulet.
2. Est-ce que tu peux me dire ce que tu as donné à ton père pour son anniversaire?	Je lui ai donné une cravate.
3. Est-ce que tu peux me dire ce que tu as offert à ta sœur pour son anniversaire?	Je lui ai offert une montre.
4. Est-ce que tu peux me dire ce que tu as acheté dans ce magasin?	J'ai acheté une veste.
5. Est-ce que tu peux me dire ce que tu as envoyé à ta cousine?	Je lui ai envoyé des photos.

DICTÉE

Activité 14. L'anniversaire de Marc. Vous allez entendre un court paragraphe. Écoutez d'abord! N'écrivez pas!

Demain, c'est l'anniversaire de Marc et je ne sais pas ce que je vais lui acheter. De quoi a-t-il besoin? Qu'est-ce qu'il aime faire? Qu'est-ce qui l'amuse? À qui est-ce que je peux demander ce que je dois lui offrir?

Maintenant, écrivez les phrases dans votre manuel de laboratoire.

Demain, / c'est l'anniversaire de Marc / et je ne sais pas / ce que je vais / lui acheter. / De quoi / a-t-il besoin? / Qu'est-ce qu'il aime faire? / Qu'est-ce qui / l'amuse? / À qui / est-ce que je peux demander / ce que je dois / lui offrir? /

Écoutez le texte encore une fois et vérifiez ce que vous avez écrit.

(Text is reread without pauses.)

LECTURE CULTURELLE

Activité 15. Lecture. Ouvrez votre livre à la page 512. Écoutez.

(See textbook page 512.)

Activité 16. Compréhension du texte. Vous allez entendre des phrases concernant le texte que vous avez écouté. Indiquez dans votre manuel de laboratoire si ces phrases sont vraies ou fausses.

Commençons.

1. La devise de la France est «Liberté, Égalité, Fraternité».
2. La statue de la Liberté a commémoré le centième anniversaire de la Révolution française.
3. Les Français ont donné cette statue aux Américains en 1789.
4. Pour les Français d'aujourd'hui, la liberté reste une valeur fondamentale.
5. Pour beaucoup de Français, les libertés individuelles sont plus importantes que les libertés publiques.
6. Certains Français pensent que le progrès technologique peut menacer les libertés individuelles.
7. En général, les Français n'aiment pas révéler les détails de leur vie privée.

Maintenant vérifiez vos réponses. Les phrases suivantes sont vraies: 1, 4, 5, 6 et 7. Les phrases fausses sont: 2 et 3.

Fin de la Leçon 33.
End of Lesson 33.
(music)

SONG CASSETTE TRANSCRIPT

The lyrics for the ten *Chansons françaises* are provided here, along with English translations. The following songs are included on Tape 19, Side B:

1. Un Canadien errant
2. Chevaliers de la table ronde
3. La mère Michel
4. Auprès de ma blonde
5. Marche des Rois
6. Il est né, le divin Enfant
7. Ah! vous dirai-je, Maman
8. À la claire fontaine
9. Il était une bergère
10. La Marseillaise

Vocals: Josée Vachon, Véronique Epiter-Smith, Kevin D. P. McDermott
Piano: Elizabeth Skavish
Guitar: Josée Vachon

A correlation chart demonstrating how certain songs might be used when teaching the material of certain units follows.

Un Canadien errant	Unit 2: adjectives Unit 7: irregular adjectives, negations
Chevaliers de la table ronde	Unit 2: **Il y a** + article Unit 3: prepositions of location Unit 9: **si** + present Unit 10: subjunctive
La mère Michel	Unit 4: imperative, passé composé Unit 11: two object pronouns, interrogative pronouns
Auprès de ma blonde	Unit 2: **avoir** Unit 3: **faire** Unit 5: geographical terms Unit 9: conditional
Marche des Rois	Unit 6: **suivre**, object pronouns Unit 7: imperfect
Il est né, le divin Enfant	Unit 1: **être** Unit 4: imperative Unit 5: expressions of quantity Unit 7: imperfect
Ah! vous dirai-je, Maman	Unit 7: imperfect Unit 10: infinitives, present participle Unit 11: **ce qui**
À la claire fontaine	Unit 4: passé composé Unit 6: object pronouns Unit 8: reflexive verbs
Il était une bergère	Unit 3: comparative Unit 8: pronoun **y**
La Marseillaise	Unit 4: imperative, passé composé

Un Canadien errant

Refrain:
Un Canadien errant, banni de ses foyers **(bis)**
Parcourait en pleurant des pays étrangers. **(bis)**

Un jour, triste et pensif
Assis au bord des flots **(bis)**
Au courant fugitif
Il adressa ces mots: **(bis)**

«Si tu vois mon pays,
Mon pays malheureux, **(bis)**
Va, dis à mes amis
Que je me souviens d'eux. **(bis)**

«Ô jours si pleins d'appas,
Vous êtes disparus ... **(bis)**
Et ma patrie, hélas!
Je ne la verrai plus!» **(bis)**

Plongé dans les malheurs,
Loin de mes chers parents, **(bis)**
Je passe dans les pleurs
D'infortunés moments. **(bis)**

Un Canadien errant *(A wandering Canadian)*

Refrain:
A wandering Canadian, banished from his home,
Crying, traveled through foreign countries.

One day, sad and pensive,
Seated on the banks of a stream
To the fleeting current
He addressed these words:

"If you see my country,
My unfortunate country,
Go, tell my friends
That I remember them."

0 days so filled with charms,
You are gone...
And my country, alas,
I will never see again!

Fallen deep into sorrow,
Far from my dear parents,
I spend my unhappy moments
In tears.

Chevaliers de la table ronde

Chevaliers de la table ronde,
Goûtons voir si le vin est bon. **(bis)**
Goûtons voir, oui, oui, oui,
Goûtons voir, non, non, non,
Goûtons voir si le vin est bon. **(bis)**

Si je meurs, je veux qu'on m'enterre
Dans la cave où il y a du bon vin. **(bis)**
Dans la cave, oui, oui, oui,
Dans la cave, non, non, non,
Dans la cave où il y a du bon vin.

Les deux pieds contre la muraille
Et la tête sous le robinet. **(bis)**
Et la tête, oui, oui, oui,
Et la tête, non, non, non,
Et la tête sous le robinet. **(bis)**

Sur ma tombe, je veux qu'on inscrive:
Ici gît le Roi des Buveurs. **(bis)**
Ici gît, oui, oui, oui,
Ici gît, non, non, non,
Ici gît le Roi des Buveurs. **(bis)**

Chevaliers de la table ronde

(Knights of the round table)

Knights of the round table
Let's taste the wine to see if it is good.
Let's taste to see, yes, yes, yes,
Let's taste to see, no, no, no,
Let's taste the wine to see if it is good.

If I die, I want to be buried
In the cellar where there is good wine.
In the cellar, yes, yes, yes,
In the cellar, no, no, no,
In the cellar where there is good wine.

My two feet against the stone wall,
And my head under the tap.
And my head, yes, yes, yes,
And my head, no, no, no,
And my head under the tap.

On my grave, I want to have written:
Here lies the King of Drinkers.
Here lies, yes, yes, yes,
Here lies, no, no, no,
Here lies the King of Drinkers.

La mère Michel

C'est la mère Michel
Qui a perdu son chat,
Qui crie par la fenêtre
Qu'est-ce qui le lui rendra?
C'est le père Lustucru
Qui lui a répondu:
Allez, la mère Michel,
Votre chat n'est pas perdu.

C'est la mère Michel
Qui lui a demandé:
Mon chat n'est pas perdu!
Vous l'avez donc trouvé?
Et le père Lustucru
Qui lui a répondu
Donnez une récompense,
Il vous sera rendu.

Et la mère Michel
Lui dit: c'est décidé.
Rendez-le-moi, mon chat;
Vous aurez un baiser.
Et le père Lustucru
Qui n'en a pas voulu,
Lui dit: Pour un lapin
Votre chat est vendu.

La mère Michel *(Mother Michel)*

It's Mother Michel
Who has lost her cat
And shouts out the window
What will get it back for her?
It's old Lustucru
Who answered her:
Come on, Mother Michel,
Your cat is not lost.

It's Mother Michel
Who asked him:
My cat is not lost!
So, you have found it?
And it's old Lustucru
Who answered her:
Give a reward
And you'll get it back.

And Mother Michel
Said to him: It's a deal.
Give me back my cat;
You will have a kiss.
And old Lustucru,
Who did not want a kiss,
Told her: Your cat
Has been sold for a rabbit.

Auprès de ma blonde

Dans les jardins d'mon père
Les lilas sont fleuris **(bis)**
Tous les oiseaux du monde
Viennent y faire leurs nids.

Refrain:
Auprès de ma blonde
Qu'il fait bon, fait bon, fait bon,
Auprès de ma blonde
Qu'il fait bon dormir.

Tous les oiseaux du monde
Viennent y faire leurs nids,
La caille, la tourterelle
Et la jolie perdrix.

La caille, la tourterelle
Et la jolie perdrix
Et ma jolie colombe
Qui chante jour et nuit.

Et ma jolie colombe
Qui chante jour et nuit,
Elle chante pour les filles
Qui n'ont pas de mari.

Elle chante pour les filles
Qui n'ont pas de mari.
Pour moi ne chante guère
Car j'en ai un joli.

Pour moi ne chante guère
Car j'en ai un joli.
— Mais dites-moi donc belle
Où est votre mari?

— Mais dites-moi donc belle
Où est votre mari?
— Il est dans la Hollande,
Les Hollandais l'ont pris!

— Il est dans la Hollande,
Les Hollandais l'ont pris!
— Que donneriez-vous, belle,
Pour avoir votre mari?

— Que donneriez-vous, belle,
Pour avoir votre mari?
— Je donnerais Versailles,
Paris et Saint Denis.

— Je donnerais Versailles,
Paris et Saint Denis,
Les tours de Notre Dame,
Le clocher de mon pays.

Les tours de Notre Dame,
Le clocher de mon pays.
Et ma jolie colombe
Qui chante jour et nuit.

Auprès de ma blonde *(Next to my fair beloved)*

In my father's gardens
The lilacs are in bloom
All the birds of the world
Go there to build their nests.

Refrain:
Next to my fair beloved
It's so sweet, so sweet, so sweet,
Next to my fair beloved,
It's so sweet to sleep.

All the birds of the world
Go there to build their nests.
The quail, the turtledove
And the pretty partridge.

The quail, the turtledove
And the pretty partridge
And my pretty dove
Who sings night and day.

And my pretty dove
Who sings night and day,
She sings for the girls
Who have no husband.

She sings for the girls
Who have no husband.
For me, she hardly ever sings
For I have a fine husband.

For me, she hardly ever sings
For I have a fine husband.
—But tell me then, my dear,
Where is your husband?

—But tell me then, my dear,
Where is your husband?
—He is in Holland,
The Dutch seized him!

—He is in Holland,
The Dutch seized him!
—What would you give, my dear,
To have your husband back?

—What would you give, my dear,
To have your husband back?
—I would give Versailles,
Paris, and Saint Denis.

I would give Versailles,
Paris, and Saint Denis,
The towers of Notre Dame,
The church tower of my home.

The towers of Notre Dame,
The church tower of my home.
And my pretty dove
Who sings night and day.

Marche des Rois

Ce matin, j'ai rencontré le train
De trois grands Rois qui allaient en voyage;
Ce matin, j'ai rencontré le train
De trois grands Rois dessus le grand chemin.
Tout chargés d'or, les suivaient d'abord
De grands guerriers et les gardes du trésor;
Tout chargés d'or les suivaient d'abord
De grands guerriers, avec leurs boucliers.

Ébahi d'entendre ceci,
Je me suis rangé pour voir les équipages.
Ébahi d'entendre ceci,
De loin en loin les ai toujours suivis.
L'astre brillant, qui était devant,
Servait de guide en menant les trois Rois mages;
L'astre brillant qui était devant,
S'arrêta net quand il fut vers l'enfant.

Marche des Rois *(March of the Kings)*

This morning, I met the procession
Of three great Kings who were traveling;
This morning, I met the procession
Of three great Kings on the main road.
All laden with gold, great warriors
And the guards of the treasure
Followed after them,
All laden with gold, great warriors
with their shields
Followed after them.

Astounded to hear this,
I stood aside to see their finery.
Astounded to hear this,
Further and further I kept on following them.
The bright star which was ahead
Served as guide by leading the three Kings;
The bright star which was ahead
Stopped short when it stood over the child.

Il est né, le divin Enfant

Refrain:
Il est né, le divin Enfant,
Jouez, hautbois, résonnez, musettes;
Il est né, le divin Enfant;
Chantons tous son avènement.

Depuis plus de quatre mille ans,
Nous le promettaient les prophètes;
Depuis plus de quatre mille ans,
Nous attendions cet heureux temps.

Qu'il est beau, qu'il est charmant,
Que ses grâces sont parfaites!
Qu'il est beau, qu'il est charmant,
Qu'il est doux, ce divin enfant!

Une étable est son logement,
Un peu de paille est sa couchette;
Une étable est son logement,
Pour un Dieu quel abaissement!

Ô Jésus, ô Roi tout puissant;
Si petit enfant que vous êtes,
Ô Jésus, ô Roi tout puissant,
Régnez sur nous entièrement.

Il est né, le divin Enfant *(He is born, the holy Child)*

Refrain:
He is born, the holy Child,
Play, oboes, sound forth bagpipes;
He is born, the holy Child;
Let us all sing of His coming.

For more than four thousand years
Prophets had been promising him to us;
For more than four thousand years
We were waiting for this happy time.

How beautiful he is, how charming he is,
How perfect are his graces!
How beautiful, how charming
How sweet this holy child is!

A stable is his home
A little straw his bed;
A stable is his home,
For a God, what a humbling condition!

0 Jesus, o all powerful King;
However small you are,
0 Jesus, o all powerful King,
Be our only ruler.

Ah! vous dirai-je, Maman

Ah! vous dirai-je, Maman,
ce qui cause mon tourment?
Depuis que j'ai vu Silvandre
me regarder d'un air tendre,
mon coeur dit à tout moment:
Peut-on vivre sans amant?

L'autre jour dans un bosquet
il me cueillait un bouquet;
il en orna ma houlette,
me disant: «Belle brunette,
Flore est moins belle que toi,
l'Amour moins épris que moi.»

Je rougis et par malheur
un soupir trahit mon coeur.
Le cruel, avec adresse,
profita de ma faiblesse:
Hélas! maman un faux pas
me fit tomber dans ses bras.

Je n'avais pour tout soutien
que ma houlette et mon chien.
Amour, voulant ma défaite,
écarta chien et houlette:
Ah! qu'on goûte de douceur
quand l'amour prend soin d'un cœur!

Ah, vous dirai-je, Maman *(Ah, Mother, shall I tell you)*

Ah, Mother, shall I tell you
What causes my torment?
Since I saw Silvandre
Look at me so tenderly,
My heart keeps saying:
Can one live without a lover?

The other day, in a grove
He was picking flowers for me;
He tied them to my staff,
Saying to me: "My beautiful brunette,
Flora is less beautiful than you
Love less smitten than me."

I blushed and unfortunately
A sigh betrayed my heart.
The cruel man shrewdly
Took advantage of my weakness:
Alas! Mother, I tripped and
Fell into his arms.

My only support was
My staff and my dog.
Love, wanting my defeat,
Pushed dog and staff away:
Ah! What sweetness
When love takes care of one's heart!

À la claire fontaine

À la claire fontaine
M'en allant promener,
J'ai trouvé l'eau si belle
Que je m'y suis baigné.
Il y a longtemps que je t'aime,
jamais je ne t'oublierai.

Sous les feuilles d'un chêne
Je me suis fait sécher;
Sur la plus haute branche
Le rossignol chantait.
Il y a longtemps que je t'aime,
Jamais je ne t'oublierai.

Chante, rossignol, chante,
Toi qui as le cœur gai;
Tu as le cœur à rire,
Moi je l'ai à pleurer!
Il y a longtemps que je t'aime,
Jamais je ne t'oublierai.

J'ai perdu ma maîtresse
Sans l'avoir mérité,
Pour un bouquet de roses
Que je lui refusai.
Il y a longtemps que je t'aime,
Jamais je ne t'oublierai.

Je voudrais que la rose
Fût encore au rosier
Et moi et ma maîtresse
Dans les mêmes amitiés.
Il y a longtemps que je t'aime,
Jamais je ne t'oublierai.

À la claire fontaine *(At the crystal fountain)*

At the crystal fountain,
As I was taking a walk,
I found the water so lovely
That I bathed in it.
I have loved you for a long time,
Never will I forget you.

Under the leaves of an oak tree
I dried myself off;
On the highest branch
The nightingale was singing.
I have loved you for a long time,
Never will I forget you.

Sing, nightingale, sing,
You who have a merry heart;
You feel like laughing,
I feel like crying!
I have loved you for a long time,
Never will I forget you.

I lost my beloved
Without deserving it,
For a bunch of flowers
Which I denied her.
I have loved you for a long time,
Never will I forget you.

I wish the rose
Were still on the rose bush
And that my beloved and I
Were still in love.
I have loved you for a long time,
Never will I forget you.

Il était une bergère

Il était une bergère,
Et ron et ron, petit patapon,
Il était une bergère
Qui gardait ses moutons,
Ron ron, qui gardait ses moutons.

Elle fit un fromage,
Et ron et ron, petit patapon,
Elle fit un fromage
Du lait de ses moutons,
Ron ron, du lait de ses moutons.

Le chat qui la regarde,
Et ron et ron, petit patapon,
Le chat qui la regarde
D'un petit air fripon,
Ron ron, d'un petit air fripon.

Si tu y mets la patte,
Et ron et ron, petit patapon,
Si tu y mets la patte
Tu auras du bâton
Ron ron, tu auras du bâton.

Il n'y mit pas la patte,
Et ron et ron, petit patapon,
Il n'y mit pas la patte
Il y mit le menton,
Ron ron, il y mit le menton.

La bergère en colère,
Et ron et ron, petit patapon,
La bergère en colère
Battit le petit chaton,
Ron ron, battit le petit chaton.

Il était une bergère *(There was once a shepherdess)*

There was once a shepherdess,
And purr, purr, petit patapon*,
There was once a shepherdess
Who was tending her sheep,
Purr, purr, who was tending her sheep.

She made a cheese,
And purr, purr, petit patapon,
She made a cheese
From the milk of her sheep,
Purr, purr, from the milk of her sheep.

The cat who watches her,
And purr, purr, petit patapon,
The cat who watches her
With a mischievous look,
Purr, purr, with a mischievous look.

If you put your paw in,
And purr, purr, petit patapon,
If you put your paw in
You will get beaten,
Purr, purr, you will get beaten.

He didn't put his paw in,
And purr, purr, petit patapon,
He didn't put his paw in
He put his chin in
Purr, purr, he put his chin in.

The angry shepherdess,
And purr, purr, petit patapon,
The angry shepherdess
Beat the little kitten
Purr, purr, beat the little kitten.

La Marseillaise

Allons enfants de la Patrie,
Le jour de gloire est arrivé.
Contre nous, de la tyrannie,
l'étendard sanglant est levé,
l'étendard sanglant est levé.
Entendez-vous, dans les campagnes
Mugir ces féroces soldats?
Ils viennent jusque dans nos bras
égorger vos fils, vos compagnes.
Aux armes citoyens! Formez vos bataillons!
Marchons, marchons!
Qu'un sang impur
Abreuve nos sillons!

La Marseillaise *(The Marseillaise)*

Come, children of our country,
The day of glory is here.
Tyranny's bloody banner
Has been raised against us
Do you hear in the fields these savage
Soldiers roaring?
They are coming upon us
To slaughter your sons, your companions.
Citizens, to arms! Form your battalions
And march on! march on!
May their vile blood
Water our fields.

LAB MANUAL ANSWER KEY

Unité Préliminaire

PREMIÈRE PARTIE

7. **Consonnes et voyelles**
   vowel sound: 3, 5, 8
   consonant sound: 1, 2, 4, 6, 7

11. **Bonjour!**
   Voici Annie et Nicole. Et voilà Pascal. Bonjour, Annie. Bonjour, Nicole. Qui est-ce? C'est Pascal. Au revoir, Annie. À bientôt.

7. **Identification de structures**
   une personne: 5, 8
   un groupe: 1, 3, 6
   impossible à dire: 2, 4, 7

10. **Compréhension**
   only number left: cinq

16. **Au Canada**
   Vous habitez à Paris? J'habite à Québec avec Paul et Jacques. Nous habitons à Québec, mais nous ne travaillons pas à Québec. Je travaille à Montréal. Paul et Jacques étudient à l'Université Laval.

DEUXIÈME PARTIE

8. **Orthographe**

1.	hôtel	6.	Michèle
2.	garçon	7.	Mélanie
3.	forêt	8.	Danièle
4.	Léon	9.	Françoise
5.	Joël	10.	Valérie

10. **Géographie**

1.	Paris	4.	Cherbourg
2.	Nancy	5.	Avignon
3.	Bordeaux	6.	Montpellier

12. **Salutations**
   —Bonjour, Mademoiselle. —Bonjour, Monsieur. —Comment allez-vous? —Je vais très bien. Et vous? —Je vais comme ci, comme ça.

Unité 1

LEÇON 1

2. **Compréhension du texte**
   vrai: 1, 2, 4
   faux: 3, 5

LEÇON 2

2. **Compréhension du texte**
   vrai: 2, 3, 4, 5, 8
   faux: 1, 6, 7

11. **Compréhension: Les nombres**
   13, 16, 22, 30, 50, 60, 69, 73, 80, 92

12. **Compréhension: Les adresses**

1.	86	5.	82
2.	61	6.	76
3.	14	7.	95
4.	98	8.	24

14. **Compréhension: La montre de Claire**
   oui: 1, 3, 5, 6
   non: 2, 4, 7, 8

17. **Voyages**
   J'aime voyager. Je voyage assez souvent. Maintenant je suis à Québec. Je voudrais aussi visiter Montréal. Est-ce que vous voyagez souvent? Est-ce que vous aimez voyager?

LEÇON 3

2. **Compréhension du texte**
oui: 1, 4, 5
non: 2, 3

14. **Compréhension orale: Quelle est la date?**
    1. le 23 avril
    2. le 12 décembre
    3. le 13 juin
    4. le premier juillet
    5. le 25 août
    6. le 5 janvier
    7. le premier février
    8. le 18 mai

16. **Tennis**
Avec qui est-ce que tu joues au tennis? Tu joues avec Paul et Philippe, n'est-ce pas? Pourquoi est-ce que tu joues avec eux? Pourquoi est-ce que tu ne joues pas avec moi? Moi aussi, je joue bien!

Vivre en France 1

1. **La bonne réponse**
    1. a. Je suis photographe.
    2. b. Non, je suis marié.
    3. b. À Montréal.
    4. c. Allô! Ici André Lucas.
    5. c. Oui, un moment. Ne quittez pas, s'il vous plaît.
    6. b. Je suis né le 18 septembre.
    7. a. Oui, bien sûr. À lundi.
    8. a. Bonjour, Thérèse, comment allez-vous?

2. **En France**
Nom: Lavoie
Prénom: Denise
Nationalité: américaine
Lieu de naissance: Boston
Adresse: 39, rue du Four
Numéro de téléphone: 43-29-20-52

Unité 2

LEÇON 4

2. **Compréhension du texte**
vrai: 2, 4, 5, 6
faux: 1, 3

6. **Identification de structures**
un homme: 1, 3, 4, 6, 7
une femme: 2, 5, 8

9. **Compréhension: Qui est-ce?**
    1. un professeur
    2. un ami
    3. une jeune fille
    4. une étudiante
    5. une femme
    6. un jeune homme

17. **Jacqueline**
Voici Jacqueline. C'est une amie. Elle a des disques, mais elle n'a pas de chaîne-stéréo. Moi, j'ai une mini-chaîne, mais elle ne marche pas. Et toi, est-ce que tu as une chaîne-stéréo?

LEÇON 5

2. **Compréhension du texte**
vrai: 1, 2, 3, 7, 8
faux: 4, 5, 6

4. **Identification de structures**
un homme: 1, 6, 9
une femme: 2, 3, 7, 10
des personnes: 4, 5, 8

13. **Suzanne**
Suzanne est une grande fille brune. Elle habite à Paris, mais elle n'est pas française. Elle est américaine. Elle a un copain. C'est un étudiant anglais. Et vous, est-ce que vous avez des amis anglais?

LEÇON 6

2. **Compréhension du texte**
    1. Patrice
    2. Michèle
    3. Henri
    4. Jean-François
    5. Nathalie

10. Identification de structures
présent: 2, 4, 7
futur: 1, 3, 5, 6, 8

13. Compréhension orale
logique: 1, 2, 5, 6, 7
illogique: 3, 4, 8

17. Temps libre
Où allez-vous? Moi, je vais à la piscine avec Jean-Michel. Nous allons nager et jouer au volley. À quatre heures, nous allons aller chez lui et nous allons jouer aux cartes. Aimez-vous le bridge?

Vivre en France 2

1. La bonne réponse
1. c. Non, vous tournez à gauche.
2. a. Non, c'est tout près.
3. b. Il se trouve à côté de la pharmacie.
4. a. Il se trouve avenue des Acacias.
5. c. Vous devez traverser la rue Jacob et continuer tout droit.
6. b. C'est au sud.
7. c. Oui, il y a un commissariat dans l'avenue de la Libération.
8. c. Oui, continuez tout droit. C'est à cent mètres à gauche.

2. En France
See map on p. 196 of Lab Manual. Pierre's house should be indicated with an X directly across the boulevard Carnot from the hospital.

Unité 3

LEÇON 7

2. Compréhension du texte
vrai: 1, 4, 5
faux: 2, 3, 6

6. Compréhension orale
1. 1.000
2. 120
3. 300
4. 150
5. 10.000
6. 8.000
7. 500
8. 2.000

15. Mes voisins
Mes voisins ont deux enfants. Leur fils Robert est étudiant. C'est mon copain. Leur fille Alice est mariée. Son mari travaille au laboratoire de l'université.

17. Compréhension du texte
vrai: 2, 4
faux: 1, 3, 5

LEÇON 8

2. Compréhension du texte
vrai: 2, 3, 6
faux: 1, 4, 5

6. Compréhension orale
1. un manteau
2. une cravate
3. une chemise
4. un anorak
5. un costume
6. une robe
7. des chaussures
8. un chemisier
9. un pantalon

14. Au magasin
Je vais acheter cette cravate rouge. Elle coûte soixante-dix francs. Elle n'est pas très bon marché, mais elle est jolie. Je vais aussi acheter cette chemise bleue et ces chaussures noires. Et toi, quelles chaussures préfères-tu?

16. Compréhension du texte
vrai: 2, 4, 6
faux: 1, 3, 5

LEÇON 9

2. Compréhension du texte
vrai: 1, 5
faux: 2, 3, 4

8. Compréhension orale
1. la chambre
2. le salon
3. la cuisine
4. la salle de bains
5. la salle à manger
6. le jardin

16. Le week-end
Qu'est-ce que vous faites le weekend? Quand il pleut, je fais le ménage. Mais quand il fait beau, je ne reste pas chez moi. Ce week-end, je vais faire une promenade à bicyclette. Je vais aller chez Roger, mon nouvel ami. Il habite un bel appartement dans une vieille maison.

18. Compréhension du texte
vrai: 1, 2, 3
faux: 4, 5

Vivre en France 3

1. La bonne réponse
1. c. Deux cents francs, s'il vous plaît.
2. b. Il est à 5 francs 10.
3. c. Oui, voilà mon passeport.
4. c. Non, mais il y a une banque dans l'avenue du Maine.
5. a. Non, j'ai seulement un billet de 500 francs.
6. b. Allez à la caisse numéro deux.
7. a. En espèces.
8. c. En livres sterling, s'il vous plaît.

2. En France
Devises: dollars canadiens
Taux de change: 5 francs 80
Montant: 300 dollars
Forme: chèques de voyage
Pièce d'identité: passeport

Unité 4

LEÇON 10

2. Compréhension du texte
vrai: 3, 5, 6
faux: 1, 2, 4, 7, 8

12. Compréhension: Les problèmes de l'existence
Answers will vary.

15. Sylvestre
Mon cousin Sylvestre a dix-neuf ans. Il a l'intention d'aller en France. Il a besoin d'argent. Voilà pourquoi il vend son auto. Avez-vous envie d'acheter cette auto? Réfléchissez à ma question!

17. Compréhension du texte
vrai: 1, 3, 4
faux: 2

LEÇON 11

2. Compréhension du texte
vrai: 1, 3, 5, 6, 8
faux: 2, 4, 7

6. Identification de structures
présent: 2, 4, 6, 8, 11, 12
passé composé: 1, 3, 5, 7, 9, 10

16. Samedi dernier
Qu'est-ce que vous avez fait samedi dernier? Moi, j'ai téléphoné à Julien. L'après-midi, nous avons joué au tennis. Le soir, nous avons dîné dans un restaurant italien. Après, nous avons rendu visite à un copain. Vraiment, nous n'avons pas perdu notre temps!

18. Compréhension du texte
vrai: 1, 2, 4, 7
faux: 3, 5, 6

LEÇON 12

2. Compréhension du texte
vrai: 2, 5, 6, 7, 8
faux: 1, 3, 4

9. Identification de structures
présent: 1, 4, 8, 10
passé composé: 2, 3, 5, 6, 7, 9

10. Compréhension orale

1. entrer	4. descendre
2. arriver	5. rester
3. partir	6. sortir

12. Compréhension: Dates historiques
1. le premier septembre 1715
2. le 15 août 1769
3. le 4 juillet 1776
4. le 11 novembre 1918
5. le 7 décembre 1941
6. le 25 août 1944
7. le 4 avril 1968

16. Au Canada
L'année dernière, Georges est allé au Canada avec sa cousine Sylvie. Ils sont partis de Paris le dix juillet. Ils ont visité Québec où ils sont restés deux semaines. Là-bas, Georges a rencontré une étudiante canadienne avec qui il est souvent sorti.

18. Compréhension du texte
vrai: 3
faux: 1, 2, 4

Vivre en France 4

1. La bonne réponse
1. c. Parce que c'est moins cher qu'à l'hôtel.
2. b. Nous sommes restés dans une pension.
3. c. Oui, elle a l'air conditionné et la télé.
4. a. C'est 500 francs par jour.
5. c. Non, je préfère utiliser ma carte de crédit.
6. a. Une semaine.
7. a. À huit heures du matin.
8. b. Une chambre avec salle de bains.

2. En France
Chambre no.: 76
Nom du client: Monsieur Clément
Durée du séjour: Dix jours
Prix: 400 francs par nuit

Unité 5

LEÇON 13

2. Compréhension du texte
Per Eriksen: 1, 5
Susan Morrison: 3, 7
Karin Schmidt: 8
Andrew Mitchell: 2, 6, 9
Peter de Jong: 4, 10

6. Identification de structures
passé: 1, 4, 7, 8, 9
futur: 2, 3, 5, 6, 10

14. Catherine
Je viens de téléphoner à Catherine. Elle vient de passer une semaine à Québec. Maintenant, elle est à Montréal. Elle est là-bas depuis samedi. Elle revient aux États-Unis le premier juillet.

16. Compréhension du texte
vrai: 1, 3, 5, 6, 7
faux: 2, 4

LEÇON 14

2. Compréhension du texte
oui: 2, 3, 5, 7, 8
non: 1, 4, 6

13. Compréhension
1. le fromage
2. le gâteau
3. le sucre
4. le pain
5. la glace
6. le beurre
7. le poisson
8. la bière
9. le vin

16. Au restaurant
Guillaume et Suzanne sont au restaurant. Guillaume regarde le menu. Il va prendre du poulet et de la salade. Il va boire du vin. Suzanne va prendre de la salade, mais elle ne va pas prendre de poulet. Elle va prendre du jambon et boire de l'eau minérale.

18. Compréhension du texte
vrai: 2, 4
faux: 1, 3, 5

LEÇON 15

2. Compréhension du texte
vrai: 1, 2, 5
faux: 3, 4

5. Questions personnelles
Answers will vary.

11. Compréhension: Au restaurant
Client 7: des carottes
Cliente 2: de la bière
Client 3: de la sole
Cliente 4: une poire

15. Au restaurant
Nous déjeunons souvent dans ce restaurant. La viande et les légumes sont toujours très bons. François va commander du poulet avec des frites. Moi, je vais prendre de la sole parce que je suis au régime.

17. Compréhension du texte
vrai: 1, 2, 4
faux: 3, 5

Vivre en France 5

1. La bonne réponse

1. c. Bien sûr. Voulez-vous un croque-monsieur?
2. b. Voilà! Ça fait 48 francs.
3. a. Je vais prendre le lapin farci.
4. a. Donnez-moi une crème caramel.
5. b. Il y a des œufs mayonnaise.
6. c. Non, je vais prendre du jambon.
7. c. Oui, donnez-moi de l'eau minérale, s'il vous plaît.
8. c. Attendez une seconde. Je vais préparer l'addition.

2. En France
Hors d'œuvre: la salade de tomates
Plat principal: le poulet rôti
Légumes: les petits pois
Salade: une salade verte
Dessert: la tarte aux cerises
Boisson: de l'eau minérale

Unité 6

LEÇON 16

2. Compréhension du texte
vrai: 1, 2, 3, 4
faux: ——

6. Compréhension orale
logique: 1, 4, 5, 6
illogique: 2, 3

20. Ce soir
Ce soir, mes amis veulent aller au cinéma. Je veux sortir avec eux, mais je ne peux pas. Demain, j'ai un examen très difficile. Je dois rester chez moi. À mon université, il faut beaucoup étudier si on ne veut pas rater ses examens.

22. Compréhension du texte
vrai: 3, 4, 6
faux: 1, 2, 5

LEÇON 17

2. Compréhension du texte
vrai: 1, 3
faux: 2, 4, 5, 6

5. Compréhension orale
logique: 1, 3, 4, 6, 7, 8
illogique: 2, 5

10. Identification de structures
Philippe: 4, 6, 7
Annie: 2, 5
Jacques et Pierre: 1, 3, 8

17. Monique et Henri
Connais-tu Monique? Moi, je la connais bien. Je l'ai rencontrée l'année dernière à Paris. Je vais l'inviter à la fête. Elle va venir avec son cousin Henri. Je ne le connais pas, mais ses amis le trouvent très sympathique. Il fait des études d'ingénieur à l'Université de Grenoble.

19. Compréhension du texte
vrai: 1, 5, 6, 7
faux: 2, 3, 4

LEÇON 18

2. Compréhension du texte
vrai: 1, 2, 4, 8
faux: 3, 5, 6, 7

8. Identification de structures
Sylvie: 2, 3, 5, 7
Marc et Éric: 1, 4, 6, 8

16. J'ai besoin de mon livre
Tu connais Christine, n'est-ce pas? Elle m'a parlé de toi quand je lui ai rendu visite hier. Je lui ai prêté un livre, et maintenant j'ai besoin de ce livre. Je veux lui téléphoner. Donne-moi son numéro de téléphone, s'il te plaît!

18. Compréhension du texte
vrai: 2, 3, 5
faux: 1, 4, 6

Vivre en France 6

1. La bonne réponse
1. a. Il y a un livre.
2. b. Je dois envoyer un télégramme.
3. c. Je voudrais l'envoyer en recommandé.
4. c. Oui! Tiens, ces cartes postales sont pour toi.
5. b. J'attends une lettre de mon copain Pierre.
6. c. Bien sûr, mais dis-moi, à qui est-ce que tu écris?
7. c. J'ai l'intention d'écrire à ma cousine qui habite au Canada.
8. a. Mets-le ici, à côté du nom de la ville.

2. En France

	valeur unitaire	quantité	total
TIMBRES	4,00	1	4,00
	,50	1	,50
	2,20	2	4,40
AÉROGRAMMES	3,70	3	11,10
Total			20,00

Unité 7

LEÇON 19

2. Compréhension du texte
vrai: 2, 3, 5, 7, 9
faux: 1, 4, 6, 8, 10, 11, 12

14. Où habites-tu?
Answers will vary.

15. Ma voisine
J'habite dans un immeuble qui n'est pas très moderne mais que je trouve confortable. Je connais tous mes voisins. J'ai une voisine qui est très sympathique et que j'invite souvent chez moi. C'est une étudiante qui a passé plusieurs années dans une université américaine.

17. Compréhension du texte
vrai: 2, 3, 5
faux: 1, 4, 6

LEÇON 20

2. Compréhension du texte
vrai: 1, 2, 4, 5, 6
faux: 3

12. Identification de structures
événement spécifique: 1, 4, 5, 7
événement habituel: 2, 3, 6, 8

16. Le fils des voisins
Quand j'avais douze ans, j'habitais dans un petit village. Je passais tous mes week-ends avec Henri, le fils des voisins. C'était mon meilleur ami. Nous allions souvent à la plage et parfois nous faisions des promenades à bicyclette.

18. Compréhension du texte
vrai: 2, 3, 4, 6
faux: 1, 5, 7, 8

LEÇON 21

2. Compréhension du texte
vrai: 2, 3, 5, 6, 7, 10
faux: 1, 4, 8, 9

5. Identification de structures
circonstance: 1, 2, 3, 4, 6, 7
événement spécifique: 5, 8, 9, 10, 11, 12, 13, 14

13. **Hier soir**
Hier soir, je suis sorti avant le dîner. Il faisait un temps épouvantable. Il neigeait et la visibilité était très mauvaise. Quand je suis rentré, j'ai vu quelqu'un qui attendait un taxi, mais il n'y avait pas de taxi. J'ai reconnu mon ami Jean-Claude. Je l'ai invité chez moi et nous avons dîné ensemble.

15. **Compréhension du texte**
vrai: 1, 2, 3, 4
faux: 5

Vivre en France 7

1. **La bonne réponse**
   1. b. Je pense que c'est une pièce de Pirandello.
   2. c. On peut aller à la séance de vingt heures.
   3. a. Un excellent spectacle de variétés.
   4. c. Oh, tu sais, moi, je ne connais rien à l'art moderne.
   5. a. Non, je dois étudier.
   6. c. Volontiers, est-ce qu'il y a un café près d'ici?
   7. a. C'est entendu!
   8. b. Oui, je vais aller à un concert avec mes copains.

2. **En France**

Rendez-vous

avec qui?	Jean-Claude
quelle date?	23 mai
à quelle heure?	9 h 50
où?	l'Odéon
nom de film?	*Hannah et ses sœurs*

Unité 8

LEÇON 22

2. **Compréhension du texte**
Anne-Marie: 2, 6, 7
François: 5
Henri: 3, 4, 9
Josiane: 1, 8, 10

5. **Compréhension**
logique: 1, 2, 4, 5, 6, 8
illogique: 3, 7

14. **À la mer**
Allez-vous souvent à la mer? Quand j'étais jeune, j'y allais tous les étés. C'est là que j'ai appris à faire de la voile. J'en faisais très souvent. Maintenant je n'en fais plus parce que je n'ai pas de bateau. Si j'ai de l'argent, je vais en acheter un cet été.

16. **Compréhension du texte**
vrai: 2, 4, 5
faux: 1, 3

LEÇON 23

2. **Compréhension du texte**
vrai: 2, 4, 5
faux: 1, 3, 6, 7, 8

6. **Compréhension orale**

1. les yeux	4. les pieds
2. les cheveux	5. la tête
3. les oreilles	6. la bouche

15. **Le dimanche**
À quelle heure est-ce que vous vous levez le dimanche? Moi, je ne me lève jamais avant dix heures. Je me rase, je me lave, je m'habille et j'écoute la radio. L'après-midi, je me promène avec mon amie Marie-Laure. Nous nous promenons souvent à la campagne. Et vous, est-ce que vous vous promenez avec vos amis?

17. **Compréhension du texte**
vrai: 2, 3, 5, 6
faux: 1, 4

LEÇON 24

2. **Compréhension du texte**
vrai: 2, 3, 6, 7, 8
faux: 1, 4, 5

7. **Compréhension orale**
logique: 1, 2, 3, 4, 5, 7
illogique: 6, 8

12. Identification de structures
présent: 3, 4, 6, 7, 10
passé: 1, 2, 5, 8, 9

16. Guy et Suzanne
Aujourd'hui, Guy s'est levé tôt. Ils s'est rasé et il s'est habillé. Après il a téléphoné à Suzanne. Ils se sont donné rendez-vous au café de l'université pour trois heures. Guy est arrivé un peu en retard, mais Suzanne ne s'est pas impatientée. Guy et Suzanne se sont promenés jusqu'à sept heures. Est-ce qu'ils s'aiment? C'est possible.

18. Compréhension du texte
vrai: 1, 3, 4, 5, 8
faux: 2, 6, 7

Vivre en France 8

1. La bonne réponse

1. c. Non, mais j'ai pris un bon bain de soleil.
2. b. Je vais tous les soirs au Stade Municipal.
3. c. Oui, et nous avons fait plusieurs longues randonnées à pied.
4. a. Je faisais de l'aviron.
5. b. Écoutez, j'aimerais bien . . . mais je ne sais pas nager!
6. b. Oui, je crois que j'ai la grippe.
7. c. Oui, je crois que j'ai trop mangé.
8. a. Je suis tombé de vélo.
9. c. Je mange modérément et je fais du jogging tous les jours.
10. b. J'ai couru pendant quinze kilomètres.
11. c. Hélas, non! Je me suis cassé la jambe le jour de mon arrivée.
12. a. Je me suis foulé le poignet.

2. En France

Nom et prénom:	Sylvie Lambert		
Sports pratiqués:	jogging	Niveau:	bon
	tennis		faible
	judo		excellent
	équitation		assez bon
État de santé:	excellent		

Unité 9

LEÇON 25

2. Compréhension du texte
vrai: 1, 6, 7
faux: 2, 3, 4, 5, 8

5. Compréhension orale
Answers will vary.

7. Identification de structures
masculin: 1, 3, 4, 5, 10
féminin: 2, 6, 7, 8, 9

14. Réactions personnelles
Answers will vary.

16. Étienne et ses sœurs
Connais-tu Étienne? C'est un garçon très travailleur et très ambitieux. Ses sœurs sont assez différentes. Christine est une fille très sportive mais elle n'est pas très intellectuelle. Catherine est une fille très idéaliste et très généreuse. Voilà pourquoi elle a beaucoup d'amis loyaux.

18. Compréhension du texte
vrai: 1, 2, 4
faux: 3, 5

LEÇON 26

2. Compréhension du texte
Michèle: 2, 5, 7
Anne-Marie: 3
Jacques: 1, 8
Martin: 4, 6

13. Compréhension orale
Pierre: médecin
Philippe: ouvrier
Marie-Thérèse: ingénieur
Antoine: vendeur
Hélène: journaliste
Albert: employé
Henriette: cadre
Thomas: écrivain

17. **Voyage en Italie**
Si j'ai de l'argent cet été, je ferai un voyage en Italie avec mon ami Charles. Nous irons d'abord à Rome. Quand nous serons là-bas, nous verrons mes cousins. J'espère qu'ils pourront nous trouver un hôtel bon marché. Je leur enverrai un télégramme quand je saurai la date de notre départ.

19. **Compréhension du texte**
vrai: 2, 3, 4
faux: 1, 5, 6

LEÇON 27

2. **Compréhension du texte**
Paul: 5
Jacqueline: 1, 8
Robert: 2, 3
Marie-France: 4, 6, 7

7. **Identification de structures**
certitude: 1, 5, 7, 8, 10, 11
hypothèse: 2, 3, 4, 6, 9, 12

14. **Après l'université**
Qu'est-ce que je ferais si je n'étais pas étudiant? Je ne resterais pas ici. Si j'avais de l'argent, je ferais un grand voyage. Je verrais de nouveau pays. J'irais au Japon ou en Chine. Je reviendrais en France après deux ou trois ans.

16. **Compréhension du texte**
vrai: 1, 3, 4, 5
faux: 2, 6

Vivre en France 9

1. **La bonne réponse**
   1. b. Non, il est occupé.
   2. c. Bien sûr, allez à la porte F.
   3. c. Je ne pense pas. On m'a dit que l'avion était direct.
   4. b. Mais oui! Allez au comptoir d'Air Maroc.
   5. c. Non, donnez-moi un aller simple.
   6. a. Non, il y a une correspondance à Saint-Pierre-des-Corps.
   7. b. Non, il a une demi-heure de retard.
   8. b. Allez au guichet 2.
   9. c. Je ne sais pas. Vous pouvez demander au bureau de renseignements.
   10. c. Non, je vais les garder avec moi.

2. **En France**
Nom: Thomas
Prénom: Janine
Compagnie aérienne: Air France
Vol no: 102
Destination: Chicago
Date de départ: 2 septembre
Date de retour: 8 septembre
Mode de paiement: carte de crédit

Unité 10

LEÇON 28

2. **Compréhension du texte**
vrai: 2, 3, 5, 7
faux: 1, 4, 6, 8, 9

12. **Pour apprendre l'anglais**
Au lieu d'aller en vacances cet été, je vais travailler. Je veux gagner de l'argent pour passer deux mois en Angleterre. C'est en travaillant à Madrid que j'ai appris l'espagnol. C'est en allant en Angleterre que j'apprendrai l'anglais.

14. **Compréhension du texte**
vrai: 1, 2, 3, 4, 8
faux: 5, 6, 7

LEÇON 29

2. **Compréhension du texte**
vrai: 1, 2, 4, 7
faux: 3, 5, 6

13. **Identification de structures**
le sujet: 1, 4, 5, 7
une personne différente: 2, 3, 6, 8

17. **Les courses**
Je vais aller au supermarché. Il faut que j'achète de la bière. Ensuite, je veux passer à la bibliothèque. Il faut que je prenne un livre. Non, il n'est pas nécessaire que vous veniez avec moi. Mais, j'aimerais bien que vous me prêtiez votre voiture.

19. **Compréhension du texte**
vrai: 3, 5, 6, 8
faux: 1, 2, 4, 7

LEÇON 30

2. **Compréhension du texte**
vrai: 1, 2, 5, 6, 7
faux: 3, 4, 8, 9, 10

9. **Identification de structures**
Je sais: 1, 3, 6, 9, 10
Je doute: 2, 4, 5, 7, 8

18. **Compréhension orale**
indicatif: 1, 4, 5, 7,
subjonctif: 2, 3, 6, 8, 9, 10, 11, 12

20. **Visite à Genève**
Je suis content que tu ailles à Genève cet été, mais j'ai peur que tu ne puisses pas rencontrer mon frère. Je sais qu'il voyage beaucoup et je doute qu'il soit chez lui en juillet.

22. **Compréhension du texte**
vrai: 1, 2, 6, 8
faux: 3, 4, 5, 7

Vivre en France 10

1. **La bonne réponse**
   1. c. Je l'ai achetée dans une boutique de soldes rue de Sèvres.
   2. a. Non, elle est en laine!
   3. b. Je cherche des mocassins.
   4. a. Je chausse du trente-huit.
   5. c. J'aime la veste mais je n'aime pas le pantalon.
   6. c. Désolé, mais je n'ai pas mon porte-feuille sur moi.
   7. a. Je vais mettre mon blouson de cuir.
   8. b. Non, il est trop serré.
   9. c. Non, elle a acheté une Toyota d'occasion.
   10. a. Elle portait une ceinture blanche.

2. **En France**

	Description
VÊTEMENTS	
blouson	cuir noir
deux chemises de coton	blanches; manches longues
cravate	soie bleue unie
CHAUSSURES	
une paire de mocassins	cuir rouge; pointure 39
AUTRES OBJETS	
sac	grand, en plastique
portefeuille	?

Unité 11

LEÇON 31

2. **Compréhension du texte**
vrai: 3, 4, 5, 6
faux: 1, 2, 7, 8

14. **Mon vélo**
Je n'ai pas mon vélo. Je l'ai prêté à Thomas. Demande-le-lui. S'il ne te le donne pas, dis-lui que je vais le chercher demain.

16. **Compréhension du texte**
vrai: 1, 4, 6
faux: 2, 3, 5

LEÇON 32

2. **Compréhension du texte**
vrai: 1, 2, 5, 6
faux: 3, 4

15. **Mes disques**
J'ai plusieurs disques. Lequel veux-tu écouter? Personnellement, je préfère celui qui est sur la petite table. C'est celui que mon frère Julien m'a donné pour mon anniversaire.

17. **Compréhension du texte**
vrai: 2, 4
faux: 1, 3, 5

LEÇON 33

2. **Compréhension du texte**
vrai: 2, 3, 4, 7, 8, 9, 11
faux: 1, 5, 6, 10, 12

6. **Identification de structures**
une personne: 2, 5, 7, 9
une chose: 1, 3, 4, 6, 8, 10

8. **Identification de structures**
une personne: 1, 2, 4, 7, 9
une chose: 3, 5, 6, 8, 10

14. **L'anniversaire de Marc**
Demain, c'est l'anniversaire de Marc et je ne sais pas ce que je vais lui acheter. De quoi a-t-il besoin? Qu'est-ce qu'il aime faire? Qu'est-ce qui l'amuse? À qui est-ce que je peux demander ce que je dois lui offrir?

16. **Compréhension du texte**
vrai: 1, 4, 5, 6, 7
faux: 2, 3

PAS DE PROBLÈME: VIDEO TRANSCRIPT

Correlation of *Pas de problème* with *Contacts 5/e*

The **Pas de problème** video brings French culture and the French language alive in the classroom. As students watch the video modules, they will not be able to understand every word, but they will be able to follow the story line and observe how phrases and structures they have learned are used in real conversation.

By reading the script in advance, the teacher can see at a glance which conversational exchanges may cause comprehension difficulties. These points may be presented via overhead transparency prior to showing the module.

The following chart shows how **Pas de problème** is correlated with the progression of **Contacts 5/e.** It is probably most effective to show the video at the end of each corresponding unit as a way of contextualizing key themes and structures.

Video Module	*Correlation with* ***Contacts 5/e***	*Video Theme*	*Related Topics in* ***Contacts 5/e***
I, part 1 (up to *Les Sports*)	Unité 1	Meeting people Playing tennis	Unité préliminaire: Vivre en France Unité 1: activities (*-er* verbs)
I, part 2 (*Les Sports* to end)	Unité 2	Preferred sports Movies	Unité 2: preferences (use of *le* in a general sense) Unité 2: Leçon 6: Note culturelle
II	Unité 3	Phone calls Getting around the city Le Quartier Latin	review: Unité 1: Vivre en France review: Unité 2: Vivre en France Unité 3, Leçon 9: Note culturelle
III	Unité 4	Shopping for clothes Making suggestions Paris	review: Unité 3, Leçon 8 Unité 4, Leçon 10 (imperative) Unité 4, Leçon 11: Note culturelle
IV	Unité 5	Shopping for croissants Talking about food Meals	Unité 5, Leçon 14 Unité 5, Leçon 14 (partitive) Unité 5, Leçon 15
V	Unité 6	Ordering in a café Obligations Knowing people Talking about others Taking the train	review: Unité 5: Vivre en France Unité 6, Leçon 16 *(pouvoir, devoir, vouloir, il faut)* Unité 6, Leçon 17 *(connaître)* Unité 6, Leçons 17, 18 (pronouns) anticipation: Unité 9: Vivre en France

Video Module	*Correlation with* ***Contacts 5/e***	*Video Theme*	*Related Topics in* ***Contacts 5/e***
VI	Unité 7	Areas of France	Unité 7, Leçon 19: Note culturelle
		Talking about past events	review: Unité 4 (passé composé)
			Unité 7, Leçons 20, 21 (imperfect)
VII	Unité 7	Post office	review: Unité 6: Vivre en France
		Knowing things	Unité 7, Leçon 19 *(savoir)*
		Giving directions	review: Unité 2: Vivre en France
		Describing shops	review: Unité 4, Leçon 10 *(vendre)*
			review: Unité 5, Leçon 14 (partitive)
VIII	Unité 8	Talking about the recent past	review: Unité 5, Leçon 13 *(venir de)*
		Common activities	Unité 8, Leçons 23, 24 (reflexives)
		Opening things	Unité 8, Leçon 23 *(ouvrir)*
		Car repair	[unfamiliar topic]
IX	Unité 9	Descriptions	Unité 9, Leçon 25 (adjectives and adverbs)
		Discussing the future	Unité 9, Leçon 26 (future)
		Expressing conditions	Unité 9, Leçon 27 (conditional)
		Paris monuments	review: Unité 4, Leçon 11: Note culturelle
X	Unité 10	Shopping for food	review: Unité 4, Leçons 14, 15 (partitive; fruits and vegetables)
		Giving instructions	Unité 10, Leçon 28 (infinitive constructions)
		Expressing uncertainty	Unité 10, Leçons 29, 30 (subjunctive)
XI	Unité 11	Talking about others	Unité 11, Leçon 31 (review of object pronouns)
		Explaining things	Unité 11, Leçon 33 *(ce qui, ce que)*
		Parking tickets	[unfamiliar topic]
XII	Review	Leisure activities	review: Unité 7: Vivre en France
		Talking about others	review: Unité 6, Leçon 16 *(autre, tout)*
		Describing destinations	review: Unité 8, Leçon 22 *(y)*
		Expressing obligations	review: Unité 10, Leçons 29, 30 (subjunctive)

PERSONNAGES

Jean-François, 22 ans, québécois, à Paris depuis quelques jours seulement.
Marie-Christine, 21 ans, française, étudiante à Paris depuis deux ans.
Bruno, 23 ans, sénégalais, étudiant à Paris depuis trois ans.
Alissa, 21 ans, réunionnaise, à Paris avec ses parents depuis dix ans.
Moustafa, 22 ans, tunisien, étudiant à Paris depuis deux ans.
Yves, 20 ans, français.

MODULE I *Au tennis* RT 5:16

Jean-François: Bon alors, la Tour Eiffel ... place de la Concorde ... le métro? Il est là.

Voix-off: Cet après-midi, Jean-François joue au tennis avec son ami René. Il passe chez lui pour chercher ses affaires de tennis. Il retrouve René au tennis du Bois de Vincennes.

Jean-François: Salut, René.
René: Salut, Jean-François. Tu vas bien?
Jean-François: Oui, ça va, merci. On joue jusqu'à quelle heure?
René: On joue jusqu'à cinq heures.
Jean-François: Ah bien, c'est très bien, parce que je travaille ce soir.
René: Eh bien moi, je vais au cinéma avec ma cousine.
Jean-François: Super! T'as de la chance.
René: Et peut-être quelques amis. Alors, on y va?
René: À toi le service. Honneur aux Canadiens.
Jean-François: Je suis Québécois.
René: Mais alors?
Jean-François: Attention, je joue pas très bien, et en plus....
René: Eh, on verra bien!
Jean-François: Attention, au service là!
René: Faute! Elle est mauvaise.
Jean-François: Comment ça, faute?
René: Regarde Jean-François, la marque est là. Elle est faute.
Jean-François: OK, tu recules, je t'envoie une autre, hein? Ça c'est pas faute, hein. Ça c'est faute!
René: Mais alors, Jean-François, tu joues ou non?
Jean-François: Oui, pourquoi?
René: Tu ne fais pas attention.
Jean-François: Si, si, je fais attention.
René: Qu'est-ce que tu regardes là-bas?
Jean-François: Dis moi, René.
René: Mais alors, quoi?
Jean-François: Comment je peux faire la connaissance de cette fille?
René: Mais pas de problème. Oh, oh, Marie-Christine! Viens voir.
Marie-Christine: Oh, salut, René. Ça va?
René: Oui, et toi? Je te présente Jean-François, mon ami québécois. Ma cousine Marie-Christine.
Marie-Christine: Bonjour!
Jean-François: Bonjour!
Marie-Christine: Viens, Nathalie. Je te présente mon cousin René. Il fait beau aujourd'hui.
Jean-François: Oui.
René: Bonjour, Nathalie.
Nathalie: Bonjour.
René: Jean-François.
Nathalie: Bonjour.
Jean-François: Bonjour.
Marie-Christine: Jean-François vient au cinéma avec nous ce soir?
René: Non, non; il travaille.
Jean-François: Ben, non René ... Je ...
René: Ah, bon!
Jean-François: Je suis libre.

René: OK, OK.
Marie-Christine: Formidable!

(On screen) Les sports

Voix-off: Les Français aiment beaucoup les sports. Ils aiment l'air ... et la terre. Ils aiment la montagne ... et la forêt. Ils aiment la mer ... et les rivières. Ils aiment le ski en hiver, le vélo en été, et la pétanque en toute saison. Ils aiment monter ... et descendre. Ils aiment un bon effort ... et une bonne fatigue.

Voix-off: Problème

Marie-Christine: Oh, bonjour! Ça va?
Jean-François: Ouais. Où est René?
Marie-Christine: Il travaille. Un devoir de science politique important.
Jean-François: Et Nathalie?
Marie-Christine: Elle ne peut pas venir non plus. C'est l'anniversaire de sa tante; elle est obligée de dîner en famille.
Jean-François: Donc, il n'y a que nous deux?
Marie-Christine: Ouais.
Jean-François: Tu aimes les films d'aventures?
Marie-Christine: Pas particulièrement. Mais j'adore les mélodrames.
Jean-François: Ah, ben, allons y.
Jean-François: Deux places pour "Céremonie secrète" s'il vous plaît, Madame.
Caissière: Je regrette, Monsieur. La salle est complète. Il n'y a plus de place.
Jean-François: Mais c'est pas vrai!? Qu'est-ce qu'on va faire?

Voix-off: Il n'y a plus de billets pour le film. Qu'est-ce qu'on va faire?

MODULE II *Le coup de fil* RT 4:34

Voix-off: Aujourd'hui, Jean-François retrouve Marie-Christine pour faire des courses ensemble. Marie-Christine habite rive gauche, dans le 6ème arrondissement. C'est le quartier des étudiants, des librairies, et des universités.

Jean-François: Rue Dufour, rue Bonaparte, vers la place Saint Sulpice. Rue Bonaparte? À gauche dans la rue Saint Sulpice. Par là ... OK, à droite ici, rue de Tournon. C'est là. Ah, ben voilà. Le 16 rue de Tournon. C'est bien ici qu'elle habite Marie-Christine? Ce n'est pas possible, la porte s'ouvre pas. Excusez-moi Madame, vous savez comment on fait pour ouvrir la porte?
Une passante: Mais si. Il faut le code. Appelez donc vos amis au téléphone et demandez le code.
Jean-François: Merci Madame.
Jean-François: Ce n'est pas possible qu'elle parle si longtemps. Excusez-moi Mademoiselle, j'ai un coup de fil urgent à donner ... Hein, c'est vrai. Excusez-moi encore, mais c'est urgent. Vous pouvez accélérer! Merci.
Jean-François: Bon! Où est-ce qu'on met l'argent? Là? Vous savez comment ça fonctionne le téléphone?
Homme: Elles marchent avec des cartes, ces cabines-là.
Jean-François: Avec des cartes?
Homme: On achète une télécarte.
Jean-François: Et où est-ce que je peux acheter une télécarte?
Homme: Dans un bureau de tabac, par exemple. C'est pas difficile.
Jean-François: Mais moi il faut que je téléphone tout de suite! ... Bon ... Merci ... Oui, Marie-Christine, c'est quoi le code de la porte d'entrée? 0-4-5-8-9. OK merci; j'arrive tout de suite. Allez, au revoir.

(On screen) La télécarte

Voix-off: La nouvelle génération de cabines téléphoniques emploie exclusivement la nouvelle télécarte. Télécarte: Dans toutes les agences de France-Télécom, dans tous les tabacs, et dans beaucoup d'autres points de vente. Commencez par introduire la télécarte. Le message apparaît à l'écran digital. L'appareil annonce le nombre d'unités qui reste. Suivez les instructions affichées. À la fin de votre communication, n'oubliez pas d'enlever votre carte. Télécarte, la nouvelle clé du nouveau monde des communications.

Voix-off: Problème

Jean-François, *(fredonnant)*: Françoise est une fille charmante. Françoise est une femme élégante. Mais alors, qu'est-ce qui se passe? Il n'y a plus d'unités? Dis donc! Qu'est ce que je vais faire?

Voix-off: La carte n'a plus d'unités! Dis donc, qu'est-ce que je vais faire?

MODULE III *Le métro* RT 3:48

Voix-off: Paris est une grande ville, mais les transports en common sont faciles à employer et pas chers. Aujourd'hui, Marie-Christine et Jean-François traversent la ville pour visiter un grand magasin.

Marie-Christine: Tiens, comment tu trouves ce pull dans la vitrine?
Jean-François: Oh! Ça va. Oui.
Marie-Christine: Comment, ça va? C'est très chic.
Jean-François: Ça va.
Jean-François: Ben, écoute, il faut aller dans un grand magazin. Tu veux aller aux Galeries Lafayette?
Marie-Christine: Oui, mais c'est un peu loin. Écoute, prenons le métro. Il est là. Tu es d'accord?
Jean-François: D'accord. C'est quelle ligne?
Marie-Christine: Je ne sais pas exactement.
Marie-Christine: Écoute. Oui, prenons la direction Porte de la Chapelle.
Marie-Christine: Certainement la ligne numéro 12. Nous allons jusqu'à la Madeleine. Et puis, je ne sais pas.
Jean-François: Et puis à la Madeleine, on doit prendre la ligne numéro 8, direction Créteil, jusqu'à l'Opéra.
Marie-Christine: Nous avons donc une correspondance à la Madeleine.
Passant: Excusez-moi, m'sieur dame, mais vous avez un autobus direct.
Marie-Christine: Ah bon? Et où est l'arrêt, s'il vous plait?
Passant: Là-bas, en face.
Marie-Christine: Ah, merci.
Jean-François: Est-ce que je peux utiliser ma carte orange?
Marie-Christine: Oui, bien sûr.
Jean-François: C'est bien.
Marie-Christine: Allons y.

(On screen) Le transport en commun

Voix-off: Une voiture à Paris? Quelle idée! Il y a beaucoup trop de circulation. Prenez plutôt un taxi. Ou encore mieux, pensez aux transports en commun. Prenez l'autobus, par exemple. Et quand vous êtes à Montmartre, prenez le funiculaire. Quand les rues sont bouchées, prenez le batobus. Ou bien, prenez le métro avec ses 368 stations et ses soixante kilomètres de quais. Mais attention, le métro ferme à une heure du matin. Ne manquez pas le dernier métro.

Voix-off: Problème.

Voix-off: Jean-François et Marie-Christine ont fini leurs courses.

Marie-Christine: Tu prends le métro?
Jean-François: Oui.
Marie-Christine: Bon, je prends l'autobus. Bye!
Jean-François: À bientôt!
Jean-François: Ça marche pas, mon ticket, dans le métro....
Marie-Christine: Fais voir. Mais c'est ta carte orange. As-tu pris l'autobus avec?
Jean-François: Mais oui, on a pris l'autobus ensemble.
Marie-Christine: As-tu mis le ticket dans la petite machine?
Jean-François: Oui! C'est pas ça qu'il fallait faire?
Marie-Christine: Mais non. On ne met jamais son ticket de carte orange dans la petite machine de l'autobus, ou ça ne marche plus dans le métro.
Jean-François: Ah, qu'est-ce que je vais faire maintenant?

Voix-off: Le ticket de la carte orange ne marche plus. Qu'est-ce que je vais faire maintenant?

MODULE IV *La boulangerie* RT 5:53

Voix-off: Ce matin, Jean-François et Marie-Christine doivent trouver des amis au café, mais Jean-François trouve que le petit déjeuner au café est trop cher. Pas de problème! Marie-Christine lui suggère d'acheter des croissants dans une boulangerie. Pendant ce temps, elle fait du café.

Jean-François: Excusez moi, vous pourriez m'indiquer une boulangerie? La boulangerie de la rue des Abbesses est fermée.
Artiste: Euh ... oui ... euh ... deuxième à gauche ... voilà....
Jean-François: Ah ... OK..? Euh ... Qu'est-ce que c'est ?
Artiste: Ben.. c'est ... heu ... oui, oui, vous voyez ... vous voyez bien là, c'est le Sacré-Cœur ... Quoi! ... Puis, euh ... Voilà.
Jean-François: Ah bon. Neuf heures moins le quart. Merci, hein.
Artiste: Très bien. Bonne journée Monsieur.
Jean-François: Excusez-moi Monsieur, la boulangerie est fermée. Il n'y en a pas d'autres ?
Artiste: Euh ... donc ... euh ... deuxième ... deuxième à droite; en descendant là.
Jean-François: Et ben, ça commence à prendre forme votre dessin.
Artiste: Oui ... Euh .... vous trouvez?
Jean-François: Oui, on voit bien Montmartre.
Artiste: Bon, oui ... oui ... d'accord.
Jean-François: Merci!
Artiste: Ben, merci.
Jean-François: Au revoir.
Jean-François: J'ai pas de chance. Y a pas d'autres boulangeries dans le quartier?
Artiste: Oh, c'est pas facile le mercredi ... hein? Euh ... je suis occupé ... euh ... Vous n'êtes pas d'ici?
Jean-François: Non, non, euh ... je suis québécois.
Artiste: Ah ...bon, d'accord! Bon ... euh ... descendez ... descendez ... euh ... tout droit ... euh ... la rue des Mannes, là ... Vous allez trouvez en bas ... en bas des escaliers hein? Voilà.
Jean-François: Merci encore, hein?
Artiste: Oui ... allez, bon voyage!
Jean-François: Enfin, une boulangerie ouverte!

(On screen) La boulangerie

Voix-off: Trois heures du matin. Monsieur Jacques chauffe son four. À chacun son travail. Le boulanger prépare le pain. Le pâtissier prépare les croissants. Avec de bons œufs et de la bonne farine, on fait de bonnes choses! Des croissants, du pain, des pâtisseries, des pains aux raisins. Et tout cela pour le plaisir de mon petit déjeuner!

Voix-off: Problème

Homme: Bonjour Madame.
Boulangère: Bonjour Monsieur.
Homme: Est-ce que vous auriez trois croissants s'il vous plaît?
Boulangère: Absolument. Voici les derniers.
Homme: C'est des croissants au beurre?
Boulangère: Tout à fait. Au beurre, spécialité maison. Voilà.
Homme: Combien je vous dois?
Boulangère: Douze francs. Merci beaucoup!
Homme: Merci.
Boulangère: Au revoir, bonne journée.
Jean-François: Bonjour, vous avez pas encore deux croissants, s'il vous plaît.
Boulangère: Ah, je suis navrée, j'en aurai dans une demie-heure, pas avant.
Jean-François: Oh, non ! Mais qu'est-ce que je vais faire maintenant?

Voix-off: Il n'y a plus de croissants. Qu'est-ce que je vais faire maintenant?

MODULE V *Au Café* — RT 4:32

Voix-off: Pas loin de l'opéra de la Bastille, Bruno et Alissa attendent au café l'arrivée de leur amie Marie-Christine, et de Jean-François, qu'ils ne connaissent pas encore.

Marie-Christine: Bonjour! Bonjour Bruno!
Bruno: Ça va?
Marie-Christine: Bonjour Alissa, tu vas bien?
Bruno: T'es un peu à la bourre je trouve.
Marie-Christine: Ouais, hein? Ben je vous presente mon ami québéquois, Jean-François.
Jean-François: Salut.
Alissa: Enchantée.
Bruno: Bruno.
Jean-François: Salut Bruno.
Alissa: Alors vous avez trainé là?
Marie-Christine: Oui, on s'excuse....
Jean-François: Je suis très content de vous connaître. Je ne connais pas beaucoup de Français, encore ...
Bruno *(à Jean-François)*: Tu sais, je ne suis pas français moi. Je suis sénégalais.
Alissa: Arrête.
Bruno: Ça va, je lui dis ce que je suis. Ah, il doit connaître.
Alissa: Bienvenue en France.
Jean-François: Merci.
Bruno: Ça te plaît?
Jean-François: Ouais.
Bruno: T'as visité un peu?
Jean-François: Ouais, ouais. J'ai vu pas mal de choses.
Garçon de café: Messieurs dames, bonjour. Vous desirez?
Tous: Bonjour!

Alissa: Un café crème, s'il vous plaît.
Marie-Christine: Un café noir.
Bruno: Peut-être, un chocolat pour moi.
Garçon de café: Un chocolat chaud?
Jean-François: Moi aussi!
Garçon de café: Deux chocolats chauds, un café au lait ... crème, et un petit café noir.
Jean-François: Merci!
Alissa: Ah, il fait beau, y a du soleil.
Jean-François: Ouais.
Alissa: Génial!
Garçon de café: Excusez moi. Le café crème c'est pour?
Jean-François: Madame.
Alissa: Ici.
Garçon de café: Voilà Madame.
Alissa: Oui, merci. Mademoiselle! *(s'adressant à Jean-François)*
Garçon de café: Le chocolat? C'est ici.
Bruno: Merci.
Garçon de café: Vous, c'était un petit café noir.
Marie-Christine: Oui, merci.
Jean-François: Moi, un chocolat.
Garçon de café: Voilà un chocolat. Merci.
Jean-François: Voilà, merci.
Alissa: Et, au fait, vous savez qu'avec le pont du Premier Mai, on va avoir quatre jours. On pourrait faire quelque chose, non?
Jean-François: C'est quoi le pont?
Marie-Christine: Bien, c'est jeudi, vendredi, samedi, dimanche....
Jean-François: Ah bon.
Bruno: Faisons un petit voyage?
Marie-Christine: Oui, on a le temps, mais faut pas que ça nous coûte trop cher.
Jean-François: De toute façon, on n'a pas de voiture?
Marie-Christine: On peut y aller en train, hein.
Jean-François: C'est pas ça le problème. Mais il faut savoir où on va.
Bruno: Oui, on va où pour le week-end?
Marie-Christine: Moi, j'aime bien Trouville.
Alissa: Il paraît que la Bourgogne, c'est sympa.
Bruno: Moi, mon ami Noël m'a invité avec des amis dans sa maison en Normandie. Est-ce que quelqu'un connaît?
Alissa: Non, non.
Jean-François: Ben moi, finalement je vais rester à Paris. Je vais faire du tennis.
Marie-Christine: Bon, moi je crois que je vais rester aussi ... travailler.
Bruno: Ben, Alissa tu viens avec moi?
Alissa: Oui.

(On screen) Le temps libre

Voix-off: Et vous, qu'est-ce que vous préférez pour votre temps libre? Préférez-vous les plaisirs de la ville? Le bois de Boulogne, le cinéma, les musées, un concert, ou l'opéra? Ou préférez-vous partir en voyage? Par exemple à la mer, ou peut-être à la campagne, ou encore voir une belle cathédrale ou un beau château?

Voix-off: Problème

Alissa: Bon. Peut-être, on pourrait ... tu vois ... Toi, tu prends toutes mes affaires. Tu vas là, et puis comme ça, je vais chercher les trucs, OK?

Bruno: OK.
Alissa: Bon, à tout de suite.
Alissa: Eh, Bruno! Bruno?
Bruno: Il part à quelle heure le train pour Nogent?
Alissa: Il part à deux heures et demie. Tiens, regarde.
Bruno: Deux heures et demie?
Alissa: Ouais.
Bruno: C'est quel train?
Alissa: C'est celui là, le 13717.
Bruno: Le numéro 24, 24, 24 ... Zut! Il circule que les dimanches et fêtes.
Alissa: Mais on va prendre quel train?

Voix-off: Le train choisi ne circule que les dimanches et fêtes. Mais on va prendre quel train?

MODULE VI *Le château Saint-Jean* RT 5:12

Voix-off: Bruno et Alissa ont finalement décidé de prendre le train de 15 heures 05, qui passe par Chartres. En attendant, ils ont appelé leur ami Noël. Noël a promis de venir les chercher à la gare et de les amener au château Saint-Jean.

Noël: Salut Bruno! Ça va?
Bruno: Comment vas-tu, et toi? Noël, Alissa. Alissa, Noël.
Alissa: Bon ben, on peut se tutoyer ... et puis, on peut se faire la bise.
Noël: Bien sûr.
Bruno: Ça va gars?
Noël: Ça va. Vous montez?
Alissa: Waow! Il est superbe!
Noël: Et voilà. Ça valait la peine?
Bruno: Regarde Alissa, les merles.
Alissa: C'est beau.
Noël: Je pense que vous allez aimer notre château médiéval. Il n'y a pas beaucoup de châteaux comme celui-ci en Normandie.
Bruno: Tu vois, ça c'est de la construction solide. Tu prends une photo?
Alissa: Non, non, je regarde.
Noël: C'est pas mal ça, hein?
Bruno: Je pense que les soldats devaient avoir froid ici, non.
Alissa: Oui, surtout en hiver. Est-ce qu'il y a du chauffage dans ce château?
Noël: Venez voir. Vous allez voir comment on se réchauffe au moyen âge. Ça, c'est la salle des gardes, mais maintenant c'est une salle d'exposition. Regardez sa belle cheminée.
Alissa: Qu'est-ce qu'elle est grande! Mais il faut beaucoup de bois pour cette cheminée là.
Noël: Bien sûr, mais quand il fait froid sur les remparts du château, on est content de retrouver la bonne chaleur de la salle des gardes. Vous voulez voir les autres parties du château?
Alissa: Ah, oui.
Noël: Alors, suivez le guide.
Alissa: OK. Alors, ça s'appelle le chateau Saint-Jean?
Noël: Tout à fait. Venez voir. Du haut des tours, il y a une vue spectaculaire sur Nogent et la vallée de l'Huisne.
Alissa: Merci.
Bruno: C'est magnifique!
Alissa: Ben oui ...
Bruno: Dis moi, où est-ce que se trouve ta maison?
Noël: Là-bas, à gauche, derrière la forêt.

Bruno: Là bas, à gauche derrière la forêt?
Noël: Oui, mais on ne peut pas la voir d'ici. On va aller faire un tour en voiture.

(On screen) Le château

Voix-off: Les châteaux de France, témoignages vivants d'un passé long et riche. Châteaux du moyen âge en Alsace, le long de la Seine, ou dans le Midi. Châteaux du dix-huitième siècle dans la région de Bordeaux. Châteaux de la Renaissance dans la vallée de la Loire. Châteaux du dix-septième siècle près de Paris. Et à Nogent-le-Rotrou, le château Saint-Jean.

Voix-off: Problème

Bruno: Eh ben, dis donc, tu as une région vraiment formidable, le gars. Franchement Alissa, le point de vue est assez extraordinaire, non? Ça vaut bien une photo.
Alissa: Oui, tu as raison. Donne moi l'appareil, je vais prendre ... tiens mets toi là. Je vais prendre avec la colline derrière. Ça va être superbe. Oh, non! Zut ... tu as usé tout mon film.
Bruno: Ben, écoute, il fallait bien prendre des photos.
Alissa: Ben oui, mais moi je voulais à tout prix une photo d'ici. Comment je vais faire?
Bruno: Ils en ont peut-être à l'entrée.
Alissa: Bon, je vais voir.
Noël: C'est pas la peine. J'ai déja demandé la semaine dernière. Ils n'en ont pas.
Alissa: Mais où est-ce que je peux trouver une pellicule?

Voix-off: Bruno a employé toute la pellicule. Où est-ce que je trouve une pellicule?

MODULE VII *La Poste* RT 5:01

Voix-off: Après leur visite au château Saint-Jean, Bruno et Alissa descendent en ville et vont chacun de son côté. Alissa part acheter une pellicule et Bruno va chercher des cartes postales.

Voix-off: Problème

Bruno: Alissa!
Alissa: Alors, tu as trouvé tes cartes?
Bruno: Ouais.
Alissa: Ah, elles sont jolies.
Bruno: Tu trouves?
Alissa: Ah,oui.
Bruno: Maintenant, il faut que je trouve la poste pour envoyer mes cartes postales et en plus, ce cadeau que j'ai acheté pour ma mère au Sénégal.
Alissa: Ah! Sympa.
Bruno: Tu sais où elle se trouve, toi, la poste?
Alissa: Non, pas plus que toi. Pourquoi tu n'as pas demandé?
Bruno: Tout simplement parce que je n'y ai pas pensé. (À un passant) Excusez moi, Monsieur, s'il vous plaît, vous savez où se trouve la poste?
Passant: Oui, tout à fait. Vous allez jusqu'au feu, là, et ensuite, vous tournez à droite.
Bruno: Au feu, à droite?
Passant: Voilà, tout à fait.
Bruno: A côté du Monoprix?
Passant: Voilà.
Bruno: Merci.

Passant: Je vous en prie.
Alissa: Bon, attends. Pendant que tu cherches la poste, moi, je vais encore trainer dans les magasins. On se retrouve ici dans une demi-heure. OK?
Bruno: D'accord.
Alissa: Allez, bonne chance.
Bruno: Tchao.
Bruno: Excusez-moi, Mesdames, vous savez où se trouve la poste, s'il vous plaît?
Femme: Oui, bon. Vous descendez cette rue, là; vous allez trouver Monoprix. Vous descendez toute la rue piétonne.
Bruno: Cette rue là?
Femme: Oui là juste en face. Oui, là, juste en face de vous; ensuite, sur la gauche, vous allez trouver un grand bâtiment; et vous allez trouver la poste. C'est juste en bas de la rue piétonne, hein.
Bruno: C'est à peu près combien de mètres?
Femme: Oh, ben là, y a cinq cent mètres à peu près.
Bruno: OK, merci bien.
Femme: Au revoir.
Bruno: Excusez moi, m'sieur dame, vous savez où se trouve la poste s'il vous plaît?
Passants: La poste, elle se trouve ... là bas ... dans le .... en descendant ...
Bruno: Juste là?
Passants: Juste là.
Bruno: Merci mille fois. Au revoir ... Zut! zut, zut, zut! Elle se trouve où, cette poste?

(On screen) La boutique

Voix-off: L'âme de la France profonde, c'est la boutique et le petit magasin. Dans les boutiques, on vend de la porcelaine pour les jours de fête. Dans les petits magasins, on vend des articles pour tous les jours. Dans les pharmacies, on vend des médicaments, du savon, et du shampooing. Ailleurs, on vend de la bijouterie et des pizzas, des cadeaux et des fleurs. On vend des journaux, de la viande, de l'électro-ménager. On vend des livres, des vêtements, ou des lunettes. Même dans les agences, les banques, ou les cafés, le client est sûr d'être reçu comme un vieil ami.

Voix-off: Problème

Bruno: Bonjour, Madame.
Employée: Bonjour, Monsieur.
Bruno: J'ai deux cartes postales et ce colis à envoyer au Sénégal.
Employée: Très bien, merci. Deux cartes, ça fait sept francs pour les cartes, hein? Neuf cent grammes votre colis, ça fait 62 francs. Donc, 69 francs la totalité.
Bruno: Soixante-neuf francs? Mais, c'est pas possible. C'est trop cher! J'ai pas assez d'argent sur moi. Comment est-ce que je vais faire?

Voix-off: Ça coûte trop cher d'envoyer le paquet. Comment est-ce que je vais faire?

MODULE VIII *En panne* — RT 4:30

Voix-off: Après leurs achats à Nogent-le-Rotrou, Alissa et Bruno retrouvent Noël, qui les conduit chez lui, à travers le beau paysage percheron, avec ses collines, ses champs et ses petites fermes.

Bruno: Tu es vraiment gentil de t'occuper de nous, Noël.
Alissa: Qu'est-ce qu'elle est belle ta Normandie!
Bruno: On arrive bientôt chez toi, Noël?
Noël: Mais qu'est-ce que c'est que ce bruit?

Alissa: Mais qu'est-ce qu'elle a, ta voiture?
Bruno: Il est peut-être en panne d'essence?
Noël: Ça doit être ça. Allez, tout le monde dehors, et on pousse.
Alissa: D'accord ... Psht, allez.
Bruno: N'importe quoi!!!
Alissa: Allez, allez ...
Noël: Bonjour Émile.
Garagiste: Bonjour Noël.
Noël: Le plein, s'il te plaît.
Garagiste: Ouais ... Cent cinquante francs.
Noël: Voilà.
Garagiste: Merci. Bonne route.
Noël: Merci ... Qu'est-ce qui se passe encore? Émile!
Garagiste: Oui.
Noël: Ça marche pas.
Garagiste: Tu ouvres le capot, je vais regarder.
Noël: J'espére que ça ne coûte pas trop cher. Je viens d'acheter une nouvelle batterie.
Garagiste: Je pense pas que ça soit la batterie. Ah ben! Voilà le problème!

(On screen) La voiture

Voix-off: Entre les Français et leur automobile, c'est le grand amour. Malgré la limitation à 130 kilomètres à l'heure sur l'autoroute et à 90 kilomètres à l'heure sur les routes nationales, les Français gardent toujours la passion de la vitesse. Malgré le prix élevé de l'essence et les pannes éventuelles, ils restent amoureux de leur Peugeot, de leur Citroën, ou de leur Renault. De la simple deux chevaux à la voiture de l'avenir, de l'auto-école aux embouteillages parisiens, l'automobile reste reine, car son chauffeur se croit toujours roi.

Voix-off: Problème

Garagiste: Ah ben, voilà le problème.
Alissa: Noël! Je crois que tu viens de griller tout ton système électrique! C'est ça, hein?
Garagiste: Ouais, c'est ça.
Noël: Zut! Alors, Émile, tu peux la réparer?
Garagiste: Oui, mais pas aujourd'hui, hein. Faut me retéléphoner demain soir. Je vais la réparer pour demain soir.
Alissa: On va rester sans voiture? Mais qu'est-ce qu'on va faire sans la voiture ?

Voix-off: La voiture est tombée en panne, et Émile ne peut pas la réparer tout de suite. Qu'est-ce qu'on va faire sans la voiture?

MODULE IX *Au Centre Pompidou* RT 6:06

Voix-off: Yves et Moustafa, deux amis de Bruno et Alissa, arrivent au Centre Pompidou, pour faire des recherches à la bibliothèque publique.

Voix-off: Problème

Yves: Elle est chouette la musique, hein?
Moustafa: Et au fait, Bruno et Alissa seront là dimanche pour la fête de la musique?
Yves: Ben, j'espère. Ils ont eu des problèmes de voiture, mais normalement ils seront là dimanche, enfin, comme prévu.
Moustafa: Ah!

Yves: Allez, viens ... Allez, viens; c'est par là. Sur quel projet tu travailles en ce moment?
Moustafa: C'est un truc sur l'architecture.
Yves: Ah! Intéressant. Bon alors, je crois ... je crois que c'est au premier étage.
Moustafa: Bon. On va s'y mettre.
Yves: Ouais! Allez! Je commence à travailler tout de suite.
Moustafa: Je vais chercher les livres dont j'ai besoin.
Un lecteur: Bonjour.
Yves: Bonjour.
Moustafa: Eh, Yves, tu peux m'aider un moment?
Yves: Si tu veux. Il s'agit de quoi?
Moustafa: Je dois faire un rapport sur la construction nouvelle. Mais je n'y connais pas grand chose. Comment tu fais, toi, quand tu as un nouveau sujet à rechercher?
Yves: Mais, je sais pas moi. Souvent je commence par regarder dans le dictionnaire ou dans une encyclopédie, pour avoir une idée très générale du sujet.
Moustafa: Ça, je l'ai déjà fait. J'ai fait toute une liste des projets récents à Paris.
Yves: Cherche autre chose. Sur un projet précis. Par exemple, la pyramide du Louvre.
Moustafa: Tiens, par exemple. Regarde ce que je trouve: "La pyramide du Louvre a été construite en 1989 par l'architecte I.M. Pei. C'est la nouvelle entrée du musée."
Yves: Montre la photo. Elle est un peu petite. On voit mal. C'est difficile d'analyser sa construction avec une petite photo comme ça. Ils ont peut-être des vidéos. Tu devrais voir ça.
Moustafa: Ah, bonne idée! Tu viendras voir avec moi? Yves! C'est formidable, tu ne trouves pas?
Yves: Oui, c'est bien, mais moi je préfère voir les choses de mes propres yeux. Tu sais, la pyramide du Louvre n'est qu'à quelques minutes d'ici. Si on allait la voir ?
Moustafa: Et mon rapport?
Yves: Tu finiras ça demain.
Moustafa: D'accord.

(On screen) L'architecture à Paris

Voix-off: La tradition millénaire de nouvelle architecture à Paris renaît en 1977 avec la mise en service du Centre Pompidou. Situé rue Beaubourg dans le cœur du vieux Paris, cet édifice ultra-moderne est contesté dès le début. L'esplanade devant le Centre Pompidou devient très vite le lieu de rencontre des jeunes. A l'intérieur, le Musée national d'art moderne attire tous ceux qui sont intéressés par le modernisme. La bibliothèque est un des lieux les plus visités de Paris. De l'escalator extérieur du Centre Pompidou, on voit bien un Paris où le nouveau se trouve à côté de l'ancien: la tour Saint-Jacques ... et la tour Montparnasse, l'Opéra ... et l'opéra de la Bastille ... le palais du Louvre et sa pyramide, l'arc de triomphe ... et l'arche de la Défense.

Voix-off: Problème

Yves: C'est grandiose.
Moustafa: Yves, dis, écoute, c'est une bonne idée que tu as eue. Je pourrai mettre dans mon rapport une description de l'intérieur de la pyramide.
Yves: Ah oui, pas mal ton idée.
Moustafa: Monsieur, s'il vous plaît ...
Passant: Oui?
Yves: L'entrée se trouve de quel côté?
Passant: Ah ben, juste derrière vous, là. Mais alors, vous avez mal choisi votre jour, parce qu'aujourd'hui, le mardi, le musée est fermé. Alors faudra revenir hein? D'accord?
Moustafa: Franchement, on n'a pas de chance. Qu'est-ce que nous allons faire?

Voix-off: La pyramide du Louvre est fermée le mardi. Qu'est-ce que nous allons faire?

MODULE X *Au marché, rue Mouffetard* RT 3:54

Voix-off: C'est bientôt l'anniversaire d'Yves! Pour fêter ses 21 ans, Yves a décidé de préparer un repas pour ses amis. Malgré le mauvais temps, il se rend au marché de la rue Mouffetard, dans le 5ème arrondissement, pour faire ses courses.

Yves: Bonjour Madame.
Poissonière: Bonjour Monsieur.
Yves: Quel sale temps, hein?
Poissonière: Oh là, là, oui alors.
Yves: Je ne suis pas un grand cuisinier, mais j'aimerais faire un poisson pour des amis. Qu'est-ce que je peux faire qui ne soit pas trop difficile à préparer?
Poissonière: Eh bien, je peux vous proposer des truites, à faire à la poêle ...
Yves: Oui.
Poissonière: Ou bien des tranches de thon à préparer au barbecue ...
Yves: Bon.
Poissonière: Ou encore des filets de saumon, à préparer au four.
Yves: Ah! Est-ce que c'est pas trop difficile à préparer le saumon?
Poissonière: Non, pas du tout.
Yves: Bon, comment est-ce que je le prépare exactement?
Poissonière: Alors, vous mettez des filets dans un plat en terre beurré. Vous salez, vous poivrez, vous mettez un verre de vin blanc. Vous mettez à four moyen une dizaine de minutes.
Yves: D'accord.
Poissonière: Et puis vos servez à vos amis. Vous verrez, ils seront très contents.
Yves: Bon, euh ... formidable! Bien, écoutez, je vais en prendre pour quatre personnes.
Poissonière: D'accord.
Yves: Combien est-ce que je vous dois?
Poissonière: Soixante-seize francs.
Yves: Eh bien, voilà. Parfait, formidable!
Poissonière: Voilà, Monsieur.
Yves: Merci.
Poissonière: Merci.
Yves: Merci.

(On screen) Au marché

Voix-off: Excusez-moi, Monsieur Dame, votre table est prête. Si Madame veut bien prendre place. Si Monsieur veut bien s'asseoir. Aujourd'hui, nous vous proposons des tomates et des pommes de terre, des fraises et des framboises, des champignons et des artichauts, des concombres et des radis. Par la suite, vous prendrez peut-être un peu de charcuterie? Désirez-vous des saucisses et du pâté, ou encore même un poulet rôti? Vous prendrez un fromage sans doute? Préférez-vous un fromage de chèvre, de vache, ou de brebis? Pour finir, une pâtisserie? Une part de gâteau, par exemple? Je vous souhaite un bon appétit, Monsieur Dame.

Voix-off: Problème

Marchand *(en voix-off)*: Artichaut vert et tendre. Mangez de l'artichaut; allons, artichaut vert et tendre, allons-y!
Yves: Bon! Avec le saumon, il me faut du riz.
Marchand: Bonjour Monsieur.
Yves: Bonjour Monsieur. Bon! Ben, est-ce que vous vendez du riz?
Marchand: Ah non, je regrette; nous ne faisons pas le riz ici. Nous faisons que les légumes.

Yves: Vous ne vendez pas du riz?
Marchand: Ah, non! Nous ne faisons que les légumes seulement. Non.
Yves: Qu'est-ce que je vais faire?

Voix-off: On ne vend pas de riz ici. Qu'est-ce que je vais faire?

MODULE XI *Le papillon* RT 3:46

Voix-off: Une voiture dans une grande ville n'est pas sans problème. D'abord, il faut chercher à se garer. Et si jamais on reste trop longtemps, on risque de trouver un papillon sous son essuie-glace.

Conducteur: Oh! C'est pas vrai. Dix petites minutes de retard et voilà ce que je reçois! Eh, eh, vous avez vu ça? Dix minutes et on me donne un papillon. Non, mais je regrette d'avoir loué cette voiture, moi!
Moustafa: Mais ce n'est pas grave Monsieur. Vous avez mis ... Vous avez pris votre ticket au parcmètre?
Conducteur: Ben mon ticket, évidemment il est là. Regardez!
Moustafa: C'est pas votre journée, c'est tout.
Conducteur: Ben, je pense bien! Et puis comment est-ce que je vais payer ça? Je sais comment faire en Belgique, mais c'est la première fois que je conduis en France, ah!
Moustafa: Monsieur, vous devez aller dans un bureau de tabac. Vous achetez un timbre et vous le collez sur votre papillon. C'est une contravention à combien?
Conducteur: Mais comment voulez-vous que je sache? Je n'en ai jamais reçue, je vous dis, tenez!
Moustafa: Bon, il y a des contraventions à 75 francs, 230 francs et 450 francs.
Conducteur: Quatre cent cinquante francs?
Moustafa: Eh oui, c'est ce qu'il paraît, mais vous avez peut-être plus de chance que vous ne croyez. Si j'ai bien compris ce qui est écrit ici, vous n'aurez à payer que 75 francs, Monsieur, au bureau de tabac qui se trouve là-bas.
Conducteur: Et en plus je dois payer ça dans le tabac. Non mais, mais c'est honteux, je suis embarassé, moi, moi je ne fume même pas!
Moustafa: Je vous souhaite une bonne journée Monsieur.
Conducteur: Ben merci. Le tabac ... le tabac ... le tabac ...

(On screen) Le Tabac

Voix-off: Le tabac, cette institution particulièrement française, que ne fait-il pas? C'est d'abord un café. Puis c'est un bar. Bien sûr, au tabac on vend non seulement des cigarettes, mais aussi des allumettes et des briquets. On vend des timbres-poste et des bonbons. On vend même les timbres fiscaux ... par exemple pour payer les contraventions automobiles.

Conducteur: Un timbre fiscal à 75 francs, s'il vous plaît.
Employé: Bonjour Monsieur. Oui.
Conducteur: Vous ne trouvez pas que c'est un peu cher pour dix minutes de stationnement?
Employé: Un petit peu cher, oui. Ben, pour pas grand chose, mais ça va quand même. Soixante-quinze, quatre-vingt et cent. Merci.
Conducteur: Merci. Au revoir.
Employé: C'est moi. Au revoir.

Voix-off: On y vend même les billets de Loto et de Loto Sportif. Du matin jusqu'au soir, le tabac reste vivant.

Voix-off: Problème

Passant: Excusez moi ...
Moustafa: Mais, je vous en prie Monsieur.

Passant: S'il vous plait, pourriez-vous m'indiquer la poste?
Moustafa: Mais oui, bien sûr. Vous traversez le pont et vous prenez la première à droite, et c'est tout de suite derrière le grand bâtiment. Ah, mais ... vous n'avez pas de chance, elle est fermée depuis un quart d'heure.
Passant: Ah, bon! C'est vraiment embêtant. J'avais vraiment besoin de timbres. Où est-ce que je pourrais en trouver donc?

Voix-off: La poste est déjà fermée et il faut des timbres. Mais où est-ce que je peux donc en acheter?

MODULE XII *La Fête de la musique* RT 5:33

Marie-Christine: Ah oui, ah d'accord.
Jean-François: C'est bien.
Marie-Christine: Et alors, qu'est-ce qu'on fait ce soir?
Jean-François: Tu connais la Fête de la musique?
Marie-Christine: Ah oui, super.
Jean-François: On y va?
Marie-Christine: D'accord, c'est une bonne idée.

Voix-off: Tous les ans, au mois de juin, Paris fait la fête à la musique. Partout, pendant deux jours, il y a de la musique de toutes les sortes. Ce soir, Marie-Christine et Jean-François, Bruno et Alissa, et Yves et Moustafa vont tous à la Fête de la Musique.

Yves: Salut Alissa, ça va?
Alissa: Oh! Salut Yves. Qu'est-ce que tu fais là? D'où tu sors?
Yves: Pour la Fête de la musique!
Alissa: Ah, ben ouais, c'est sympa!
Moustafa: Alissa, bonjour.
Alissa: Ben, Moustafa, alors. Qu'est-ce que tu fous dans le coin?
Moustafa: Ah, ça fait plaisir de vous voir.
Bruno: Ah, regarde comment il est beau!
Moustafa: Arrête.
Alissa: Attendez.
Yves: Bon, alors, on va voir un autre concert ailleurs. Y'en a un autre là bas qui est très bien.
Alissa: Eh! C'est sympa ça. Vous avez regardé? C'est vraiment bien. Ils jouent vraiment bien. Restez, ils vont commencer.
Bruno: Oui, regarde.
Yves: Oui, on y va.
Alissa: Ouais, ouais.
Yves: OK, on y va.

Voix-off: Yves et Moustafa doivent rencontrer leur amie Betty.

Yves: Bon, Moustafa!
Moustafa: Ouais.
Yves: Faudrait qu'on aille retrouver Betty.
Moustafa: Ah oui, c'est vrai. Bon Alissa, faut qu'on y aille, hein?
Alissa: Faut que vous y alliez?
Bruno: Ben, écoute, tchao, à bientôt. Vous allez où?
Yves: On va retrouver une copine à un autre concert.
Alissa: Bon OK, on s'appelle? Allez, bisous. Tchao les mecs!
Bruno: Bravo

Yves: Salut Betty.
Betty: Ah, salut.
Yves: Tu vas bien?
Betty: Ça va très bien.
Moustafa: Bonjour, Betty, ça va?
Betty: Ah, moi, avec la musique, ça va toujours bien. Et dites moi, qu'est-ce qu'il y a comme concerts ce soir?
Yves: Écoute, on vient de voir du flamenco juste à coté, et puis, qu'est-ce qu'il y a d'autre?
Moustafa: Alors, il y a Joe Cocker à la République, de la musique d'Amérique latine à l'hôtel de Sully, du jazz au musée Picasso, et plein de groupes de rock partout ...
Betty: C'est formidable. Mais dis moi, comment tu sais à quelle heure et dans quel endroit chaque concert avait lieu?
Moustafa: J'ai mon programme!
Betty: C'est formidable; on va danser?

Voix-off: Problème

Betty: C'est vraiment super, tu ne trouves pas?
Yves: Ils jouent vraiment bien.
Betty: Si on allait leur dire qu'on a aimé leur concert?
Moustafa: Si tu veux.
Betty: Excusez moi. J'aime vraiment ce que vous faites. J'aimerais savoir si vous avez déja fait des disques?
Musicien: Non, pas encore, malheureusement. Mais on va bientôt faire une émission à la télévision sur la musique pour les jeunes.
Betty: Et à quelle heure ça passe?
Musicien: Ça, je ne sais pas encore.
Betty: Bon! Mais que va-t-on faire alors?

Voix-off: Le guitariste ne sait pas à quelle heure il passe à la télévision. Ben, que va-t-on faire alors?

(On screen) Le monde francophone

Voix-off: Comme Paris, tout le monde francophone sait faire la fête.

(On screen) ***Le Québec*** On fait la fête au Québec.
(On screen) ***La Martinique*** On sait faire la fête à la Martinique.
(On screen) ***Le Sénégal*** On aime faire la fête au Sénégal.
(On screen) ***Tahiti*** Et à Tahiti aussi, on fait la fête.

TRANSPARENCY MASTERS

The thirty transparency masters contain illustrations that can be used as the basis for activities to practice the structures and vocabulary presented in CONTACTS. Overhead transparencies can be prepared, or from them they can be simply dittoed or xeroxed for individual handouts. A list of transparency masters follows as well as a correlation chart suggesting transparencies to be used in conjunction with various lessons.

Transparencies

Maps
1. France
2. Communauté européene, Départements et territoires d'outre-mer
3. Afrique
4. Amériques

Scenes and Word Sets
5. L'heure
6. Les verbes réfléchis
7. Une chambre d'étudiante
8. À la gare
9. À l'aéroport
10. La circulation
11. Dans un magasin
12. La description des gens
13. La famille
14. Les vêtements
15. La maison
16. Les prépositions
17. Le temps et les saisons
18. Faisons les courses
19. Bon appétit!
20. Deux accidents

Transparency Masters

Realia
21. Tours
22. Le Guide Michelin
23. Menu: Le Grand Turc
24. Menu: Le Matador
25. Les sorties
26. Les horaires

Scenes and Word Sets
27. Quelques activités
28. Au bord de la mer
29. En ville
30. Un cambriolage

The following is a lesson-by-lesson correlation of the transparency masters.

Lesson	*Page*	*Transparency Master*	*Activity*
1	p. 21	4. Amériques	Geography
	p. 30	5. Quelle heure est-il?	Telling time
2	p. 33	3. Afrique	Geography
	p. 42	5. Quelle heure est-il?	Telling time

Lesson	Page	Transparency Master	Activity
	p. 44	8. À la gare	Telling time
3	p. 47	2. Communauté europèene; DOM et TOM	Geography
	pp. 50, 51	8. À la gare	Asking questions
4	p. 67	7. Une chambre d'étudiante	Naming (classroom) objects, asking questions
	p. 67	10. La circulation	Discussing transportation
	p. 67	11. Dans un magasin	Naming objects (AV equipment)
5	pp. 80, 82	12. La description des gens; 6. À la gare	Describing people
6	pp. 91, 93	27. Quelques activités	Discussing leisure activites
	p. 96	20. Deux accidents; 29. En ville	Discussing locations and transportation
	p. 96	10. La circulation	Discussing transporation
VF II	p. 104	21. Tours; 29. En ville	Giving directions
7	p. 111	11. Dans un magasin	Discussing prices (vary the ones shown)
	p. 118	13. La famille	Discussing family relationships
8	p. 122	14. Les vêtements; 6. À la gare; 9. À l'aéroport	Describing clothing
	pp. 128, 129	11. Dans un magasin	Comparing prices
9	pp. 136, 139	15. La maison	Discussing rooms of house, furniture, location
	pp. 138, 139	16. Les prépositions; 7. Une chambre d'étudiante	Discussing location
	p. 143	17. Le temps et les saisons	Discussing weather
VF III	p. 147	14. Les vêtements	Discussing clothing prices (add price tags)
10	p. 154	12. La description des gens	Discussing age
	p. 154	13. La famille	Discussing age
11	p. 166	1. La France	Passé composé of **visiter** + cities
12	pp. 178ff	28. Au bord de la mer	Describing vacation in passé composé
VF IV	p. 193	22. Le Guide Michelin	Choosing hotels
13	p. 202	2. Communauté europèene; 3. Afrique; 4. Amériques	Naming countries
	p. 202	8. À la gare; 9. A l'aéroport	Discussing nationalities
14	pp. 212, 216	18. Faisons les courses; 19. Bon appétit!	Naming foods & beverages
15	pp. 222, 230	19. Bon appétit!; 18. Faisons les courses	Naming foods for various meals; fruits & vegetables
VF V	p. 235	23. Menu: Le Grand Turc	Ordering foods
	p. 236	24. Menu: Le Matador	Ordering foods
16	p. 246	25. Les sorties	Using **vouloir/pouvoir** to discuss leisure plans
17	p. 259ff	18. Faisons les courses	Asking/answering questions about shopping, using direct-object pronouns
19	p. 290	21. Tours	Talking about city life
21	p. 318ff	20. Deux accidents; 30. Un cambriolage	Describing events and circumstances of event
	p. 318ff	14. Les vêtements	Describing what people were wearing
VF VII	pp. 333, 334	25. Les sorties	Choosing leisure activities; telling time
22	p. 340	17. Le temps et les saisons; 27. Quelques activités	Describing activities
23	p. 355	12. La description des gens	Naming parts of body
	pp. 358, 360	6. Les verbes réfléchis	Describing daily routine; telling time
VF VIII	p. 379ff	28. Au bord de la mer	Describing beach activities
		17. Le temps et les saisons	Describing leisure activities
		12. La description des gens	Describing aches and pains

Lesson	*Page*	*Transparency Master*	*Activity*
25	p. 388ff	12. La description des gens	Describing people
27	p. 418ff	2. Communauté européene; DOM et TOM	Discussing vacation destinations using conditional
		28. Au bord de la mer	Discussing vacation activities using conditional
VF IX	p. 426	9. À l'aéroport	Using air travel vocabulary
	p. 427ff	8. À la gare; 26. Les horaires	Using train vocabulary
30	p. 464	2. Communauté européene	Discussing the EC
	p. 470	20. Deux accidents	Describing emotions
VF X	p. 476	14. Les vêtements	Describing clothing

1. France

FRANCE

COMMUNAUTÉ EUROPÉENE: 1992

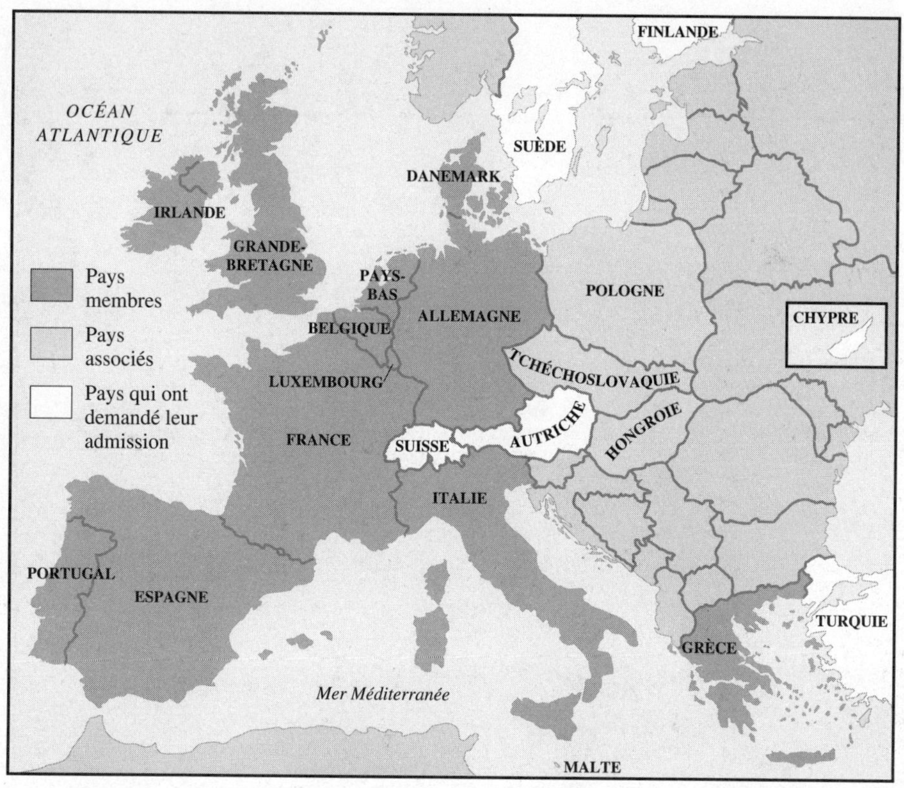

DÉPARTEMENTS ET TERRITOIRES D'OUTRE-MER

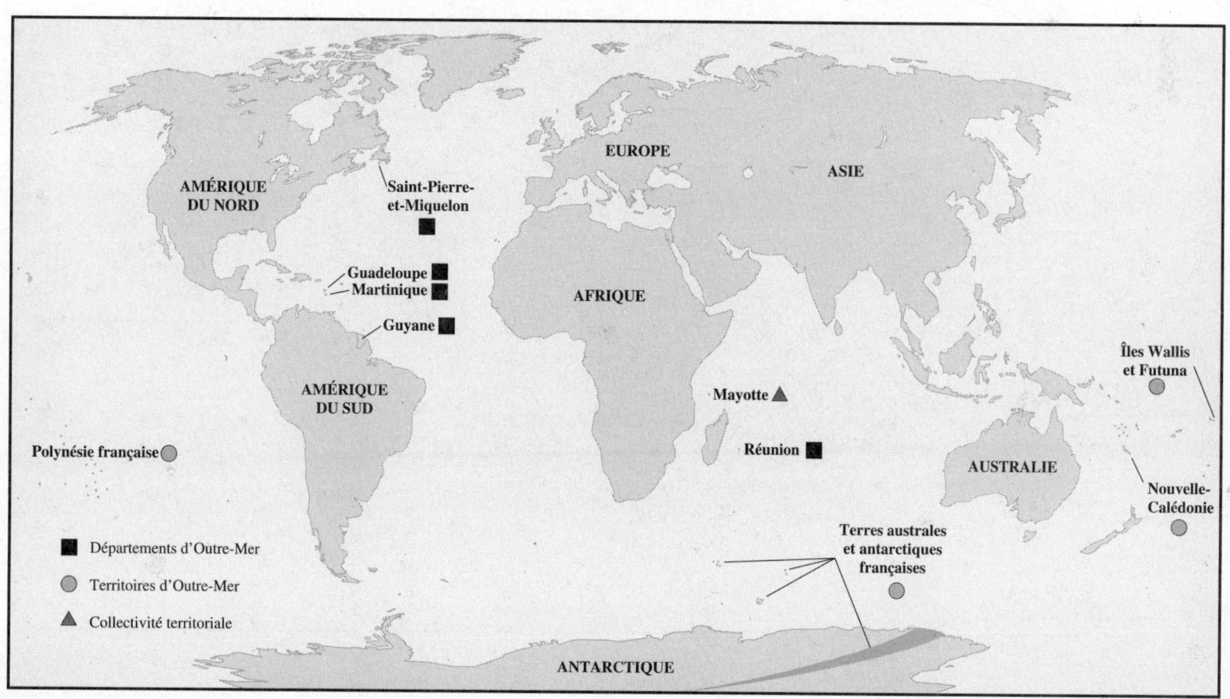

AFRIQUE

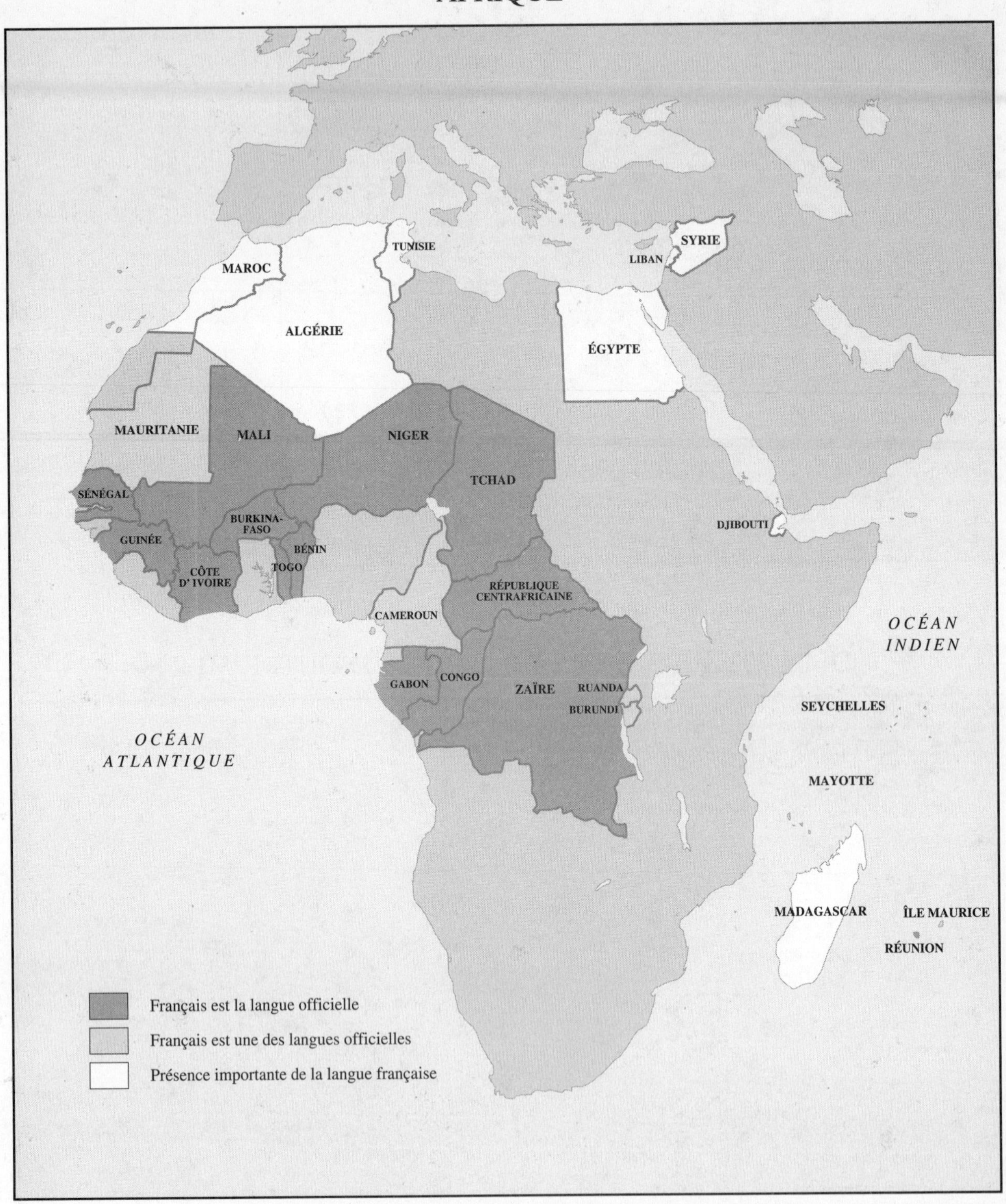
MAROC
TUNISIE
ALGÉRIE
SYRIE
LIBAN
ÉGYPTE
MAURITANIE
MALI
NIGER
TCHAD
SÉNÉGAL
BURKINA-FASO
GUINÉE
BÉNIN
CÔTE D'IVOIRE
TOGO
DJIBOUTI
RÉPUBLIQUE CENTRAFRICAINE
CAMEROUN
GABON
CONGO
ZAÏRE
RUANDA
BURUNDI
SEYCHELLES
MAYOTTE
OCÉAN INDIEN
OCÉAN ATLANTIQUE
MADAGASCAR
ÎLE MAURICE
RÉUNION
Français est la langue officielle
Français est une des langues officielles
Présence importante de la langue française

AMÉRIQUES

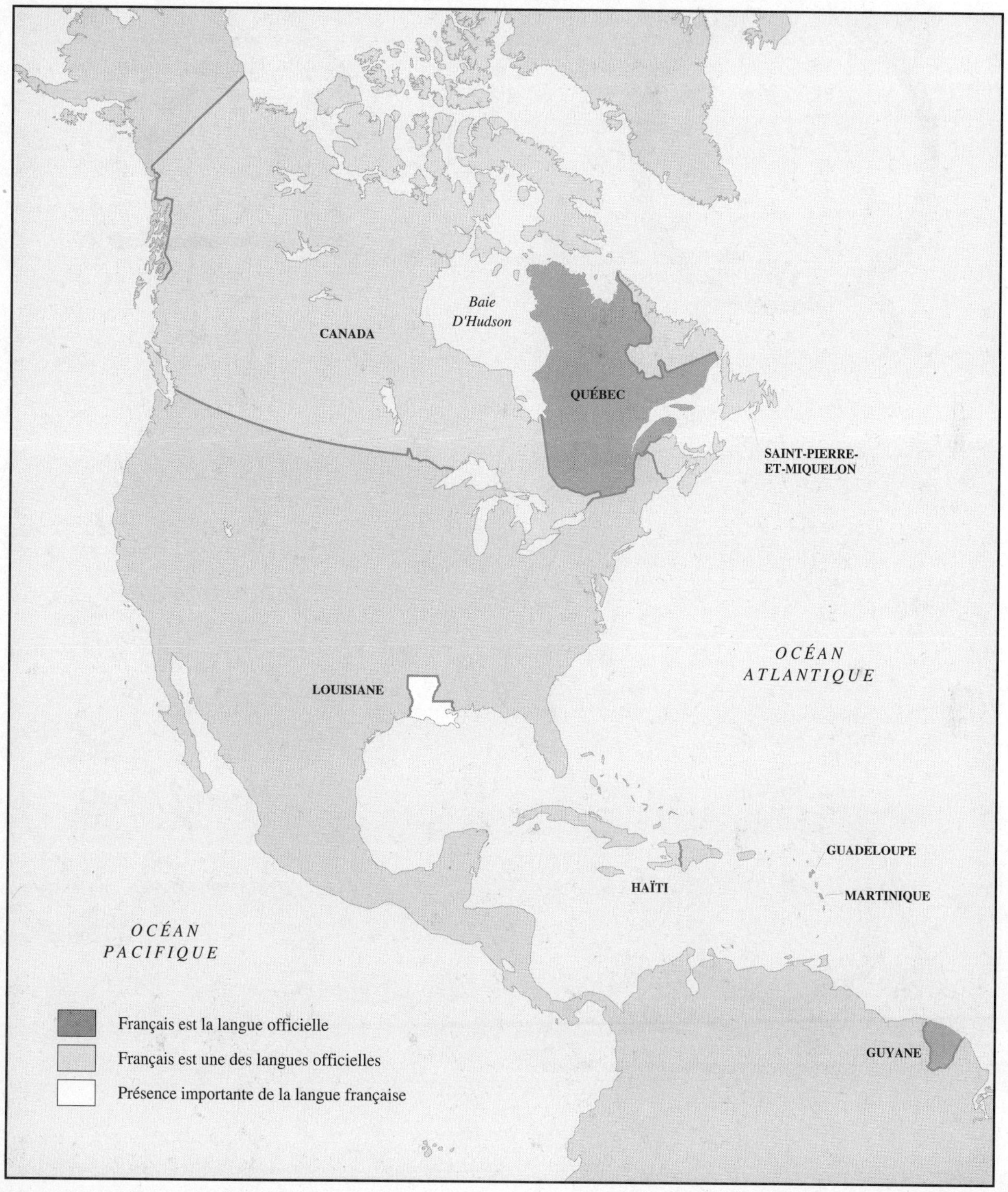
Baie
D'Hudson
CANADA
QUÉBEC
SAINT-PIERRE-
ET-MIQUELON
OCÉAN
ATLANTIQUE
LOUISIANE
GUADELOUPE
HAÏTI
MARTINIQUE
OCÉAN
PACIFIQUE
GUYANE
Français est la langue officielle
Français est une des langues officielles
Présence importante de la langue française

5. L'heure

6. Les verbes réfléchis

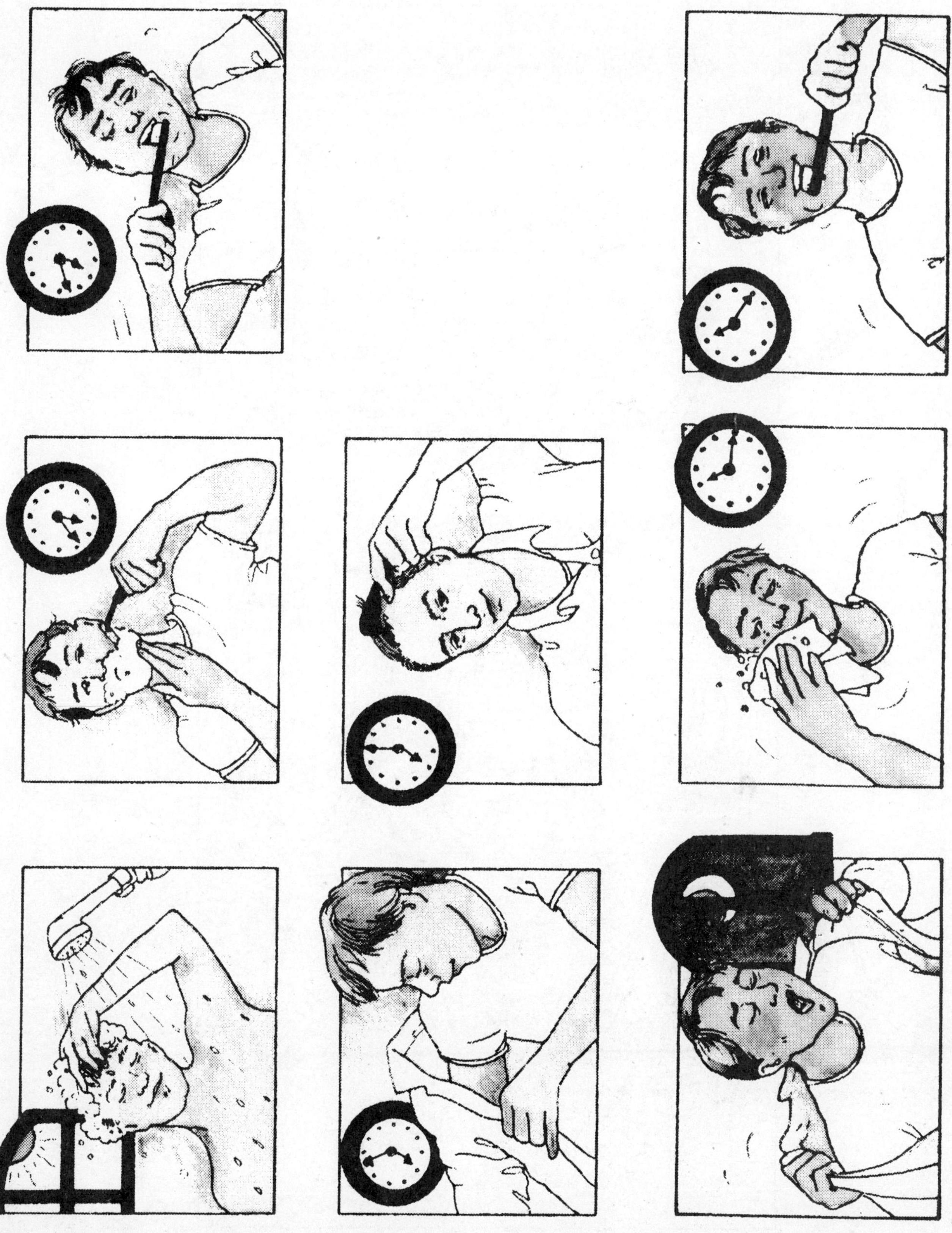

7. Une chambre d'étudiante

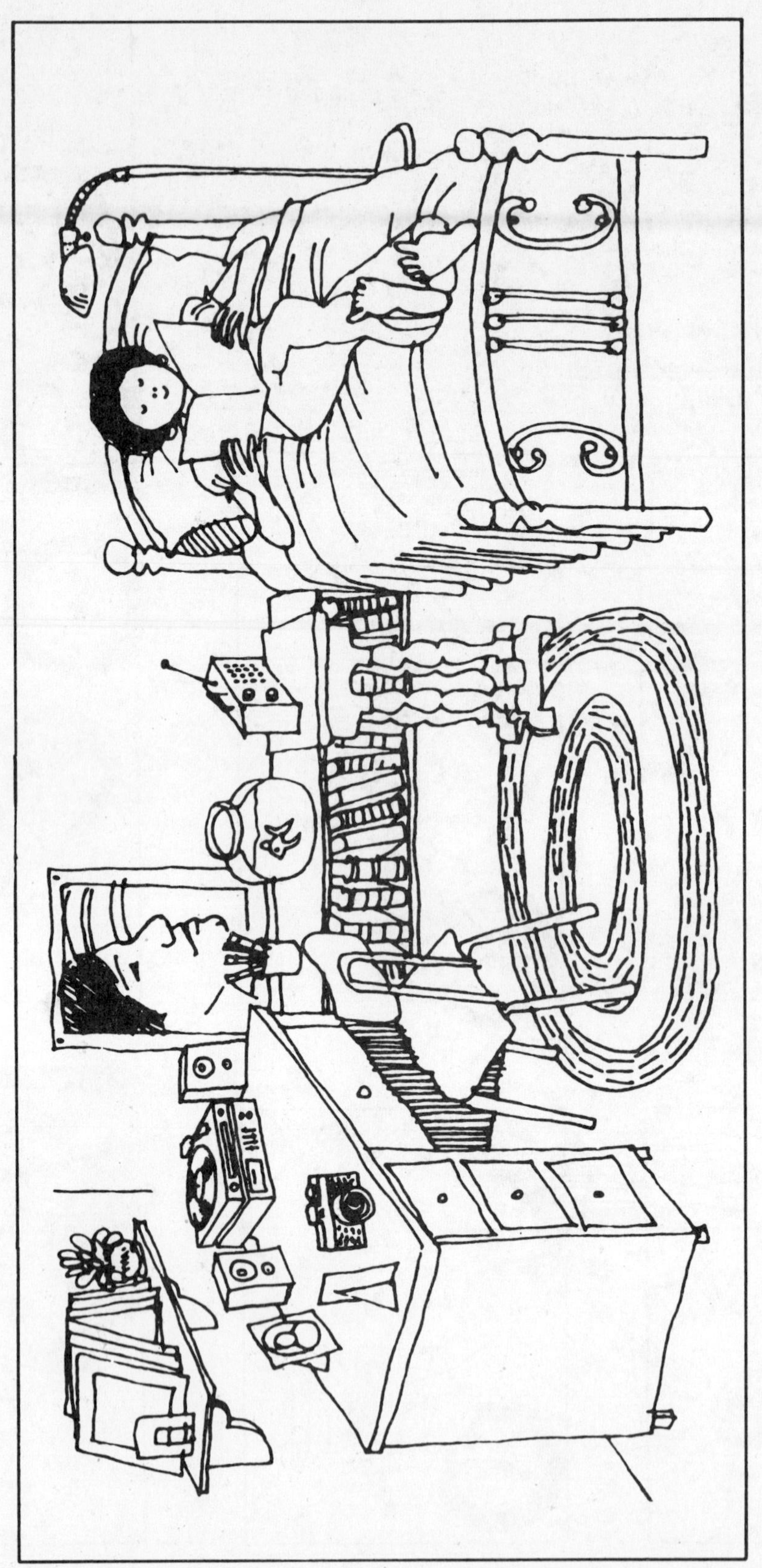

8. À la gare

VOIE 15
NICE
ARRIVÉE 13.10
DÉPART 16.30
VOIE 14
LYON
ARRIVÉE 15.45
DÉPART 17.05
BILLETS

9. À l'aéroport

10. La circulation

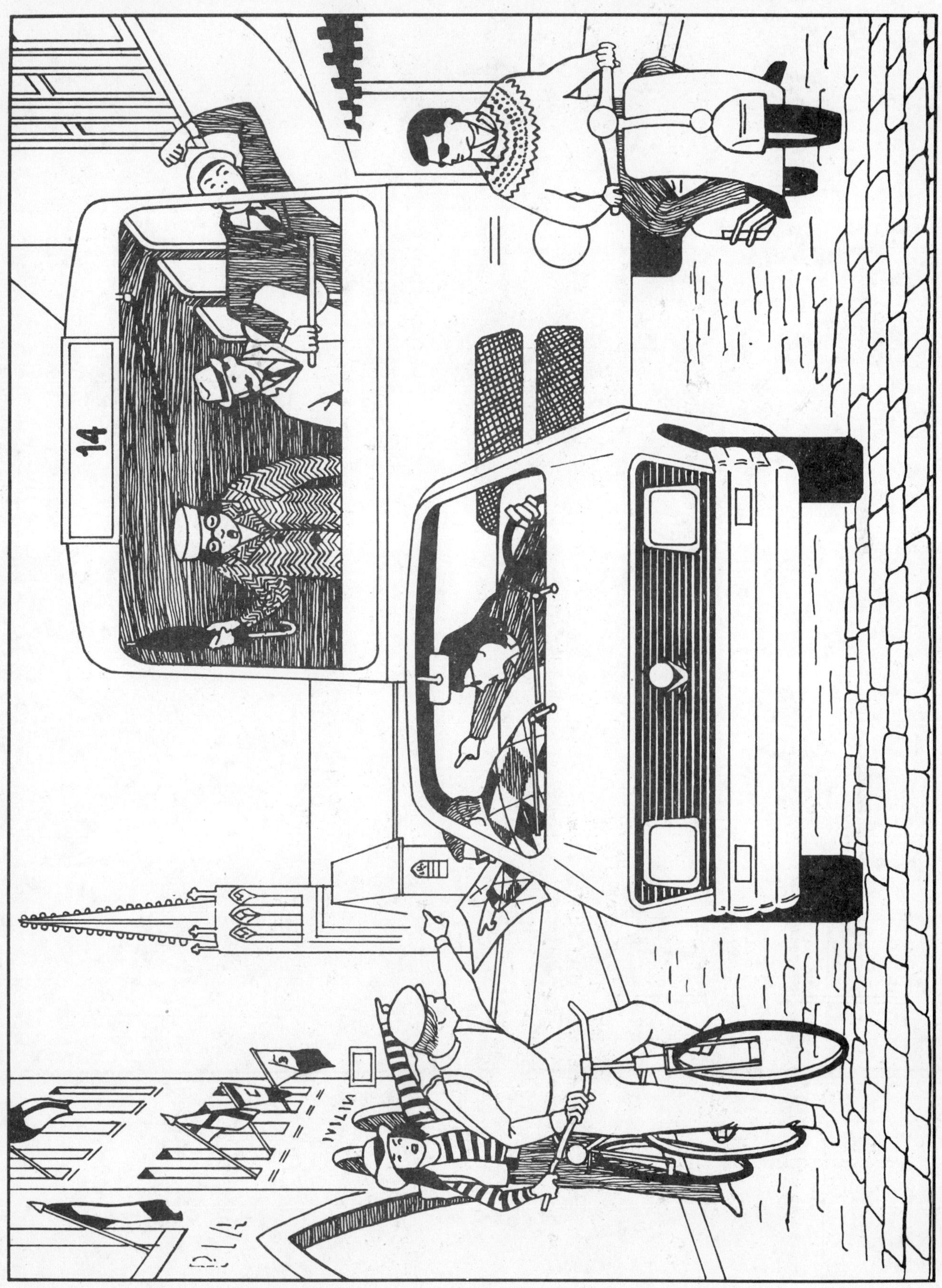

11. Dans un magasin

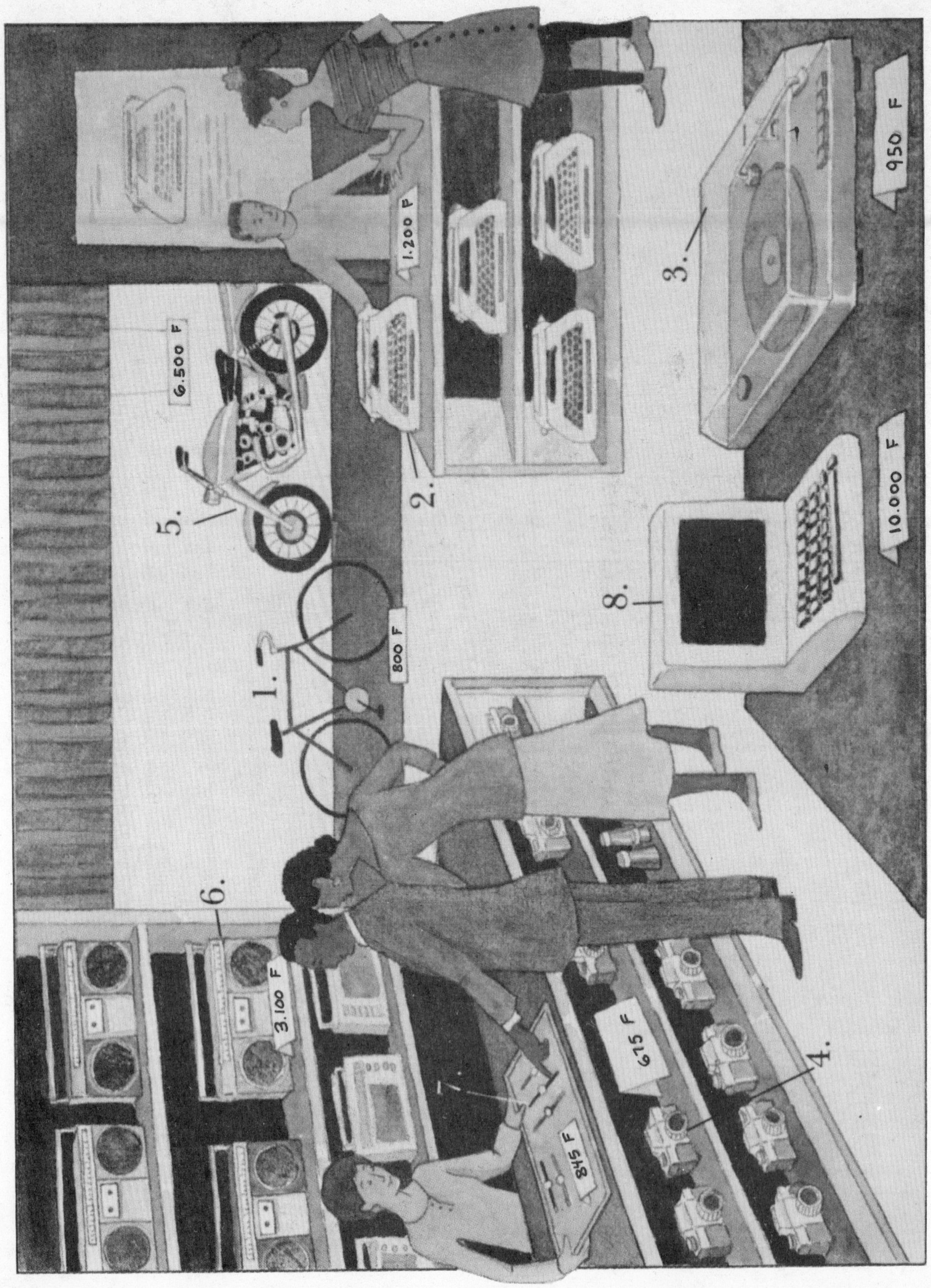

12. La description des gens

13. La famille

15. La maison

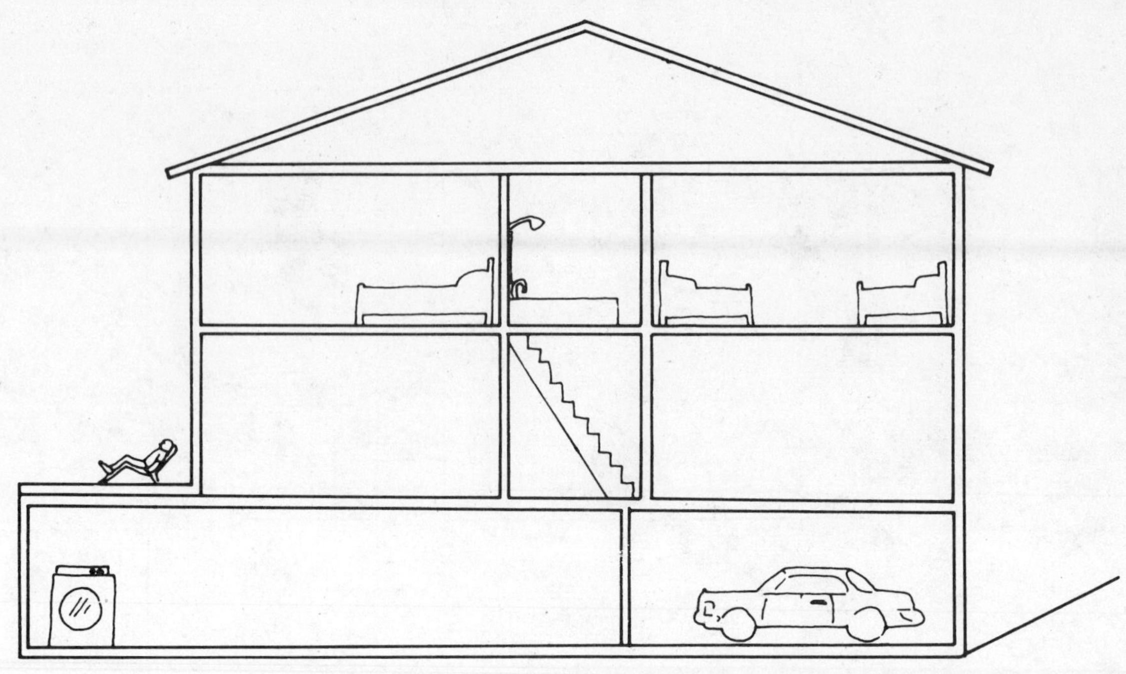

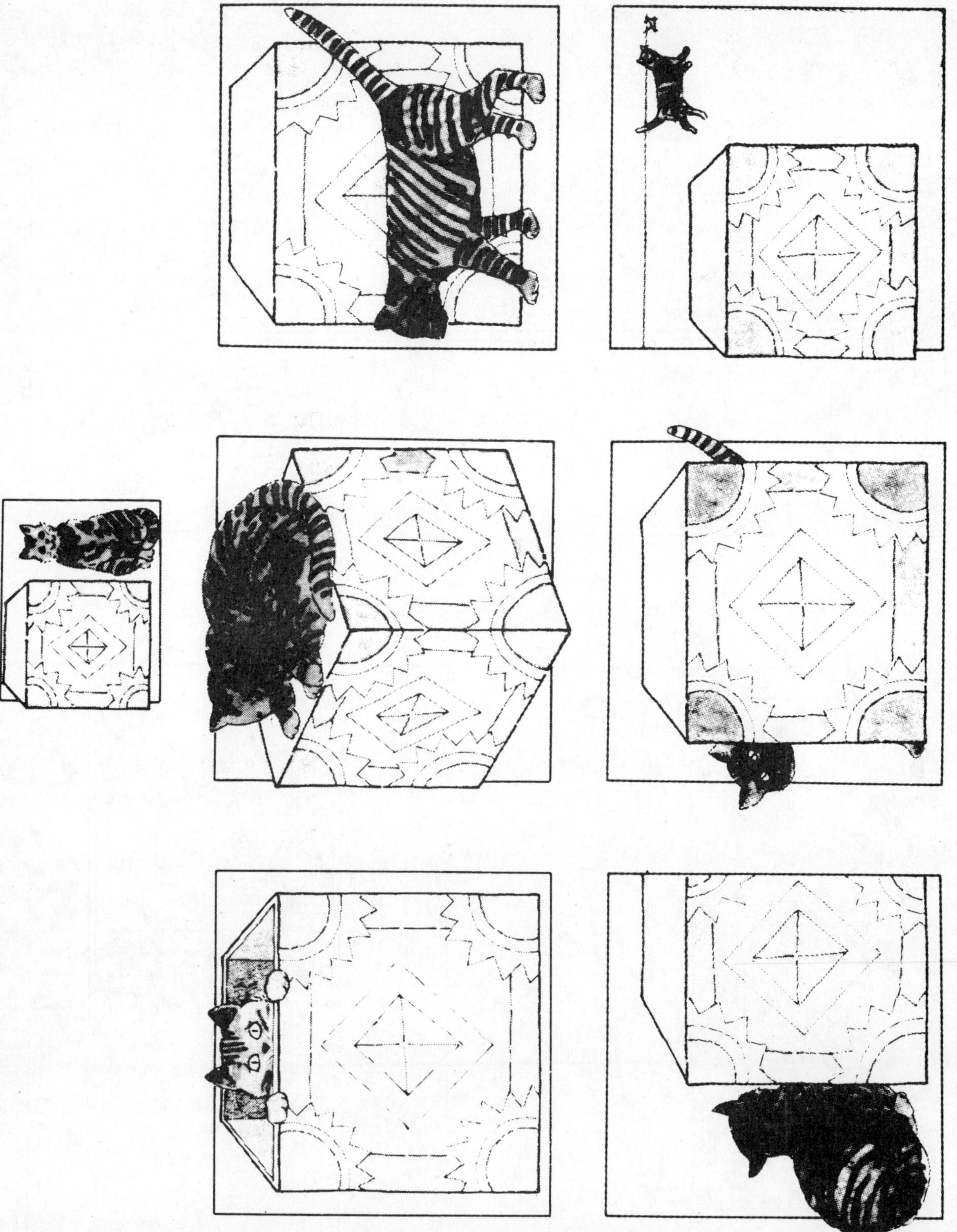

17. Le temps et les saisons

18. Faisons les courses

19. Bon appétit!

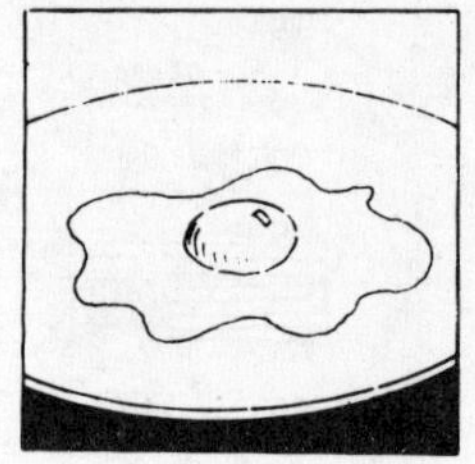

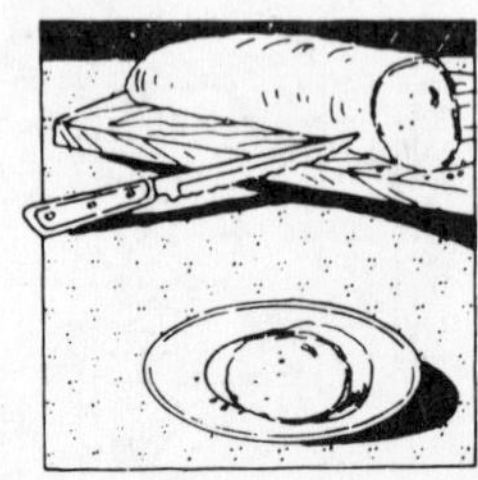

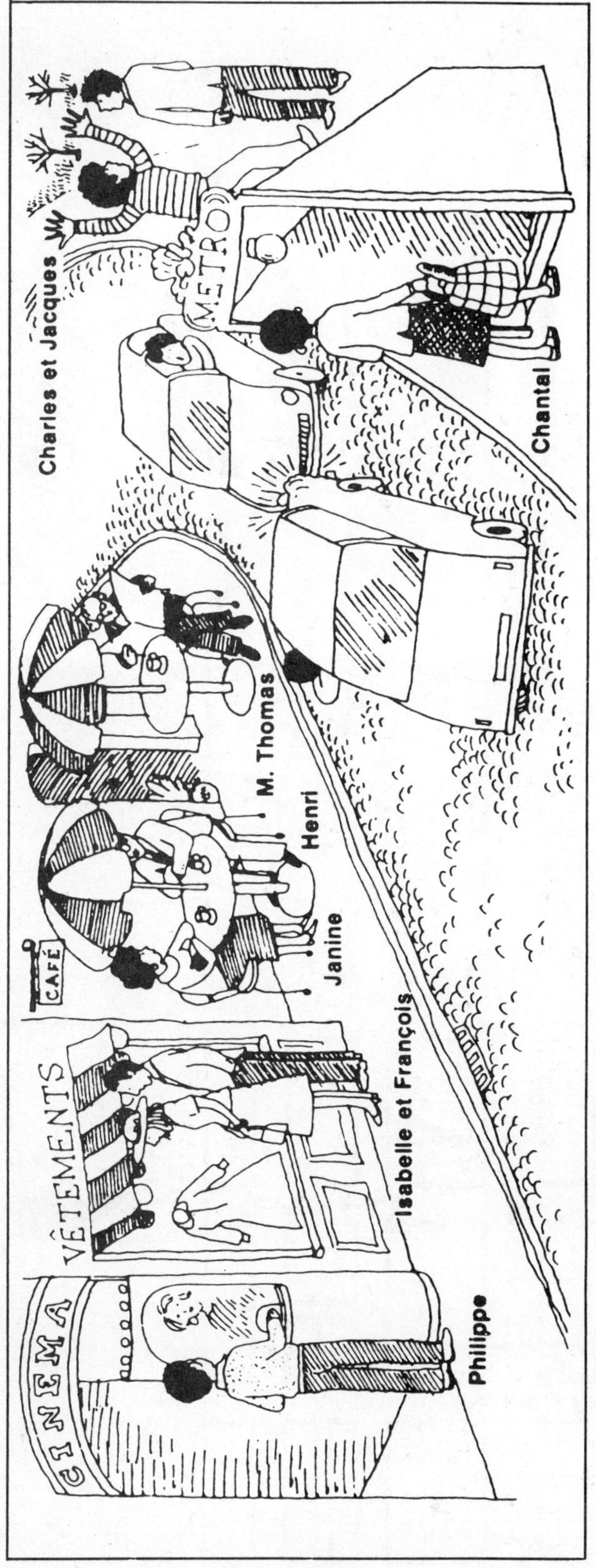
CINEMA
VÊTEMENTS
CAFÉ
METRO
Philippe
Isabelle et François
Janine
Henri
M. Thomas
Charles et Jacques
Chantal

TAXI
CAFE
Paul
Monique
Simon
Sylvie
Alain
Jacques
Claudette
M. Bonin

21. Tours

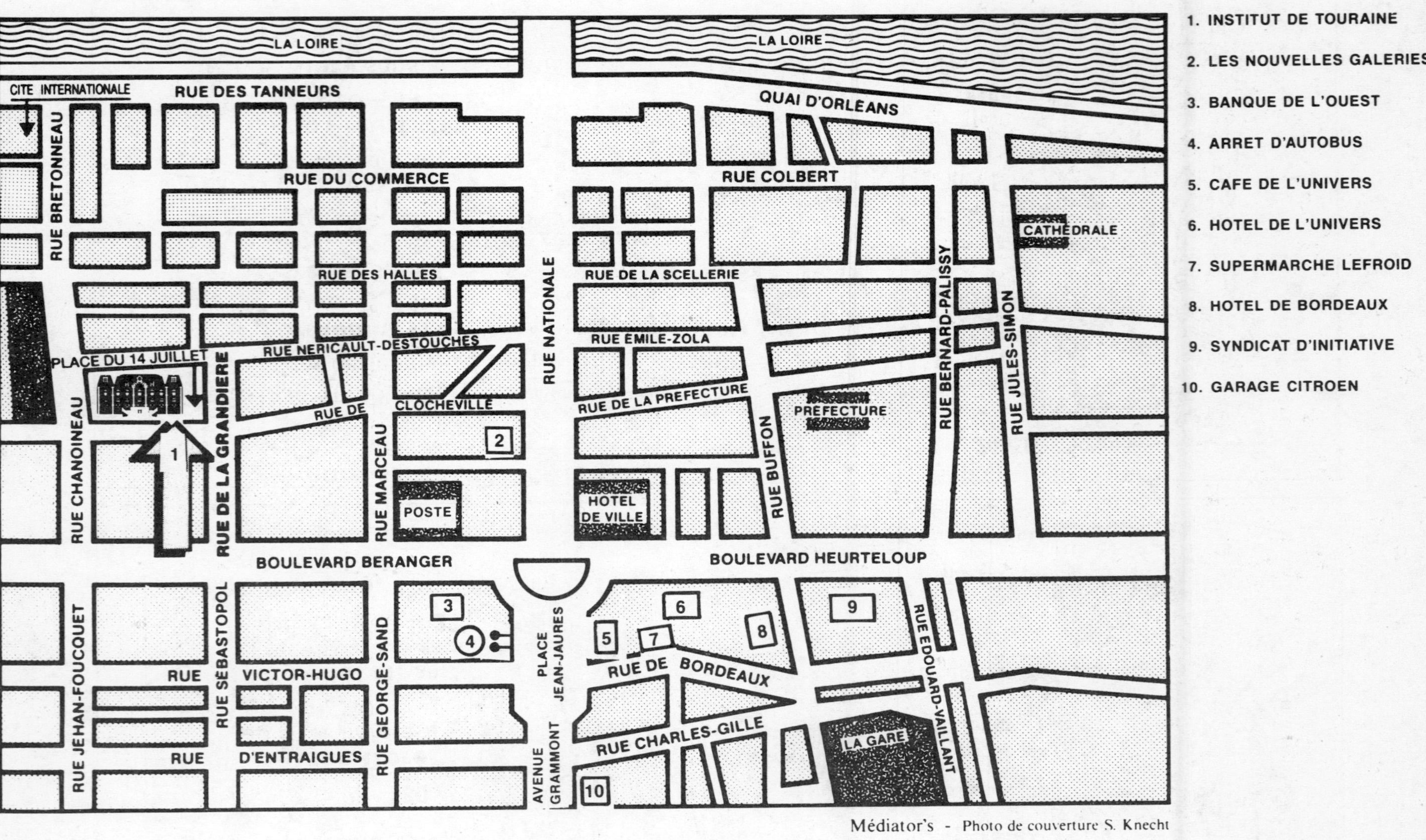

LA LOIRE
LA LOIRE
CITE INTERNATIONALE
RUE DES TANNEURS
QUAI D'ORLEANS
RUE BRETONNEAU
RUE DU COMMERCE
RUE COLBERT
CATHEDRALE
RUE DES HALLES
RUE DE LA SCELLERIE
RUE BERNARD-PALISSY
RUE JULES-SIMON
RUE NATIONALE
RUE NERICAULT-DESTOUCHES
RUE EMILE-ZOLA
PLACE DU 14 JUILLET
RUE DE
CLOCHEVILLE
RUE DE LA PREFECTURE
PREFECTURE
RUE CHANOINEAU
RUE DE LA GRANDIERE
RUE MARCEAU
POSTE
HOTEL DE VILLE
RUE BUFFON
BOULEVARD BERANGER
BOULEVARD HEURTELOUP
PLACE JEAN-JAURES
RUE JEHAN-FOUCQUET
RUE SEBASTOPOL
RUE
VICTOR-HUGO
RUE
D'ENTRAIGUES
RUE GEORGE-SAND
AVENUE GRAMMONT
RUE DE BORDEAUX
RUE CHARLES-GILLE
RUE EDOUARD-VAILLANT
LA GARE
1. INSTITUT DE TOURAINE
2. LES NOUVELLES GALERIES
3. BANQUE DE L'OUEST
4. ARRET D'AUTOBUS
5. CAFE DE L'UNIVERS
6. HOTEL DE L'UNIVERS
7. SUPERMARCHE LEFROID
8. HOTEL DE BORDEAUX
9. SYNDICAT D'INITIATIVE
10. GARAGE CITROEN
Médiator's - Photo de couverture S. Knecht

ANNECY **P** **74000** H.-Savoie **74** ⑥ **G. Alpes** – **51 593 h. alt. 448.**

Carlton sans rest, **5 r. Glières** ✆ **50 45 47 75** – ☎. AE ⓓ VISA — AY **g**
SC : ☕ 25 – **50 ch** 200/300.

Splendid H. sans rest, **4 quai E.-Chappuis** ✆ **50 45 20 00, Télex 385233** – TV ☎. VISA — BY **s**
SC : ☕ 25 – **50 ch** 150/320.

Faisan Doré, 34 av. Albigny ✆ **50 23 02 46** – wc wc ☎ – 35 — CV **e**
SC : **R** *(fermé 1er nov. à fin janv. et dim. hors sais.)* 80/160 – ☕ 28 – **46 ch** 180/300 – P 320/340.

Crystal H. sans rest, **20 r. L.-Chaumontel** ✆ **50 57 33 90** – TV wc wc ☎ **P**. VISA — AX **e**
SC : ☕ 19,50 – **22 ch** 178/200.

Réserve, 21 av. Albigny ✆ **50 23 50 24,** ←, **« Jardin »** – TV wc wc ☎ **P**. ⓓ E VISA — CV **v**
fermé 23 juin au 5 juil. et 20 déc. au 19 janv. – SC : **R** 80/180 ♨ – ☕ 22 – **12 ch** 200/280 – P 290/310.

Semnoz sans rest, **1 fg Balmettes** ✆ **50 45 04 12** – wc wc ☎. AE E VISA. ✻
fermé 20 déc. au 15 janv., sam. et dim. en hiver – SC : ☕ 21 – **24 ch** 190/240. — AY **b**

Ibis M, **12 r. Gare** ✆ **50 45 43 21, Télex 385585** – TV wc ☎ – 35. E VISA — AY **a**
SC : **R** carte environ 85 ♨ – ☕ 20 – **83 ch** 183/245.

Parmelan, 41 av. Romains ✆ **50 57 14 89,** – wc ☎ **P**. ✻ — BU **d**
Pâques-1er oct. – SC : **R** (dîner seul.) 56/84 – ☕ 19 – **30 ch** 95/190.

Parc sans rest, **43 chemin des Fins, vers le parc des sports** ✆ **50 57 02 98,** – wc wc ☎ **P**. VISA — BU **r**
fermé 22 au 30 juin et 1er déc. au 5 janv. – SC : ☕ 18 – **24 ch** 84/139.

Paris sans rest, **15 bd J.-Replat** ✆ **50 57 35 98** – wc ☎. AE. ✻ — AX **y**
fermé 15 oct. au 15 nov. – **SC :** ☕ 15,50 – **12 ch** 85/160.

Coin Fleuri sans rest, **3 r. Filaterie** ✆ **50 45 27 30** – wc wc ☎ — BY **t**
SC : ☕ 20 – **14 ch** 95/170.

d'Aléry sans rest, **5 av. d'Aléry** ✆ **50 45 24 75** – wc ☎. E VISA — AY **k**
SC : ☕ 15,50 – **18 ch** 100/203.

LE GRAND TURC

Tarif des Consommations

Boissons

(un) express	*6F*
(un) café-crème	*7F*
(un) chocolat	*10F*
(un) thé-nature[3]	*7F*
(un) thé-citron	*8F*
(un) Coca-Cola	*10F*
(un) Orangina	*10F*
(un) Perrier	*8F*
(un) citron pressé[5]	*12F*

(une) bière pression[1]	*10F*
(une) bière en bouteilles	*15F*
(un) jus de pomme[2]	*12F*
(un) jus de raisin[4]	*12F*

Sandwichs

(un) sandwich au jambon	*15F*
(un) sandwich au fromage	*15F*
(un) sandwich au pâté	*15F*

[1] *draft beer*
[2] *apple juice*
[3] *plain tea*
[4] *grape juice*
[5] *fresh lemonade*

LE MATADOR

menu à 120 francs

Hors d'oeuvre

melon	
ou salade de concombres	ou saucisson
ou salade de tomates	ou oeufs mayonnaise
ou salade de thon	ou jambon d'Auvergne

Plat principal

steak au poivre	
ou lapin farci	ou poulet rôti
ou côtelette de porc	ou filet de sole

Légumes

pommes frites	
ou haricots verts	ou petits pois

Salade verte ou Fromage

Dessert

glace	
ou yaourt	ou fruit
ou crème caramel	ou tarte aux pommes

Boisson

vin rouge	ou vin blanc
ou bière pression	ou eau minérale

Service 15% compris

CLUNY-PALACE

Les aventures de l'Arche perdue
avec Harrison Ford

séances à 16h et 19h30

PUBLICIS

ALIENS,
de retour

film américain
avec Sigourney Weaver

séances à 19h et 21h30

SAINT-GERMAIN-STUDIO

Hannah
et ses soeurs

comédie américaine
de Woody Allen

séance unique à 20 heures

Le retour
de Zorro

séances à 19h, 21h et 23h

séances à 18h45 21h00 23h15

La Pagode

Au revoir, les enfants
un film de Louis Malle

séances à 18h30 et 20h45

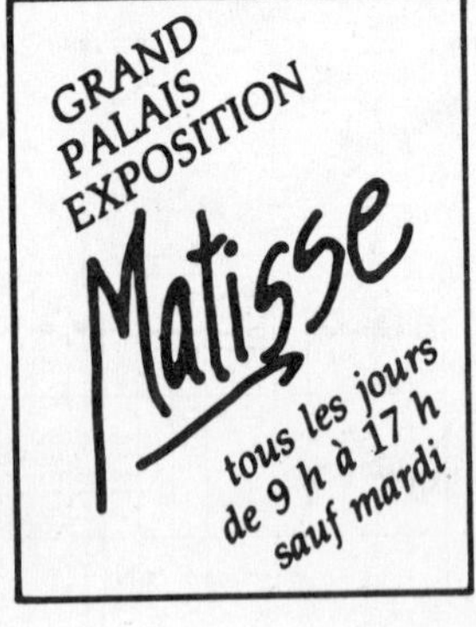

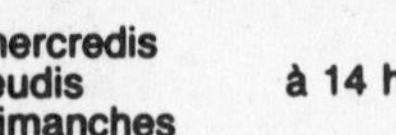

PRIX DES BILLETS TGV AU 31 MARS 1988

RELATIONS AU DÉPART DE PARIS	TARIF NORMAL RÉSERVATION (12 F) INCLUSE		SUPPLÉMENT ÉVENTUEL	
	2e classe	1re classe	2e classe	1re classe
PARIS → AIX-LES-BAINS	261 F	385 F	42 F	70 F
→ ANNECY (1)	275 F	407 F	42 F	70 F
→ ANTIBES	434 F	644 F	56 F	84 F
→ AVIGNON	319 F	472 F	56 F	84 F
→ BEAUNE	178 F	261 F	28 F	42 F
→ BELLEGARDE	265 F	391 F	42 F	70 F
→ BERN	309 F	457 F	42 F	70 F
→ BESANÇON	196 F	288 F	28 F	42 F
→ BOURG-EN-BRESSE	221 F	326 F	42 F	56 F
→ CANNES	430 F	639 F	56 F	84 F
→ CHALON-SUR-SAÔNE	189 F	277 F	28 F	42 F
→ CHAMBÉRY (1)	265 F	391 F	42 F	70 F
→ CULOZ	254 F	374 F	42 F	70 F
→ DIJON	162 F	237 F	28 F	42 F
→ DÔLE	182 F	266 F	28 F	42 F
→ FRASNE	207 F	304 F	28 F	42 F
→ GENÈVE	275 F	407 F	42 F	70 F
→ GRENOBLE	283 F	418 F	42 F	70 F
→ LAUSANNE	273 F	403 F	42 F	70 F
→ LE CREUSOT TGV	189 F	277 F	28 F	56 F
→ LYON	236 F	347 F	42 F	70 F
→ MÂCON TGV	211 F	310 F	42 F	56 F
→ MARSEILLE	362 F	536 F	56 F	84 F
→ MONTBARD	131 F	191 F	28 F	28 F
→ MONTÉLIMAR	290 F	428 F	56 F	70 F
→ MONTPELLIER	355 F	526 F	56 F	84 F
→ MOUCHARD	193 F	283 F	28 F	42 F
→ NICE	441 F	655 F	56 F	84 F
→ NÎMES	337 F	499 F	56 F	84 F
→ SAINT-ÉTIENNE	236 F	347 F	42 F	70 F
→ SAINT-RAPHAËL	419 F	623 F	56 F	84 F
→ TOULON	387 F	574 F	56 F	84 F
→ VALENCE	272 F	401 F	42 F	70 F
→ VALLORBE	218 F	320 F	28 F	56 F

HORAIRES ET SUPPLEMENTS TGV

HORAIRES ET SUPPLEMENTS TGV HORAIRES ET SUPPLEMENTS TGV

- ○ TGV sans supplément.
- ★ TGV avec supplément.
- ● TGV à supplément seulement pour les voyageurs descendant à Lyon.

PARIS → LYON → VALENCE → MARSEILLE → TOULON → NICE

N° du TGV		803	843	807	813	809/811	▲ 845	815	819
Restauration		▣	1/2	▣		▣ 1/2	▣	▣	1/2
Paris - Gare de Lyon	D	7.00	7.30	7.40	10.13	10.23	10.41	11.42	12.55
Le Creusot TGV	A			9.05					
Lyon - Part-Dieu	A	9.00	9.30				12.43		
Valence	A	9.54		10.39	13.11			14.33	15.47
Montélimar	A			11.02	b		†	b	
Avignon	A	10.50		11.40	14.11	14.08		15.27	16.42
Marseille	A	11.46		12.37	15.11	15.03		16.22	17.39
Toulon	A	a	12.44	a	16.10	15.52	15.56	a	a
St-Raphaël	A		13.35	a		c	16.46	a	
Cannes	◖ A		13.59	a		c	17.09	a	
Antibes	◖ A		14.09	a		c	17.21	a	
Nice	A		14.25	a		c	17.37	a	

N° du TGV		(1) 847	805	823	849	827	831	835	841	645
Restauration		1/2			1/2		1/2	▣	▣ 1/2	▣
Paris - Gare de Lyon	D	13.24	13.29	13.55	15.05	15.40	16.49	17.47	18.36	20.00
Le Creusot TGV	A						18.16			
Lyon - Part-Dieu	A				17.05		18.57			22.00
Valence	A		16.20			18.33	19.53	20.40	21.33	22.56
Montélimar	A						b	21.02	b	
Avignon	A		17.15	17.40		19.29	20.49	21.39	22.29	
Marseille	A		18.10	18.36		20.25	21.44	22.35	23.25	
Toulon	A	18.39	a	a	20.21	a	a	23.21	a	
St-Raphaël	A	19.30	a		21.12	a	a			
Cannes	◖ A	19.55	a		21.35	a	a			
Antibes	◖ A	20.05	a		21.45	a	a			
Nice	A	20.22	a		22.01	a	a			

27. Quelques activités

28. Au bord de la mer

29. En ville

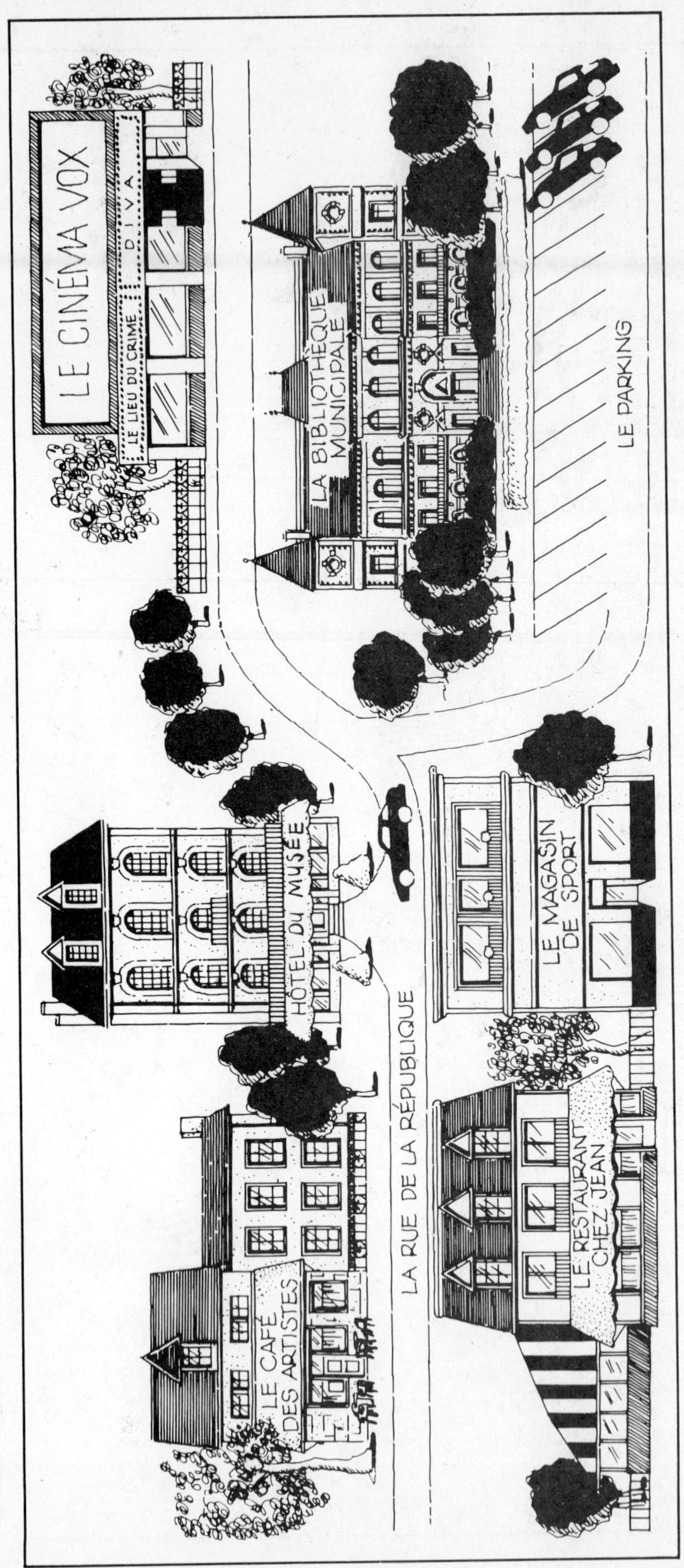
LE CINÉMA VOX
LE LIEU DU CRIME
DIVA
LA BIBLIOTHÈQUE MUNICIPALE
LE PARKING
HÔTEL DU MUSÉE
LE MAGASIN DE SPORT
LA RUE DE LA RÉPUBLIQUE
LE CAFÉ DES ARTISTES
LE RESTAURANT CHEZ JEAN

30. Un cambriolage